O9-ABF-493

HAUTE-ALPES

**THE RIVIERA AND THE
ALPES MARITIMES**
Pages 60–99

ALPES-DE-HAUTE-
PROVENCE

Digne-les-Bains

THE RIVIERA AND THE
ALPES MARITIMES

Monaco

Nice

Cannes

Iles de Lérins

THE VAR AND THE
ILES D'HYERES

ulon

Iles d'Hyeres

**THE VAR AND THE
ILES D'HYÈRES**
Pages 100–125

EYEWITNESS TRAVEL

PROVENCE
& THE CÔTE D'AZUR

EYEWITNESS TRAVEL

PROVENCE
& THE CÔTE D'AZUR

MAIN CONTRIBUTOR: ROGER WILLIAMS

DK

LONDON, NEW YORK,
MELBOURNE, MUNICH AND DELHI
www.dk.com

PROJECT EDITOR Jane Simmonds
ART EDITOR Jane Ewart
SENIOR EDITOR Fay Franklin
EDITORS Tom Fraser, Elaine Harries, Fiona Morgan
Designers Claire Edwards, Pippa Hurst, Malcolm Parchment

CONTRIBUTORS
John Flower, Jim Keeble, Martin Walters

PHOTOGRAPHERS
Max Alexander, John Heseltine, Kim Sayer, Alan Williams

ILLUSTRATORS
Stephen Conlin, Richard Draper, Steve Gyapay,
Chris D Orr Illustration, John Woodcock

Film outputting bureau Cooling Brown, England
Reproduced by Colourscan, Singapore
Printed and bound in China by
Toppan Printing Co. (Shenzhen Ltd)

First American Edition 1995
06 07 08 09 10 9 8 7 6 5 4 3 2 1

**Reprinted with revisions 1995, 1997, 2000,
2001, 2002, 2003, 2004, 2006**

Published in the United States by
DK Publishing, Inc., 375 Hudson Street,
New York, New York 10014

Copyright 1995, 2006 © Dorling Kindersley Limited, London

ISSN 1542-1554
ISBN-10: 0-75661-549-6
ISBN-13: 978-0-75661-549-9

THROUGHOUT THIS BOOK, FLOORS ARE REFERRED TO IN ACCORDANCE
WITH EUROPEAN USAGE, I.E., THE "FIRST FLOOR" IS ONE FLIGHT UP.

Front cover main image: fields of lavender by rustic farmhouse, Var.

**The information in this
Dorling Kindersley Travel Guide is checked annually.**
Every effort has been made to ensure that this book is as up-to-date
as possible at the time of going to press. Some details, however,
such as telephone numbers, opening hours, prices, gallery hanging
arrangements and travel information are liable to change. The
publishers cannot accept responsibility for any consequences arising
from the use of this book, nor for any material on third party
websites, and cannot guarantee that any website address in this
book will be a suitable source of travel information. We value the
views and suggestions of our readers very highly. Please write to:
Publisher, DK Eyewitness Travel Guides,
Dorling Kindersley, 80 Strand, London WC2R 0RL, Great Britain.

◁ Abbaye de Sénanque, Vaucluse

ANTOINE MA 508

CONTENTS

HOW TO USE THIS
GUIDE 6

Poppy field outside Sisteron

INTRODUCING
PROVENCE

Busy Pampelonne beach to the
south of fashionable St-Tropez

Marseille fisherman and his catch

Goat cheese in chestnut leaves

TRAVELLERS' NEEDS

One of the perfumes of Provence

SURVIVAL GUIDE

Typical Provençal countryside between Grasse and Castellane

Tarascon's château by the Rhône

Fondation Maeght outside St-Paul-de-Vence

HOW TO USE THIS GUIDE

This guide will help you get the most from your stay in Provence. It provides both expert recommendations and detailed practical information. *Introducing Provence* maps the region and sets it in its historical and cultural context. *Provence Area by Area* describes the important sights, with maps, photographs and detailed illustrations. Suggestions for food, drink, accommodation, shopping and entertainment are in *Travellers' Needs*, and the *Survival Guide* has tips on everything from the French telephone system to getting to Provence and travelling around the region.

PROVENCE AREA BY AREA

In this guide, Provence has been divided into five separate regions, each of which has its own chapter. A map of these regions can be found inside the front cover of the book. The most interesting places to visit in each region have been numbered and plotted on a *Regional Map*.

Each area of Provence can be quickly identified by its colour coding.

1 Introduction
The landscape, history and character of each region is described here, showing how the area has developed over the centuries and what it has to offer the visitor today.

A locator map shows the region in relation to the whole of Provence.

2 Regional Map
This gives an illustrated overview of the whole region. All the sights are numbered and there are also useful tips on getting around by car and public transport.

Features and story boxes highlight special or unique aspects of a particular sight.

3 Detailed information on each sight
All the important towns and other places to visit are described individually. They are listed in order, following the numbering on the Regional Map. Within each town or city, there is detailed information on important buildings and other major sights.

4 Major Towns
An introduction covers the history, character and geography of the town. The main sights are described individually and plotted on a Town Map.

A Visitors' Checklist gives contact points for tourist and transport information, plus details of market days and local festival dates.

The town map shows all main through roads as well as minor streets of interest to visitors. All the sights are plotted, along with the bus and train stations, parking, tourist offices and churches.

5 Street-by-Street Map
Towns or districts of special interest to visitors are shown in detailed 3D, with photographs of the most important sights. This gives a bird's-eye view of towns or districts of special interest.

A suggested route for a walk covers the most interesting streets in the area.

For all the top sights, a Visitors' Checklist provides the practical information you will need to plan your visit.

6 The top sights
These are given two or more pages. Important buildings are dissected to reveal their interiors; museums have colour-coded floorplans to help you locate the most interesting exhibits.

The gallery guide explains the layout of the museum and gives details on the arrangement and display of the collection.

Stars indicate the works of art or sights that no visitor should miss.

INTRODUCING PROVENCE

DISCOVERING PROVENCE

This is a land for all the senses: the sight of timeless light-suffused landscapes, the scents of lavender and olive groves, the taste of sun-drenched produce and grapes, the sound of sea gently lapping and the feel of the sun – so good you can almost taste it.

Famous regional lavender perfume

From the glamorous resorts of the Riviera to tiny islands, from bustling cities to *villages perchés*, to magnificent Roman remains and to the picturesque rural Provence with its sun-baked villages and endless seas of purple lavender, this is also a land of startling contrasts.

Spectacular view of the Riviera from Nice

RIVIERA AND ALPES MARITIMES

- Nice, Cannes and Monaco
- Sensual Grasse
- Vallée des Merveilles

The fabled Riviera has been the playground of painters, composers, writers and celebrities for more than a century. The beautiful landscapes enchanted all the major French Impressionists and still weave their magic for visitors on every budget.

Try to break the bank at **Monte Carlo**'s casino *(see pp92–3)*, go celebrity spotting at the **Cannes Film festival** *(see pp68–69)*, stroll along the Promenade des Anglais in **Nice** *(see pp80–1)*, the Riviera's largest city, follow in the footsteps of Picasso in the charming *vieille ville* of **Antibes** *(see p72)*, or relax in the warmth of **Menton** *(see pp98–9)*, the lemon capital which enjoys the best climate in France.

Inland, medieval towns stretch lazily over the hills, such as the much photographed, gastronomic town of **Mougins** *(see p66)*. Among fragrant fields of roses and jasmine, discover the world perfume capital, **Grasse** *(see pp66–7)*, the birthplace of Chanel No 5.

The back country of the Alpes Maritimes is a scenic delight, largely undiscovered by tourists. Gorges plunge, rivers sparkle and mountain peaks glisten with snow. The crowning delight is the aptly named **Vallée des Merveilles** *(see p97)*, cradled among craggy peaks where ibex and goats roam.

VAR AND ILES D'HYERES

- Stylish St Tropez
- Côtes de Provence vineyards
- Iles d'Hyères, Golden Islands

St Tropez *(see pp118–22)*, or St-Trop as the French call it, is the most glamorous resort on the Provence coast. Its gorgeous sandy beaches act as a magnet for stars and sybarites. Nearby, wonderful beaches seem to appear at the roadside out of nowhere. **Fréjus** *(see p125)* has safe swimming and pristine beaches, while **Bandol** *(see p112)* has sandy coves, sheltered by an arc of wooded hills.

Around Bandol the land is cloaked with the **Côtes de Provence** *(see pp108–9)* vineyards. These wines are excellent, especially the reds, and opportunities for tasting are plentiful. The jewel of the bay of Hyères is its islands, the **Iles d'Hyères** *(see pp114–5)*, known as the *"Iles d'Or"* or "Golden Islands". They are an intense green set amid a sea of brilliant blue, the best islands of the western Riviera.

St Tropez harbour, full of glitz and glamour

The hilltop village of Roussillon, known as the "red village"

BOUCHES-DU-RHONE AND NIMES

- Amazing natural history in the Camargue
- Superb Roman ruins at Nîmes and Pont du Gard
- Marseille and smaller ports

The breathtaking, contrasting landscapes of this region have been immortalized on canvas by Van Gogh and Cézanne. To the west is the **Camargue** *(see pp136–9),* one of France's greatest wildlife reserves. *Gardians* or Camargue cowboys herd the black bulls astride their white horses, birdwatchers twitch with pleasure at the rich variety of birdlife, and flora and fauna enthusiasts are rewarded with unique collections.

Nîmes *(see pp132–3)* is full of southern charm with a Spanish accent. It is the site of some of Europe's best preserved Roman buildings including their version of Rome's Colosseum, **Les Arènes** *(see p132).* Nearby is the extraordinary feat of Roman engineering, the **Pont du Gard** *(see p131),* which, at 48 m (157 ft), is the highest bridge ever built by the Romans. Glorious **Arles** *(see pp144–6)* is, for many, the jewel of Provence.

This area is also home to **Marseille** *(see pp150–2),* Provence's largest city, and France's biggest port and oldest city. It has recently benefitted from a facelift and is more sparkling and dynamic than ever. Elegant, cultured **Aix-en Provence** *(see pp148–9)* should not be missed nor should the lovely little resort, **Cassis** *(see p153).*

Colourful, fresh produce at Aix-en-Provence market

VAUCLUSE

- *Villages perchés* of Gordes and Roussillon
- Avignon, Provençal jewel
- Châteauneuf-du-Pape

Dominated by the snow-capped peak of **Mont Ventoux** *(see p160),* this lovely region is redolent of rosemary, herbs, lavender and pine wherever you go. The hilltop villages can often only be reached by winding roads, but your efforts are well rewarded. **Gordes** *(see p169)* clings spectacularly to its mountaintop eyrie and **Roussillon** *(see p169)* basks in its ochre light.

Avignon *(see pp166–8),* on the banks of the Rhone, is a gateway to Provence. This fascinating city of ramparts bursts with culture and energy. In this extraordinarily fertile region, don't miss the Côtes-du-Rhone wines, especially from **Châteauneuf -du-Pape** *(see p164),* nor melons from **Cavaillon** *(see p170),* France's largest market garden.

ALPES-DE-HAUTE-PROVENCE

- Secret Provence
- Striking Gorges du Verdon
- Plateau de Valensole lavender fields

Provence's least-known and least populated area has a climate blending Provençal warmth and clear, cool Alpine air. The terrain is sprinkled with dramatic gorges, deeply carved valleys, bizarre rock formations and sparkling lakes framed by the soaring Alps.

The **Gorges du Verdon** *(see pp184–5)* is one of France's top sights. This breathtaking gorge carves into the rock up to 700 m (2,300 ft) deep. The whole area is a paradise for lovers of the outdoors – walking, white-water canoeing and hang-gliding. In the north is the highest peak in the Provencal Alps, **Mont Pelat** *(see p179).* In the south is France's most important lavender-growing area, the **Plateau de Valensole** *(see pp182–3).* To see this vision of purple magnificence at its best, visit in the summer.

The distinctive mauve of lavender fields in the Plateau de Valensole

Putting Provence on the Map

Provence is situated in the sun-blessed south-east corner of France, edged to the south by the Mediterranean. Its most illustrious stretch of coastline, roughly from Menton to Bandol, is also known as the Côte d'Azur although, the nearer to Italy it gets, the more likely it is to be referred to as the Riviera. To the east are Italy and the Alps, to the west, the Rhône river. The region covers an area of over 30,000 sq km (18,650 sq miles) with a population of about 4.25 million.

KEY

☐ Area covered by this guide

⛴ Ferry service

✈ Airport

═ Motorway

═ Major road

— Railway line

| 0 kilometres | 100 |
| 0 miles | 100 |

View of the impressive Palais des Papes in Avignon next to the Rhône

Den Haag
ek van
Holland
brugge

AMSTERDAM

Rotterdam

NETHERLANDS

Antwerpen

BRUXELLES

BELGIUM Liège

Köln

Aachen

LUXEMBOURG

LUXEMBOURG

Thionville

Reims

Metz

Troyes

Hannover

Essen

Strasbourg

Stuttgart

GERMANY

München

Salzburg

Mulhouse

Basel

Dijon

Zürich

Bodensee

LIECHTENSTEIN

Innsbruck

AUSTRIA

BERN

SWITZERLAND

Lac Léman

Genève

Lyon

Grenoble

Milano

Torino

ITALY

Venezia

Valence

Rhône

Nîmes

Avignon

PROVENCE

tpellier

Arles

Aix-en-Provence

Marseille

Nice

Monaco

Cannes

Toulon

Genova

La Spezia

Bologna

Livorno

Firenze

Piombino

Bastia

Orbetello

CORSICA

Civitavecchia

ROMA

Ajaccio

See inside back cover

MEDITERRANEAN SEA

A PORTRAIT OF PROVENCE

In a comparatively short time, Provence has changed its face. A generation or two ago it was, to the French, a place of indolent southern bumpkins. To foreigners, it was an idyllic spot, but one reserved, it seemed to many, for the rich or artistic. Now, Provence, more than any other region, is where the French would choose to live and work, and its holiday routes buzz with traffic all year round.

The high-tech industry based here can attract top-flight staff, not just from France but from all over the world.

Still, Provence remains an essentially rural region. At its edges, it has a lively Latin beat: almost Spanish among the *gardians* of the Camargue in the west, Italian in Nice to the east. The rest of the region is mostly traditional and conservative. Only in games of *boules* or discussions about European bureaucracy does the talk become animated. But, once engaged in conversation, Provençals are the most generous and warmest of hosts. There is an all-pervading Frenchness, of course, which means that people are polite and punctual.

Monaco Grand Prix poster

Shopkeepers always greet you as you enter, but will close at the stroke of noon. Other institutions open and close on the dot, too. Lunch, in Provence, is sacrosanct.

Traditions are important to the people of Provence. Local crafts are not quaint revivals, but respected, time-honoured occupations. Artists who came here for the light and the scenery found other inspirations, too. Picasso himself learned the potter's art at the wheel of a Provençal craftsman. Homes will have hand-turned local chestnut or oak furniture, *terre rouge* clay pots, Moustiers *faïence*, Biot glassware and furnishings using the traditional *indiennes* patterns of Arles and Nîmes.

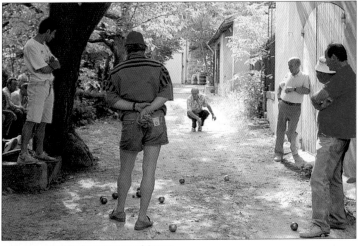

A leisurely game of *boules* at Châteauneuf-du-Pape

◁ One of the many narrow, Italianate streets in the Old Town of Nice

Vendor of delicious cakes and pastries in Sisteron

The home is run as it has been for generations. Provençal kitchens, at the heart of family life, are famous. Combining simplicity with bounty, they mix the aroma of herbs with the generosity of wine. In the envious and admiring eyes of visitors, they are the epitome of taste.

Good taste is inbred. In this rural community, the familiarity of the weather, the seasons and the harvests are sources of constant discussion. Gardens, full of fruit trees, vegetables and flowers, are a matter of pride. Even city-dwellers know how the best produce should be grown, and may well have access to a country relation's plot. Market stalls are beautifully laid out and carefully scrutinized and, no matter how abundant the fruit, the vegetables or the wine, they are all grist for debate.

The most heated discussions today are fuelled by the European Union, whose legislation, the farmers say, has set aside acres of productive Provençal land. They see ancient vineyards being grubbed up, no new ones to be planted. They cite towns such as Cavaillon, once among the richest in the country because of its fruit and vegetables, now no longer in the same league, with its landowners' wealth in similar decline.

The harvest cycle is close to the gods, whose benificence can affect the crops as surely as any EU bureaucrat. As Catholic as the rest of France, the people of Provence are also touched with a mystic sense that has been influenced by Mithraism and Islam, as well as by pagan gods. Religious beliefs are so well mixed that it is often difficult to separate them. Carnival and Corpus Christi extend Easter, which has more importance here than in many other parts of Europe. Christmas, too, is an elaborate affair. The rituals begin as early as 4 December, St Barb's day, with the planting of grains of wheat, a pagan symbol of renewal and rebirth.

Superstitions linger in the countryside. An egg, salt, bread and matches, humble representations of elemental

Fish, straight from the sea to the market

concepts, may be given to a newborn baby, while carline thistles may be seen nailed to front doors for good luck.

Provence has a typically Mediterranean landscape: the mountains drop down to the sea; communities perch on crags or cling to remote hillsides. It is little wonder that traditions live on here. For centuries, too, it was a place for outlaws from France, who could assume new identities here and carry on with their lives.

Harvesting linden blossoms to make *tilleul* infusion

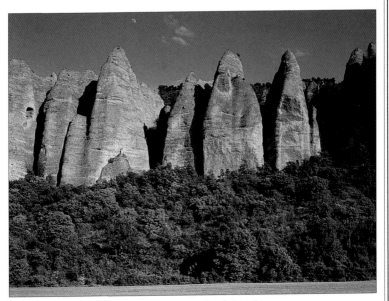

The dramatic, isolated crags of Les Pénitents des Mées, in Alpes-de-Haute-Provence

Strangers were not to be trusted, and remained outsiders for ever. A seemingly trivial slight might spark a feud which could last for generations. There are still villages where one family does not speak to another, even though each has long forgotten why. This attitude, and its tragic implications, was finely portrayed by Yves Montand, with Gérard Depardieu as the shunned outsider, in Claud Berri's films of Marcel Pagnol's *Jean de Florette* and *Manon des Sources*. The more cosmopolitan coast is the territory of *film noir*. Here, the tradition of silence and family ties has not always been beneficial. Jean-Paul Belmondo and Alain Delon romanticized it in *Borsalino;* Gene Hackman revealed its dark underside in *The French Connection.*

In 1982, the Antibes-based novelist Graham Greene published an exposé of corruption in nearby Nice. In 1994, Yann Piat, anti-drugs campaigner and member of parliament, was assassinated in Hyères.

The fact that Piat was a woman made no difference to her enemies, ironic in a region where women are not treated as equals. Alphonse Daudet noted the Provençal male's "incurable contempt" for women. Still, the Queen of Arles is elected for her virtues as an upholder of the traditional Provençal values; It was this region that nurtured the 20th century's icon of French womanhood, Brigitte Bardot.

There are great rewards for the visitor who can appreciate the many facets of Provence – its traditions as well as its beauty and glamour. But, the more often you return, the more you will realize, as have some of the world's greatest artists and writers, that part of the endless allure of Provence lies within the very secrets that it refuses to surrender.

Pavement café on cours Mirabeau, Aix

The Natural History of Provence

A two-tailed pasha butterfly

A fascinating array of insects, birds, animals and flowers flourish in the varied habitats available in Provence, from the Mediterranean to coastal wetlands, rocky gorges and the remote peaks of the Alpes Maritimes. The area has the mildest climate in France: hot, mainly dry summers, and warm, mild winters near the coast. In early spring the myriad flowers are at their best, while numbers of unusual birds are at their highest in late spring. Many of the wilder areas have been made into reserves, often with routes marked out for exploration.

Mont Ventoux's lower slopes are flower-covered in the spring *(see p160)*.

The Luberon (see pp170–72) *is a huge limestone range, rich in orchids, such as this military orchid. It is also a hunting ground for birds of prey.*

Les Alpilles' *limestone ridge (see p141) attracts birds of prey, including Bonelli's eagles, Egyptian vultures and eagle owls, as well as this more mild-mannered bee-eater.*

• Orange

Carpentras •

• Avignon

Rhône

VAUCLUSE

• Arles

BOUCHES-DU-RHONE AND NIMES

The Camargue, *at the delta of the river Rhône, is one of Europe's most important wetlands (see pp136–9). Water birds that thrive here include purple herons and the magnificent greater flamingo. Lizards, such as this ocellated lizard, can also be seen here.*

• Marseille

The Côte Bleue is rich in marine life, such as octopuses, in the deeper waters.

Les Calanques *(see p153)* are narrow inlets bounded by cliffs. Pine and oak trees grow on the rocky slopes, home to woodland birds such as owls.

The Plaine de la Crau *is 50,000 ha (193 sq miles) of stony plains and steppe-like grasslands southeast of Arles, home to birds like this hoopoe, and the rare pin-tailed sandgrouse.*

The Parc National du Mercantour *is one of the finest Alpine reserves (see p97), containing wildlife such as this marmot, and chamois, ibex and mouflon (wild sheep). It is also good walking country.*

The Haute Provence Geological Reserve near Digne *(see p180)* has a spectacular collection of giant ammonites embedded in rock.

The Cime de la Bonette *(see p179)* is a lofty pass where chamois roam.

The Gorges du Verdon *area, between the Alps and the Mediterranean, is a beautiful nature reserve with a dramatic canyon at its centre (see pp184–5). A footpath along the canyon floor allows detailed examination of the rock formations, rare plants and birds.*

Barcelonnette •

ALPES-DE-HAUTE-PROVENCE

Digne-les-Bains

Var

The Gorges de la Vésubie *(see p95)* has viewpoints from which to spot migrating birds such as swallows.

THE RIVIERA AND THE ALPES MARITIMES

Nice

THE VAR AND THE ILES D'HYERES

• Fréjus

The Massif de l'Esterel's *(see p124)* high rocky coves and scrubland are home to various species of snakes.

In the Massif des Maures (see pp116–17), *dense maquis and cork oak woods contain bee-eaters, woodchat shrikes and hoopoes. They also provide sanctuary for the rare Hermann's tortoise.*

The Massif de la Ste-Baume is clothed with many broadleaved trees that are vividly coloured in autumn.

Toulon

KEY

☐	National park
☐	Regional natural park
☐	Protected site
☐	Reserve

0 kilometres   25

0 miles   25

The Iles d'Hyères (see pp114–15), *scattered a ferry-ride away from the most southerly point of Provence, are best known for their abundant sea life, including fish such as this wrasse. Geckos and rare birds like the great spotted cuckoo can be seen.*

Perched Villages

Some of the most attractive architectural features of Provence are the *villages perchés* or perched villages. They rise like jagged summits on the hilltops where they were built for safety in the political turmoil of the Middle Ages. From their lofty heights they kept vigil over the hinterland as well as the coast. They were built around castle keeps and wrapped in thick ramparts, a huddle of cobbled streets, steps, alleys and archways. Few were able to sustain their peasant communities beyond the 19th-century agrarian reforms, and a century of poverty and depopulation followed. Today many of the villages have been restored by a new generation of artists, craftworkers and holiday-makers.

The mountainous site *of Peillon (see p95) is typical of the way perched villages blend organically with the landscape.*

RUE DE LA FOURTOUINE

GRANDE PLACE

RUE DES DORIERS

RUE DES BAUQUES

RUE DE LA CASTRE

RUE GRANDE

COURTINE ST PAUL

BASTION ST REMY

REMPAR

ST-PAUL-DE-VENCE
St-Paul is a typical *village perché*, with many of the key features preserved. The medieval ramparts were completely reinforced by Francis I in the 16th century. Today it is again besieged – as one of the most popular tourist sights in France *(see p75)*.

Complicated entrances confused invaders and provided extra security against attack.

The chapel was always the focal point of the village.

Side entrances *were never obtrusive or elaborate, but were usually small and, as in Eze (see p88), opened onto narrow, winding lanes. Sometimes there were more gates or abrupt turns within the walls to confuse attacking soldiers, making the town easier to defend.*

Castles and keeps *(donjons), and sometimes fortified churches, were always sited with the best viewpoint in the village, and provided sanctuary in times of crisis. Many, like the castle at Eze (see p88), were often attacked and are now in ruins.*

The chapel *sustained the religious life of the community. As in Les Baux (see p142), it was usually built near the keep of the castle, part of a central core of communal buildings, and was often fortified. The bell would be rung to warn of impending attack.*

Fountains *were essential to the village, often being the sole source of water. Many, like this one in Vence (see p74), were elaborately embellished.*

The arcades *lent support to the buildings in the narrow, winding streets, as here in Roquebrune (see p98). They also gave shelter from sun and rain.*

Fountain

Arched and stepped streets

RUE GRANDE

LE PONTIS

RUE GRANDE

DU HAUT FOUR

PLACE DE L'HOSPICE

REMPARTS OUEST

EST

A narrow gateway was easily secured.

Ramparts and bastions provided solid defences.

The ramparts *surrounded the entire village with thick stone walls, often with houses built into them. The defences, like those of St-Paul (see p75), were strengthened in the 16th century under Francis I and by Vauban, Louis XIV's military architect. Today they offer excellent panoramas.*

Main gates *were always narrow so they could be closed off and defended in times of attack. Some gates had the additional protection of portcullises. This example is one of four 12th-century gates built into the ramparts of the ancient village of Bargemon (see p106) in the Var.*

Rural Architecture in Provence

Shutters to keep out the sun and wind

Traditional architectural features are reminders of how influential the weather is on living conditions in rural Provence. Great efforts are made to ease the biting gusts of the Mistral and the relentless heat of the summer sun. Thick stone walls, small windows and reinforced doors are all recognizable characteristics. Traditional farmhouses were built entirely from wood, clay, stone and soil, all locally found materials. Rows of hardy cypress trees were planted to act as a windbreak on the north side; plane and lotus trees provided shade to the south.

Bories (see p169) *are drystone huts built using techniques dating back to 2,000 BC.*

THE PROVENÇAL MAS

Found across rural Provence, the *mas* is a low, squat stone farmhouse. Protection and strength are vital to its construction – walls are made of compact stone blocks and the wooden doors and shutters are thick and reinforced. Outbuildings often included a cellar, stables, a bread oven and dovecote.

Canal roof tiling, *or* tuiles romaines, *is typical of the south.*

Dovecot

Chimneys are stone-built, low and squat, and lie close to the roof.

Roughly cut stone bricks are used to make the walls.

The most exposed part of the roof is unthatched.

The roof is gently sloping and thatched with marsh reeds.

The north wall is rounded for protection against the Mistral.

The gardian's cabin *was the original dwelling place of the bull herdsman or* gardian *of the Camargue. It is a small, narrow structure, consisting of a dining room and bedroom, divided by a reed screen and furnished simply.*

The windows are small and reinforced.

Walls are made of compressed clay and straw, known as cob.

The tiled roofs *are gently sloping and are influenced by Roman design, with a decorative frieze (génoise) under the eaves. The tiles are made of thick, red terracotta and curved in shape – a double or triple layer of tiles are set in mortar and protrude beyond the wall.*

Windows are built *on three sides of the mas but none on the north to avoid the Mistral's full blast. They are kept small to prevent the winter winds coming in, but large enough to let light in.*

Interlocking clay tiles form canals, allowing rainwater to run down and drain off the roof.

The Mistral winds blow so fiercely that the mas was often built facing the southeast to minimize the wind's impact. Roofs are built low to the ground, covering the living quarters and annexes. The gentle slope prevents the tiles blowing and sliding off.

The walls are rendered smooth with plaster.

Stone ice houses *were built near the mas and used for storage during the winter months. Blocks of ice were cut and put in the huts, insulated with hay.*

IRONWORK BELL TOWERS

Wrought-iron bell towers have been a speciality in Provence since the 16th century. Their light, open framework allows strong winds to blow through and the sound of the bells to carry for miles. The design and complexity depends on the size and purpose of the building. These examples illustrate the skills of local craftsmen across the region.

Highly ornate bell tower in Aix

The bell tower of St-Jérôme in Digne

The Hôtel de Ville bell tower in Orange

Notre Dame's bell tower in Sisteron

Architectural Styles in Provence

From the imperial grandeur of Roman constructions to the modern domestic designs of Le Corbusier, Provence has a magnificent array of architectural styles. The Middle Ages saw a flourishing of great Romanesque abbeys and churches and from the 16th to the 18th centuries, as prosperity increased, châteaux and town houses were built. With the expansion of towns in the 19th century came an increase in apartment blocks and public buildings to accommodate the fast-growing population. Today, successful restoration has taken place, but often in haste. The demands of tourism have taken their toll, particularly on the coast, resulting in ugly developments.

An 18th-century fountain in Pernes-les-Fontaines

ROMAN ARCHITECTURE (20 BC–AD 400)

The quality of Roman architecture is illustrated by the many extant amphitheatres, triumphal arches and thermal baths found across the region, all built with large blocks of local limestone.

Ornate high-relief

The triumphal arch of Glanum (pp140–41) *is the original entrance to the oldest Roman city in Provence. Carvings on the outer arch show Caesar's victory over the Gauls and Greeks.*

Doric columns on second storey

Both storeys have 60 arcades

Nîmes Arènes, built in the 1st century AD (p132)

Nîmes' well-preserved Maison Carrée (p132)

ROMANESQUE ARCHITECTURE (11–12TH CENTURIES)

The high point of Provençal architecture came after the Dark Ages. It was a combination of Classical order and perfection, inspired by Roman design and new styles from northern and southern Europe. This style is characterized especially in religious buildings by elegant symmetry and simplicity.

Multiple arches

Elaborate religious carvings

This church entrance in Seyne (see p178) *is an example of 13th-century Romanesque architecture. The slight point of the multiple arches hints at a move away from strict Romanesque purity.*

Clustered pillar

Decorated capital with interlaced leaves

Capital from the Abbaye du Thoronet (p108)

The Abbaye de Sénanque, founded in 1148 (pp164–5)

LATE MIDDLE AGES (13TH–16TH CENTURIES)

Feuding and religious wars led to people withdrawing to towns, protected by fortified walls and gates. Communication between houses was often by underground passages. Streets were roughly paved and water and sewage were carried away by a central gutter.

Tour de la Campana in the Palais des Papes (pp44–5)

Street in St-Martin-Vésubie (p95) showing central gutter

Crenellation or battlements

Portcullis used against invaders

Aigues-Mortes (see pp134–5) *was built by Louis IX in the 13th century, according to a strict grid pattern. This strategically placed fort overlooks both sea and land.*

CLASSICAL ARCHITECTURE (17TH–18TH CENTURIES)

The severity and order of the Classical style was relieved by elaborate carvings on doorways and windows. Gardens became more formal and symmetrical.

The 17th-century Barbentane château, fronted by formal gardens (p130)

Tablet with symbol of authority

Carved Regency doorway

Refined stone

Neo-Classical pillar

The Musée des Tapisseries *in Aix (see p148) has elaborately carved wooden entrance doors.*

Pavillon de Vendôme detail, Aix-en-Provence (p149)

MODERN ARCHITECTURE (1890–PRESENT DAY)

The magnificent hotels and villas of the Belle Epoque have given way to more utilitarian housing and public buildings. But the numerous modern art galleries represent the highest standards of 20th-century architecture.

Le Corbusier's Cité Radieuse (p152)

Rounded pavilion

Cupola above a round corner tower

The palatial Négresco hotel in Nice (p84)

The Musée d'Art Contemporain in Nice (see p85) *was built in 1990. It is made up of square towers, linked by glass passageways.*

Artists of Provence

Provence inspired many of the most original 19th-
and 20th-century painters. They were attracted by
the luminescent quality of the light here, and the
consequent brilliance of the colours. Cézanne,
who was a native, and Van Gogh, a convert, were
both fired by the vibrant shades of the landscape.
The Impressionists Monet and Renoir came early,
and followers included Bonnard, Signac and Dufy.
The two giants of 20th-century painting, Matisse
and Picasso, both settled here. The artistic tradition
is kept alive by small galleries in almost every town,
as well as major museums throughout the region.

Jean Cocteau *(1889–1963) spent
many years on the coast and created
his museum in Menton (see p99).
Noce imaginaire (1957) is one of his
murals from the Salle des Mariages.*

Victor Vasarely *(1908–
97) restored the château
in Gordes. His Kinetic and
Op Art can be seen in Aix-
en-Provence (see p149).*

Hans Van Meegeren
*(1889–1947), the Dutch
master-forger of Vermeer,
was living in Roquebrune
(see p98) when found out.*

**REGIONS OF
PROVENCE**

Gordes · Roquebrune · Menton · Arles · Aix-en-Provence · Martigues · St-Tropez · Vallauris

Vincent Van Gogh *(1853–90)
painted* Van Gogh's Chair *(1888)
in Arles (see pp144–6). His two
years here and in St-Rémy (see
pp140–41) were his most prolific.*

Paul Cézanne *(1839–
1906), in his desire to
scour the "depth of reality",
often painted his native
Aix (see pp148–9).*

Paul Signac *(1863–1935)
came to St-Tropez in 1892,
painting it in his palette of
rainbow dots (see pp118–22).*

Félix Ziem *(1821–1911) was born in
Burgundy but was a great traveller. He adored
Venice, and found the same romantic
inspiration by the canals of Martigues (see
p147), where he painted* Camargue, Côté Soleil.

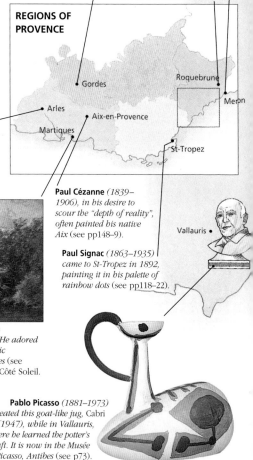

Pablo Picasso *(1881–1973)
created this goat-like jug,* Cabri
*(1947), while in Vallauris,
where he learned the potter's
craft. It is now in the Musée
Picasso, Antibes (see p73).*

0 kilometres   3
0 miles   3

Marc Chagall *(1887–1985),
Russian painter of light-hearted
and biblically inspired works,
lived in St-Paul-de-Vence
from 1949 (see p75).*

Raoul Dufy *(1877–1953)
appreciated the pleasures of the
coast. A twilight stroll beneath the
palm trees is fondly evoked in* La
Jetée, Promenade à Nice *(1928).*

• Vence

• Cagnes-sur-Mer

Henri Matisse
*(1869–1954) captured
the Riviera's light and colour
even in homely settings such as*
Intérieur au Phonographe
(1924) (see pp82–3).

• Biot

Pierre Auguste Renoir
*(1841–1919) sought relief
from his rheumatism at
Cagnes in 1906 and found
new inspiration (see p78).*

Fernand Léger *(1881–
1955) is celebrated for his
vivid Cubist and industrial
works in oils and ceramics,
on show in Biot (see p74).*

Antibes

Nicolas de Staël *(1914–55) was born in
Russia. When successful, he bought a house
in the Luberon for his wife, but chose to live
with his mistress in Antibes (see p72). His*
Paysage Méditerranéen *was painted in 1953.*

ARTISTS IN PROVENÇAL HISTORY

Provence was home to great artists long
before the advent of modern art. In the
Middle Ages, the Schools of Avignon and
Nice flourished. The latter was dominated
by the Bréa family, whose works can be
seen in churches throughout the
region. Sculptor Pierre Puget
(1620–94) is called the
"Michelangelo of Provence".
His birthplace, Marseille,
has several of his works *(see
p150–2).* But Jean-Honoré
Fragonard (1732–1806) is
most Provençal
of them all – his Romantic
paintings are filled with
Grasse flowers *(see p66).*

**Crucifixion (1512) by Louis
Bréa, monastery of Notre-
Dame, Cimiez *(see p84)***

Writers in Provence

The Nobel Laureate Frédéric Mistral (1830–1914) was the champion of the Provençal language, but better known are the local writers who have captured the Provençal character: Alphonse Daudet, Jean Giono, Emile Zola and Marcel Pagnol. French writers such as Dumas and Hugo used Provençal backdrops for their fiction; foreign writers also found inspiration in the region.

Victor Hugo

1892 The last part of *Thus Spake Zarathustra* by German Friedrich Nietzsche is published. He devised it after traversing the path in Eze *(see p88)* which was later named after him.

1895 Jean Giono is born in Manosque *(see p182)*. Work like *The Man who Planted Trees* evokes the region.

Frédéric Mistral

An early edition of The Count of Monte Cristo

Alphonse Daudet

1869 Alphonse Daudet publishes *Collected Letters from my Windmill*, set in a windmill at Fontvieille *(see p143)*.

1870 Death in Cannes of Prosper Mérimée, author of *Carmen*, Bizet's opera.

1844 Alexander Dumas publishes *The Count of Monte Cristo*, set in the Château d'If, Marseille *(see p152)*.

1904 Frédéric Mistral wins the Nobel Prize with his poem, *Mirèio*.

1840	1855	1870	1885	1900
1840	1855	1870	1885	1900

1862 *Les Misérables* by Victor Hugo is published. The early chapters are set in Digneles-Bains *(see p180)*.

1868 Edmond Rostand, author of *Cyrano de Bergerac* (1897) is born in Marseille *(see pp150–51)*.

1907 Provençal poet, René Char, is born in L'Isle sur-la-Sorgue.

EARLY WRITERS

For centuries, troubadour ballads and religious poems, or *Noels*, formed the core of literature in Provence. While certain unique individuals stand out, it was not until 1854, with Mistral's help, that Provençal writers found their own "voice".

1327 Petrarch *(see p45)* falls in unrequited love with Laura de Noves in Avignon, inspir-ing his *Canzonière* poems.

1555 Nostradamus, from St-Rémy, publishes *The Centuries*, prophecies outlawed by the Vatican.

1764 Tobias Smollett "discovers" Nice. (He published his book, *Travels through France and Italy*, in 1766).

1791 Marquis de Sade, the original sadist, publishes *Justine*, written while imprisoned in the Bastille.

Petrarch's Laura de Noves

Edith Wharton

1915 Edith Wharton, American author of *The Age of Innocence*, visits Hyères *(see p115)* with André Gide. A street is named after her.

1887 Journalist Stéphen Liégeard introduces the term, *Côte d'Azur*.

Emile Zola

1885 *Germinal* published by Emile Zola, boyhood friend of Cézanne, as part of his 20-novel cycle, *The Fortunes of the Rouge* (1871–93), set partly round Aix.

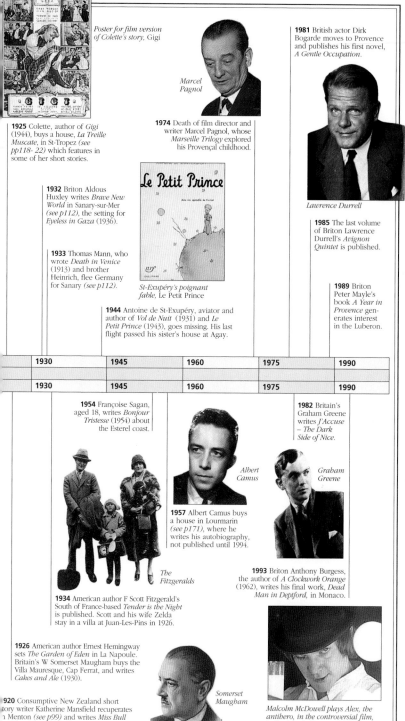

Poster for film version of Colette's story, Gigi

Marcel Pagnol

1925 Colette, author of *Gigi* (1944), buys a house, *La Treille Muscate*, in St-Tropez *(see pp118- 22)* which features in some of her short stories.

1974 Death of film director and writer Marcel Pagnol, whose *Marseille Trilogy* explored his Provençal childhood.

1932 Briton Aldous Huxley writes *Brave New World* in Sanary-sur-Mer *(see p112)*, the setting for *Eyeless in Gaza* (1936).

1933 Thomas Mann, who wrote *Death in Venice* (1913) and brother Heinrich, flee Germany for Sanary *(see p112)*.

St-Exupéry's poignant fable, Le Petit Prince

1944 Antoine de St-Exupéry, aviator and author of *Vol de Nuit* (1931) and *Le Petit Prince* (1943), goes missing. His last flight passed his sister's house at Agay.

1981 British actor Dirk Bogarde moves to Provence and publishes his first novel, *A Gentle Occupation*.

Lawrence Durrell

1985 The last volume of Briton Lawrence Durrell's *Avignon Quintet* is published.

1989 Briton Peter Mayle's book *A Year in Provence* generates interest in the Luberon.

1930	1945	1960	1975	1990
1930	1945	1960	1975	1990

1954 Françoise Sagan, aged 18, writes *Bonjour Tristesse* (1954) about the Esterel coast.

1982 Britain's Graham Greene writes *J'Accuse – The Dark Side of Nice.*

Albert Camus

Graham Greene

1957 Albert Camus buys a house in Lourmarin *(see p171)*, where he writes his autobiography, not published until 1994.

The Fitzgeralds

1993 Briton Anthony Burgess, the author of *A Clockwork Orange* (1962), writes his final work, *Dead Man in Deptford*, in Monaco.

1934 American author F Scott Fitzgerald's South of France-based *Tender is the Night* is published. Scott and his wife Zelda stay in a villa at Juan-Les-Pins in 1926.

1926 American author Ernest Hemingway sets *The Garden of Eden* in La Napoule. Britain's W Somerset Maugham buys the Villa Mauresque, Cap Ferrat, and writes *Cakes and Ale* (1930).

1920 Consumptive New Zealand short story writer Katherine Mansfield recuperates in Menton *(see p99)* and writes *Miss Bull* and *Passion* among other pieces.

Somerset Maugham

Malcolm McDowell plays Alex, the antihero, in the controversial film, A Clockwork Orange *(1966).*

The Beaches of Provence

From the untamed expanses of the Rhône delta to the hot spots of the Riviera, via the cliffs and coves of the Var, the coastline of Provence is extremely varied. Resort beaches around the towns of the Riviera, such as Menton, Nice and Monte-Carlo, are crowded and noisy in the height of summer. They often charge a fee, but are usually well-kept and offer good watersports facilities. It is, however, possible to seek out quieter corners away from the crowds if you know where to look.

The Côte d'Azur *beaches offer warmth and sunshine all year long, as advertised in this 1930s poster by Roger Broders.*

The Camargue beaches (see pp136–8) *at the mouth of the Rhône delta, are often deserted. The long, flat sands are ideal for horse riding, but there is a shortage of amenities.*

The Côte Bleue *is dotted with fishing ports and elegant summer residences. Pine trees line the beaches.*

Stes-Maries-de-la-Mer ①

Plage de Piémanson

Carry-le-Rouet

CÔTE BLEUE

Marseille

CAMARGUE

CALANQUES ②

Bandol

Sanary ③

S

Les Calanques (see p153) *are beautiful and dramatic fjord-like inlets situated east of Marseille. The sheer white cliffs, some 400 m (1,312 ft) high, drop vertically into the tempting, blue water.*

Cap Sicié *is a small peninsula that juts out from the Var mainland. It is famed for its strong winds and waves, ideal for experienced windsurfers.*

PROVENCE'S TEN BEST BEACHES

Best sandy beach ①
Plage de Piémanson, east of the Camargue, is remote enough for nudist bathing.
Best deep-sea diving ②
The deep Calanques waters are ideal for exploring.
Best sea fishing ③
Bandol and Sanary are charming resorts, where the tuna boats make their daily catch.
Best small resort beach ④
Le Lavandou offers all amenities on a small scale.

Best trendy beach ⑤
Tahiti-Plage in St-Tropez is the coast's showcase for fun, sun, fashion and glamour.
Best family beaches ⑥
Fréjus-Plage and the beach of St-Raphaël are clean, safe and have excellent facilities.
Best star-spotter's beach ⑦
Cannes' beautiful setting, with its scenic harbour, casino and stylish beaches, attracts the rich and famous.

Best teen and twenties beach ⑧
The all-night bars, cafés and nightclubs of Juan-les-Pins make this a lively resort.
Best activity beach ⑨
Watersports fanatics gather at the Ruhl-Plage in Nice for the jet-skiing and parasailing.
Best winter beach ⑩
Menton is the warmest resort on the Riviera and the sun shines all year round, ideal for relaxing winter holidays.

0 kilometres   25

0 miles   25

The Riviera *is the most popular destination for sun-worshippers, with its big, traditional resorts and private golden beaches.*

The Côte Varoise *has a beach to suit all tastes, offering popular family resorts, small fishing ports and excellent snorkelling.*

The Esterel *coast stretches from Cannes to St-Raphaël. Its most striking features are the red cliffs and rocks, deep ravines and secluded coves.*

PROVENCE THROUGH THE YEAR

Provence is at its prettiest in spring, when flowers bring livelihoods to perfume-makers and pleasure to passers-by. It can also be surprisingly cold as this is when the Mistral blows its strongest.

Summer fruit and vegetables are both abundant and beautiful, filling the local markets. The midsummer heat is added to by the fires of St Jean and the Valensole plains are striped with lavender, the indelible colour of the region.

Medieval-style grape harvest or *vendange*

To entertain the thousands of holiday makers, July and August are filled with music festivals. Come autumn, vineyards turn to copper and the grapes are harvested. Snows blanket the mountains from December and skiers take to the slopes. Throughout the year, every town and village celebrates with a *fête*, often with traditional costume and lively activities. For information, contact the local tourist office *(see p237)*.

The first strawberries of the year

SPRING

By the time March begins, lemons have already been harvested and the almond blossom faded. The landscape is brightened with pear, plum and apricot blossom and the first vegetables of spring are ready for the markets: beans, asparagus and green artichokes known as *mourre de gats*. By May, fruit markets are coloured with the first ripe cherries and strawberries of the year.

Southern mountain slopes warm to the sunshine and come alive with alpine flowers but the northern slopes remain wintery. Broom turns hillsides deep yellow and bees start to make honey from the sweet-smelling rosemary flowers. Flocks of sheep begin the journey of transhumance up to the summer pastures, and on the vast plains maize, wheat and rape push their way up through the softening earth.

MARCH

Exposition International de la Fleur *(end-March–April)*, Cagnes-sur-Mer *(p78)*. One of the region's many flower festivals to celebrate spring.
Festin des Courgourdons *(last Sun)*, Nice *(pp84-5)*. Folklore and sculpted gourd *fête*.

APRIL

Procession aux Limaces *(Good Friday)*, Roquebrune-Cap-Martin *(p98)*. The streets are lit with shell lamps and a parade of locals dressed as disciples and legionnaires recreate the entombment of Christ.
Fête de la St-Marc *(end April)*, Châteauneuf-du-Pape *(p164)*. Wine contest. (The year's vintage is blessed on the 1st weekend in August.)
Fête des Gardians *(last Sunday in April)*, Arles *(pp144–6)*. The town is taken over by the *gardians* or cowboys who look after the Camargue cattle herds
Feria Pascale *(Easter)*, Arles *(pp144–6)*. Arletans turn out in

their traditional costume for a *feria*. The *farandole* is danced to the accompaniment of the *tambourin* drum and *galoubet* flute to mark the beginning of the famous bullfighting season.

MAY

Pèlerinage des Gitans avec Procession à la Mer de Sainte Sarah *(24–25 May)*, Stes-Maries-de-la-Mer *(pp228–9)*.
Festival International du Film *(two weeks in May)*, Cannes *(pp68–9)*. The most prestigious annual film festival.
La Bravade *(16–18 May)*, St-Tropez *(see p228)*.
Fête de la Saint-Marc *(end Apr–mid-May)*, Villeneuve-Loubet *(p74)*. Classical and regional music.
Grand Prix Automobile de Formula 1 (weekend after Ascension), Monaco *(p94)*. The only Grand Prix raced on public roads laps up an impressive 3,145 km (1,954 miles).
Feria *(Pentecost)*, Nîmes *(see pp132–3)*. The first major bullfighting event of the year.

Rodeo-style horse games at the Fête des Gardians in Arles

AVERAGE DAILY HOURS OF SUNSHINE

Hours

12 — 9 — 6 — 3 — 0

Jan Feb Mar Apr May Jun Jul Aug Sep Oct Nov Dec

Sunshine Chart
The summer months are guaranteed to be hot, with the intensity climaxing in July. Even in the winter, coastal towns can have up to 150 hours of sunshine a month, but be warned: it is often the icy Mistral that blows the clouds away in early spring.

SUMMER

The Côte d'Azur is essentially a playground in summer, particularly in August when the French take their holidays. Rafters take to the rivers and scuba divers explore the varied sea-life. For laid-on entertainment, there are music festivals throughout the region.

Three national celebrations are also manifest: fireworks and bonfires brighten the skies on the **Fête de St-Jean** (June 24). **Bastille Day** (July 14) is celebrated with fireworks while **Assumption Day** (August 15) is a time for great feasting.

JUNE

Fête de la Tarasque *(last w/e)*, Tarascon *(p140)*. According to local legend, the Tarasque monster once terrorized the region. An effigy of the monster is paraded through the town.
Festival d'Art Lyrique *(June and July)*, Aix-en-Provence *(pp148–9)*. Extensive programme of classical music concerts and opera is staged in the courtyard theatre of the Archbishop's Palace.

JULY

Festival de la Sorgue *(end Jun–end Jul)*, Fontaine-de-Vaucluse & l'Isle-sur-la-Sorgue *(see p165)*. Concerts, shows, boat races and floating markets on the river Sorgue.
Festival d'Avignon *(last three weeks)*, Avignon *(see p229)*.
Chorégies d'Orange *(all*

Celebrating the Fête de St-Jean with fireworks over Marseille harbour

The legendary Tarasque

month) Orange. This long-established opera season is held in the accoustically perfect Roman theatre *(pp162–3)*.
Jazz à Juan *(last 2 weeks)*, Juan-les-Pins *(p72)*. One of the top jazz festivals in Provence.
Festival du Jazz *(mid-month)*, Toulon *(p112–13)*. A week of free concerts in different squares every day throughout the town.
Recontres Internationales de la Photographie *(first two weeks)*, Arles *(p144–6)*. The National School of Photography was set up in 1982 as a result of this festival and each year the town is transformed into a photographic arena.

AUGUST

Corso de la Lavande *(first weekend)*, Digne-les-Bains *(see p229)*.
Les Journées Médiévales *(biennial, weekend before Assumption)*, Entrevaux

(p187). The quiet streets come to life with a 16th- and 17th-century music *fête*.
Fête du Jasmin *(first weekend)*, Grasse *(pp66–7)*. Floats, music and dancing in the town.
Procession de la Passion *(5 Aug)*, Roquebrune-Cap-Martin *(p98)*. Over 500 locals take part in staging Christ's passion, enacted since the Virgin saved the town from plague in 1467.
Le Festival de Musique *(all month)*, Menton *(pp98–9)*. Chamber music in the square.

Holiday-makers on the crowded beaches of the Côte d'Azur

AVERAGE MONTHLY RAINFALL

Rainfall Chart
*Spring and autumn
are the wettest times,
with the amount of
rainfall increasing as
you head inland.
November rain is the
most violent, often
with storms and
flooding. Summer is
virtually rain-free,
causing drought in
some forest areas.*

AUTUMN

When summer is over it is
time for the *vendange*, the
grape harvest. In the
Camargue, rice is ready to be
brought in. Walnuts are
picked and, in the Maures,
sweet chestnuts are collected.
The woods also yield rewards
for mushroom hunters, while
in Vaucluse and the Var truffles
are harvested from oak woods
and sold on the market stalls,
notably at Richerenches.

The hunting season begins
in November. Small birds, such
as thrushes, and ducks fall from
flight into the pot and wild
boar are bagged, their feet kept
as talismans. Sheep are brought
down to their winter pastures.

A grape picker at work during the autumn harvest

On the hunt for truffles in the
woods of Haute Provence

SEPTEMBER

Fête des Prémices du Riz
(early Sep), Arles *(pp144–6)*.
This festival of the rice harvest
coincides with the last Spanish-
style bullfights of the year.

Féria des Vendanges *(second
week)*, Nîmes *(pp132–3)*. An
enjoyable combination of
wine, dancing and bullfights.
**Festival de la Navigation de
Plaisance** *(mid-Sep)*, Cannes
(pp68–9). Yachts from around
the world meet in the harbour.
Fête du Vent *(mid-Sep)*,
Marseille *(pp150–2)*. Kites
from all over the world
decorate the sky for two days
down on the Plages du Prado.

OCTOBER

Fête de Sainte Marie Salomé
(Sunday nearest 22 Oct), Stes-
Maries-de-la-Mer. A similar festival to the Gypsy Pilgrimage
held in May *(see p228–9)* with
a procession through the
town's streets to the beach and
the ritual blessing of the sea.
**Foire Internationale de
Marseille** *(end of Sep–early
Oct)*, Marseille *(pp150–52)*.
Thousands of visitors pour into
the city to enjoy the annual fair.
Various activities and sports are
organized with crafts, music
and folklore entertainment from
over 40 different countries.

NOVEMBER

Fête du Prince *(19 Nov)*,
Monaco *(pp90–94)*. The
second smallest independent
state in Europe celebrates its
national day with a firework
display over the harbour.
**Festival International de la
Danse** *(biennial, late-Nov or
early Dec)*, Cannes *(pp68–9)*.
A festival of contemporary
dance and ballet with an
impressive programme of
international performances.

Performers at the Festival International de la Danse in Cannes

AVERAGE MONTHLY TEMPERATURE

Temperature Chart
The Mistral has a substantial effect on the temperature. During the winter and early spring, it can drop 10°C (18°F) in only a few hours. The summer heat can be uncomfortable, but the evenings cool down and are perfect for sitting outside.

WINTER

There is an old saying in Provence used to describe winter: *"l'hiver a ges d'ouro,"* "winter has no hours". It is a time to open the jams of the summer, to make the geese and duck *confits* and to turn the olive harvest into oil.

Snow soon cuts off mountain passes and, at weekends, locals and visitors take to the many ski resorts, warmed by juniper or wild strawberry liqueurs.

Christmas is heralded by the sale of *santons*, the figurines used to decorate Provence's distinctive cribs. Epiphany is another important festival, when the Three Kings are fêted with crown-shaped pastries.

DECEMBER

Foire aux Santons *(all month)*, Marseille *(pp150–52)*. The largest fair honouring the symbolic clay figures that are an integral part of Christmas.
Fête du Vin *(early December)*, Bandol *(p112)*. Every wine-grower in the town has their own stand and there is free wine-tasting. A different theme is chosen every year with activities and much merriment.
Noël and midnight mass *(24 Dec)*, Les Baux-de-Provence *(pp142–3)*. A traditional festive feast of the shepherds before mass.

JANUARY

Rallye de Monte-Carlo *(late Jan, pp92–3)*. A major event in the motor sporting calendar.
Festival du Cirque *(end of month)*, Monaco *(p94)*. Circus shows from around the globe.

Relaxing in the winter sun in the Alpes-de-Haute-Provence

FEBRUARY

Fête du Citron, *(late Feb–early Mar)*, Menton *(pp98–9)*. Floats and music fill the town during the lemon festival.
Fête du Mimosa *(third Sunday)*, Bormes-les-Mimosas

(pp116–17). The annual festival in celebration of the perched village's favourite flower.
Carnaval de Nice, *(all month)*, Nice *(see p228)*.

PUBLIC HOLIDAYS

New Year's Day (1 Jan)
Easter Sunday and Monday
Ascension (sixth Thursday after Easter)
Whit Monday (second Monday after Ascension)
Labour Day (1 May)
VE Day (8 May)
Bastille Day (14 Jul)
Assumption Day (15 Aug)
All Saints' Day (1 Nov)
Remembrance Day (11 Nov)
Christmas Day and Boxing Day (25–26 Dec)

The Taj Mahal re-created at the Fête du Citron in Menton

THE HISTORY
OF PROVENCE

Virgin and Child, Aix-en-Provence

Few regions of France have experienced such a varied and turbulent history as Provence. There is evidence, in the form of carvings, tools and weapons, of nomadic tribes and human settlements from 300,000 BC. The introduction of the vine, so important today, can be credited to the Phoenicians and Greeks who traded along the coast. Perhaps more crucially, Provence was the Romans' "Province" and few regions of their vast empire have retained such dramatic buildings; the theatre at Orange, the arenas of Arles and Nîmes, the Pont du Gard and the imposing trophy of La Turbie are all testimony to past Roman power.

The Middle Ages proved a stormy period of feuding warlords and invasions; the many well-fortified hilltop villages that characterize the region were a desperate attempt at defence. The presence of the papacy dominated the 14th century, and the magnificent palace that the popes built in Avignon remains today. The arts flourished too, especially under King René in his elegant capital of Aix. Following his death in 1480, Provence lost its independence and its history became enmeshed with that of France. Religious war took its toll and the Great Plague killed tens of thousands in 1720.

A beguiling climate and improved transport in the 19th century began to attract artists and foreign nobility. Tiny fishing villages grew into glamorous Riviera resorts. The allure remains for millions of tourists while economic investment means it is also a boom area for the technology industry.

16th-century map of Marseille and its harbour

◁ **Detail of an illuminated 13th-century manuscript showing a troubadour playing to a royal audience**

Ancient Provence

Rock carvings, fragments of paintings and remains from primitive settlements suggest that Provence was first inhabited a million years ago. Carvings in the Grotte de l'Observatoire in Monaco and the decorated Grotte Cosquer near Marseille are among the oldest of their kind in the world. Nomadic tribes roamed the land for centuries, notably the Celts from the north and the Ligurians from the east. Not until the arrival of the Phoenicians and the Greeks did trade flourish in a more structured way and Provençal society become more stable.

Stone fertility figurine (1,000,000 BC)

"Double Head" Carving
This stone figure (3rd century BC) probably decorated a Celtic sanctuary.

The **bories** at Gordes date back to 3,500 BC.

Celtic Doorway
(3rd century BC) The niches in the pillars held the embalmed heads of Celtic heroes.

The **Grotte des Fées** at Mont de Cordes contain prehistoric carvings often associated with modern astrological symbols.

St-Blaise, once a heavily fortified Greek trading centre, has only minimal remains.

The **Grotte Cosquer**, with paintings dating to 30,000 BC, is accessible only from the sea.

THE FOUNDATION OF MARSEILLE

When Greek traders arrived in 600 BC, their captain, Protis, attended a feast in honour of the local chief's daughter, Gyptis. She chose Protis as her husband. The chief's dowry to Protis and Gyptis was the strip of land on which Marseille grew.

Wine jars, bound for Greece from 1,000 BC onwards, were found in Les Calanques near Marseille.

TIMELINE

1,000,000 BC Earliest human presence in Provence at Grotte de l'Observatoire in Monaco; use of bone as a tool

400,000 BC Fire first used in Nice

60,000 BC Neanderthal hunters on the Riviera

1,000,000 BC	5,000		4,000	3,50

30,000 BC Appearance of *Homo sapiens* (modern man); cave painting at Grotte Cosquer

Cave painting from Grotte Cosquer

3,500 BC First borie villages

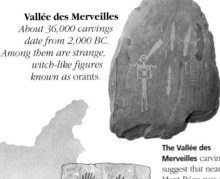

Vallée des Merveilles
About 36,000 carvings date from 2,000 BC. Among them are strange, witch-like figures known as orants.

The Vallée des Merveilles carvings suggest that nearby Mont Bégo was a focus for worship.

The **Grotte de l'Observatoire** in Monaco yielded evidence of symbolic human burials from prehistoric times.

The **"Fairy Stone"**, *Peïro de la fado* in Provençal, is the only true prehistoric dolmen in Provence.

WHERE TO SEE ANCIENT PROVENCE

Many museums, such as the Musée Archéologique, Nîmes *(see p132)*, have excellent collections of ancient artifacts. The well-preserved *bories* in the Luberon *(p169)* illustrate early village communities; the Grotte de l'Observatoire in Monaco *(p94)* is an example of an even more primitive settlement.

Borie Village at Gordes
These dry-stone dwellings (p169) have for centuries been used by nomadic shepherds.

Grotte de l'Observatoire
Skeletons uncovered here have characteristics linking them with southern African tribes.

ANCIENT SITES OF PROVENCE

Most sites lie along the coast, but there are some pockets of settlement inland near Tende, in the Luberon, and in the inaccessible Vallée des Merveilles, which stands at about 2,500 m (8,200 ft).

Standing Stone
Prehistoric stelae, like this carved stone from the Luberon, are scattered throughout Provence.

Hannibal crossing the Alps

2,500–2,000 BC Carvings at Vallée des Merveilles

218 BC Hannibal passes through region to reach Italy

3,000	2,500	2,000	1,500	1,000	500 BC

2,000 BC Tombs carved at Cordes

600 BC Greek traders settle at St-Blaise. Founding of Marseille

380 BC Celtic invasions of Provence

Gallo-Roman Provence

Mosaic from Vaison-la-Romaine (40 BC)

The Romans extended their empire into Provence towards the end of the 2nd century BC. They enjoyed good relations with the local people and within 100 years created a wealthy province. Nîmes and Arles became two of the most significant Roman towns outside Italy; colonies at Glanum and Vaison-la-Romaine flourished. Many fine monuments remain and museums, for instance at Vaison-la-Romaine, display smaller Roman treasures.

Christ's followers are reputed to have brought Christianity to the region when they landed at Les-Saintes-Maries-de-la-Mer in AD 40.

Pont Julien *(3 BC)*
This magnificently preserved triple-arched bridge stands 8 km (5 miles) west of Apt.

Two temples, dedicated to the emperor Augustus's adopted sons, Caius and Lucius, date from 30 BC.

Marble Sarcophagus *(4th century)*
The Alyscamps in Arles (see p146), once a vast Roman necropolis, contains many carved marble and stone coffins.

Triumphal Arch at Orange
Built in about 20 BC this is, in spite of much restoration, one of the best preserved Roman triumphal arches. Carvings depict the conquest of Gaul and sea battle scenes.

The fortified gate was built by the original Greek community that occupied Glanum from the 4th century BC.

ROMAN GLANUM

The impressive ruined site at Glanum reveals much earlier Roman and Greek settlements. This reconstruction shows it after it was rebuilt in AD 49.

TIMELINE

118 BC Provincia founded – first Gallo-Roman Province

125 BC Roman legions defend Marseille against Celto-Ligurian invaders

Consul Marius

49 BC Emperor Julius Caesar lays siege to Marseille for supporting his rival, Pompey. Romans rebuild Glanum

40 BC Vaison-la-Romaine ranks among Roman Gaul's wealthiest towns

100 BC	AD 1	100

123 BC Romans make Entremont first Provençal settlement

121 BC Foundation of Aquae Sextiae, later to become Aix-en-Provence

102 BC Consul Marius defeats invading German tribes; over 200,000 killed

14 BC Emperor Augustus defeats Ligurians in Alpes Maritimes. Trophy at La Turbie erected *(see p89)*

3 BC Pont Julien built

AD 40 "Boat of Bethany" lands at Les-Saintes-Maries-de-la-Mer

2nd-century BC Venus d'Arles

THE HISTORY OF PROVENCE

Les-Stes-Maries-de-la-Mer
Mary Magdalene, Mary Salome and Mary Jacobea reputedly sailed here in AD 40. The town where they landed is named in their honour and continues to attract pilgrims (see p138).

WHERE TO SEE GALLO-ROMAN PROVENCE

Arles *(see pp144–6)* and Nîmes *(pp132–3)*, with their amphitheatres and religious and secular buildings, offer the most complete examples of Roman civilization. Orange *(p161)* and Vaison-la-Romaine *(p158)* contain important monuments, and the Pont du Gard *(p131)* and Le Trophée des Alpes *(p89)* are unique.

Théâtre Antique d'Orange
Built into a hill, this Roman theatre would have held up to 7,000 spectators (pp162–3).

Cryptoporticus
The foundations of Arles' forum, these horseshoe-shaped underground galleries were probably used as grain stores (p146).

The baths occupied four rooms, each used for bathing at a different temperature.

The Forum, the commercial centre of the Roman town, was surrounded by a covered gallery.

Jewellery from Vaison-la-Romaine
1st-century AD jewellery was found in excavations of the Roman necropolis.

Roman Flask
Well-preserved ancient Roman glassware and everyday items have been found in many areas of Provence.

---

413 Visigoths seize Languedoc

476 Western Roman Empire collapses

200	300	400	500

300 Arles reaches height of its prestige as a Roman town

Abbaye St-Victor, founded 416, in Marseille

Medieval Provence

13th-century manuscript illustration

With the fall of the Roman Empire, stability and relative prosperity began to disappear. Although Provence became part of the Holy Roman Empire, the local counts retained considerable autonomy and the towns became fiercely independent. People withdrew to hilltops to protect themselves from attack by a series of invaders, and *villages perchés (see p20–21)* began to develop. Provence became a major base for Christian Crusaders, intent on conquering Muslim territories in Africa and Asia.

The Great Walls, finally completed in 1300, 30 years after Louis IX's death, were over 1.6 km (1 mile) long and formed an almost perfect rectangle.

St-Trophime Carving
The monumental 12th-century portal at St-Trophime in Arles (see p144) is adorned with intricate carvings of saints and scenes from the Last Judgment.

Louis IX's army consisted of 35,000 men plus horses and military equipment.

Louis IX

St Martha and the Tarasque
The 9th-century legend of St Martha and the Tarasque, a dragon, proved the strength of Christianity. The beast is said to have fled at the sight of her crucifix. (See p140.)

THE SEVENTH CRUSADE

Hoping to drive the Muslims out of the Holy Land, Louis IX (St Louis) of France set sail from his new port, Aigues-Mortes *(see p134–5)*, in 1248. It was a spectacular occasion, with banners waving and his army singing hymns.

TIMELINE

536 Provence ceded to the Franks

737–9 Anti-Frankish rebellions in Avignon, Marseille and Arles brutally suppressed by Charles Martel

855 Kingdom of Provence created for Charles the Bald, grandson of Charlemagne

949 Provence divided into four counties

600 **700** **800** **900**

Saracen warrior and Provençal maiden

800 First wave of Saracen invasions

924 Hungarians sack Nîmes

Charles the Bald

Troubadour Ivory *(c.1300)*
The poetry of Provençal troubadours tells how knights wooed virtuous women through patience, courtesy and skill.

WHERE TO SEE MEDIEVAL PROVENCE

The highlights are undoubtedly the Romanesque abbeys and churches, especially the "three sisters": Silvacane *(p147)*, Le Thoronet *(p108)* and Sénanque *(p164)*. Fortified *villages perchés*, such as Gordes *(p169)* and the spectacular 11th-century citadel at Les Baux-de-Provence *(p142)*, testify to the unrest and horrific violence that scarred this period of Provence's history.

Notre-Dame-de-Beauvoir Chapel
At the top of a path from Moustiers (see p186), the chapel has a fine Romanesque porch and nave.

1500 ships set sail for the Holy Land on 28 August 1248.

Les Pénitents des Mées
These are said to be 6th-century monks turned to stone for gazing at Saracen women (p181).

St Christopher Fresco
The Tour Ferrande in Pernes-les-Fontaines (see p164) contains religious frescoes from 1285. They are among the oldest in France.

Silvacane Abbey *(1175–1230)*
This beautiful, austere Cistercian abbey was Provence's last great Romanesque abbey.

---

974 Saracens defeated at La Garde-Freinet

Seal of Simon de Montfort

1213 Battle of Muret: de Montfort defeats count of Toulouse and King of Aragon

1209 French military leader Simon de Montfort marches on Provence

1246 Charles of Anjou marries Béatrice, heiress of Provence, to become Count of Provence

1248 Louis IX embarks on Seventh Crusade from Aigues-Mortes

1000	**1100**	**1200**	**1300**

1032 Provence becomes part of Holy Roman Empire

1096–1099 First Crusade

1186 Counts of Provence declare Aix their capital

1187 Remains of St Martha discovered at Tarascon

1295 Death of Guiraut Riquier, the "Last Troubadour"

1112 Raymond-Bérenger III, Count of Barcelona, marries the Duchess of Provence

1125 Provence shared between Barcelona and Toulouse

1274 Papacy acquires Comtat Venaissin

1280 Relics of Mary Magdalene found at St-Maximin-la-Ste-Baume

Papal Avignon

14th-century carving, Palais des Papes

When the papacy temporarily abandoned war-torn Italy, Avignon became the centre of the Roman Catholic world. From 1309 until 1377 seven French popes ruled unchallenged. When a new Italian pope, Urban VI, was elected, the French cardinals rebelled. In 1378 they chose a rival pope, Clement VII, thus causing a major schism that lasted until 1403.

During the 14th century the papal court in Avignon became a wealthy centre for both learning and the arts, extending its influence across the region.

The Palais Vieux (1334–42), built by Benedict XII in typically austere Cistercian style, is more of a fortress than a church.

Benedict XII's cloister

Grand Tinel

Consistory Hall

Bargème, Northern Var
Instability across Provence led to villages like Bargème building strong fortifications.

Papal Throne
The Pope's Room in the Palais des Papes contains copies of the original 14th-century furniture, like this carved wooden throne.

Great Courtyard

Prophets Fresco *(1344–5)*
Matteo Giovanetti from Viterbo was the principal fresco-master of Clement VI. His realism contrasts with earlier medieval artists.

TIMELINE

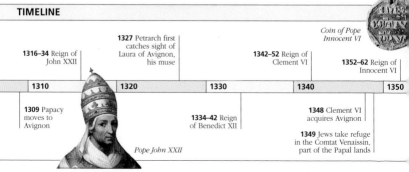

1316–34 Reign of John XXII

1327 Petrarch first catches sight of Laura of Avignon, his muse

1342–52 Reign of Clement VI

Coin of Pope Innocent VI

1352–62 Reign of Innocent VI

1310	1320	1330	1340	1350

1309 Papacy moves to Avignon

1334–42 Reign of Benedict XII

1348 Clement VI acquires Avignon

1349 Jews take refuge in the Comtat Venaissin, part of the Papal lands

Pope John XXII

Death of Clement VI
Clement VI came to Avignon to "forget he was pope". In 1348 he bought the town for 80,000 florins and built the splendid Palais Neuf.

WHERE TO SEE PAPAL PROVENCE

Avignon is surrounded by evidence of religious and aristocratic splendour. With the presence of the wealthy papacy – a kind of miniature Vatican – abbeys, churches and chapels flourished. The Musée du Petit Palais *(see p168)* in Avignon contains examples of work by the artists who were encouraged to work at the papal court.

Villeneuve Charterhouse
Innocent VI established this, the oldest charterhouse in France, in the 1350s (p130).

Châteauneuf-du-Pape
John XXII's early 14th-century castle became the popes' second residence. The keep and walls are still standing today (p164).

Pope's Room

Stag Room Frescoes
The hunting scenes are a reminder that monastic life was not only about learning and prayer.

Stag Room

The Great Chapel, covering 780 sq m (8,400 sq ft), contains the restored papal altar.

The Palais Neuf was built by Clement VI in 1342–52.

Great Audience Hall

PALAIS DES PAPES
The maze of corridors and rooms in the Palais des Papes *(see p168)*, built over 18 years (1334–52), were richly decorated by a skilled artists and craftsmen introduced from Italy. The building's scale is overwhelming.

Petrarch *(1304–74)*
The great Renaissance poet Petrarch considered papal Avignon to be a "sewer" and a place of corruption.

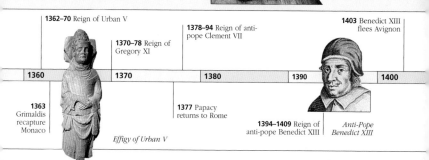

1362–70 Reign of Urban V

1370–78 Reign of Gregory XI

1378–94 Reign of anti-pope Clement VII

1403 Benedict XIII flees Avignon

| 1360 | 1370 | 1380 | 1390 | 1400 |

1363 Grimaldis recapture Monaco

1377 Papacy returns to Rome

1394–1409 Reign of anti-pope Benedict XIII

Anti-Pope Benedict XIII

Effigy of Urban V

René and the Wars of Religion

Pietà, Notre-Dame-de-l'Assomption

The end of the 15th century saw the golden age of Aix *(see pp148–9)*, then Provence's capital. Under the patronage of King René, art and culture flourished and the Flemish-influenced Avignon School was formed. After René's death, Provence was annexed by the French king, Louis XI. Loss of independence and subsequent involvement with French politics led to brutal invasions by Charles V. The 16th-century Wars of Religion between "heretic" Protestants and Catholics resulted in a wave of massacres, and the wholesale destruction of churches and their contents.

Detail of the Triptych
René's favourite château of Tarascon (p140) on the Rhône is realistically painted.

King René, himself a poet, painter and musician, was a great influence on Provençal culture.

Nostradamus
Born in St-Rémy (pp140–41), the physician and astrologer is best known for his predictions, Les Centuries *(1555).*

Massacres of Protestants and Catholics
The religious wars were brutal. Thousands of Protestants were massacred in 1545, and 200 Catholics died in Nîmes in 1567.

BURNING BUSH TRIPTYCH
Nicolas Froment's painting (1476) was commissioned by King René. The star of the Cathédrale de St-Sauveur, Aix, it depicts a vision of the Virgin and Child surrounded by the eternal Burning Bush of Moses.

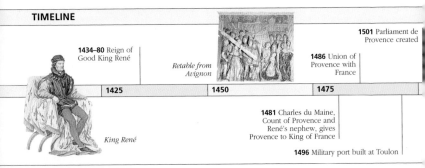

TIMELINE

1434–80 Reign of Good King René

Retable from Avignon

1501 Parliament de Provence created

1486 Union of Provence with France

1425	1450	1475

King René

1481 Charles du Maine, Count of Provence and René's nephew, gives Provence to King of France

1496 Military port built at Toulon

The Annunciation
The Master of Aix, one of René's artistic circle, painted this Annunciation. Dark symbolism, including the owl's wings of the angel Gabriel, undercuts this usually joyful subject.

The Bush, burning but unconsumed, was a pagan and Christian symbol of eternal life.

WHERE TO SEE 15TH- AND 16TH-CENTURY PROVENCE

Architecture from this period can be seen today in the fine town houses and elegant streets of Aix *(pp148–9)* and Avignon *(pp166–8)*. The Musée Granet, also in Aix, contains several interesting examples of religious paintings. A collection of period furniture is exhibited in the Musée Grobet-Labadié in Marseille *(p151)*.

Holy Roman Emperor, Charles V, by Titian
Between 1524 and 1536, Charles V (Charles I of Spain) attacked Provence frequently as part of his war against France.

Château at Tarascon
This 13th-century château (p140) was partly rebuilt by Louis II and then completed by King René, his son.

The saints John the Evangelist, Catherine of Alexandria and Nicolas of Myra are behind Queen Jeanne.

Rhinoceros Woodcut by Albrecht Dürer
In 1516, Marseille's Château d'If (p152) was briefly home to the first rhinoceros to set foot in Europe. It was in transit as a gift for the Pope, but died later in the journey.

Queen Jeanne, René's second wife, is shown kneeling in adoration.

Moses is seen receiving the word of God from an angel.

1524 Invasion of Charles V

1545 Massacre of Protestants in Luberon villages

1577 First soap factory in Marseille

1598 Edict of Nantes signals end of Wars of Religion

1525	1550	1575	1600

1525 Jews in Comtat Venaissin forced to wear yellow hats

1562 Wars of Religion commence

Protestant martyrdom

Classical Provence

Provence in the 17th and 18th centuries saw a decrease in regional allegiance and growth of national awareness. Towns grew and majestic monuments, town houses *(hôtels)* and châteaux proliferated. But despite economic development in the textile industry and the growth of the ports of Toulon and Marseille, the period was bleak for many, culminating in the devastating plague of 1720. The storming of the Bastille in Paris in 1789 sparked popular uprisings and revolutionary marches on Paris.

Pavillon de Vendôme
Jean-Claude Rambot made the Atlantes for this building (1667) in Aix (see pp148–9).

Boat-Building in Toulon
Toulon, a strategic port, was famous for its boat-building. Galley slaves, chained to their oars, were a great tourist attraction in the 17th century.

The death toll was over 100,000 in the last plague in Europe.

Santon Crib Scene
The santon ("little saints" in Provençal) cribs were first made after the Revolution, when the churches were shut. They soon became a very popular local craft.

Corpses were hauled in carts to mass graves.

THE GREAT PLAGUE

Vue du Cours pendant la Peste by Michel Serre depicts the 1720 plague in Marseille, brought by a cargo boat from Syria. Over half of Marseille's population died. All contact with the city was banned and huge walls were built to halt the epidemic, but it still spread as far as Aix, Arles and Toulon.

TIMELINE

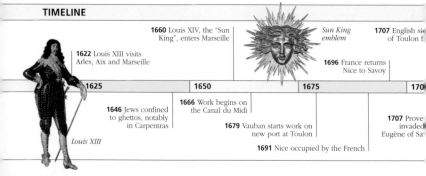

1622 Louis XIII visits Arles, Aix and Marseille

1660 Louis XIV, the "Sun King", enters Marseille

Sun King emblem

1707 English si of Toulon f

1696 France returns Nice to Savoy

1625   **1650**   **1675**   **170**

1646 Jews confined to ghettos, notably in Carpentras

1666 Work begins on the Canal du Midi

1679 Vauban starts work on new port at Toulon

1707 Prove invaded Eugène of Sa

Louis XIII

1691 Nice occupied by the French

Napoleon Seizes Toulon
Junior officer Napoleon Bonaparte first made his name when he took Toulon from occupying English troops in 1793.

Cours Belsunce, built in 1670 in the Italian style, was lined with trees and Baroque palaces.

Monks, led by the devout Jean Belsunce, the Bishop of Marseille, gave succour to the dying.

Marshal Sébastien Vauban
Louis XIV's brilliant military architect, Vauban, fortified towns and ports including Toulon and Antibes.

Moustiers Faïence
Brought to France from Italy in the 17th century, traditional faïence features pastoral scenes in delicate colours.

WHERE TO SEE CLASSICAL PROVENCE

Avignon (*see pp166–8*) and Aix (*pp148–9*) have period town houses with fine doorways and staircases. Jewish synagogues and remains of Jewish enclaves can be found in Cavaillon (*p170*), Forcalquier (*p182*) and Carpentras (*p164*). The 18th-century Jardin de la Fontaine in Nîmes (*pp132–3*) can still be visited.

Pharmacy at Carpentras
The 18th-century Hôtel-Dieu (hospital) houses a chapel and a pharmacy containing faïence apothecary jars.

Fontaine du Cormoran
The best known of the 36 fountains in Pernes-les-Fontaines (p164) is the 18th-century carved Cormoran fountain.

---

713 Treaty of Utrecht cedes Orange to France

1791 Avignon and Comtat Venaissin annexed to France

1793 Breaking of siege of Toulon catapults Napoleon Bonaparte to fame

1718 Nice becomes part of new Kingdom of Sardinia

1779 Roman mausoleum at Aix demolished

1725	1750	1775	1800

1720 Great Plague strikes Marseille and spreads throughout Provence

1771 Aix parliament suppressed

1787 Provençal silk harvest fails

1792 Republicans adopt Rouget de Lisle's army song: *La Marseillaise*

The Great Plague, Marseille

1789 Storming of the Bastille, Paris; Provençal peasants pillage local châteaux and monasteries

The Belle Epoque

Marseille soap advert, 1880

From the start of the 19th century the beguiling climate, particularly the mild winters, of coastal Provence attracted foreign visitors, from invalids and artists to distinguished royalty and courtesans. Railways, grand hotels, exotic gardens, opulent villas and the chic promenade des Anglais in Nice were built to meet their needs. Queen Victoria, the Aga Khan, King Leopold of Belgium and Empress Eugénie – Napoleon III's wife and doyenne of Riviera royalty – all held court. Artists and writers came in droves to revel in the light and freedom.

Homage à Mistral
Frédéric Mistral created the Félibrige group in 1854 to preserve Provençal culture.

Printing in Marseille
Cheap labour, ample paper supplies and good communications fostered the development of printing.

Casino tables were sometimes draped in black mourning when a gambler succeeded in breaking the bank with a major win.

Grasse Perfume
More modern methods of cultivation and distillation played an important role in the expanding 19th-century perfume-making industry.

MONTE-CARLO CASINO INTERIOR

From being the poorest state in Europe in 1850, Monaco boomed with the opening of the first Monte-Carlo casino in 1865, as seen in Christian Bokelman's painting. The fashionable flocked to enjoy the luxury and glamour, while fortunes were won and lost *(see pp92–4)*.

TIMELINE

1814 Napoleon lands at Golfe-Juan

1830 Beginnings of tourism around Nice

1861 Monaco sells Roquebrune and Menton to France

1860 Nice votes for union with France

1820   1840   18

Paul Cézanne

1839 Marseille-Sète railroad begun. Birth of Cézanne

1854 Founding of Félibrige, the Provençal cultural school

1859 Mistral publishes his epic poem, Mirèio

Vineyard blight
Ravaged by phylloxera, vines in Provence and across France were replaced by resistant American root stocks.

Tourism
By the late 19th century, sun and sea air were considered beneficial to health.

Belle Epoque decor had interiors lavish with ornate chandeliers, gilt and coloured marble.

High society included famous courtesans as well as their rich and royal lovers.

Van Gogh's Provence
Van Gogh produced turbulent works in the Clinique St-Paul in St-Rémy (see pp140–41).

WHERE TO SEE BELLE EPOQUE PROVENCE

Although many have been destroyed, villas and hotels built in the extravagant Belle Epoque style still survive on the Côte d'Azur. The Négresco in Nice *(see pp84–5)* is especially fine. Other period pieces include the Cathédrale Orthodoxe Russe, also in Nice, and, on glamorous Cap Ferrat, the Musée Ephrussi de Rothschild *(pp86–7)*. In Beaulieu the Villa Kerylos, Rotunda and lush exotic gardens are all typical of the era *(p88)*.

Hôtel Carlton, Cannes
Built in 1911, this ostentatious Riviera landmark is still an exclusive hotel overlooking the beach (pp68–9).

Monte-Carlo Opéra
Charles Garnier designed this opera house (pp92–3), as well as the Casino.

1879 Monte-Carlo Opéra opens

Casino at Monte-Carlo

1909 Earthquake centred on Rognes in the Bouches-du-Rhône causes widespread damage

1880 | **1900** | **1920**

1869 Opening of Suez Canal brings trade to Marseille; railway extended to Nice

1888–90 Van Gogh works in Provence

1904 Mistral wins Nobel prize for Literature for *Mirèio*

Provence at War

After the economic drain caused by World War I, Provence enjoyed increasing prosperity as the tourist industry boomed. While much of the interior remained remote and rural, the vogue for sea-bathing drew crowds to resorts such as Cannes and Nice from the 1920s onwards. Provence continued to build on its image as a playground for the rich and famous, attracting visitors from Noël Coward to Wallis Simpson. The 1942–44 German occupation brought an end to the glamorous social life for many, and some towns, including St-Tropez and Marseille, were badly damaged by Germans and Allies.

Tourism
As swimming in the sea and sunbathing became fashionable pursuits, resorts along the Riviera attracted many new visitors. In the 1930s a nudist colony opened on the Ile du Levant.

Monaco Grand Prix
This race around the principality's streets was started on the initiative of Prince Louis II in 1929. It is still one of the most colourful and dangerous Formula 1 races.

Antoine de Saint-Exupéry
France's legendary writer-pilot disappeared on 31 July 1944 while on a reconnaissance flight (see p29).

Precious ammunition
and arms were dropped from Allied planes or captured from the Nazis.

LA RÉSISTANCE

After 1942 the Résistance (or *maquis* after the scrubland that made a good hiding place) was active in Provence. The fighters were successful in Marseille and in preparing the coastal areas for the 1944 Allied invasion.

TIMELINE

Coco Chanel

F Scott Fitzgerald

1920

1924 Scott and Zelda Fitzgerald spend a year on the Riviera

1925 Coco Chanel arrives on the Riviera

1928 Camargue National Park created

1925

1930 Novelist DH Lawrence dies in Vence

1930 Pagnol begins filming *Marius, Fanny* and *César* trilogy in Marseille

1930

Many who joined the Résistance had scarcely left school. Training was often only by experience.

Marcel Pagnol (1905–74)
Pagnol immortalized Provence and its inhabitants in his plays, novels and films, depicting a simple, rural life (see p29).

Allied Landings
On 14 August 1944, Allied troops bombarded the coast between Toulon and Marseille and soon gained ground.

Marseille Exhibition
The 1922 exhibition was an invitation to enjoy the cosmopolitan delights of Marseille.

WHERE TO SEE 1920s TO 1940s PROVENCE

The now slightly seedy sub-urbs of Hyères *(see p115)* retain evidence of graceful living after World War I. Toulon harbour's bristling warships *(pp112–13)* are a reminder of the French navy's former power. The activities of the Résistance are well documented in the Musée d'Histoire 1939–45 in Fontaine-de-Vaucluse *(p165)*.

Les Deux Garçons, Aix
This still chic café was frequent-ed by Churchill and Cocteau among others (pp148–9).

Citadelle, Sisteron
Rebuilt after the Allied bombing in 1944, the citadel has displays on its turbulent history (p178).

1942 Nazis invade southern France; French fleet scuttled in Toulon harbour

1940 Italians occupy Menton

1943 *Maquis* resistance cells formed

1935	1940	1945

1939 Cannes Film Festival inaugurated, but first festival delayed by war

Liberation of Marseille

1944 American and French troops land near St-Tropez; liberation of Marseille

Post-War Provence

Scooter rider in St-Tropez

Paid vacations, post-war optimism, and the St-Tropez sun cult all made the Riviera the magnet it has remained for holiday-makers. The region still offers a rich variety of produce – olive oil, wine, fruit, flowers and perfume – though industry, especially in the high-tech sector, grows apace. The environment has suffered from overdevelopment, pollution and forest fires. The 1960s saw massive North African immigration, and today unemployment creates racial and political tension.

Port-Grimaud
The successful "Provençal Venice", a car-free leisure port, was built by François Spoerry in 1966 in regional village style (see p123).

Bus Stop by Philippe Starck
The modern architecture of Nîmes typifies many bold projects in the region.

Beach at Nice
Though many are pebbly, the Riviera beaches still attract dedicated sun-worshippers.

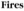

Fires
The devastating forest fires which ravage the region are fought with planes scooping up sea water.

TIMELINE

1946 Picasso starts painting in the Grimaldi Castle, Antibes

1952 Le Corbusier's Cité Radieuse built

Grace Kelly

1954 Matisse dies

1956 Grace Kelly marries Monaco's Prince Rainier III

1956 Roger Vadim films *And God Created Woman*, starring Brigitte Bardot, in St-Tropez

1959 Floods in Fréjus

1961 Art festival of new Ecole de Nice

1962 Lower Durance engineered to develop hydro-electric power

1962 Algerian Independence – French North Africans *(pieds-noirs)* settle in Provence

1970 Sophia-Antipolis technology park opens near Antibes

Picasso

1970 Autoroute du Soleil completed

1971 The "French Connection" drug ring is exposed

1973 Picasso dies at Mougins

1950	1960	1970

Winter Sports

Skiing has become increasingly popular (see p96). Isola 2000, near Nice, a purpose-built, futuristic resort, was built in 1972.

WHERE TO SEE MODERN PROVENCE

Some of the most striking modern architecture includes Le Corbusier's Cité Radieuse in Marseille (see p152), the Musée d'Art Contemporain in Nice (p85) and the Norman Foster-designed Carré d'Art in Nîmes (p132). Large-scale rebuilding programmes in towns such as St-Tropez (pp118–22) and Ste-Maxime (p123) have concentrated on new buildings that blend well with the existing ones.

Colombe d'Or, St-Paul
Once an artists' café, this is now one of many chic venues for the rich and famous (see p75).

St-Tropez
Successful post-war restoration means it is often difficult to tell new buildings from old.

Fondation Maeght
The building reflects the modern use of traditional Provençal style and materials (pp76–7).

Brigitte Bardot   Kim Novak

CANNES FILM FESTIVAL

First held in 1946, the festival *(see p68)* has become the world's annual film event, a glamorous jamboree of directors, stars and aspiring starlets. *And God Created Woman*, starring Brigitte Bardot, became a *succès de scandale* in 1956.

1977 First section of Marseille underground railway opened

1981 TGV link with Paris completed

1992 Floods in Vaison-la-Romaine

1998 Jacques Médecin dies in Uruguay, self-exiled after a year in jail in France

Jacques Médecin

2005 Prince Rainier III dies and is succeeded by his only son, Prince Albert II

1980	1990	2000	2010

1982 Princess Grace is killed in car accident

TGV train

1990 Jacques Médecin, Mayor of Nice, flees to Uruguay to avoid trial for corruption and tax arrears

2002 Euro replaces Franc as legal tender

PROVENCE
AREA BY AREA

Provence at a Glance

From natural wonders and historic architecture to the cream of modern art, Provence is a region with something for everyone. Even the most ardent sun-worshipper will be tempted into the cool shade of its treasure-filled museums and churches. Visitors who come in the footsteps of the world's greatest artists will be equally dazzled by the wild beauty of the Gorges du Verdon and the Camargue. In a region packed with delights, those shown here are among the very best.

Papal Avignon's medieval archi-tectural splendour *(see pp166–7)*

The beautifully preserved Roman theatre at Orange *(see pp162–3)*

• Avignon   VAUCLUSE

BOUCHES-DU-RHONE
AND NIMES

• La Camargue

Marseille •

Wildlife in its natural habitat in the Camargue *(see pp136–7)*

The massive basilica of St-Maximin-la-Ste-Baume, housing relics of St Mary Magdalene *(see pp110–11)*

0 kilometres   20

0 miles   20

Unspoiled and tranquil, the Iles d'Hyères *(see pp114–5)*

Outstanding modern art at the Fondation Maeght, St-Paul-de-Vence *(see pp76–7)*

Musée Matisse, in the artist's beloved Nice *(see pp82–3)*

Musée Ephrussi de Rothschild, a "dream villa" among the pines of Cap Ferrat *(see pp86–7)*

ALPES-DE-HAUTE-PROVENCE

THE RIVIERA AND THE ALPES MARITIMES

THE VAR AND THE ILES D'HYERES

Monaco

St-Paul-de-Vence

Nice

See inset above

Nice

Monaco

Cannes

Iles de Lérins

St-Tropez

oulon

Iles d'Hyères

The dramatic Gorges du Verdon *(see pp184–5)*

St-Tropez's Musée de l'Annonciade, displaying its art collection in a former chapel *(see pp120–21)*

THE RIVIERA AND THE ALPES MARITIMES

The French Riviera is, without doubt, the most celebrated seaside in Europe. Just about everybody who has been anybody for the past 100 years has succumbed to its glittering allure. This is the holiday playground of kings and courtesans, movie stars and millionaires, where the seriously rich never stand out in the crowd.

There is a continual complaint that the Riviera is not what it used to be, that the Cannes Film Festival is mere hype, that grand old Monte-Carlo has lost all sense of taste and that Nice isn't worth the trouble of finding a parking space. But look at the boats in Antibes harbour, glimpse a villa or two on Cap Martin, or observe the baubles on the guests at the Hôtel de Paris in Monte-Carlo. Money and class still rule.

The Riviera is not just a millionaire's watering hole: a diversity of talent has visited, seeking patrons and taking advantage of the luminous Mediterranean light. This coast is irrevocably linked with the life and works of Matisse and Picasso, Chagall, Cocteau and Renoir. It lent them the scenery of its shores and the rich environment of hill villages like St-Paul-de-Vence. St-Paul has echoed to the voices of such luminaries as Bonnard and Modigliani, F Scott Fitzgerald and Greta Garbo. Today, its galleries still spill canvases on to its medieval lanes.

The Alpes Maritimes, which incorporates the principality of Monaco, is renowned for its temperate winter climate. The abundance of flowers here attracted the perfume industry and the English – who created some of the finest gardens on the coast. Inland, the mountainous areas of Provence offer a range of skiing activities in superb mountain scenery, and a chance to try traditional Alpine food.

Relaxing on the promenade des Anglais, Nice

◁ **View of Roquebrune village from the castle**

Exploring the Riviera and the Alpes Maritimes

The rocky heights of the pre-Alps lie in tiers,
running east to west and tumbling down to
the Riviera's dramatic, Corniche-hemmed coast.
On bluffs and pinnacles, towns and villages keep
a watchful eye on the distant blue sea. Towards
the Italian border, the Alpine ridges run from
north to south, cut by torrents and gorges
which provide snowy winter slopes for skiers.
Much of the higher ground is occupied by the
Parc National du Mercantour *(see p97)*, home
of the ibex and the chamoix. Its jewel is the
prehistoric Vallée des Merveilles, less than two
hours from the contrasting bustle of the Riviera.

GETTING AROUND

The A8 from Italy runs inland, parallel to the coast.
Between this highway and
the sea, from Nice to Menton,
are three corniches. The
Grande Corniche follows the
Roman road, Julia Augusta,
via La Turbie. The Moyenne
Corniche passes through Eze,
and the Corniche Inférieure
visits all coastal resorts. The
inland roads are narrow and
winding, so allow more time
for your journey. Grasse and
Cannes are linked by a
regular bus service, and
bikes can be hired at some
railway stations. Other bus
links are also good. The
largest airport in the region
and second busiest in France,
is at Nice, west of the city.

**Expensive yachts in the colourful
harbour at Antibes**

SIGHTS AT A GLANCE

Saint-Étienne-
de-Tinée

Auron

Entraunes

LE P

D2205

Valberg   Be

GORGES DU C

Guillaumes

D2202

D902

PUGET-
THÉNIERS ❷   N202

Digne-les-
Bains   To
             sur

Roquest

A L P E S

Sisteron

Mont Cheiron
1777m

Le Logis-
du-Pin   D2

N85

GOURDON

St-Vallier-
de-Thiey

GRASSE ❺ m

Grottes de
St-Cézaire

❸ ST-CÉZAIRE-
SUR-SIAGNE   N85

MOUG

CAN

Draguignan

| 0 kilometres | 10 |
| 0 miles | 10 |

View from Roquebrune towards Nice

Isola 2000
Isola

D2205

29

ATIONAL DU MERCANTOUR

N204

30 TENDE

Saint-Sauveur-
sur-Tinée

Saint-Martin-
Vésubie

St-Dalmas

Roquebillière

Pointe de
Trois-Communes
2082m

31 SAORGE

l'Authion
1889m

28 FORÊT

Villars-
sur-Var

Lantosque

DE TURINI

Breil-sur-Roya

D2205

D2204

N204

St-Jean-
la-Rivière

Peïra-Cava

D2566

Ventimiglia

N202

27

LUCÉRAM **26**

32 SOSPEL

Plan-du-Var

D2565

Escarène

Esteron

San
Remo

PEILLE **25**

Ste-
Agnes

A8

GORBIO **33**

PEILLON **24**

35 MENTON

LA TURBIE **22**

34 ROQUEBRUNE-
CAP-MARTIN

BEAULIEU

N98

23 MONACO

14 VENCE

20

21 EZE

NICE **17**

19 VILLEFRANCHE

ST-PAUL-
E-VENCE **15**

CAGNES-
SUR-MER

18 CAP FERRAT

ENEUVE-
LOUBET **13**

16

KEY

BIOT **12**

Cros-de-Cagnes

Motorway

N98

Major road

10 ANTIBES

Secondary road

VALLAURIS

Minor road

Golfe-
Juan

9 JUAN-LES-PINS

Scenic route

Cap d'Antibes

Main railway

Minor railway

8 ILES DE LÉRINS

International border

Regional border

△ Summit

The sunshine and relaxing
atmosphere of a café in Nice

Upstream view of the upper Gorges du Cians

Gorges du Cians ❶

🚉 Nice. 🚌 Touët-sur-Var. 🚍 Nice, Touët-sur-Var, Valberg. 🛈 Valberg (04 93 23 24 25).

Among the finest natural sights in the region, these gorges are a startling combination of deep red slate and vivid mountain greenery. They follow the course of the river Cians, which drops 1,600 m (5,250 ft) in 25 km (15 miles) from Beuil to Touët-sur-Var. At Touët, through a grille in the floor of the church nave, you can see the torrent below.

Approaching from the lower gorges, olives give way to scrubland. It is not until Pra d'Astier that the gorges become steep and narrow: at their narrowest, the rock walls entirely obliterate the sky. Higher still up the gorge, you may spot saffron lilies in June.

At the upper end of the gorges, overlooking the Vallée du Cians, is the 1,430-m (4,770-ft) eyrie of Beuil. Now a military sports centre, it was first fortified by the counts of Beuil, members of the aristocratic Grimaldi family (see p91). They lived here until 1621, despite staff revolt: one count had his throat cut by his barber and another was stabbed by his valet. The last, Hannibal Grimaldi, was tied to a chair and strangled by two Muslim slaves. Stones from their château were used to build the Renaissance chapel of the White Penitents in the 1687 Eglise St-Jean-Baptiste.

Puget-Théniers ❷

Road map E3. 🏠 1,700. 🚍 🚌
🛈 RN 202 (04 93 05 05 05).

This attractive village lies at the foot of a rocky peak, nestling at the confluence of the Roudole and the Var beneath the ruins of a château that belonged to the Grimaldi family (see p91). The old town has some fine manorial homes with overhanging roofs, but the chief attraction is the 13th-century parish church **Notre-Dame de l'Assomption** built by the Templars. The delightful altarpiece, *Notre-Dame de Secours* (1525), is by Antoine de Ronzen. Inside the entrance, the altarpiece of the Passion (1515–1520) is by Flemish craftsmen, possibly working with the architect and sculptor Matthieu d'Anvers.

Beside the main road, the striking statue of a woman with her hands tied is called *L'Action Enchaînée*, by Aristide Maillol (1861–1944). It commemorates the local revolutionary and master of insurrection, Louis-Auguste Blanqui. He was born in the town hall in 1805 and became one of the

L'Action Enchaînée, in Puget-Théniers square

socialist heroes of the Paris Commune in 1871. A year later he was imprisoned for life and served seven years, having already spent 30 years in jail.

St-Cézaire-sur-Siagne ❸

Road map E3. 🏠 2,500. 🚌
🛈 3 rue de la République (04 93 60 84 30). 🕑 Tue & Sat.

Dominating the steep-sided Siagne valley, St-Cézaire has been occupied since pre-Roman times. The walls and towers of the village are reminders of its feudal past. At its heart is the 13th-century **Chapelle du Cimetière**, which houses a Gallo-Roman tomb discovered nearby – a fine example of Provençal Romanesque design. From the medieval part of the village, a path leads to a viewpoint. To the northeast of the village are the **Grottes de St-Cézaire-sur-Siagne** – iron-rich caves filled with beautiful rock crystallization. Dramatic stalactites and stalagmites have formed on the cave ceilings and floor. If touched, the stalactites become remark-

Antoine Ronzen's altarpiece *Notre-Dame de Secours* (1525), Puget-Théniers

ably resonant, but leave this to the guide. Both the stalactites and stalagmites have created enchanting shapes, reminiscent of flowers, animals and toadstools. Red oxide in the limestone gives a rich colour to the caves' chambers: the Fairies' Alcove, Great Hall, Hall of Draperies and Organ Chamber, all connected by narrow underground passages, one of which ends abruptly, 40 m (130 ft) below ground, at the edge of an abyss.

Grottes de St-Cézaire-sur-Siagne

St-Cézaire-sur-Siagne. **Tel** 04 93 60 22 35. ☐ Jun–Sep: daily; Oct–May: Sun. ☑ **www**.lesgrottesdesaintcezaire.fr

Inside the remarkable Grottes de St-Cézaire-sur-Siagne

The village of Gourdon, on the edge of a rocky cliff

Gourdon ❹

Road map E3. 🏠 395. 🚹 pl Victoria (04 93 09 68 25). **www**.gourdon-france.com

For centuries, villages were built on hilltops, surrounded by ramparts. Gourdon is a typical *village perché (see pp20–21)*, its shops filled with regional produce, perfume and local art. From the square at its precipitous edge, there is a spectacular view of the Loup valley and the sea with Antibes and Cap Roux in the distance.

There are good views, too, from the terrace of the Château de Gourdon, built in the 12th century by the *Seigneurs* du Bar, overlords of Gourdon, on the foundations of what was once a Saracen fortress. Its

vaulted rooms are remnants of Saracen occupation. The terrace gardens were laid out by André Le Nôtre when the château was restored in the 17th century. Although it is still privately owned, it has two museums. The **Musée Historique** has an Aubusson tapestry, a writing desk belonging to Marie-Antoinette, and a self-portrait by Rembrandt. There is also an adjoining **Musée d'Arts Décoratifs et de la Modernité** with 1930s furniture, lamps by Jacques Le Chevallier and Paul Dupré-Lafon, and some Salvador Dali sculptures.

🏛 Musée Historique et Musée d'Arts Décoratifs

Château de Gourdon. **Tel** 04 93 09 68 02. ☐ Jun–Sep: daily; Oct–May: Wed–Mon pm only. ☑

JOURNEY IN THE GORGES DU LOUP

The village of Gourdon is on the edge of the Gorges du Loup, the most accessible of many dramatic gorges running down to the coast. The route up to the Gorges du Loup begins at Pré-du-Loup, just east of Grasse, and leads to Gourdon. From Gourdon, the D3 goes up into the gorge and offers the best views, turning back down the D6 after 6.5 km (4 miles).

Descending on the left bank, the road passes the great pothole of Saut du Loup and the Cascades des Demoiselles, where the river's lime carbonate content has partly solidified the vegetation. Just beyond is the 40-m (130-ft) Cascade de Courmes, which has a treacherously slippery stairway under it.

The D2210 continues to Vence, passing via Tourrettes-sur-Loup, an art and craft centre on a high plateau. The 15th-century church has a triptych by the Bréa School and a 1st-century altar dedicated to the Roman god Mercury.

The 40-m (130-ft) Cascade de Courmes

Grasse ❺

Road map E3. 🏘 49,000. 🚌 🅸
22 cours Honoré Cresp (04 93 36 66
66). 🚃 Tue–Sun. **www**.grasse-
riviera.com

Once known for its leather
tanning industry, Grasse
became a perfume centre in
the 16th century. The
tanneries have vanished, but
three major perfume houses
are still in business. Today,
perfume is mainly made from
imported flowers, but each
year, this attractive, fragrance-
filled town holds a Jasmine
festival *(see p31)*. The best
place to find out more is the
**Musée Inter- national de la
Parfumerie**. It also displays
bergamotes, decorated
scented *papier-mâché* boxes.
At **Molinard** there is also a
museum and visitors have the
opportunity to create their
own perfume.
   Grasse became fashionable
after 1807–8 when Princess
Pauline Bonaparte recuperated
here. Queen Victoria often
wintered at the Grand Hotel.
   Artist Jean-Honoré
Fragonard (1732– 1806) was
born here and the walls of
the **Villa-Musée Fragonard** are
covered with his son's murals.
The artist's *Washing of the
Feet* hangs in the 12th-century
**Ancienne Cathédrale Notre-
Dame-du-Puy**, in the old town.
The cathedral also houses
three works by Rubens. The
**Musée d'Art et d'Histoire de
Provence** has Moustiers ware.
18th–19th century Provençal
costumes and jewellery can be
seen at the **Musée Provençal
du Costume et du Bijou**.

🏛 **Musée International de la
Parfumerie**
8 place du Cours, Honoré Cresp.
Tel 04 93 36 80 20.
◻ Jun–Sep: daily; Oct & Dec–May:
Wed–Sun. ⬤ public hols. 🈳🅰♿🅸

🏛 **Molinard**
60 bd Victor Hugo. **Tel** 04 92 42 33
11. ◻ Mon–Sat. ⬤ public hols. 🈳

🏛 **Villa-Musée Fragonard**
23 bd Fragonard. **Tel** 04 93 40 32
64. ◻ daily. ⬤ public hols. 🈳🅸

🏛 **Musée d'Art et d'Histoire
de Provence**
2 rue Mirabeau. **Tel** 04 93 36 01
61. ◻ Jun–Sep daily; Oct & Dec-
–May: Wed–Sun. ⬤ public hols. 🈳

**Exterior of the Musée International
de la Parfumerie in Grasse**

Mougins ❻

Road map E3. 🏘 19,000. 🚌 🅸
15 av Charles Mallet (04 93 75 87 67).

This old hilltop town *(see
pp20–21)*, huddled inside the
remains of 15th-century
ramparts and fortified Saracen
Gate, is one of the finest in
the region. Mougins is a smart
address: it has been used by
royalty and film stars as well
as Yves St Laurent and Picasso,
who spent his last years in a
house opposite the Chapelle
de Notre-Dame-de-Vie.
   Mougins is also one of the
smartest places in France to
eat. Among its many high-class
restaurants, is Roger Vergé's
Moulin de Mougins *(see
pp210–11)*, set in an old mill
just outside the village. Diners
can also browse through his
quality kitchen equipment
shop, open until midnight.
   The **Musée de la Photographie** has a fine permanent
collection of work by Villers,
Doisneau and Lartigue, who
lived at nearby Opio. The
radiator-shaped **Musée de
l'Automobiliste**, some 5 km (3
miles) south of Mougins, has
a classic car collection,
notably Bugattis, on show.

🏛 **Musée de la Photographie**
Porte Sarrasine. **Tel** 04 93 75 85 67.
◻ Wed–Sun; Jul– Sep: daily.
⬤ 1 May, Nov. 🈳

🏛 **Musée de l'Automobiliste**
Aire des Breguières, autoroute A8.
Tel 04 93 69 27 80. ◻ daily. ⬤
mid-Nov–mid-Dec. 🈳♿🅸

Jacques-Henri and Florette Lartigue, Musée de la Photographie, Mougins

The Perfumes of Provence

For the past 400 years, the town of Grasse has been the centre of the perfume industry. Before that it was a tannery town, but in the 16th century, Italian immigrant glove-makers began to use the scents of local flowers to perfume soft leather gloves, a fashion made popular by the Queen, Catherine de' Médici. Enormous acres of lavender, roses, jonquils, jasmine and aromatic herbs were cultivated. Today, cheaper imports of flowers and high land prices mean that Grasse focuses on the creation of scent. The power of perfume is evoked in Patrick Süskind's disturbing novel, *Perfume*, set partly in Grasse, in which the murderous perfumer exploits his knowledge of perfume extraction to grisly effect.

Catherine de'Médici, 1581

Picking early morning jasmine

Jasmine waiting to be processed

CREATING A PERFUME

Essences are extracted by various methods, including distillation by steam or volatile solvents, which separate the essential oils. *Enfleurage* is a costly and lengthy method for delicate flowers such as jasmine and violet. The blossoms are layered with lard which becomes impregnated with scent.

Steam distillation *is one of the oldest extraction processes originally developed by the Arabs. It is now used mainly for flowers such as orange blossom. Flowers and water are boiled together in a still and the essential oils are extracted by steam in an essencier, or oil decanter.*

Vast quantities *of blossoms are required to create the essence or "absolut" perfume concentrate. For example, almost a ton of jasmine flowers are needed to obtain just one litre of jasmine essence.*

The best perfumes *are created by a perfumer known as a "nose" who possesses an exceptional sense of smell. The nose harmonizes fragrances rather like a musician, blending as many as 300 essences for a perfume. Today, scents can be synthesized by using "head-space analysis" which analyzes the components of the air above a flower.*

Cannes ❼

Lord Brougham, British lord chancellor, put Cannes on the map in 1834 when he stopped on his way to Nice. He was so entranced by the climate of what was then a tiny fishing village that he built a villa and started a trend for upper-class English visitors. Today, Cannes may not attract blue blood but it has become a town of festivals, the resort of the rich and famous. It is busy all year round, its image reinforced by the Film Festival (*see p30*). With its casinos, fairs, beach, boat and street life, there is plenty to do, even though Cannes lacks the great museums and monuments of less glamorous resorts.

Cannes beach and Hôtel Carlton

Exploring Cannes

The heart of the city is built lround the Bay of Cannes and the palm-fringed seafront boulevard de la Croisette. Here there are luxury boutiques and hotels and fine views of La Napoule Bay and the Esterel heights. The eastern end of the bay curves out to Pointe de la Croisette and the summertime Palm Beach Casino, built on the ruins of the medieval Fort de la Croix, which has a night-club, restaurant and swimming pool. The town's other gaming house is **Casino Croisette**, which is open all year.

Brougham persuaded King Louis-Philippe to donate two million francs to build the Cannes harbour wall. Between La Pantiero and rue Félix Faure are the allées de la Liberté. Shaded by plane trees and surveyed by a statue of Lord Brougham, this open space is ideal both for *boules* and the colourful morning flower market. It provides a fine view of the harbour, which is filled with pleasure craft and fishing boats. Behind the allées is the rue Meynadier, where you can buy delicious pasta, bread and cheese. This leads you to the sumptuous **Marché Forville**. Succulent regional produce turns up here fresh every day. The small streets and lanes meander up from the *marché* to the old Roman town of Canoïs Castrum. This area was named after the reeds that grew by the seashore, and is now known as Le Suquet. The church in the centre of the old town, **Notre-Dame de l'Espérance**, was completed in 1648.

The Cannes Film Festival has been held here every May since 1946. The main venue is the **Palais des Festivals**, but there are cinemas all over town, some of which are open to the public and film screening starts as early as 8:30am. The beach has been a focus for paparazzi since 1953, when Brigitte Bardot pouted so beautifully that the world's press were

Famous handprint

moved to put her on its front pages.

The main hotels in Cannes have their own beaches with bars and restaurants, where prices match their standing. Celebrities are most likely to be seen at the Carlton, Majestic and Martinez. There is a small charge to enter most beaches in Cannes, where imported sand covers the natural pebbles, and sun-loungers cost extra. Just next to the festival building is a free public beach.

🏛 Palais des Festivals et des Congrès

1 la Croisette. **Tel** *04 93 39 01 01.*
🏛 *04 93 39 24 53.*
Built in 1982, this unmistakable modern slab, known as The Bunker, stands beside the Vieux Port at the west end of the promenade. It is the chief venue for the *Palmes d'Or* and other internationally recognised awards sufficiently prestigious for the film business to take them seriously, and much business goes on, so that the festival is not all hype and publicity. Some 78,000 official tickets are distributed to professionals only. Apart from its use for the great Film Festival, the building also houses a casino and a nightclub, and is a regular conference venue. In the nearby allée des Stars, handprints of such famous celebrities as the film director Roman Polanski are immortalized in pavement cement.

Models Carla Bruni and Karen Mulder at the Cannes Film Festival

Cannes Old Town, known locally as Le Suquet, overlooking the harbour

🏨 Hôtel Carlton

58 la Croisette. **Tel** 04 93 06 40 06.
See Where to Stay p195.
This ultimate symbol of comfort and grace contains 338 rooms and apartments. It was designed and built in 1911 by the architect, Henri Ruhl. The huge Rococo-style dining room, where the colonnades rise to an ornately decorated ceiling with finely wrought cornices, is unchanged. The hotel's wedding-cake exterior is studded with tiny balconies, and the window frames, cornices and attic pediments are decorated with stucco. The hotel's twin black cupolas are said to be modelled on the breasts of the notorious Belle Otéro, a half-gypsy courtesan who captivated Ruhl. The Carlton was so revered that in World War II, a *New York Times* journalist asked a commanding officer to protect what he considered the world's finest hotel.

CARLTON HOTEL CANNES

The height of luxury

VISITORS' CHECKLIST

Road map E4. 🏠 69,000.
🚉 rue Jean-Jaurès. 🚌 pl de l'Hôtel de Ville. 🛈 Palais des Festivals (04 92 99 84 22). 🛒 daily. 🎬 Film Festival (May). **www**.cannes.com

🏛 Musée de la Castre

Château de la Castre, Le Suquet.
Tel 04 93 38 55 26. ◯ Feb–Dec: Wed–Mon. ⬤ some public hols. 🎫
The old Cannes castle, erected by the Lérins monks in the 11th and 12th centuries, houses this museum. Set up in 1877, it contains some fine archaeological and ethnographical collections from all over the world, ranging from South Sea Island costumes to Asian art and African masks. Also housed in the Cistercian St-Anne chapel is a collection of superb musical instruments. The 11th-century **Tour de la Castre** is worth climbing for the view.

CANNES

0 metres   250
0 yards   250

Key to Symbols see back flap

Iles de Lérins

Although only a 15-minute boat ride from the glitter of Cannes, the Iles de Lérins reflect a contrasting lifestyle, with their forests of eucalyptus and Aleppo pine and their tiny chapels. The two islands, separated only by a narrow strait, were once the most powerful religious centres in the south of France. St-Honorat is named after the Gallo-Roman, Honoratus, who visited the smaller island at the end of the 4th century and founded a monastery. Ste-Marguerite was named after his sister, who set up a nunnery there. Its fort is well known as the prison of the mysterious 17th-century Man in the Iron Mask, who spent 11 years here.

Lerina liqueur

★ Fort Ste-Marguerite
Built under Richelieu and strengthened by Vauban in 1712, its ground floor has a maritime museum.

ILE STE-MARGUERITE

Port for ferries to and from Cannes

Etang du Batéguier

Allée des Eucalyptus

Eglise St-Michel

ILE ST-HONORAT

Chapelle St-Sauveur

St-Honorat et les Saints de Lérins
This icon of St-Honorat can be found in the Abbaye de Lérins.

Chapelle St-Caprais
St-Caprais was the disciple of St-Honorat during his first visit to Provence.

| 0 metres | 1000 |
| 0 yards | 1000 |

The Man in the Iron Mask
The mystery man was imprisoned in Fort Royal from 1687 to 1698, then moved to the Bastille, where he died in 1703.

Remains on Ste-Marguerite
Excavations on the coast near the fort have revealed houses, mosaics, wall paintings and ceramics which date back to around the 3rd century BC.

Allée du Grand Jardin

Allée de la Convention
Both the islands have many paths leading through the densely wooded interior as well as round the coast.

Chapelle St-Cyprien

La Chapelle de la Trinité

Abbaye de Lérins
The old church and monks' quarters were incorporated in the 19th-century building.

★ Monastère Fortifié
Built in 1073 by Abbot Aldebert, to protect the monks from Saracen pirates, this "keep" gives views as far as Esterel.

STAR SIGHTS

★ Fort Ste-Marguerite

★ Monastère Fortifié

Juan-les-Pins ⑨

Road map E3. 👥 *80,000*
(Commune of Antibes). 🚉 🚌 ℹ️
55 bd Guillaumont (04 92 90 53 05).
www.antibes-juanlespins.com

To the east of Cannes is the hammerhead peninsula of Cap d'Antibes, a promontory of pines and coves where millionaires' mansions grow. Its finest beach is tucked in the west side of the cape in Golfe-Juan, where Napoleon came ashore from Elba in 1815. This is a 20th-century resort, promoted by American railroad heir Frank Jay Gould, who attracted high society in the 1920s and 1930s when writers F Scott Fitzgerald and Ernest Hemingway stayed.

Today, in the high season, it is filled with a young crowd. The area at the junctions of boulevards Baudoin and Wilson is filled with colourful bars. Action centres round the 1988 casino, the Palais des Congrès, and Penedès pine grove, which reaches down to the shore and gives shelter to the World Jazz Festival *(see p33)* in July.

Nightlife in Juan-les-Pins

Antibes ⑩

Road map E3. 👥 *80,000*. 🚉 🚌
🚤 ℹ️ *11 place du Gen de Gaulle
(04 92 90 53 00).* 🗓️ *Tue–Sun.*
www.antibes-juanlespins.com

Originally the ancient Greek trading post of Anti- polis, Antibes became heavily fortified over the centuries, notably by Vauban in the 17th century, who built the main port and Fort Carré, where Napoleon lived and was temporarily imprisoned.

There are some pleasant lanes splashed with colourful flowers in the old town, and a

Spectacular pleasure yachts in Antibes harbour

picturesque market place in cours Masséna. The town's high points include the 12th-century towers of the church and Grimaldi castle on the site of Antipolis. The **Cathédrale Notre-Dame**, which took over the town's watchtower as a belfry, has a wooden crucifix from 1447, a 16th-century Christ and a fine Louis Bréa altarpiece depicting the Virgin Mary, dating from the same period.

The Château Grimaldi nearby houses the **Musée Picasso**, in which over 50 drawings, paintings, prints and ceramics by the artist when he used the museum as a studio during 1946 are displayed. Also on show is Antoine Aundi's *La Vierge de Douleur* (1539), with one of the earliest views of Antibes.

The modern art collection includes works by Ernst, Léger, Miró and Nicolas de Staël in the last two years of his life.

Further south, the **Musée d'Histoire et d'Archéologie** housed in the fortified Bastion St-André houses Greek and Etruscan finds from the Mediterranean, including a 3rd-century BC inscription to the spirit of Septentrion, a boy who danced at the Antipolis theatre.

🏛 **Musée Picasso**
Château Grimaldi. **Tel** *04 92 90 54 20.*
🗓️ *Tue–Sun.* 🔴 *public hols.* 📷 🚫

🏛 **Musée d'Histoire et d'Archéologie**
Bastion St-André. **Tel** *04 92 90 54 35.* 🗓️ *Tue–Sun.* 🔴 *public hols.*
📷 ♿ 🚫

Vallauris ⑪

Road map E3. 👥 *26,000*. 🚌
ℹ️ *square 8 mai 1945 (04 93 63 82 58).*
🗓️ *Tue–Sun.*
www.vallauris-golfe-juan.com

In summer, the wares of potters spill on to the avenue of this pottery capital. Picasso revitalized this industry, the history of which is traced in the **Musée Magnelli**, together with some fine Pre-Columbian ceramics. In the square is *L'Homme au Mouton* (1943). *La Guerre et la Paix* (1951) is on the ceiling of the chapel that houses the **Musée National Picasso**.

Local pottery from Vallauris

🏛 **Musée Magnelli**
Pl de la Libération. **Tel** *04 93 64 16 05.*
🗓️ *Wed–Mon.* 🔴 *1 Jan, 25 Dec.* 📷

🏛 **Musée National Picasso**
Pl de la Libération. **Tel** *04 93 64 16 05.*
🗓️ *Wed–Mon.* 🔴 *1 Jan, 25 Dec.*

78-year-old Pablo Picasso with a man-sized dalmatian companion

Pablo Picasso (1881–1973)

Picasso, the giant of 20th-century art, spent most of his later life in Provence, inspired by its luminous light and brilliant colours. He came first to Juan-les-Pins in 1920, and returned to Antibes in 1946 with Françoise Gilot. He was given a studio in the seafront Grimaldi palace, where, after wartime Paris, his work became infused with Mediterranean light and joyful images. No other artist has succeeded with so many art forms, and the Antibes collection is a taste of his versatility. He died at Mougins, aged 92.

Violin and Sheet of Music *(1912), now in Paris, is a Cubist collage from the period when Picasso experimented with different forms.*

Les Demoiselles d'Avignon *(1907), now in New York, was the first Cubist painting. Its bold style shocked the art world of the day.*

La Joie de Vivre *(1946), is one of Picasso's main works from the Antibes period, using favourite mythological themes. He is the bearded centaur playing the flute, and Françoise Gilot is the Maenad who dances while two fauns leap about and a satyr plays a panpipe.*

The Goat *(1946), also in Antibes, is one of his best-known images. In 1950 he made his famous goat sculpture using a wicker basket as the ribcage.*

L'Homme au Mouton *(1943) was sculpted in an afternoon. It stands in the main square of Vallauris, also home of* La Guerre et la Paix *(1951).*

Biot ⑫

Road map E3. 🚶 8,000. 🚌 🚘 ℹ️
46 rue St-Sébastien (04 93 65 78 00).
🎪 Tue & Fri.
www.biot-coteazur.com

The picturesque village of
Biot was the main pottery
town in the region until Pablo
Picasso revived the industry in
Vallauris after World War II.
Today, Biot is renowned for its
bubble-flecked glassware, with
eight glass works. Visitors to
La Verrerie de Biot can marvel
at master craftsmen at work.

Biot was once the domain
of the Knights Templar (see
p123), and some fortifications
remain, such as the 1566 Porte
des Migraniers (grenadiers).

The church has two fine
16th-century works: L'Ecce
Homo, attributed to Canavesio,
and La Vierge au Rosaire,
attributed to Louis Bréa.

The modern **Musée
National Fernand
Léger** is built on the
land the artist
bought to use as a
studio. It contains
many works in his
Cubism-influenced
bold style.

Detail of Léger mosaic from the eastern façade of the museum, Biot

🏛 **Musée National
Fernand Léger**
Chemin du Val-de-
Pome. **Tel** 04 92 91 50
30. ⭘ Wed–Mon. ⬤
1 Jan, 1 May, 25 Dec. 🎫 ♿ 🏠 🖵

🏛 **La Verrerie de Biot**
Chemin des Combes. **Tel** 04 93 65
03 00. ⭘ daily. ⬤ 25 Dec. ♿ 🏠

Villeneuve-Loubet ⑬

Road map E3. 🚶 13,000. 🚌
ℹ️ rue de l'Hôtel de Ville. 🎪 Wed &
Sat. **www**.ot-villeneuveloubet.org

This old village is dominated
by a restored medieval castle
which belonged to the
Villanova family. It is also
where France's most
celebrated chef,
Auguste Escoffier,
(1846–1935) was
born. The man
who invented the
bombe Néro and
pêche Melba was
chef de cuisine
at the Grand Hotel,
Monte-Carlo before
Mr Ritz persuaded
him to become
head chef at the
Savoy in London. The **Musée
de l'Art Culinaire**, in the house
of his birth, contains many
showpieces in almond paste
and icing sugar, and over

**Chef Auguste Escoffier,
born in Villeneuve-Loubet**

1,800 menus, some dating
back to 1820. The **Marineland**
leisure park includes a
children's farm and shark-filled
aquarium.

🏛 **Musée de l'Art
Culinaire**
3 rue Escoffier. **Tel** 04 93 20 80 51.
⭘ Mon–Sat. ⬤ Nov; public hols. 🎫

🐬 **Marineland**
306 av Mozart. **Tel** 04 93 33 49 49.
⭘ daily. 🎫 ♿ 🏠 🍴

Vence ⑭

Road map E3. 🚶 17,000. 🚌 ℹ️
place du Grand-Jardin (04 93 58 06
38). 🎪 Tue & Fri. **www**.ville-vence.fr

A delightful old cathedral
town on a rocky ridge, Vence
has long attracted artists.
English writer DH Lawrence
died here in 1930.

The old town is entered by
the Porte de Peyra (1441),
beside the place du Frêne,
named after its giant ash tree
planted to commemorate the
visits of King François I and
Pope Paul III. The 16th-
century castle of the lords of
Villeneuve, seigneurs of
Vence, houses the museum
and the **Fondation Emile
Hughes**, named after an
illustrious former mayor.

The town's cathedral, one
of the smallest in France,
stands by the site of the forum
of the Roman city of Vintium.
Vence was a bishopric from
the 4th to the 19th centuries.
Its notable prelates included
Saint Véran (d AD 492), and
the former wit and ladies'
confidant, Bishop Godeau
(1605–72). The 51 oak and
pear choir stalls are carved

THE CREATION OF BIOT GLASSWARE

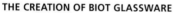

Biot is the capital of glassblowing on the coast. Local
soils provide sand for glass-
making, and typical Biot
glass is sturdy, with tiny air
bubbles (known as verre à
bulles). The opening of
Léger's museum led to an
increased interest in all local
crafts, and to the arrival of
the Verrerie de Biot workshop in 1956. This revived
old methods of making oil
lamps, carafes and narrow-
spouted porrons, from which
a jet of liquid can be poured
straight into the mouth.

with satirical figures. Marc Chagall designed the mosaic of *Moses in the Bulrushes* in the chapel (1979).

Henri Matisse *(see pp82–3)* decorated the **Chapelle du Rosaire** between 1947 and 1951 to thank the Dominican nuns who nursed him through an illness. The stations of the cross are reduced to black lines tinted with stained glass.

The Galerie Beaubourg exhibits interesting modern art in a private house and garden.

🏛 **Fondation Emile Hughes**
Château de Villeneuve. *Tel 04 93 58 15 78.* ◯ *Tue–Sun.* ◯ *1 Jan, 1 May, 25 Dec.* ▨ ▯

🏛 **Chapelle du Rosaire**
Av Henri Matisse. *Tel 04 93 58 03 26.* ◯ *Tue & Thu: am; Mon–Thu & Sat: pm* ◯ *mid-Nov–mid-Dec, publ hols.* ▨ ♿

St-Paul-de-Vence ⑮

Road map E3. 🏠 *2,900.* 🚏 *Vence.* 🛈 *2 rue Grande (04 93 32 86 95).* **www**.stpaulweb.com

This classic medieval *village perché (see pp20–21)* was built behind the coast to avoid Saracen attack. In 1537 it was re-ramparted, under François I, to stand up to Savoy, Austria and Piedmont. A celebrity village, it was first "discovered" by Bonnard, Modigliani and other artists of the 1920s. Since that time, many of the rich and famous literati and glitterati have flocked to St-Paul. A photographic display in the local museum includes Simone de Beauvoir, Jean-Paul Sartre, F Scott Fitzgerald, Catherine

Simone Signoret and Yves Montand in St-Paul-de-Vence

Deneuve, Sophia Loren and the elusive Greta Garbo.

Most famously, these personalities slept, dined, and, in the case of Yves Montand and Simone Signoret, even had their wedding reception at the **Colombe d'Or** *auberge (see p211)*. Today it has one of the finest 20th-century private art collections, built up over the years in lieu of payment of bills. The priceless dining-room décor includes paintings by such world-famous artists

as Miró, Picasso and Braque. In the 12th-century Gothic church, there is a painting, *Catherine of Alexandria*, attributed to Tintoretto. There are also gold reliquaries and a fine local 13th-century enamel Virgin. The **Musée d'Histoire Locale de St-Paul** nearby features waxwork costumed tableaux of scenes from the town's rich past, and the old castle keep opposite is now used as the town hall.

The main street runs from the 13th-century entrance gate of Porte Royale and past the Grande Fontaine to Porte Sud. This gives on to the cemetery, a resting place for Chagall, the Maeghts, Escoffier and many locals. It also offers wonderful views.

Just outside St-Paul, on La Gardette Hill, is Josep Lluis Sert's striking concrete and rose **Fondation Maeght** *(see pp76–7)*, one of Europe's finest modern art museums.

🏛 **Musée d'Histoire Locale de St-Paul**
Pl de la Mairie. *Tel 04 93 32 41 13.* ◯ *daily.* ◯ *1 Jan, 25 Dec; 2 wks Nov.* ▨

Entrance to Chapelle du Rosaire in Vence, decorated by Henri Matisse

Fondation Maeght

Nestling amid the umbrella pines in the hills above St-Paul-de-Vence, this small modern art museum is one of the world's finest. Aimé and Marguerite Maeght were Cannes art dealers who numbered the likes of Chagall, Matisse and Miró among their clients and friends. Their private collection formed the basis for the museum, which opened in 1964. Like St-Paul itself, the Maeght has been a magnet for celebrities: Duke Ellington, Samuel Beckett, André Malraux, Merce Cunningham and, of course, a galaxy of the artists themselves have mingled at fundraising events. The museum now receives over 250,000 visitors each year.

★ **Cour Giacometti**
Slender bronze figures by Alberto Giacometti, such as L'Homme Qui Marche I (1960), inhabit their own shady courtyard or appear about the grounds as if they have a life of their own.

La Vie *(1964)*
Marc Chagall's painting is full of humanity: here is love, parenthood, religion, society, nature; all part of a swirling, circus-like tableau of dancers and musicians, acrobats and clowns.

Les Poissons
is a mosaic pool designed by Georges Braque in 1962.

Les Renforts *(1965)*
One of many works of art that greet arriving visitors, Alexander Calder's creation is a "stabile" – a counterpart to his more familiar mobiles.

L'Eté *(1909)*
Pierre Bonnard settled in Provence for the last 22 years of his life, becoming a close friend of Aimé Maeght. Matisse called Bonnard "the greatest of us all".

Cowled roofs
allow indirect light to filter into the galleries. The building was designed by Spanish architect Josep Lluis Sert.

For hotels and restaurants in this region see pp194–197 and pp210–213

La Partie de Campagne (1954)
Fernand Léger lends his unique vision to the classic artistic scene of a country outing.

VISITORS' CHECKLIST

St-Paul-de-Vence. **Tel** 04 93 32 81 63. ⬜ Jul–Sep: 10am–7pm; Oct–Jun: 10am–12:30pm, 2:30–6pm. 🚫 📷 🚻 ♿ **Library**. **www**.fondation-maeght.com

★ **Labyrinthe de Miró**
Joan Miró's l'Oiseau Lunaire (1968) is one of the many statues in this multi-levelled maze of trees, water and gargoyles.

Oiseau dans le Feuillage (1961)
Georges Braque's bird nestles amongst "foliage" made of newsprint. Braque was highly influential in the creation of the Fondation, but died before he could see the museum finally opened to the public.

GALLERY GUIDE

The permanent collection is comprised entirely of 20th-century art. The only items on permanent view are the large sculptures in the grounds. The indoor galleries display works from the collection in rotation but, in summer, only temporary exhibitions are held.

Chapelle St-Bernard was built in memory of the Maeghts' son, who died in 1953 aged 11. The altarpiece is a 15th-century Christ; above it is a stained-glass window by Braque.

Main entrance and information

STAR SIGHTS

★ Cour Giacometti

★ Labyrinthe de Miró

Renoir's studio at Les Collettes

Cagnes-sur-Mer ⑯

Road map E3. 🚶 *43,000.* 🚌 🚉
ℹ️ *6 bd Maréchal Juin (04 93 20 61
64).* 🛒 *Tue–Sun.* **www**.cagnes.com

There are three parts to
Cagnes-sur-Mer: Cros-de-
Cagnes, the fishing village
and beach; Cagnes-Ville, the
commercial centre; and Haut-
de-Cagnes, the upper town.

Haut-de-Cagnes is the place
to head for. This ancient hilltop town is riven with lanes,
steps and vaulted passages. It
is dominated by the **Château
Grimaldi** but also has some
fine Renaissance houses and
the church of St-Pierre, with a
Gothic nave in which the
Grimaldis are entombed.

East of Cagnes-Ville is Les
Collettes, built among ancient
olive trees by Pierre-Auguste
Renoir (1841–1919). He came
here in the 1890s, hoping that
the climate would relieve his
rheumatism. He built the
house in 1907 and stayed for
the rest of his life. A picture of
Renoir in his last year shows
him still at work, a brush tied
to his crippled hand.

Now the **Musée Renoir** at
Les Collettes is almost exactly
as it was when the artist died.
In the house are eleven of
Renoir's paintings, as well as
works by his friends Bonnard
and Dufy. Visitors can also
explore his beloved olive
groves, the setting for the fine
bronze *Venus Victrix* (1915-16).

🏛 **Musée Renoir**
19 chemin des Collettes. **Tel** 04 93 20
61 07. ⬜ Dec–Oct: Wed–Mon. ⬤ 1
Jan, 1 May, 2 wks Nov, 25 Dec. ⬛⬛

Château Grimaldi

In the Middle Ages the Grimaldi family held sway over
many of the Mediterranean coastal towns. The castle
that towers over Haut-de-Cagnes was built by Rainier in
1309 as a fortress-prison; in 1620 his descendant, Jean-
Henri, transformed it into the handsome palace which
shelters behind its dramatic battlements. Mercifully, the
château survived the worst ravages of the Revolution and
later occupation by Piedmontese troops in 1815. It now
houses an eclectic mixture of
museums, from olives to
modern art.

**Stairs to
the tower**

**Second
floor**

The chapel contains
a wealth of religious
ornamentation, both
ancient and modern.

GALLERY GUIDE

*The olive tree museum is on
the ground floor, along with
exhibits about life in the medieval castle. The Suzy Solidor
collection is displayed in a
former boudoir on the first
floor. Selections from the permanent collection of modern
Mediterranean art, as well as
temporary exhibitions, are on
the first and second floors.*

KEY TO FLOORPLAN

⬜	Donation Suzy Solidor
⬜	Musée d'Art Modern Méditerranéen
⬜	Musée de l'Olivier
▨	Permanent collection
▨	Temporary exhibition space
⬜	Non-exhibition space

★ **Donation Suzy Solidor**
*This 1930s chanteuse was
painted by 244 artists during
her lifetime. The 40 works
on display include portraits
by Jean Cocteau* (above)
and Kisling (top).

Renaissance Courtyard
This central space rises past two levels of marble-columned galleries to the open sky. Among its lush greenery is a 200-year-old pepper tree.

VISITORS' CHECKLIST

Cagnes-sur-Mer. **Tel** 04 92 02 47 30. ☐ Dec–mid-Nov: 10am–noon, 2–6pm (5pm winter) Wed–Mon. ● 1 Jan, 1May, mid-Nov–2 Dec, 25 Dec. 🖼

First floor

★ La Chute de Phaëton attributed to Carlone
The Piedmontese soldiers occupying the château in the 19th century had little respect for this spectacular 1620s illusionistic ceiling – and used it for target practice.

Ground floor

Musée de l'Olivier
A massive wooden oil mill, vast terracotta jars and other artifacts illustrate the time-honoured Provençal tradition of olive cultivation.

Maison aux Crénaux is a house built within the fortified town walls.

To place du Château

Main entrance and ticket office

STAR SIGHTS

- ★ La Chute de Phaëton attributed to Carlone

- ★ Donation Suzy Solidor

Street-by-Street: Nice ⑰

A dense network of pedestrian alleys, narrow buildings and narrow buildings and pastel, Italianate façades make up the Old Town. Its streets contain many fine 17th-century Italianate churches, among them St-François-de-Paule, behind the Opéra, and l'Eglise du Jésus in the rue Droite. Most of the seafront, at quai des Etats-Unis, is taken up by the Ponchettes, a double row of low houses with flat roofs, a fashionable walk before the promenade des Anglais was built. To the east of this lies the Colline du Château, occupied in the 4th century by Greeks who kept fishing nets on the quay.

★ Cathédrale Ste-Réparate
Built in 1650 by the Nice architect J-A Guiberto in Baroque style, this has a fine dome of glazed tiles and an 18th-century tower.

Palais de Justice
This awesome building was inaugurated on 17 October 1892, replacing the smaller quarters used before Nice became part of France. On the same site was a 13th-century church and convent.

★ Cours Saleya
The site of an enticing vegetable and flower market, it is also a lively area at night.

Opera House
Built in 1855, the ornate and sumptuous Opéra de Nice has its entrance just off the quai des Etats-Unis.

Chapelle de la Miséricorde

Designed in 1740 by Guarino Guarinone, this Baroque masterpiece has a fine Rococo interior. The Nice altarpieces are by Louis Bréa and Jean Miralhet.

VISITORS' CHECKLIST

Road map F3. 🚗 349,000.
✈ 7 km (4.5 miles) SW. 🚉 av
Thiers. 🚌 5 blvd Jean Jaurès.
🚢 quai du Commerce.
ℹ 5 prom des Anglais (08 92 35
35 35). 🕑 Tue–Sun. 🎭 Carnival
(before Lent), Nice Jazz Festival
(July). www.nicetourisme.com

★ Palais Lascaris

18th-century statues of Mars and Venus flank the staircase. The trompe l'oeil ceiling is by Genoese artists.

Tourist Train

It passes the market, old town and castle gardens.

KEY

- - - Suggested route

```
0 metres          100
0 yards           100
```

STAR FEATURES

- ★ Cathédrale Ste-Réparate
- ★ Palais Lascaris
- ★ Cours Saleya

Les Ponchettes

One of Nice's most unusual architectural features is the row of low white buildings along the sea-front once used by fishermen, now a mix of galleries and ethnic restaurants.

Musée Matisse

Henri Matisse (1869–1954) first came to Nice in 1916, and lived at several addresses in the city before settling in Cimiez for the rest of his life. His devotion to the city and its "clear, crystalline, precise, limpid" light culminated, just before his death in 1954, with a bequest of works. Nine years later they formed the museum's core collection, sharing space with archaeological relics in the Villa des Arènes, next to the Cimiez cemetery, which holds the artist's simple memorial. Since 1993 the entire villa, complete with its new extension, has been devoted to celebrating his life, work and influence.

★ **Nu Bleu IV** *(1952)*
The celebrated "cut-outs" were made in later life when Matisse was bedridden.

Matisse in his Studio *(1948)*
The museum's photographic collection offers a unique insight into the man and his work. Robert Capa's picture shows him drafting the murals for the Chapelle du Rosaire at Vence (see pp74–5).

First floor

To stairs up to villa

Ground floor

★ **Fauteuil Rocaille**
A gilded Rococo armchair, painted by Matisse in 1946, is among many of his personal belongings that are on display in the museum.

Main Entrance

STAR EXHIBITS

- ★ Nature Morte aux Grenades
- ★ Fauteuil Rocaille
- ★ Nu Bleu IV

GALLERY GUIDE

The ground and first floors of the villa are used to display works from the museum's ever-expanding permanent collection. The new subterranean wing is used for changing thematic exhibitions devoted to Matisse and his contemporaries.

KEY TO FLOORPLAN

- ☐ Permanent collection
- ☐ Temporary exhibition space
- ☐ Non-exhibition space

Liseuse à la Table Jaune *(1944)*
The tranquillity of this work belies the troubles that beset Matisse in World War II, including a major operation and the arrest of his wife for Resistance work.

VISITORS' CHECKLIST

164 av des Arènes de Cimiez, Nice. *Tel 04 93 53 40 53.*
◻ 10am–6pm Wed–Mon (5pm Oct–Mar). ● 1 Jan, 1 May, 25 Dec. ♿ 🅿 📷
www.musee-matisse-nice.org

Torse Debout
This bronze of 1909 was given to the museum in 1978 by the artist's son, Jean.

Mezzanine, new wing

Children's workshop

Lower ground floor, new wing

The upper floors of the villa hold a library and resource centre for students and researchers.

Exit

Trompe l'Oeil Façade
The decorative stonework that adorns the 17th-century Villa des Arènes is, in fact, a masterful disguise of plain walls, only visible close to.

★ Nature Morte aux Grenades *(1947)*
Ripe pomegranates feature in a favourite setting: an interior with a window to "skies …as brilliantly blue as Matisse's eyes", as the poet Aragon put it.

Exploring Nice

Nice is France's largest tourist resort and fifth biggest city. It has the second busiest airport in France and more banks, galleries and museums than anywhere else outside the capital. Each year, Nice hosts a lavish pre-Lent carnival, ending with a fireworks display and the Battle of the Flowers *(see p228)*. The city has its own dialect and its own cuisine of *socca*, chickpea pancakes, but the ubiquitous pizza ovens lend a rich Italian flavour.

Beach and promenade des Anglais

A glimpse of the city

Nice lies at the foot of a hill known as the Château, after the castle which once stood there. The daily flower and vegetable market in the cours Saleya is a shoppers' paradise. The fashionable quarter is the Cimiez district, up on the hills overlooking the town, where the old monastery of **Notre-Dame** is worth a visit. Lower down, next to the handsome **Musée Matisse** *(see p82–3)*, are the remains of a Roman amphitheatre and baths. Artifacts are on show at the nearby archaeological museum.

The city's most remarkable feature is the 19th-century promenade des Anglais which runs right along the seafront. It was built in the 1820s, using funds raised by the English colony. Today it is an eight-lane 5-km (3-mile) highway. Until World War II, Nice was popular with aristocrats. Queen Victoria stayed here in 1895, and in 1912, Tsar Nicholas II built the onion-domed **Cathédrale Orthodoxe Russe** in St-Philippe. The old town is now gentrified, although it once had a bad reputation. In 1982 English author Graham Greene criticized Jacques Médecin, the city's right-wing mayor, who was eventually imprisoned for corruption and died in exile.

🏨 Hotel Négresco

37 promenade des Anglais. **Tel** 04 93 16 64 00. See **Where to Stay** p195. This palatial hotel was built in 1912 for Henri Négresco, once a gypsy-violin serenader, who went bankrupt eight years later.

The fountain in place Masséna

NICE

Cathédrale Ste-Réparate ⑤
Musée Mossa ④
Hotel Négresco ③
Musée d'Art Contemporain ⑦
Musée Chagall ①
Musée Masséna ②
Palais Lascaris ⑥

KEY

▭ See pp80–81

In the *salon royale* hangs a Baccarat chandelier made from 16,000 stones. The infamous American dancer Isadora Duncan spent her last months here in 1927. She died tragically outside the hotel when her trailing scarf caught in the wheel of her Bugatti and broke her neck.

🏛 Musée Masséna

65 rue de France. *Tel* 04 97 43 34 45. ⬤ *Tue–Sun.* 📷

This late 19th-century Italianate villa belonged to the great-grandson of Napoleon's Nice-born Marshal. Its Empire-style main hall has a bust of the Marshal by Canova. Among its exhibits are religious works, paintings by Niçois primitives, white-glazed faïence pottery (*see p186*) and Josephine's gold cloak.

🏛 Musée Chagall

36 Av Dr Ménard. *Tel* 04 93 53 87 20. ⬤ *Wed–Mon.* ⬤ *1 Jan, 1 May, 25 Dec.* 📷 ♿

Built in 1972, this museum houses the largest collection of Marc Chagall's work. There are 17 canvases from

Russian Orthodox cathedral

his Biblical Message series, including five versions of *The Song of Songs*. Three stained-glass windows depict the *Creation of the World* and the large mosaic reflected in the pool is of the prophet Elijah.

🔒 Cathédrale Ste-Réparate

Place Rossetti. *Tel* 04 93 62 34 40. ⬤ *daily.*

This 17th-century Baroque building has a handsome tiled dome. The interior is lavishly decorated with plasterwork, marble and original panelling.

⚓ Palais Lascaris

15 rue Droite. *Tel* 04 93 62 72 40. ⬤ *Wed–Mon.* ⬤ *1 Jan, Easter, 1 May, 2 weeks in Nov, 25 Dec.*

This salon of this stuccoed 17th-century palace has a *trompe l'oeil* ceiling, said to be by Carlone. An 18th-century pharmacy has been re-created on the ground floor.

🏛 Musée des Arts Asiatiques

405 prom des Anglais. *Tel* 04 92 29 37 00. ⬤ *Wed–Mon.* ⬤ *1 Jan, 1 May, 25 Dec.* 📷 ♿ 🏠

This museum has outstanding examples of ancient and 20th-century art from across Asia in Kenzo Tange's uncluttered white marble and glass setting.

🏛 Musée des Beaux-Arts

33 av des Baumettes. *Tel* 04 92 15 28 28. ⬤ *Tue–Sun.* ⬤ *1 Jan, Easter, 1 May, 25 Dec.* 📷 ♿

Once home to a Ukranian princess, this 1878 villa houses a collection begun with a donation by Napoleon III. Three centuries of art cover work by Jules Chéret, Carle Van Loo, Van Dongen, and Impressionists and Post-impressionists such as Bonnard, Dufy and Vuillard.

🏛 Musée d'Art Contemporain

Promenade des Arts. *Tel* 04 93 62 61 62. ⬤ *Tue–Sun.* ⬤ *1 Jan, Easter, 1 May, 25 Dec.* 📷 ♿ 🏠

Based in a strikingly original building with marble-faced towers and glass passageways, the collection reflects the history of the *avant-garde*, including Pop Art by Andy Warhol and work by Ecole de Nice artists such as Yves Klein.

Hillside view over Cap Ferrat

Cap Ferrat ⑱

Road map F3. 🚉 Nice. 🚌 Beaulieu. 🚌 St-Jean-Cap-Ferrat. ℹ St-Jean-Cap-Ferrat (04 93 76 08 90).

The Cap Ferrat peninsula is a playground for the rich, with exclusive villas, luxury gardens and fabulous yachts in the St-Jean marina.

King Léopold II of Belgium started the trend in the 19th century when he built Les Cèdres on the west side of the cape overlooking Villefranche. Today, the 14-ha (35-acre) park is open to the public and a 3-ha (7-acre) lake on Leopold's estate has been turned into the **Parc Zoologique**, complete with chimps' tea parties. In 1906 he built the Villa Mauresque for his personal priest; it was bought by Somerset Maugham 20 years later. The Duke and Duchess of Windsor added *cachet* when they rented a villa here in 1938, and post-war residents have included David Niven and Edith Piaf. High hedges and gates protect these exotic villas, but one of the finest, **Musée Ephrussi de Rothschild** (*see pp86–7*), is open to the public.

There is a superb view from the little garden around the 1837 lighthouse at the end of the cape. A pretty shoreside walk leads around the Pointe St-Hospice, east of the port at **St-Jean-Cap-Ferrat**, a former fishing village with old houses overlooking the harbour.

🦌 Parc Zoologique

Cap Ferrat. *Tel* 04 93 76 04 98. ⬤ *daily.* 📷 ♿ 🏠 📷

Yves Klein's *Anthropométrie* (1960) in the Musée d'Art Contemporain

Musée Ephrussi de Rothschild

Beatrice Ephrussi de Rothschild (1864–1934) could have led a life of indolent luxury, but her passions for travel and fine art, combined with an iron will, led to the creation of the most perfect "dream villa" of the Riviera, Villa Ile-de-France. She competed with King Léopold II of Belgium for the land, and later supervised every aspect of the villa's creation. It was completed in 1912 but Béatrice had only four years in which to enjoy its beauty. After the death in 1916 of her beloved husband, whom she called "Frousse", she never lived there again. The villa remains a monument to a woman of spirit and vision.

★ Fragonard Room
The unrivalled collection of working drawings by Jean-Honoré Fragonard (1732–1806) includes this sketch, wryly named If he were as faithful to me.

Béatrice, Aged 19
Her meek appearance belies a woman who, a contemporary once observed, "commands flowers to grow during the Mistral".

The Salon Louis XV–XVI opens out on to the French garden, combining the pleasures of a sea breeze with the comfort of elegant surroundings.

Béatrice's Boudoir
Béatrice's writing desk is a beautiful piece of furniture dating from the 18th century. It once belonged to Marie-Antoinette.

STAR SIGHTS

- ★ Fragonard Room
- ★ Salon Louis XV–XVI
- ★ Gardens

Villa Ile-de-France
Béatrice christened her villa in memory of an ocean voyage on the luxury liner of the same name. Its stucco walls are coloured in her favourite shade of rose pink.

Covered Patio
Combining Moorish and Italian elements, this airy space rises the full height of the villa. The marble columns, mosaic flooring and diffused light complement the Renaissance religious works and 16th–17th-century tapestries on the walls.

VISITORS' CHECKLIST

1 av Ephrussi de Rothschild, St-Jean-Cap-Ferrat. ☎ 04 93 01 33 09. ☐ Jul & Aug: 10am–7pm daily; Sep–Jun: 10am–6pm daily. ● 25 Dec. 🎟 📷 1st floor collections only (obligatory). ☐ ☐ ☐ ground floor only. www.villa-ephrussi.com

First-floor apartments

Entrance to villa and assembly point for guided tours

Cabinet des Singes
Béatrice's love of porcelain animals is epitomized by this tiny room. Its screens are painted with monkeys dancing to the music of the diminutive 1740s Meissen monkey orchestra.

To ticket office and car park

★ Salon Louis XV–XVI
Like every room in the villa, the decor here is lavish, with wood ornamentation from the Crillon in Paris, Savonnerie carpets, and chairs upholstered in 18th-century Beauvais tapestries.

★ Gardens
The French garden is designed to resemble the prow of a ship. At parties, staff wore sailors' uniforms to enhance the illusion. Other garden themes include Florence and Japan, complete with a miniature Pagoda.

Villefranche ⑲

Road map F3. 👥 *7,000*. 🚗 🚊
ℹ️ *Jardin François Binon (04 93 01 73 68)*. 🛒 *Sat*.
www.villefranche-sur-mer.com

This unspoilt town overlooks a beautiful natural harbour, deep enough to be a naval port, with a lively waterfront lined by bars and cafés.

The medieval **Chapelle St-Pierre** on the quay, once used for storing fishing nets, was renovated in 1957, when Jean Cocteau added lavish frescoes. Steep lanes climb up from the harbour, turning into tunnels beneath the tightly packed buildings. The vaulted rue Obscure has provided shelter from bombardment as recently as World War II. The Baroque **Eglise St-Michel** contains a 16th-century carving of St Rock and his dog and a 1790 organ.

Within the sturdy grey walls of the 16th-century Citadelle de St-Elme are the chapel, open-air theatre and museums.

🏠 **Chapelle St-Pierre**
Quai Amiral Courbet. **Tel** *04 93 76 90 70*. 🕐 *Tue–Sun*. ⬤ *Easter Mon, mid-Nov–mid-Dec, 25 Dec*. 🈲

Fishing in the natural harbour at Villefranche

Beaulieu ⑳

Road map F3. 👥 *4,000*. 🚗 🚊
ℹ️ *pl Clemenceau (04 93 01 02 21)*.
🛒 *Mon–Sat*.
www.ot-beaulieu-sur-mer.fr

Hemmed in and protected by a rock face, this is one of the Riviera's warmest resorts in winter, with two beaches: the Baie des Fourmis and, by the port, Petite Afrique. The casino, formal gardens and the Belle Epoque Rotunda, now a conference centre and museum, add to Beaulieu's old-fashioned air. Among its hotels is La Réserve, founded by Gordon Bennett, the owner of the *New York Herald*. As a stunt, in 1871, he sent journalist HM Stanley to rescue the Scottish missionary and explorer Dr Livingstone, who was looking for the source of the Nile.

Beaulieu is the site of the **Villa Kerylos**. Built by archeologist Théodore Reinach, it resembles an ancient Greek villa. Authentic techniques and precious materials were used to create lavish mosaics, frescoes and inlaid furniture. There are also numerous original Greek ornaments, and a new antique sculpture gallery.

🏛️ **Villa Kerylos**
Imp. Eiffel. **Tel** *04 93 76 44 09*.
🕐 *daily*. ⬤ *25 Dec*. 🈲 🈲

Eze ㉑

Road map F3. 👥 *2,450*. 🚗 🚊 ℹ️
pl Général de Gaulle (04 93 41 26 00).

Eze is a dramatic *village perché (see pp20–21)*, a cluster of ancient buildings some 427 m (1,400 ft) above the sea. At its summit are the bat-filled ruins of a 14th-century castle. Around it, is the **Jardin Exotique**, offering views as far as Corsica.

The flower-decked, car-free streets lead to an 18th-century church. Its bust of Christ is made from olive wood that survived the terrible fires that raged close by in 1986.

🌿 **Jardin Exotique**
Rue du Château. **Tel** *04 93 41 10 30*.
🕐 *daily*. ⬤ *25 Dec*. 🈲

Steps of the elegant Belle Epoque Rotunda (1886), Beaulieu

For hotels and restaurants in this region see pp194–197 and pp210–213

La Turbie ②

Road map F3. 🏚 *2,600.* 🚌 ℹ️ *La Mairie (Jun–Sep: 04 93 41 21 15; Oct–May: 04 92 41 51 61).* 🚌 *Thu.*

High above Monte-Carlo is one of the finest views on the Riviera, reached by a stretch of the Grande Corniche which crosses ravines and tunnels through mountains. The village of La Turbie, scented with bougainvillea, has two medieval gateways. Its oldest houses, dating from the 11th–13th centuries, are on the Roman via Julia.

🏛 Musée du Trophée des Alpes

Av Albert 1er. **Tel** *04 93 41 20 84.* ☐ *May–mid-Sep: daily; mid-Sep–Apr: Tue–Sun.* ⚫ *1 Jan, 1 May, 1 & 11 Nov, 25 Dec.* 🛒 📷

The most spectacular feature of La Turbie is the Trophée des Alpes, a huge Roman monument, built out of white local stone, which marked the division between Italy and Gaul. Its construction was ordered in 6 BC by the Roman Senate to honour Augustus's

View of Le Trophée des Alpes from the village of La Turbie

Monument detail

victory in 13 BC over 44 fractious Ligurian tribes. The original trophy was 50 m (164 ft) tall and had niches with statues of each of the campaign's victors. There were stairs leading to all parts of the structure.

When the Romans left, the trophy was gradually dismantled. In the 4th century, St Honorat chipped away at the monument because it had become the object of pagan worship. Later it served both as a fort and as a stone quarry. It was partly destroyed on the orders of Louis XIV, who feared it would fall into enemy hands during the invasion of Provence by Savoy in 1707. Restoration was first begun in 1905, and continued in 1923 by an American, Edward Tuck. To-day, the triumphal inscription of Roman victory has been restored to its original position.

A small museum on the site documents the history of the trophy, with fragments of the monument, pieces of sculpture, inscriptions, drawings and a small-scale model.

The spectacular panorama from the terraces of the trophy takes in Cap Ferrat and Eze. Monaco, at 480 m (1,575 ft) below, seems breathtakingly close, like an urban stage set seen from a seat in the gods.

Among visitors impressed with La Turbie and its trophy, was the poet Dante (1265–1321), and his comments are inscribed on a plaque in rue Comte-de-Cessole. From the end of this street there is a fine view of the monument.

🔔 Eglise St-Michel-Archange

☐ *daily.* ♿

The 18th-century Nice Baroque church was built with stones plundered from the trophy. Inside there is an altar of multi-coloured marble and a 17th-century onyx and agate table, which was used for communion. Its religious paintings in-clude two works by the Niçois artist Jean-Baptiste Van Loo, a portrait of St Mark at-tributed to Veronese, and a Piéta from the Bréa School.

LE TROPHÉE DES ALPES

This triumphal monument had a square podium, a circular colonnade and a stepped cone which was surmounted by the statue of Augustus.

6-m (20-ft) statue of Emperor Augustus

The original colonnade included niches for the statues of Augustus's campaign generals.

The inscription records the names of the 44 tribes subjugated by Augustus, with a dedication to the emperor.

Monaco ㉓

Grimaldi family crest

If you come to Monaco by car, you may well travel in on the Moyenne Corniche, one of the world's most beautiful coastal highways. Arriving amid the skyscrapers of present-day Monaco, it is hard to imagine its turbulent history, much of it centred on Monaco-Ville. The palace, cathedral and museums are all in this old part of town, set on the Rock, a sheer-sided, flat-topped finger of land extending 792 m (2,600 ft) into the sea. First a Greek and later a Roman colony, it was bought from the Genoese in 1309 by François Grimaldi. In spite of family feuds and at least one political assassination, the Grimaldis, whose crest shows two sword-waving monks, remain the world's oldest ruling monarchy.

Modern Monaco
Lack of space has led to vertical building, and a striking skyline of skyscrapers and apartment blocks.

Musée des Souvenirs Napoléoniens

Palais Princier
The Grimaldis have ruled from here since the 14th century. The palace dates from the 16th–17th centuries but its towers are Genoese of 1215. The constitution insists it is guarded by French carabiniers. (See p94).

Cathédrale
This Neo-Romanesque construction in cream-coloured stone sits on a rocky spur. Among its treasures are two early 16th-century screens by Bréa, La Pietà and St-Nicolas. (See p94).

Musée Océano-graphique

Erected on a sheer cliff, high above the Mediterranean, it has one of the best aquaria in Europe. It is also used as a scientific research institute. (See p94).

VISITORS' CHECKLIST

Road map F3. 35,000.
15 km (9 miles) SW Nice.
pl Ste Dévote (08 36 35 35 35)
2a bd des Moulins (00 377 92 16 61 16). daily. Festival du Cirque (Jan); Grand Prix (May); Fête Nationale (19 Nov).
www.monaco-tourisme.com

Théâtre du Fort Antoine

This ancient fort has been converted into a theatre which shows a wide range of productions in summer.

Monte Carlo Story is a multi-visual history in film and photographs, recorded in different languages.

Typical Old Town Villa
Hidden in a labyrinth of passages are fountains, tiny squares and elegant façades.

THE ROYAL FAMILY

Monaco was ruled from 1949 by the businesslike Prince Rainier Louis Henri Maxence Bertrand de Grimaldi. He was the 26th ruling prince, a descendant of the Grimaldi who, disguised as a monk, entered the Monaco fortress in 1297. At that time the territory extended to Antibes and Menton. Prince Rainier's wife, the former film star Grace Kelly, whom he married in 1956, died tragically in 1982. Their son, Albert, inherited the $200 million throne on Rainier's death in 2005 but it is his beautiful, sometimes wayward, sisters Stephanie and Caroline who have taken up most media attention in recent years.

Prince Rainier III and Grace Kelly at their engagement party in 1956

Monte-Carlo

**Art Deco entrance,
Le Café de Paris**

The dramatic heights of Monte-Carlo are the best-known area of Monaco. People flock to the annual car rally in January and many of the world's greatest singers perform here in the opera season. Monte-Carlo is named after Charles III, who opened the first casino in 1878, to save himself from bankruptcy. Such was his success that, five years later he abolished taxation. Although Queen Victoria thought Monte-Carlo a den of iniquity, her view was not shared by other aristocrats, including Edward VII, who were regular visitors. The stunning Casino and Opera House were built by Charles Garnier, architect of the Paris Opéra. Between Monaco-Ville and Monte-Carlo lies La Condamine, a shopping and commercial centre surrounding the luxury yachts.

View of Monte-Carlo
*It is worth pausing at
La Turbie (see p89) to
admire the panorama.*

Palais Princier

Jardin Exotique
*Plants normally grown in
balmy climates flourish here,
and its grottoes housed prehistoric animals and humans
200,000 years ago (see p94).*

La Condamine
*The quays are pleasant
yacht-watching promen-
ades laid out by Albert I.
The current prince added
a watersports pool, and
it is also a popular
setting for funfairs.*

VISITORS' CHECKLIST

Road map F3. 🚌 pl Ste Dévote
ℹ️ 2a bd des Moulins (00 377 92
16 61 16). **Grimaldi Forum**
(cultural centre) **Tel** 00 377 99 99
3000. ⬜ daily. 🏁 Monte-Carlo
Rally (Jan); Festival International de
Feux d'Artifices (Jul–Aug).
🚆 daily.

Le Café de Paris
*Ladies' man Edward VII
was a regular visitor to this
renovated Art Deco triumph.
The dessert* crêpe suzette *was
named after one companion.*

La Turbie

Eglise Ste-Dévote

Hôtel Hermitage

Centre de Congrès

Salle Garnier
*Designed by Charles Garnier
in 1878, this was where ballet
innovators such as Diaghilev
and Nijinksy congregated.*

Casino
*In a 3-day gambling
spree in 1891, Charles
Deville Wells turned
$400 into $40,000
and inspired the tune,*
The Man Who Broke
the Bank at Monte-
Carlo *(see p94).*

Exploring Monaco

After the Vatican, Monaco is the world's smallest sovereign state. It covers 1.95 sq km (0.75 sq miles), about half the size of New York City's Central Park. Its inhabitants, 20 per cent Monégasque citizens, pay no taxes and enjoy the world's highest per capita income. Monégasque, a dialect of Provençal, is reflected in street names, such as *piaca* for place, *carrigiu* for rue. But the official language is French, the Euro is used here and most of France's laws apply. Monaco's road network is complicated, so drivers should plan routes with care.

Marine explorer Jacques Cousteau

Monaco Grand Prix route

views of Monaco. Its interior is still decorated in Belle Epoque style. Roulette is played in the opulent Salons Européens; blackjack is played in the Salons Privés. Female nudes smoking cigars deck the ceiling of the Salon Rose bar.

🏛 Musée National (Poupées et Automates)
17 av Princesse Grace. **Tel** 00 377 93 30 91 26. ◯ daily. ● 1 Jan, Grand Prix, 1 May, 19 Nov, 25 Dec. 🗺 🅿
Charles Garnier built this villa, set in a rose garden with sculptures including the *Young Faun* by the Carpeaux School. It has dolls from the 18th–19th centuries. The automata are set in motion daily: some are opened to show their inner workings.

🛡 Cathédrale
4 rue Colonel Bellando del Castro. ◯ daily. 🅰
The 12th-century church of St-Nicolas was replaced by this 19th-century Neo-Romanesque building in La Turbie stone. Its old altarpiece, by Louis Bréa, is by the ambulatory, with its tombs of princes and bishops. The much-mourned Princess Grace is buried here.

🏛 Musée Océanographique
Av St-Martin. **Tel** 00 377 93 15 36 00. ◯ daily. 🗺 🅰 🅿 🍴 *Cinema*
Founded by Prince Albert I in 1910, this clifftop museum has an aquarium filled with rare marine plants and animals, a collection of shells, coral and pearls, and a life-sized model of a giant squid. Marine explorer Jacques Cousteau was director here for 30 years until 1988. The roof terrace offers a superb coastal view.

🍀 Jardin Exotique
62 bd du Jardin Exotique. **Tel** 00 377 93 15 29 80. ◯ daily. ● public hols. 🗺 🅿 🅰 (part of garden only).
These gardens are among the finest in Europe, with a vast range of tropical and sub-tropical plants. Off the gardens is the **Grotte de l'Observatoire**, where prehistoric animals lived and were hunted by humans 200,000 years ago. The **Musée d'Anthropologie Préhistorique**, accessible via the garden, displays prehistoric tools, figurines and bones.

♣ Palais Princier
Pl du Palais. **Tel** 00 377 93 25 18 31. ◯ Jun–Oct: daily. 🗺
Monaco's seat of government is an attractive castle-palace, protected by cannons donated by Louis XIV, and sentries who change daily at 11:55am. The palace, with its priceless furniture and frescoes, is only open in the summer. Concerts are held in the Cour d'Honneur.

🏛 Musée des Souvenirs Napoléoniens et Archives Historiques du Palais
Pl du Palais. **Tel** 00 377 93 25 18 31. ◯ Jun–mid-Nov: daily; mid-Dec–May: Tue–Sun. ● 1 Jan. 🗺 🅿
The palace museum combines local history with Napoleonic memorabilia. A large family tree traces links between the Bonapartes and the Grimaldis, while the ground floor is, appropriately to the nature of the man, devoted to Napoleon, with numerous busts of him.

♠ Casino
Pl du Casino. **Tel** 00 377 92 16 23 00. ◯ daily, from noon. 🅰
www.casino-monte-carlo.com
Designed in 1878 by Charles Garnier (*see p51*), the casino sits on a terrace with superb

Roulette tables in the Salle Europe of the Casino

Peillon ⓴

Road map F3. 👥 *1,100.*
ℹ️ *(04 93 91 98 34) pm only.*

At a level of 373 m (1,225 ft), this pretty *village perché* is said by locals to mark the extremity of the inhabited world. Its streets are stepped and narrow, with houses that have scarcely changed since the Middle Ages. There is an attractive cobbled square with fine views, and the 18th-century parish church has an unusual octagonal lantern. But most impressive of all are Giovanni Canavesio's frescoes in the Chapelle des Pénitents Blancs. Peillon is ideally placed for woodland walks leading to both Peille and La Turbie.

Ancient arch across Peillon street

Peille ⓶⑤

Road map F3. 👥 *2,000.* 🚉
ℹ️ *La Mairie (04 93 91 71 71).*

Peille is a charming medieval village with a view from its war memorial across the Paillon Valley and as far as the Baie des Anges. Behind the village looms the vast Pic de Baudon, rising to 1,264 m (4,160 ft).

The town is full of cobbled alleys and covered passages. At the end of place A-Laugier, beyond a Gothic fountain, two arches beneath a house rest on a Romanesque pillar.

The Counts of Provence were lords of the castle, and the 12th-century church of Ste-Marie has a picture of Peille in the Middle Ages. There is also a fine 16th-century altarpiece

The Gorges de la Vésubie in the pine-forested Vallée de la Vésubie

by Honoré Bertone. The Hôtel de Ville is in the domed 18th-century former Chapelle de St-Sébastien, and there is a museum in rue de la Turbie.

Lucéram ⓶⑥

Road map F3. 👥 *1,000.* 🚉 ℹ️ *pl Adrien Barralis (04 93 79 46 50).*

In the midst of this pretty, Italianate village is the tiled roof of the 15th-century Eglise Ste-Marguerite, which contains art by Nice's Primitive masters, notably Louis Bréa, the artist of the 10-panelled altarpiece, who made Lucéram a centre for religious painting. Other treasures include a silver statue of the Tarascon dragon and Ste Marguerite *(see p140)*. The church is the setting for a Christmas service, where shepherds, accompanied by flutes and tambourines, bring lambs and fruit as offerings.

Italian-style houses in Lucéram, set between two ravines

Vallée de la Vésubie ⓶⑦

🚉 *Nice.* 🚌 *St-Martin-Vésubie.* ℹ️ *St-Martin-Vésubie (04 93 03 21 28).*

Some of the most attractive landscape around Nice can be uncovered and enjoyed in the valley of the river Vésubie, with its dense pine forests, alpine pastures, peaks and cascades. The river rises high in the snowy Alps near the Italian border, courses past Roquebillière to the west of the Parc National du Mercantour *(see p97)* and dives through the Gorges de la Vésubie before entering the river Var, 24 km (15 miles) north of Nice airport.

The Vésubie is created from the Madone de Fenestre and the Boréon torrents, which meet at St-Martin-Vésubie. This popular summer mountaineering centre is surrounded by waterfalls, summits and lakes. In its fine 17th-century church is a 12th-century statue of Notre-Dame-de-Fenestre. Each year this statue is carried to the Chapelle de la Madone de Fenestre, in a craggy alpine setting, 12 km (8 miles) to the east, for a three-month stay.

The Gorges de la Vésubie begins at St-Jean-la-Rivière, and there is a spectacular panorama at la Madonne d'Utelle, above the fortified village of Utelle. In places, the dramatic gorge, etched with coloured rock, runs up to 244 m (800 ft) deep. Sadly, the road beside it has few stopping places from which to admire the view.

Skiing in the Alpes d'Azur

Provence offers a wide range of skiing activities in the Alpes d'Azur. Around one hour from the coast, in breathtaking mountain scenery, there are more than 20 resorts, with over 250 ski-runs. The *après-ski* includes ice-skating, riding on a snowmobile and a chance to sample traditional Alpine food such as delicious melted cheese *raclette*. In summer, Auron and Isola 2000, resorts in the Parc National du Mercantour, offer swimming, cycling and horse-riding in dramatically contrasting surroundings to the Côte d'Azur.

Snowbound Valberg, a winter resort since 1935

AURON

ALTITUDE *1,600 m (5,250 ft) – 2,100 m (6,890 ft).*
LOCATION *97 km (60 miles) from Nice via RN 202 and D 2205.*
SKI RUNS *5 black, 15 red, 13 blue, 2 green.*
SKI LIFTS *23 including 8 chair lifts and 3 cable cars.*

ISOLA 2000

ALTITUDE *2,000 m (5,250 ft) – 2,610m (8,563 ft).*
LOCATION *90 km (56 miles) from Nice via RN 202, D 2205 and D 97.*
SKI RUNS *5 black, 16 red, 18 blue, 7 green.*
SKI LIFTS *23 including a cable car and 10 chairlifts. Funicular railway.*

VALBERG

ALTITUDE *1,430 m (4,690 ft) – 2,100 m (6,890 ft).*
LOCATION *86 km (51 miles) from Nice via RN 202, CD 28, CD 202 or CD 30.*
SKI RUNS *12 black, 22 red, 13 blue, 11 green.*
SKI LIFTS *26 including 6 chair lifts.*

Climbing a frozen waterfall, or frozen fall climbing, in one of the many alpine resorts

Getting ready for a few hours of snow-shoe trekking

ALPINE ACTIVITIES

	Auron	Isola 2000	Valberg	
Cross-country skiing	•	•	•	
Disabled skiing			•	
Horse riding	•		•	
Horse-driven buggy rides	•		•	
Ice circuit driving		•		
Ice skating	•	•	•	
Kart Cross on ice		•		
Mono-skiing		•	•	
Night skiing		•	•	
Ski-jo-ring		•		
Ski jumping		•		
Ski school	•	•	•	
Ski touring	•	•	•	
Snowboarding	•	•	•	
Snow scooter circuits			•	
Snow-shoe trekking	•	•	•	
Speed ski school			•	
Aquatic centre (17 km), sauna and jacuzzi		•		

Snowboarding in the alpine resort of Isola 2000

Forêt de Turini ❷⑧

🚆 l'Escarène, Sospel. 🚌 Moulinet, Sospel. 🛈 La Bollène (04 93 03 60 54).

Between the warm coast and the chilly Alps, from the Gorges de la Vésubie to the Vallée de la Bévéra, lies this humid, 3,497-sq km (1,350-sq mile) forest. Beech, maple and sweet chestnut thrive here, and pines grow to great heights.

At the forest's northeastern edge is the 1,889-m (6,197-ft) mountain of l'Authion, site of heavy fighting in the German retreat of 1945. Casualties are recorded on a war memorial.

The neighbouring Pointe des Trois-Communes, at 2,082 m (6,830 ft), offers superb views of the pre-Alps of Nice and the peaks of the Mercantour national park.

Le Parc National du Mercantour ❷⑨

Road map E2 & F2. 🚆 Nice. 🚌 St Etienne de Tinée, Auron. 🛈 Maison du Parc (04 93 02 42 27). **www**.parc-mercantour.fr

Scoured by icy glaciers and bristling with rocky summits, this sparsely populated park covers 70,000 ha (270 sq miles). Among its unusual wildlife are the chamois, the ibex and the *mouflon*, a sheep which originated in Corsica. Sometimes visible in the mornings is the marmot, a rodent which is prey to golden eagles, and the exotic lammergeier, a bearded vulture with orange-red feathers and black wings. There are also many brightly coloured butterflies and alpine flowers.

Tower at Tende

Tende ❸⓪

Road map F2. 🚶 2,200. 🚆 🚌 av du 16 Sep 1947 (04 93 04 73 71). 🚌 Wed.

Sombre Tende once guarded the mountain pass connecting Piedmont and Provence, now bypassed by a tunnel. Its tall, balconied, green schist buildings appear piled on top of each other. Only a wall remains of the castle of

A street scene in the old border town of Tende

Lascaris' feudal lords, near the terraced cemetery above the town. Tende's unusual towers include that of the 15th-century church of **Notre-Dame-de-l'Assomption.** Lions support the pillars around the Renaissance doorway and there are green schist columns inside.

The **Vallée des Merveilles**, the most spectacular part of Mercantour national park, can be visited with a guide. For information, contact the tourist office at Tende or St-Dalmas. The most direct route is from Lac des Mesches. A 2-hour walk leads to Lac Long and Le Refuge des Merveilles. The Mont Bégo area has 36,000 engravings, dating from 2,000 BC, carved into the rock face. They reveal a Bronze Age culture of shepherds and farmers who instilled magic into the area. In Tende, the **Musée des Merveilles** is worth a visit.

Southeast of Tende, there are fine paintings in the church at La Brigue. Jean Canavasio's 15th-century frescoes of *La Passion du Christ*, and the lurid *Judas pendu* are in the nearby 13th-century **Chapelle Notre-Dame-des-Fontaines.**

🏛 **Musée des Merveilles**
Av du 16 Septembre 1947 **Tel** 04 93 04 32 50. ⬜ Wed–Mon. ⬤ publ hols, 2 wks mid-Mar & mid-Nov. 🎫 ♿ 🛈

Saorge ❸①

Road map F3. 🚶 360. 🚌 🛈 La Mairie (04 93 04 51 23).

Saorge is the prettiest spot in the Roya Valley. Set in a natural amphitheatre high over the river, its slate-roofed houses are tiered between narrow alleys, in the style of a typical stacked village or *village empilé*.

Olive-wood carvings are traditional, and carved lintels date many houses to the 15th century, when Saorge was a stronghold. It was taken by the French under Masséna in 1794.

Churches range from the dank 15th-century St-Sauveur with an Italian organ to the Baroque church of the Franciscan monastery and the octagonal tower and Renaissance frescoes of **La Madone-del-Poggio** (appointment only).

View of Saorge from the Franciscan monastery terrace

Sospel ③②

Road map F3. 🏠 2,600. 🚌 🚗 🚻
Le Pont Vieux (04 93 04 15 80). 🛒 *Thu*

This charming alpine resort on
the river Bévéra has a 13th-
century toll tower, restored
since Sospel was badly
damaged by bombs in World
War II, when the bravery of
the town's citizens earned it
the Croix de Guerre. Fort St-
Roch, built in 1932 against
possible Italian invasion, has
a museum with details of the
Maginot line. The former
cathedral, now church of St-
Michel, containing one of
François Bréa's best works,
has an attractive façade, as
does the Romanesque Palais
Ricci. The interior of the White
Penitent chapel is magnificent.

🏛 **Musée de la Ligne
Maginot des Alpes**
Fort St-Roch. *Tel 04 93 04 00 70.* ◯
*Apr–Jun, Oct: Sat, Sun & public hols
pm only; Jul–Sep: Tue–Sun pm only.* 🎫

Trompe l'oeil houses in Sospel

Gorbio ③③

Road map F3. 🏠 1,135. 🚌
🛈 *La Mairie, 30 rue Garibaldi (04 92
10 66 50).*

More than a thousand species
of flowers have been
identified in the sunny Gorbio
valley, which produces
vegetables and fruit, wine and
oil. Until the last century the
area was entirely supported
by its olive production.
　Often shrouded in mist in
the mornings, Gorbio itself is
a *village perché (see pp20–21)*,
with sea views. The old
Malaussène fountain stands
by the entrance to the narrow
cobbled lanes, and an elm tree

Early morning Gorbio, surrounded by olive groves

in the square was planted in
1713. The church has a conical
belfry, a typical feature of the
region. Each June a procession
marks the Penitents' ritual,
when the village lanes twinkle
with the lights from oil lamps
made from snail shells.
　A good hour's walk from
Gorbio is Ste-Agnès, at 671 m
(2,200 ft) it is the highest
village perché on the coast.

Roquebrune-Cap-Martin ③④

Road map F3. 🏠 12,400. 🚌 🚗 🚻
218 av Aristide Briand (04 93 35 62 87).
🛒 *Wed.* **www**.roquebrune.com

Roquebrune is said to have
the earliest feudal **château** in
France, the sole example of
the Carolingian style. Built in
the 10th century by Conrad I,
Count of Ventimiglia, to ward
off Saracen attack, it was later
remodelled by the Grimaldis
(see p91). Wealthy Englishman

View of Château de Roquebrune,
overlooking Cap Martin

Sir William Ingram, one of the
first wave of tourist residents,
bought the château in 1911
and added a mock medieval
tour anglaise.
　At the turn of the century,
Cap Martin was the smartest
resort on the Côte d'Azur,
attracting the era's glitterati.
Empératrice Eugénie, wife of
Napoléon III, and England's
Queen Victoria wintered here.
Winston Churchill, Coco
Chanel and Irish poet WB
Yeats also visited. Architect Le
Corbusier, who drowned off
the cape in 1965, has a
coastal path named after him.
　A number of important
prehistoric remains have been
found around Roquebrune,
some in caves such as the
nearby **Grottes du Vallonet**.
Just outside the village, on the
Menton road, is the majestic
olivier millénaire, one of the
oldest olive trees in the
world, which is believed to
be at least 1,000 years old.
　Every August since 1467,
in gratitude for being spared
from the plague, Roquebrune's
inhabitants take part in scenes
from the Passion *(see p33).*

⚓ **Château de Roquebrune**
Tel 04 93 35 07 22. ◯ *daily.* 🎫

Menton ③⑤

Road map F3. 🏠 30,000. 🚌
🚗 🛈 *Palais de l'Europe, 8 av Boyer
(04 92 41 76 50).* 🛒 *daily.*
www.villedementon.com

Just a mile from the border,
Menton is the most Italian of
the French resorts. Tucked in
by mountains, it is a sedate

town with a Baroque square and a promenade stretching towards Cap Martin.

Menton has several fine tropical gardens, and citrus fruits thrive in a climate mild enough for the lemon festival in February *(see p35)*. The **Palais de l'Europe** of the Belle Epoque (1909), once a casino, now a cultural centre, is beside the **Jardin Biovès**. The **Jardin Botanique Exotique** has tropical plants and is in the grounds of Villa Val Rahmeh. Above the town is the **Jardin des Colombières** designed by artist and writer Ferdinand Bac (1859–1952). This private garden reputedly has France's oldest carob tree.

The jetties offer good views of the old town, and steps lead to Parvis St-Michel, a fine square paved with the Grimaldi coat of arms, where summer concerts are held. To the left side are the twin towers of the Baroque **Basilica St-Michel**, its main altarpiece by Manchello (1565). Behind the new marina is the suburb of Garavan where the tubercular New Zealand writer Katherine Mansfield lived, in the Villa Isola Bella, from 1920-22.

⛫ Musée des Beaux-Arts
Palais Carnolès, 3 av de la Madone. ***Tel** 04 93 35 49 71.* ⬜ *Wed–Mon.* ⬤ *public hols.* ♿ *restricted.*
The 17th-century palace, now Menton's main art museum, was once summer residence of

the princes of Monaco. It has paintings by Graham Sutherland (1903–80), an honorary citizen, 13th- to 18th-century Italian, French and Flemish art, and works by Utrillo and Dufy.

⛪ Salle des Mariages
Hôtel de Ville. ***Tel** 04 92 10 50 00.* ⬜ *Mon–Fri.* ⬤ *public hols.* ♿
Jean Cocteau decorated this room in 1957 with colourful images of a fisherman and his bride, and the less happy story of Orpheus and Eurydice, and Provençal motifs such as using a fish for a fisherman's eye.

⛫ Musée Jean Cocteau
Quai de Monléon. ***Tel** 04 93 57 72 30.* ⬜ *Wed–Mon.* ⬤ *public hols.* ♿
Cocteau supervised the conversion of this former 17th-

century fort into his museum. He designed the salamander mosaic on the ground floor, and donated his first tapestry, set designs and drawings.

⛨ Cimetière du Vieux-Château
Each terrace of this former castle site accommodates a separate faith. Webb Ellis, inventor of rugby, is buried here, as is Rasputin's assassin, Prince Youssoupov.

⛫ Musée de Préhistoire Régionale
Rue Loredan Larchey. ***Tel** 04 93 35 84 64.* ⬜ *Wed–Mon.* ⬤ *public hols.*
The museum's fine local history and archaeological pieces include the skull of 30,000-year-old "Grimaldi Man".

JEAN COCTEAU (1889–1963)

Born near Paris in 1889, Cocteau spent much of his very public life around the Côte d'Azur. A man of powerful intellect and great *élan*, he became a member of the Académie Française in 1955. Among other talents, Cocteau was a dramatist (*La Machine Infernale, 1934*); the writer of *Les Enfants Terribles* (1929), and a surrealist film director. *Orphée* (1950) was partly shot against the barren landscape at Les Baux *(see p142)*. He died before his museum opened in 1967.

Mosaic at the entrance of the Musée Jean Cocteau in Menton

View over Menton from Ferdinand Bac's Jardin des Colombières

THE VAR AND THE ILES D'HYÈRES

The Var is a region of rolling lands, rocky hills, thick forests and swathes of vineyards. To the north, Provençal villages are thinly scattered by mountain streams, on hilltops and in valleys; to the south, a series of massifs slope down to the coast making this stretch of the Côte d'Azur the most varied and delightful shore in France.

Through the centre of the Var, dividing it roughly into two sections, runs the A8 autoroute. To the south of this artery the influence of the sea is unmistakable. Toulon, the departmental capital, occupies a fine deep-water harbour that is home to the French Mediterranean fleet. Beyond it are the pleasant resorts of Bandol and Sanary, where Jacques Cousteau first put scuba-diving to the test. To the east are the sandy beaches beneath the great slab of the Massif des Maures. The Var's most famous resort, St-Tropez, facing north in the crook of a bay, lies in a glorious landscape of vineyards. Beyond it, just past Fréjus, the first Roman settlement in Gaul, the land turns blood red in the twinkling inlets and coves below the beautiful Corniche de l'Esterel, which heads east towards the Riviera. The more remote areas to the north of the autoroute have always provided a retreat from the bustling activity of the coast. This is where the Cistercians built their austere Abbaye du Thoronet. Today visitors escape inland from the summer traffic around St-Tropez to the sparsely populated Haut Var, where towns seem to grow from tufa rock.

Highlights include wines from the Côtes de Provence, and fresh tuna from quayside restaurants. Music enthusiasts should spare time to hear both the organ at St-Maximin-la-Ste-Baume, Provence's finest Gothic building, and the string quartets at the festival in the hill towns near Fayence. Visitors can also go walking, sailing and sunbathing, and enjoy a rich collection of museums and architecture.

Sunrise over the boats in St-Tropez harbour

◁ **A traditional shop in the centre of Cotignac in the Haut Var**

Exploring the Var and the Iles d'Hyères

The Var Departement covers about 6,000 sq km (2,300 sq miles). It combines a stunning coastline sprinkled with red cliffs, delightful bays and the Iles d'Hyères, which spill out from its southernmost point, with dramatic chains of hills behind the coast and further inland. Although the hills have been partly depleted by forest fires, they are still home to a fascinating array of flora and fauna as well as to the many producers of Côtes-de-Provence wines.

View of the Abbaye du Thoronet

SIGHTS AT A GLANCE

KEY

▬▬	Motorway
▬▬	Major road
──	Secondary road
┄┄	Minor road
▬▬	Scenic route
╾╼	Main railway
──	Minor railway
▬▬	Regional border
△	Summit

0 kilometres   10

0 miles   10

Les Issambres beach, north of Ste-Maxime

GETTING AROUND

The uplands of the Maures and Esterel force the A8 auto-route and N7 national road inland, leaving the coast to the more scenic routes: the Corniche d'Or in the Massif de l'Esterel is thought to be France's loveliest. The combination of stunning views and tight bends means that you should allow plenty of time for your journey. The unspoiled Haut Var is easy to get to by car. Alternatively, the railway reaches as far as Draguignan, from where you can explore the region by bus. Comps-sur-Artuby is a good tour base for the Gorges du Verdon (see pp184–5).

Le Logis-du-Pin

Trigance

Artuby

Bargème

3 COMPS-SUR-ARTUBY

D955

D563

4 MONS

St-Cézaire-sur-Siagne

6 BARGEMON

5 FAYENCE

Grasse

Châteaudouble

Callas

D562

St-Paul-en-Forêt

Lac de St-Cassien

Cannes

Aups

2

issac-levue

HAUT VAR

Tourtour

Pierre de la Fée

D955

Villecroze

D560

rnes

Flayosc

7 DRAGUIGNAN

N7

Mont Vinaigre 620m

Entrecasteaux

LORGUES

D555

Le Muy

Puget-sur-Argenas

MASSIF

Carcès

9

D4

DE L'ESTEREL

N98

Pic de Cap Roux 452m

10 ABBAYE DU THORONET

8 LES ARCS

PROVENCE

CÔTES DE

11

Vidauban

D25

FRÉJUS **29**

SAINT-RAPHAEL

28

Agay

Cabasse

A8

N7

Le Luc

VAR

esse-sur-sole

A57

Fréjus-Plage

Saint-Aygulf

N98

Les Issambres

26 SAINTE-MAXIME

D75

Notre-Dame-des-Anges

D39

M497

Maures

La Garde Freinet

D558

21

MASSIF DES MAURES

GRIMAUD **25**

24 PORT-GRIMAUD

N98

23 SAINT-TROPEZ

Cogolin

Moulins de Paillas △ 322m

Collobrières

D14

Chartreuse de la Verne

Môle

D559

22

Cap Camarat

RAMATUELLE

Cavalaire-sur-Mer

20 BORMES-LES-MIMOSAS

LE LAVANDOU **19**

N98

Port-de-Miramar

Cap Benat

LES D'HYÈRES

17

Porquerolles

Île du Levant

LES

Île de Porquerolles

Île de Port Cros

A narrow street in St-Tropez old town

A traditional flute-maker at work in Barjols

Barjols ❶

Road map D4. 🏛 *2,150.* ⊟
ℹ *bd Grisolle (04 94 77 20 01).*
⊟ *Sat.* www.barjols.fr

Once renowned for its seeth-
ing tanneries, Barjols lies
peacefully among woods and
fast-flowing streams. In 1983,
after almost 400 years, the
leather industry finally
folded. The many aban-
doned factories have
now become bustling
artisans' studios.

Today, it is these
local craftsmen who
bring manufacturing
acclaim to the area.
Two traditional Prov-
ençal instruments, the
three-holed flute *(galoubet)* and
the narrow drums *(tam-
bourins)*, were still made in
Barjols until recently.

**The *Champignon*
fountain in Barjols**

These instruments resound
each January at the annual
fête of St-Marcel, the town's
patron saint. About every four
years the ceremony includes
the slaughter and roasting of
an ox in the square. This is
followed by a colourful "tripe
dance" inside and outside the
11th-century church of Notre-
Dame-de-l'Assomption, where
St-Marcel's relics can be seen.
The ceremony commemorates
the survival of the town after a
siege in 1350. For roastings
contact the tourist office.

Of the many stone fountains
dotted around the town, the
most famous is the mossy
Champignon in place Capitaine
Vincens. It stands under what
is reputed to be the largest
plane tree in Provence.

Between the church and the
old tanneries are the restored
buildings of the old *quartier
du Réal*. Exotic porticoes,
particularly on the Renaissance
Hôtel de Pontevès, add spice
to some otherwise drab streets.

Haut Var ❷

✈ Toulon-Hyères, Nice. 🚊 *Les Arcs.*
🚌 *Aups.* ℹ *Aups (04 94 84 00 69).*

The most remote and un-
spoiled lands of the Var are
situated between Barjols and
Comps-sur-Artuby, up towards
the Gorges du Verdon *(see
pp184–5)*. Much of the land
near here has been taken over
by the military.

Aups, set among undulating
hills on the plateau edge, is
the region's centre. Epicureans
may be drawn by the local
honey and the truffle market
each Thursday in winter. It is
an attractive town with a
grand old square and
castle ruins. The
15th-century St-
Pancrace church
has a well-restored
Renaissance door-
way. Also worth a
visit is the **Musée
Simon Segal**,
which is housed in a
former Ursuline
convent. The
museum contains works by
Segal and Paris painters, as
well as local scenes.

About 5 km (3 miles) northwest on the D9 is the village
of Moissac-Bellevue. Many of

its buildings date from the
16th and 17th centuries and
its church was mentioned in a
papal edict of 1225.

South from Aups is Ville-
croze. The town is set against
a natural backdrop of caves
on two levels, which local
lords in the 16th century
turned into dwellings, known
as the **Grottes Troglodytes**.
The arcaded streets and the
keep of the feudal castle give
the town a medieval flavour.
A short drive from Villecroze
leads up to the hill village of
Tourtour, a smaller, prettier
and more popular place.

**View of Entrecasteaux château
near Cotignac, Haut Var**

From Tourtour there are fine
views of Montagne Ste-Victoire,
which was one of Cézanne's
favourite painting subjects.

The valley town of Salernes
lies in the opposite direction,
10 km (6 miles) west on the
D51. Smoke pumps from the
kilns of its 15 ceramic factories.

Troglodyte dwellings in Villecroze

The 110 m (361 ft) Artuby bridge spanning the Canyon du Verdon

Salernes is one of the best-known Provençal tile-making centres, noted for *tomettes* – hexagonal terracotta floor-tiles.

Cotignac, west of Salernes, is an echo of Villecroze, with a cave-pocked cliff behind it. Behind the *Mairie*, a river springs from the rocks and beyond is an open-air theatre.

The region's most intriguing château is **Entrecasteaux**, 15 km (8 miles) east of Cotignac. The 17th-century castle is filled with the present owner's 17th- to 18th-century collection of paintings, artifacts, tapestries and furniture. The garden, by Le Nôtre, is publicly owned.

🏛 **Musée Simon Segal**
Rue Albert Premier, Aups.**Tel** 04 94 70 01 95. ⬜ *mid-Jun–mid-Sep: daily.* 🔲

🎦 **Grottes Troglodytes**
Villecroze. **Tel** 04 94 70 63 06. ⬜ Feb & Easter hols, May–Jun: daily pm; Jul–mid-Sep: daily; mid-Sep–mid-Oct: Sat–Sun pm. ⬤ Nov–Easter. 🔲

🎦 **Château d'Entrecasteaux**
83570 Entrecasteaux. **Tel** 04 94 04 43 95. ⬜ Sun–Fri. ⬤ Sat; mid-Nov–Easter. 🔲 🔳

Comps-sur-Artuby ❸

Road map D3. 🏠 *270.* 🔲 🚹 *La Mairie (04 94 50 24 00).*

The eastern approach to the Gorges du Verdon *(see pp184–5)* passes through Comps-sur-Artuby. The village nestles at the foot of a rock topped by the 13th-century chapel of **St-André**, which was restored recently. From the church there are grand views of the Artuby Gorges.

To the east lies Bargème, a village of steep streets and hollyhocks with a population of just 86. At 1,094 m (3,589 ft) it is the highest community in the Var. The village itself is closed to all traffic.

Dominating Bargème is a large, partially ruined but nevertheless remarkably well preserved 14th-century castle. Also worth a visit is the 13th-century Romanesque **Eglise St-Nicolas** which contains a carved, wooden altarpiece depicting Saint Sebastian.

Mons ❹

Road map E3. 🏠 *460.* 🔲
🚹 *pl St Sébastien (04 94 76 39 54).*

Dramatically situated on a rock-spur, Mons, with its tiny lanes and overhanging arches, has an almost magical appeal. The place St-Sébastien looks out across the entire coast, from Italy to Toulon.

Originally a Celtic-Ligurian settlement, its Château-Vieux quarter dates from the 10th century, but it was mainly built by Genoese who repopulated the village after ravages by the plague in the 14th century. The first families came in 1461 from Figounia near Ventimiglia; their legacy is the local dialect, *figoun*, which still survives thanks to the unusually isolated position of the village. Nearby is the *roche taillée*, a Roman aqueduct carved from solid rock. There are also many dolmens in the surrounding area.

The Roman-built *roche taillée* aqueduct near Mons

TRUFFLES

This richly flavoured and treasured fungal delicacy of the Var is traditionally sniffed out by trained pigs. The golfball-sized truffles are collected during the winter, when they are at their most fragrant, from underground near the roots of oak trees. Local markets specialize in truffles when they are in season, though their rarity means that they tend to be very expensive.

A trained pig hunting for truffles

View over Bargemon's terracotta rooftops to the wooded hills beyond

Fayence ❺

Road map E3. 🏛 *4,300.* 🚌
ℹ *place Léon Roux (04 94 76 20 08).*
🛒 *Tue, Thu & Sat.*

The hillside town of Fayence is the largest one between Draguignan and Grasse and is a centre for both local crafts and gliding. Dominated by a wrought-iron clock tower, it still has a few remains of its 14th-century defences including a Saracen-style gate.

The **Eglise St-Jean-Baptiste** was built in the 18th century with a baroque marble altar (1757) by a local mason, Dominique Fossatti. Its terrace offers a sweeping view over the town's glider airfield.

On the hillside opposite, in the community of Tourettes,

there is a striking château. Part modelled on the Cadet school in St Petersburg, it was constructed in 1824 for General Alexandre Fabre, who once worked as a military engineer for Tsar Alexander I of Russia. He originally intended to make the building a public museum, but failed to finish the task and so it remains private.

There are a number of attractive villages nearby. Among the best are Callian and Montauroux to the east and Seillans, 5 km (3 miles) to the west, where the German-born painter Max Ernst (1891–1976) chose to spend his last years. The prestigious Musique en Pays de Fayence festival in October brings string quartets who perform in some of the charming local churches.

Bargemon ❻

Road map E3. 🏛 *1,250.* 🚌 *Les Arcs.* 🚌 ℹ *av Pasteur (04 94 47 81 73, am only in winter).* 🛒 *Thu.* **www**.ot-bargemon.fr

This medieval village, fortified in AD 950, has three 12th-century gates and a tower from the mid-16th-century. The village is laid out around a number of squares with fountains, shaded by plane trees.

The angels' heads on the high altar of the 15th-century church, **St-Etienne**, now the Musée-Galerie Honoré Camos, are attributed to the school of Pierre Puget, like those in the **Chapelle Notre-Dame-de-Montaigu** above the town. The chapel also contains a "miraculous" oak-wood carving of the Virgin brought here from Montaigu in Belgium by a local monk in 1635.

Draguignan ❼

Road map D4. 🏛 *35,000.* 🚌 ℹ
2 ave Lazare Carnot. (04 98 10 51 05). 🛒 *Wed, Sat.*
www.ot-draguignan.fr

During the day, the former capital of the Var département has the busy air of a small market town. At night, however, the only sign of life is groups of young people in the place des Herbes. Baron Haussmann, planner of modern

TRADITIONAL POTTERY AND CRAFTS

Fayence, Cotignac, Aups and Salernes are at the centre of an exciting revitalization of Provençal crafts, which includes weaving, pottery, stone and wood carving. A regional speciality is hand-crafted domestic pottery made using traditional techniques and designs, as well as local clays in a wonderful variety of colours. Examples of all these crafts can be found in small shops and studios, or craft fairs and local markets. There are good buys to be had, but do shop around to avoid being unknowingly overcharged.

A Provençal potter at work

Paris, laid out Draguignan's 19th-century boulevards.

At the end of his plane-tree-lined allées d'Azémar, there is a Rodin bust of the prime minister Georges Clemenceau (1841–1929) who represented Draguignan for 25 years.

The main interest lies in the pedestrianized old town. Its 24-m (79-ft) clockless clock tower, built in 1663, stands on the site of the original keep and there is a good view from its wrought-iron campanile. The **Eglise St-Michel**, in the place de la Paroisse, contains a statue of St Hermentaire, first bishop of Antibes. In the 5th century he slew a local dragon, hence giving the town its name.

Draguignan has two good local museums. The **Musée des Traditions Provençales** is concerned with the region's social and economic history. It occupies buildings that date back to the 17th century. Regional country life is illustrated using reconstructed kitchens and barns. Exhibits include beautiful hand-painted wooden horses.

St Hermentaire laying the dragon

The **Musée Municipal** shows works of art from Rubens to Renoir as well as eye-catching collections of both ceramics and furniture. The adjoining library houses a lavishly illuminated 14th-century manuscript of the *Roman de la Rose*, considered to be the most important book of courtly love *(see p142)* in France (by appointment only).

Northwest of the town on the D955 is the enormous prehistoric dolmen Pierre de la Fée, or Fairy Stone *(see p39)*.

🏛 **Musée des Traditions Provençales**
15 rue Joseph-Roumanille. **Tel** 04 94 47 05 72. ◯ Tue–Sat, Sun pm. ●25 Dec, 1 May. 📷 🔲 ♿ gr. fl. only.

🏛 **Musée Municipal**
9 rue de la République. **Tel** 04 98 10 26 85. ◯ Mon–Sat. ● public hols. ♿

Pierre de la Fée, the giant dolmen outside Draguignan

Les Arcs ⑧

Road map D4. 🏠 *5,300.* 🚉 🚌 ℹ *place du Général de Gaulle (04 94 73 37 30).* 🛍 *Thu.*

Wine centre for the Côtes de Provence *(see p109)*, Les Arcs has a medieval quarter, Le Parage, based around the 13th-century Château de Villeneuve. The **Eglise St-Jean-Baptiste** (1850), in the rue de la République, contains a screen by Louis Bréa (1501) and a mechanical crib.

East of Les Arcs on the D91 is the 11th-century Abbaye de Ste-Roseline, which was named after Roseline de Villeneuve, daughter of the hard-hearted Arnaud de Villeneuve, Baron of Arcs. Legend has it that when Roseline's father stopped her while taking food to the poor, her provisions turned miraculously into roses. She entered the abbey in 1300 and later became its abbess.

The renovated Romanesque **Chapelle Ste-Roseline** contains the well-preserved body of the saint in a glass shrine. There is also an abundance of Renaissance and Baroque detail, and a celebrated Chagall mosaic *(see p29)*.

🔒 **Chapelle Ste-Roseline**
Route Ste-Roseline, between Muy and La Motte. **Tel** 04 94 99 50 30. ◯ Tue–Sun pm. ♿

Mosaic by Marc Chagall (1887–1985) in the Chapelle Ste-Roseline

Lorgues 9

Road map D4. 🏛 7,500. 🚗 ⓘ pl
Trucy (04 94 73 92 37). 🚌 Tue.

Nestling on a slope beneath
oak and pine woodland,
Lorgues is surrounded by vineyards and olive groves. Its old
town was fortified in the 12th
century. Today, two 14th-cen-
tury gates and city wall remains
can be seen. The town centre's
handsome square is shaded by
a large plane tree. Lorgues has
a grand array of 18th-century
municipal buildings and monuments and one of the longest
plane-tree avenues in France.
In the centre of town is the
stately **Collégiale St-Martin**,
consecrated in 1788. Its organ,
dating from 1857, is the finest
example of the work of the
Augustin Zeiger factory, Lyon.
Also on display is a marble
Virgin and Child (1694) which
came from the Abbaye du
Thoronet and is attributed to
the school of Pierre Puget.

Abbaye du Thoronet 10

Road map D4. 83340 Le Thoronet.
Tel 04 94 60 43 90. ☐ daily. ⬤ 1
Jan, 1 May, 1 & 11 Nov, 25 Dec. 🈶 ⓘ

Founded in 1146, Le Thoronet
was the first Cistercian
building in Provence. Lost in
deep woodland, it occupies a
typically remote site. Along

**Graceful cloisters on the north side
of the Abbaye du Thoronet**

with the two Romanesque
abbeys of Sénanque (see p164)
and Silvacane (see p147), it is
known as one of the three
"Cistercian sisters" of Provence.
The cool geometry of the
church, cloister, dormitory
and chapter house reflects the
austerity of Cistercian prin-
ciples. Only the belltower
breaks with the order's strict
building regulations: instead
of wood, it is made of stone,
to enable it to withstand the
strong Provençal winds.
Dilapidated as early as the
15th century, the abbey was
finally abandoned in 1791. In
common with many medieval
Provençal buildings, its restoration was instigated by Prosper
Mérimée, Romantic novelist
and Napoleon III's Inspector
of Historic Monuments, who
visited in 1834.
Just beside the abbey is the
modern Monastère de Beth-
léem, home to some 20 silent
Cistercian nuns whose handi-
crafts are on sale in a shop.

Côtes de Provence Tour 11

The Côtes de Provence wine-growing region
reaches from the Haut Var to the coast.
Dozens of roadside vineyards offer
tastings and a chance to buy. This
rural route suggests a few accessible
and well-regarded producers, starting at
the Maison des Vins in Les Arcs. Here
you can find out about local wines, plot your
own route, buy wine from the producers, and
even book to stay at a vineyard. The tour
passes a few interesting towns
en route. For more information on the
region's wines, see pages 208–9.

TIPS FOR DRIVERS

Tour length: 100 km (62 miles).
Stopping-off points: The
Maison des Vins should be your
first stopping point – it is open all
day and has a restaurant. Around
the route motorists should have
no difficulty in spotting places to
stop and sample, though many of
the wine producers close between
noon and 2pm. The Lac de Carcès
makes a good place for a picnic.
(See also pp250–1.)

Entrecasteaux ⑥
From Entrecasteaux, dominated
by its huge 17th-century
château, follow signs for
Les Saignes to find
Château Mentone.

les Saignes

CHATEAU
MENTONE

D50

D31

Argens

D562

D562

D13

D13

DOMAINE
DE L'ABBA

D79

Le Thoronet ④
The Domaine de l'Abbaye
vineyard is named after Le
Thoronet's beautiful abbey.

Carcès ⑤
As you head north, the Lac de
Carcès is on the left in a steep
valley. The town's castle remains
and gardens are worth seeing.

KEY

▬▬▬ Tour route

———— Other roads

La Gayole sarcophagus, dating from the 2nd or 3rd century, in the Musée du Pays Brignolais

Brignoles ⑫

Road map D4. 🏛 *13,000.* 🚌 🛈
Hôtel de Clavier, rue des Palais (04 94 69 27 51). 🛒 *Wed, Sat.*
www.ville-brignoles.fr

Bauxite mines have stained the Brignoles countryside red: vital to the region's economy, over a million tonnes of metal are mined here annually. The medieval town remains above it all, quiet and empty for most of the year. An unexpected delight is the **Musée du Pays Brignolais** in a 12th-century castle that was built as a summer retreat for the Counts of Provence. The eclectic collection includes La Gayole marble sarcophagus, which is 2carved with images in both the pagan and Christian traditions; a boat made of cement designed by J Lambot (1814–87), who gave the world reinforced concrete; and

a collection of votive offerings. St Louis, bishop of Toulouse and patron of Brignoles, was born in a palace beside the Eglise St-Sauveur in 1274. The church has a 12th-century portico and a side entrance in the rue du Grand Escalier.

🏛 **Musée du Pays Brignolais**
2 place des Comtes de Provence. **Tel** *04 94 69 45 18.* 🕐 *Wed–Sun.* ● *1 Jan, Easter, 1 May, 1 Nov, 25 Dec.* 📷

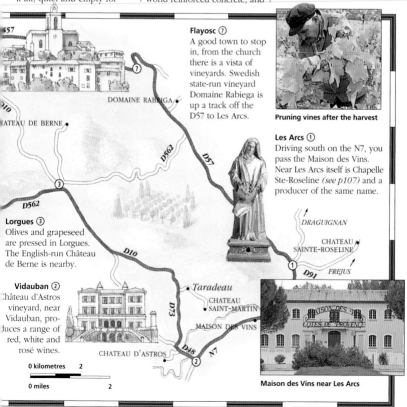

Flayosc ⑦
A good town to stop in, from the church there is a vista of vineyards. Swedish state-run vineyard Domaine Rabiega is up a track off the D57 to Les Arcs.

Pruning vines after the harvest

Les Arcs ①
Driving south on the N7, you pass the Maison des Vins. Near Les Arcs itself is Chapelle Ste-Roseline *(see p107)* and a producer of the same name.

Lorgues ③
Olives and grapeseed are pressed in Lorgues. The English-run Château de Berne is nearby.

Vidauban ②
Château d'Astros vineyard, near Vidauban, produces a range of red, white and rosé wines.

0 kilometres 2

0 miles 2

Maison des Vins near Les Arcs

St-Maximin-la-Ste-Baume ⓭

Surrounded by hills and vineyards, St-Maximin-la-Ste-Baume is dominated by the basilica Ste-Marie-Madeleine and its attached monastery. According to legend, the basilica was built on the site of the tombs of St Mary Magdalene and of St Maximin, martyred first bishop of Aix *(see pp148–9)*. The saints' remains, hidden from the Saracens *(see pp42–3)*, were rediscovered in 1279. The building, started 16 years later by Charles II, Count of Provence, is the region's finest example of Gothic architecture.

Sarcophagus of St Cedonius
This is one of four 4th-century saints' sarcophagi in the crypt, which was once the burial vault of a Roman villa.

★ Relics of St Mary Magdalene
This bronze gilt reliquary (1860) holds the skull of St Mary Magdalene. Pilgrim popes and princes took away other parts of her body.

Stairs to crypt

The apse was completed in the early 14th century; a staircase tower has become the belfry.

★ Ronzen's Retable *(1520)*
François Ronzen's wood retable and surrounding panels include the first picture of the Papal Palace in Avignon (pp44–5).

★ Organ
One of the finest in France, with some 3,000 pipes, the organ was made in 1773 by Jean-Esprit Isnard. Napoleon's brother Lucien saved it in the Revolution by having the Marseillaise played on it whenever a visiting official arrived.

Basilica Entrance

The western side of the basilica has two matching wooden doors. They feature studied carving that contrasts sharply with the surrounding façade, which appears to have been crudely chopped off. When work stopped on the building in 1532, this part was left unfinished.

VISITORS' CHECKLIST

Road map D4.
🛈 Place de l'Hôtel de Ville. *Tel* 04 94 59 84 59.
Basilica ◻ 7:30–11:30am, 3–5:30pm Mon–Sat.
✝ 10:30am Sun, 9am Wed, 6pm Thu. **Mass** 9am Mon–Sat, 8am & 11am Sun. ♿
Monastery ◻ 9am–6pm daily.
www.st.maximin.com

Hôtel de Ville

The town hall is in the pilgrims' hostelry. It adjoins the refectory and chapel of the Royal Monastery.

Milestone

Discovered along the Roman Aurelian Way (see p125), this 1st-century milestone is now on display at the entrance to the cloisters.

Former Refectory

STAR SIGHTS

★ Relics of St Mary Magdalene

★ Organ

★ Ronzen's Retable

Cloisters

The cloisters are at the centre of the Royal Monastery, so called because the French kings were its priors. The monks left in 1957 and it is now a hotel-restaurant.

Boats in the colourful, palm-fringed harbour at Sanary-sur-Mer

Bandol ⓸

Road map C4. 🏛 *7,500.* ▣ ▣
ℹ *Service du Tourisme, allée Vivien
(04 94 29 41 35).* ▣ *daily.*

This cheerful resort has a
tree-lined promenade, casino,
large yachting harbour and
tuna-fishing boats for hire.
Tucked away in a
bay, the shelter
offered by the en-
circling hills makes
for excellent grape-
growing conditions.
Indeed, Bandol has
produced superb
wines since 600 BC.
Outside town, the
**Jardin Exotique et
Zoo de Sanary-Ban-
dol** contains wildlife and
greenhouses of tropical plants.

**✗ Jardin Exotique et Zoo de
Sanary-Bandol**
Quartier Pont-d'Aran. **Tel** 04 94 29 40
38. ▢ Mon–Sat, Sun pm. ▨ ▣ ▣

Sanary-sur-Mer ⓹

Road map C4. 🏛 *18,000.*
▣ *Ollioules-Sanary.* ▣ ℹ *Maison
du Tourisme, Jardins-de-la-Ville (04 94
74 01 04).* ▣ *Wed.*
www.sanarysurmer.com

In the agreeable, clear blue
waters of Sanary-sur-Mer, the
diver Jacques Cousteau's

experiments to develop the
modern aqualung took place.
Diving and fishing (mainly for
tuna and swordfish) are still
popular pursuits in this delightful resort, where rows of pink
and white houses line the bay.
Its name derives loosely from
St-Nazaire; the lovely local
19th-century church took the
saint's name in its
entirety. Dating
from about 1300,
the landmark
medieval tower in
the town still con-
tains the cannon
that saw off an
Anglo-Sardinian
fleet in 1707. It is
now part of a hotel.
Sanary-sur-Mer
has enticed visitors for many
years. Once the home of the
British writer Aldous Huxley
(1894– 1963), it was a haven
between the wars for innum-
erable other authors. Bertolt
Brecht (1898–1956) and Thomas Mann (1875–1955) both
fled here from Nazi Germany.
To the east of Sanary, the
coast becomes dramatic and
rocky. By the peninsula's extremity at the Cap Sicié is the
Notre-Dame-du-Mai chapel,
which was built in the 17th
century. A pilgrimage destination full of votive offerings, its
stepped approach offers a
wonderful panorama over the
coast and surrounding hills.

Bandol wine label

Toulon ⓺

Road map D4. 🏛 *172,000.*
✈ ▣ ▣ ℹ *pl Raimu (04 94
18 53 00).* ▣ *Tue–Sun.*
www.toulontourisme.com

Tucked into a fine natural
harbour, Toulon is home to
France's Mediterranean fleet.
In the old town, or along the
quays of the Darse Vieille, the
matelots and the bars reinforce
the maritime connection.
In Roman times, Toulon was
renowned for its sea snails
(*murex*) which, when boiled,
produced an imperial-quality
purple dye. During the reign
of Louis XIV, Pierre Puget
(1620–94) was in charge of
the port's decoration. Two of
his best-known works now

**Ornate Baroque entrance to the
Musée de la Marine**

support the town-hall balcony. These are *Strength* and *Tiredness*, his 1657 carved marble figures of Atlantes.

The port was extensively damaged in World War II by the Allies and Nazis. Today, much of the town is under restoration. Toulon has a large opera house and several interesting museums, including the **Musée des Arts Asiatiques** located in the Villa Jules Verne, which has been entirely redesigned to house it.

🏛 Musée de la Marine

Place Monsenergue. **Tel** 04 94 02 02 01. ☐ Apr–Sep: daily; Oct–Mar: Wed–Mon. ● 15 Dec–Jan. ⌨ 🔂 📷

The museum's grand entrance is decorated with imposing statues of Mars and Bellona. It was once the gateway to the 17th-century city arsenal. This stretched for more than 240 ha (595 acres) behind it.

Inside, the museum boasts two vast model galleons, *La Sultane* (1765) and *Duquesne* (1790), used for training. Some figureheads and ships' prows are on show, as are two wooden figures that were carved by Pierre Puget, and various 18th-century naval instruments.

🏛 Hôtel des Arts

113 bd du Maréchal Leclerc. **Tel** 04 94 36 81 01. ☐ daily pm only. ● public hols. 🔂 limited.

A permanent collection of traditional and contemporary Provençal paintings makes up the core of this small but illuminating museum. Works by international artists are often included in the first-floor temporary exhibitions.

🏛 Musée du Vieux Toulon

69 cours Lafayette. **Tel** 04 94 62 11 07. ☐ Mon–Sat pms. ● Sun, public hols. This quaint museum features the young Napoleon and his

endeavours in the defence of Toulon, as well as old weapons and a number of historical sketches by Puget.

�︎ Cathédrale Ste-Marie-de-la-Sedo

Place de la Cathédrale. ☐ daily. Lying directly inland from the town hall in the Darse Vieille is the city's 11th-century cathedral. It was treated to a Classical face-lift and extended during the 17th century.

Inside, there are works by Puget and Jean Baptiste Van Loo (1684–1745) as well as a spectacular Baroque altar.

Place Victor Hugo and the opera house in Toulon

0 metres   250
0 yards   250

Key to Symbols *see back flap*

Iles d'Hyères ⓱

The Iles d'Hyères are three unspoilt islands,
found 10 km (6 miles) off the Var coast –
Porquerolles, Le Levant and Port-Cros. Their
history has been chequered due to their
important strategic position: occupiers have
included Greeks, Romans and Saracens, as
well as ruthless pirates. Today the French
Navy uses much of Le Levant. Porquerolles,
the largest island, is partly cultivated with

Bottle of the rare Côte des Iles wine vineyards, but also has expanses of pine
forest and *maquis*. Port-Cros has been a
national park since 1963, protected for its
woodlands (including holm oak, strawberry tree
and myrtle), rare birds and rich underwater habitats.

LOCATOR MAP

PORT-CROS MARINE LIFE

The wooded slopes of the island shelve
down into unpolluted sea, where
colourful fish swim among beds
of Neptune grass. A ready-
planned swimming route
makes exploration easy.

Fort du Moulin, over-
looking Port-Cros harbour

Sponge alga
Codium bursa

Mermaid's cup
*Acetabularia
mediterranea*

Bath sponge
Spongia officinalis

Neptune grass
Posidonia oceanica

Sea urchins, *Paracentrotus lividus*

Peacock's tail
Padina pavonia

Sea peacock
*Thalassoma
pavo*

Black goby
Gobius niger

Saupe
Sarpa salpa

Moray eel
*Muraena
helena*

Port-Cros Harbour
The tiny, palm-fringed harbour and village of Port-Cros nestle in a sheltered bay to the northwest of the island.

VISITORS' CHECKLIST

Road map D5. 🚂 Toulon-Hyères. 🚌 Hyères. 🚍 Hyères. 🚢 from Hyères (Tour Fondu) to Porquerolles daily (every 30 mins in summer); from Hyères and Le Lavandou to Port-Cros and Le Levant daily (Nov–Mar: 3–4 times a week). 🚢 Porquerolles (04 94 58 33 76).

Scuba diving off the coast of Port-Cros

Black-faced blenny
Trypterygion tripteronotus

Cardinal fish
Apogon imberbis

Diplodus
Diplodus sargus

Grey mullet
Chelon labrosus

Octopus
Octopus vulgaris

Damsel fish, *Chromis chromis*

Hyères ⑱

Road map D4. 🏛 53,000. 🚂 Toulon-Hyères. 🚌 🚍 🚢 ℹ av A Thomas (04 94 01 84 50). 🛒 Tue, Thu, Sat. **www**.ville-hyeres.fr

Hyères is one of the most agreeable towns on the Côte d'Azur, and the oldest of the south of France winter resorts. The town lies at the centre of well-cultivated land that provides fresh fruit and vegetables all year. It has three leisure ports, 35 km (22 miles) of sandy beach and a penin-sula facing the Iles d'Hyères.

The new town was called Hyères-les-Palmiers. A palm-growing industry was estab-lished here in 1867, soon becoming the largest in Europe. The industry is still important and hundreds of palms line the new town boulevards.

Hyères' main church is **St-Louis** in place de la Répub-lique just outside the old town. Romanesque and Provençal Gothic, it was completed in 1248. From place Massillon, rue St-Paul leads past the 11th-century **Eglise St-Paul**, full of 17th-century ex-votos. The road continues to the ruined 12th-century Château St-Bernard which has good views. In the gardens is the Cubist-inspired **Villa de Noailles** (1924), built by Robert Mallet-Stevens for the Vicomte de Noailles (tours during exhi-bitions only). The **Jardins Olbius Riquier** has a zoo and exotic plants.

🌿 Jardins Olbius Riquier
Av Ambroise Thomas. ⭕ daily. &

Moorish architecture inspired by the many palms in Hyères

Beach at Le Lavandou overlooked by hotels and exclusive villas

Le Lavandou ⑲

Road map D4. 🏠 5,500. 🚗 🚢
🛈 quai Gabriel Péri (04 94 00 40 50).
🛒 Thu. **www**.lelavandou.com

An embarkation port for the nearby Iles d'Hyères, Le Lavandou is a fishing village now almost entirely given over to tourism. This is due to its twelve sandy beaches,

each of a different colour sand. It is a centre for water sports and offers moorings for luxury yachts. Full of bars, nightclubs and restaurants, Le Lavandou is a favourite of younger, less well-heeled visitors.

It takes its name not from the lavender fields in the surrounding hills, but from a *lavoir* (wash-house) depicted in a painting of the town by Charles Ginoux dating from 1736. During the last century, when it was no more than a fishing village, Le Lavandou was popular with artists. The most famous, though not so well known outside France, was Ernest Reyer (1823–99), a composer and music critic after whom the main square is named. From this square there is a view over the Iles du Levant and Port-Cros.

Much of nearby Brégançon is in the hands of the military and the French president has a summer residence there.

Bormes-les-Mimosas ⑳

Road map D4. 🏠 5,100. 🚗
🛈 1 place Gambetta (04 94 01 38 38).
🛒 Tue & Wed.
www.bormeslesmimosas.com

Bormes is a medieval hill village on the edge of the Dom Forest, bathed in the scent of oleander and euca-

Rue Rompi-Cuou, one of the steep, old streets in Bormes-les-Mimosas

---

Tour of the Massif des Maures ㉑

The ancient mountain range of Maures takes its name from the Provençal *maouro*, meaning dark or gloomy, for the Massif is carpeted in sweet chestnuts, cork trees, oaks and pines with a deeply shaded undergrowth of myrrh and briar, though forest fires have reduced some of it to scrubland. Lying between Hyères and Fréjus, the Massif is nearly 60 km (40 miles) long and 30 km (18 miles) wide. This tour is a simple route that takes you through the wild and often deserted heart of the Massif, through dramatic countryside ranging from flat valley floors covered in cork trees to deep valleys and lofty peaks. A few of the roads are steep and winding.

Village des Tortues ③
Keep bearing left on the D75 for the "Tortoise Village", which has saved France's only remaining species of wild tortoise.

Gonfaron

Notre-Dame-des-Anges ④
Beside this priory and its chapel full of votive offerings, is the highest summit in the Massif at 780 m (2,559 ft).

← *TOULON*

Collobrières ⑤
This riverside village with its hump-backed bridge is famed for its *marrons glacés*. Nearby forests supply bottle corks.

TIPS FOR DRIVERS

Tour length: 75 km (47 miles).
Stopping-off points: Collobrières is a pleasant lunchtime stop. Allow time to visit Chartreuse de la Verne (04 94 48 08 00 for opening times), which is reached up narrow, steep roads. (See also pp250–1.)

Farm workers at Collobrières

lyptus and topped with a flower-lined walk around its castle. "Les Mimosas" was not added to its name until 1968, a century after the plant was first introduced to the south of France from Mexico. A pretty and popular village, Bormes serves a marina of more than 800 berths. Plummeting streets such as Rompi-Cuou lead to lively cafés and coastal views.

A statue of St Francis di Paola stands in front of the attractive 16th-century **Chapelle St-François**, commemorating the saint's timely arrival during a plague outbreak in 1481. The 18th-century church of **St-Trophyme** has newly restored 18th-century frescoes. The works of local painter Jean-Charles Cazin (1841–1901) are well represented in the **Musée d'Arts et Histoire**.

🏛 **Musée d'Arts et Histoire**
103 rue Carnot. **Tel** 04 94 71 56 60.
🔾 Tue–Sun (public hols & Sun: am only). 🔾 restricted.

Ramatuelle village enclosed by wooded slopes and vineyards

Ramatuelle ㉒

Road map E4. 🚶 2,000. 🚌 🚹 pl de l' Ormeau (04 98 12 64 00). 🔾 Thu & Sun.

Surrounded by vineyards, this attractive hilltop village was called "God's Gift" (Rahmatu 'llah) by the Saracens who left a gate, now well-restored, in its fortifications, as well as a penchant for figs. It is one of three particularly quaint villages on the St-Tropez peninsula (Grimaud and Gassin are the others). Gérard Philipe (1922–59), the leading young French actor during the 1950s, is buried here. Vibrant theatre and jazz festivals take place in the village annually.

Nearby, Les Moulins de Paillas (322 m, 940 ft), offers a fine panorama, as does Cap Camarat, with its lighthouse, at the tip of the peninsula, 5 km (3 miles) east of Ramatuelle.

La Garde-Freinet ②
This is famous for bottle corks and sweet chestnut confections. Half an hour's walk south of the village are ruins of a Saracen castle with impressive views.

View between Cogolin and Collobrières

Grimaud ①
This hill village offers stunning views south over the coast and west over the Massif des Maures from place du Château. It is also a thriving centre for local crafts (see p123).

ST TROPEZ →

0 kilometres 2
0 miles 2

KEY
▬▬▬ Tour route
═══ Other roads

Chartreuse de la Verne ⑥
Inhabited since the 12th century, this restored hilltop charterhouse is surrounded by chestnut woods.

Cogolin ⑦
Visitors can see the rugs for which the town is known being handmade at Manufacture des Tapis in Cogolin (see p221).

Street-by-Street: St-Tropez ㉓

St Torpès in his boat

Clustered around the old port and nearby beaches, the centre of St-Tropez, partly rebuilt in its original style after World War II *(see p52)*, is full of fishermen's houses. In the port itself, traditional fishing boats are still to be seen moored side-by-side with sleek luxury cruisers of all shapes and sizes. Behind the port-side cafés of the quai Jean-Jaurès, the narrow, bustling streets are packed with boutiques and restaurants. The town is overlooked by the church's wrought-iron belltower in the centre and the citadel just outside.

La Fontanette beach leads to a coastal walk with views over Ste-Maxime.

The Ponche quarter is a comparatively quiet and unspoiled area of St-Tropez.

Tour Vieille

The Port de Pêche
The Tour Vieille separates this port from La Glaye next door.

Place de la Ponche

LA GLAYE

RUE DE LA PONCHE

Tour du Portalet

PLACE DE L'HOTEL DE VILLE

RUE SI

QUAI FREDERIC MISTRAL

RUE DU CEP

St-Tropez Old Town
Fashionable motorcyclists pose along the narrow streets of central St-Tropez.

QUAI

Môle Jean Réveille

★ **Quai Jean-Jaurès**
The attractively painted houses and packed cafés lining the quay have enticed visitors and inspired artists for over a century.

View from the Ramparts of the Citadel
The hilltop citadel, situated east of St-Tropez, offers spectacular views over the rooftops of the town and beyond.

VISITORS' CHECKLIST

Road map E4. 🚍 5,750.
🚌 *Gare Routière (04 94 97 88 51).* 🛈 *quai Jean-Jaurès (04 94 97 45 21).* 🛒 *Tue & Sat.*
🎭 *Bravades: 16–18 May, 15 Jun.*
www.saint-tropez.st

RUE FONTANETTE

RUE DES PECHEURS

EMPARTS

To the citadel

★ Eglise Notre-Dame de l'Assumption
Its bust of St Torpès features in the bravade (see p228).

RUE D'ANNALE

RUE DE LA CITADELLE

RUE DU CLOCHER

MARTIN

RUE VICTOR LAUGIER

To place des Lices

Open Window on the Harbour at St-Tropez *(1925–6)*
Charles Camoin's painting is now in the Annonciade.

KEY

- - - Suggested route

| 0 metres | 50 |
| 0 yards | 50 |

QUAI SUFFREN

Statue of Pierre André de Suffren

To Musée de l'Annonciade *(see pp120–21)*

STAR SIGHTS

★ Quai Jean-Jaurès

★ Eglise Notre-Dame

Musée de l'Annonciade

This innovative gallery opened in 1955 in the former Chapelle de l'Annonciade by the old port in St-Tropez. Built in 1568, the building was converted into a museum by architect Louis Süe (1875–1968), funded by art collector Georges Grammont. The collection began with the paintings of Paul Signac and the other artists who followed him to St-Tropez, and now contains many stunning Post-Impressionist works from the late 19th and early 20th centuries. In 1961, 65 valuable works were stolen from the museum, but were recovered and restored a year later.

Le Rameur *(1914)*
This bold Cubist work is by Roger de la Fresnaye.

★ St-Tropez, la Place des Lices et le Café des Arts
This painting (1925) is one of several that Charles Camoin made of St-Tropez's famous square after he followed Paul Signac and settled in the town.

Temporary exhibition room

★ L'Orage *(1895)*
Paul Signac's atmospheric work vividly depicts the onset of a storm in St-Tropez harbour.

GALLERY GUIDE

Exhibition space is too limited for all works to be permanently on view, so the display changes frequently. An exhibition room holds temporary displays linked with the permanent collection.

KEY TO FLOORPLAN

☐	Ground floor
☐	Mezzanine
☐	First floor
☐	Non-exhibition space

★ Nu Devant la Cheminée *(1919)*
In this warm, intimate picture, characteristic of the artist, Pierre Bonnard uses delicate tones within a limited colour range to create an effect of light and shade.

Le Temps d'Harmonie
*In this study (1893–5)
for a larger work, Paul
Signac departs from his
more usual Pointillist
technique, using simple,
fluid lines.*

Balcony

VISITORS' CHECKLIST

Place Grammont, St-Tropez.
Tel 04 94 97 04 01. ☐ Jun–Oct:
10am–1pm, 4–10pm daily;
Dec–May:10am–noon, 2–6pm
Wed–Mon. ☐ 1 Jan, Ascension,
1 May, Nov, 25 Dec. ☒ ☐ ☐
☐ ground floor only.

La Nymphe *(1930)
This Classically
influenced bronze
sculpture, one of several
excellent works by
Aristide Maillol in
the Annonciade, is a
graceful evocation of
ideal beauty.*

Deauville, le Champ de Courses
*Raoul Dufy's racecourse, painted in
1928, is typical of his interest in
glamorous subjects.*

18th-century main
entrance

STAR PAINTINGS

- ★ St-Tropez, la Place des
  Lices et le Café des
  Arts by Charles
  Camoin

- ★ L'Orage by Paul
  Signac

- ★ Nu Devant la
  Cheminée by Pierre
  Bonnard

Exploring St-Tropez

This exceptional resort has become a victim of its own charms – the August high season attracts about 80,000 hell-bent hedonists. Following their departure, however, the genuine, peaceful nature of the village still shines through. Surrounded by slopes covered with vineyards, looking out over the millpond bay of Golfe St-Tropez and protected by an imposing citadel, its situation remains inviolate. It does, however, face the northerly Mistral which thunders through the town for much of the winter, ensuring it remains a summer haunt.

Eglise Notre-Dame de l'Assomption

Paintings by local artists for sale on the quai Jean-Jaurès

A glimpse of the town

Activity is centred north of the Musée de l'Annonciade, beside the little port. Here, local artists sell their wares and people pass the time of day in the Café de Paris, le Gorille or Senequier (see p219).

The pretty, pastel-painted houses lining the quai Jean-Jaurès can be viewed at their best from the harbour breakwater, the Môle Jean Réveille. These buildings were among the town's sights that inspired Paul Signac (1863–1935) to start painting in St-Tropez. Many other artists followed, all well represented in the Annonciade (see pp120–21).

The old town, just behind the waterfront, is flagged by the tower of the Eglise Notre-Dame de l'Assomption. To its north lies the Hôtel de Ville and the Tour Suffren, home of the former local lords. Admiral Pierre André de Suffren (1726–88), "terror of the English", is commemorated by a statue on the quay. Behind the quai Suffren is the place des Lices, a large square crowded with cafés.

Out to the east, beyond the old Ponche quarter and the unspoiled fishing port nearby, lies the 16th-century hexagonal citadel. With fine views from the ramparts, it contains the Musée Naval de St-Tropez. Further east, is La Madrague where Brigitte Bardot used to live. *And God Created Woman*, the 1959 film shot in St-Tropez starring Bardot, started the celebrity rush to the town.

🏛 Musée de l'Annonciade
See pp120–21.

⛪ Eglise Notre-Dame de l'Assomption
Rue de l'Eglise. ☐ *daily.*
This 19th-century Baroque church contains several busts of saints, including one of St Torpès after whom St-Tropez is named. Beheaded for his Christianity, his body was put in a boat with a dog and a cockerel and the boat landed here in AD 68. Every year, his bust is carried through the town in the 16 May *bravade.*

The hilltop citadel east of St-Tropez

🏛 Musée de la Citadelle
Forteresse. **Tel** 04 94 97 59 43.
☐ *daily.* ● *1 Jan, 1 May, Ascension, 17 May, 25 Dec.* 🗓 ♿ *restricted.*
Located in the dungeon of the citadel keep, to the east of the town, the Musée de la Citadelle houses temporary exhibitions on the history of St-Tropez and the navy.

🏛 Maison des Papillons
9 rue Etienne Berny. **Tel** 04 94 97 14 96. ☐ *Wed–Mon.* ● *public hols, Jan–Apr & Nov.* 🗓
Hidden in a narrow medieval lane, is this amazingly complete collection of butterflies found in France, and rare specimens from the Amazon.

Fishing boats and luxury cruisers docked at quai Jean-Jaurès

Port-Grimaud ㉔

Road map E4. 🏘 150. 🚐
ℹ️ *chemin communal (04 94 56 02 01 in summer)* or *1 bd des Aliziers, 83310 Grimaud (04 94 55 43 83).* 🛒 *Thu & Sun.*

This newly created port was dreamed up entirely by the Alsace architect François Spoerry (1912–98). In 1962 he bought up the marshy delta lands of the River Giscle west of the Golfe St-Tropez. Four years later, work began on a mini-Venice of 2,500 canalside houses with moorings covering 90 ha (222 acres). There are now three "zones", a marina and a beach. Its church, **St-François-d'Assise**, in the place d'Eglise, contains some stained glass by Victor Vasarély (1908–97) and offers a sweeping view of the port from the top of its tower.

The whole port is free of traffic and the *coche d'eau* offers a water-taxi service. As one of France's major tourist attractions, Port-Grimaud brings in about one million visitors a year.

View of Port-Grimaud from the Eglise de St-François-d'Assise

Grimaud ㉕

Road map E4. 🏘 3,300. 🚐 ℹ️ *1 bd des Aliziers (04 94 55 43 83).* 🛒 *Thu.*

The ancient, fortified, traffic-free *village perché (see pp20–21)* of Grimaud is yet another legacy of the ubiquitous Grimaldi family *(see p91)*, after which the village is named. Gibelin de Grimaldi, a doughty Genoese knight, was rewarded with a fief here after

helping William the Good of Provence drive the Saracens out of this part of France in AD 973, after 83 years of occupation. The castle dates from the 11th century and was reduced to ruins under the direction of Cardinal Richelieu as punishment for the town's Protestant leanings.

The view of the coast from its heights made it an ideal vantage point from which to watch for further invasion. This task was adopted in 1119 by the Knights Templar. These were a clandestine military and religious order of knights founded during the First Crusade to defend Christians.

Once called Rue Droite, the Rue des Templiers is the town's oldest street, lined with arcades designed to be battened down in case of attack. Legend has it that the Knights Templar stayed in Grimaud, but this fact has not been historically attested. In the same street is the pure Romanesque 12th-century church of St-Michel.

Ste-Maxime ㉖

Road map E4. 🏘 12,000. 🚐 *St-Raphaël, St Tropez.* ℹ️ *promenade Simon-Lorière (04 94 55 75 55).* 🛒 *Fri.*

Beach at Ste-Maxime

Facing St-Tropez across the neck of the Gulf, Ste-Maxime is protected by hills. Its year-round clientele reaches saturation point in summer. The attractions of this smart resort are its port, promenade, good sandy beaches, watersports, nightlife, fairs and casino.

Ste-Maxime was once protected by the monks of Lérins, who named the port after their patron saint and put up the defensive Tour Carrée des Dames which now serves as the **Musée des Traditions Locales**. The church opposite contains a 17th-century green marble altar that was brought from the former Carthusian monastery of La Verne in the Massif des Maures.

🏛 **Musée des Traditions Locales**
Place des Aliziers. **Tel** 04 94 96 70 30. 🕐 *Wed–Mon.* ● *Mon am, 1 Jan, 1 May, 25 Dec, 1 mth in winter.* 📷

Grimaud, dominated by the castle ruins

St-Raphaël ㉗

Road map E4. 🏔 *35,000.* 🚌 🚉
🛈 *rue Waldeck Rousseau (04 94 19
52 52).* 🛒 *daily.*
www.saint-raphael.com

This staid and sensible family
resort dates to Roman times
when rich families came to
stay at a spot near the modern
seafront casino. Napoleon put
the town on the map when he
landed here in 1799 on his
return from Egypt, and 15
years later when he left St-
Raphaël for exile on Elba.

Popularity came when the
Parisian satirical novelist Jean-
Baptiste Karr (1808–90) pub-
licized the town's delights. In
the old part is the 12th-century
church of St-Raphaël and the
Musée Archéologique, which
contains Greek amphorae and
other underwater finds.

🏛 **Musée Archéologique**
Place de la Vieille Eglise. **Tel** *04 94 19
25 75.* 🚪 *Tue–Sat.* 🌑 *public hols.* 📷

**Tourist poster of St-Raphaël from
the 19th century**

Massif de l'Esterel ㉘

Road map E4. ✈ *Nice.* 🚌 🚉 *Agay,
St-Raphaël.* 🛈 *rue Waldeck Rousseau,
St-Raphaël (04 94 19 52 52).*

The Esterel, a mountainous
volcanic mass, is a wilderness
compared to the popular
coast. Although it rises to no
more than 620 m (2,050 ft),
and a succession of fires have
laid waste its forests, its innate
ruggedness and the dramatic
colours of its porphyry rocks
remain intact. Until the middle of the last century it was a

Château de la Napoule, now an art centre

refuge for highwaymen and
escaped prisoners from Toulon.
Here, after being fêted on
arrival in St Raphaël, Napoleon
and his coach were robbed of
all their valuables while they
were on their way out of town
heading towards Paris.

The north side of the massif
is bounded by the N7 which
runs through the Esterel Gap,
following the Roman Aurelian
way from Cannes to Fréjus. At
the Testannier crossroads 11
km (7 miles) from Fréjus a
road leads to Mont Vinaigre;
the final 15 minutes of the
journey must be made on
foot. This is the highest point
on the massif and there is a
fine panorama from the Alps
to the Massif des Maures.

On the seaward side of the
massif the N98 from St-Raphaël
twists along the top of start-
lingly red cliffs to Agay. This
resort has the best anchorage
on the coast. It is famous for
its red porphyry, from which
the Romans cut columns for
their Provençal monuments.

Round the bay is Pointe de
Baumette where there is a
memorial to French writer and
World War II aviator, Antoine
de St-Exupéry *(see p29).* The
road continues to Anthéor and
the Pointe de l'Observatoire.
Just before here, a left turn
leads to the circuit of the Cap
Roux and Pic de l'Ours.

The coast road continues
through a series of resorts to
La Napoule at the start of the
Riviera. In La Napoule is a
14th-century château refurbished by American sculptor
Henry Clews (1876–1937),
who left work scattered about
the estate. The château is now

an art centre, the **Fondation
Henry Clews**.

The route leading inland to
the Col Belle-Barbe from the
coast passes on the right a
turn to the 452-m (1483-ft) Pic
du Cap Roux. An hour's walk
to the top is rewarded by a
sweeping coast view.

From the car park at Col
Belle-Barbe, a path leads to
the Mal Infernet, a dramatic
ravine that concludes a 40-
minute walk away at the Lac
de l'Ecureuil. Continuing
inland from Col Belle-Barbe
over the Col du Mistral up to
the Col des Trois Termes, the
path then twists south to Col
Notre-Dame. A 45-minute
walk leads on to the dramatic
Pic de l'Ours, rising to 496 m
(1,627 ft). Between here and
the coast is the 323-m (1,060-
ft) Pic d'Aurelle, which also
provides an impressive vista.

🏛 **Fondation Henry Clews**
1 av Henry Clews, Napoule. **Tel** *04
93 49 95 05.* 🚪 *daily.* 📷 📷

**Remaining timber on the fire-
ravaged Massif de l'Esterel**

Fréjus ㉙

Road map E4. 🏔 *52,000.* 🚉 *St Raphaël.* 🚌 ℹ️ *325 rue Jean-Jaurès (04 94 51 83 83).* 🏪 *Wed & Sat.* **www**.ville-frejus.fr

Visibly, though not ostentatiously, wealthy in history, Fréjus is one of the highlights of the coast. The oldest Roman city in Gaul, it was founded by Julius Caesar in 49 BC and greatly expanded by Augustus. Lying on the Aurelian way – a huge road built in the reign of Augustus from Rome to Arles – it covered 40 ha (100 acres), had a population of 30–40,000 and, as a port, was second in importance only to Marseille.

Although substantial sections of the Roman city were decimated by the Saracens in the 10th century, a few parts of their walls remain, including a tower of the western Porte des Gaules. The opposite eastern entrance, the Porte de Rome, marks one end of a 40-km (25-mile) aqueduct, the ruins of which amble alongside the

Mosaic in the Musée Archéologique in Fréjus

N7 towards the Siagnole river near Mons. Just to the north of here the remains of the semi-circular, 1st-century Théâtre can be viewed. In their midst, performances are still held. The praetorium or Plateforme – military headquarters that formed the eastern citadel – lie to the south. North of the Porte des Gaules, on the road to Brignoles, stands the large 1st–2nd-century **Arènes**, built to hold 6,000 spectators, now used for bullfights and music.

The spectacular **Cathédrale St-Léonce et Cloître** houses a Musée Archéologique with finds from all around Fréjus.

The Chapelle Notre-Dame, decorated by Cocteau, and Musée d'Histoire Locale are also well worth a visit.

South of the town is the Butte St-Antoine citadel, which at one time overlooked the harbour. The canal connecting the harbour to the sea began silting up in the 10th century; by the 18th century it was entirely filled in,

Well in the centre of the Cathedral cloisters at Fréjus

forming Fréjus-Plage. A little over 2 km (1 mile) from the town's centre, this modern resort stretches along a sandy beach towards St-Raphaël. North of the Arènes is a Buddhist Pagoda commemorating Vietnamese soldiers who died serving in the French army.

🏛 **Arènes de Fréjus**
Rue Vadon. **Tel** *04 94 51 34 31.* ⏰ *Wed–Mon.* ⬛ *1 Jan, 1 May, 25 Dec.*

⛪ **Cathédrale St-Léonce**
Place Formigé. **Tel** *04 94 51 26 30.* ⏰ *Apr–Aug: daily; Sep–Mar: Tue–Sun.* ⬛ *public hols.* 🅿️ *cloisters.* ♿

CATHÉDRALE ST-LÉONCE ET CLOÎTRE

The fortified cathedral and the marble-columned cloister date from the 12th century, while the 5th-century baptistry is one of the oldest in France.

Musée Archéologique

The choir stalls, in two rows, date from the 15th century and are ornately carved.

High altar

Renaissance doorway

The Baptistry's eight Corinthian columns are from a former pagan Roman temple.

The Cloisters originally had 2 storeys, but today only one of the upper galleries remains. Paintings cover the ceilings.

The octagonal font was originally used only to baptize adults.

Earthenware basin

BOUCHES-DU-RHÔNE
AND NÎMES

This southwestern corner of Provence has a feel that's unique in the region. It is the land of Van Gogh, brightly patterned materials and beaches of shifting sands. Its wildest point is the Camargue in the Rhône delta, a place of light and colour, lived in for centuries by gypsies and by cowboys who herd the wild horses and bulls.

Many inland towns reflect the region's Greek and Roman past. The Greeks first settled in France in circa 600 BC and founded Marseille, now a cosmopolitan cultural centre and the country's second largest city. The Romans, who arrived after them, built the theatre at Arles and the amphitheatre at Nîmes, and left the remains of Classical houses at Glanum. The skeleton of a Roman aqueduct runs beween a spring at Uzès to a water tower at Nîmes, a great feat of engineering best seen at Pont du Gard.

"A race of eagles" is how Frédéric Mistral, the Provençal writer *(see p28)* described the Lords of Baux, bloodthirsty warriors who ruled in the Middle Ages from an extraordinary eyrie in Les Baux-de-Provence. This former fief was paradoxically famous as a Court of Love *(see p142)* during the 13th century. Louis IX (Saint Louis) built the fortified city of Aigues-Mortes for the Crusaders. In the 15th century, Good King René *(see pp46–7)*, held his court in the castle of Tarascon and in Aix-en-Provence, the ancient capital of Provence. Aix's university, founded by René's father in 1409, is still the hub of this lively student town.

The area provides great walks and stunning scenery, particularly in the Alpilles and around Marseille. The films and books of Marcel Pagnol *(see 153)* and the stories of Daudet *(see p143)*, which have influenced perceptions of Provençal people and life, are set in this region. The Camargue maintains a unique collection of flora and fauna, providing, in addition to fine vistas, superb horse riding and birdwatching.

Produce on display in the colourful food market, Aix-en-Provence

◁ Joseph Sec's statue of Saul in Aix-en-Provence, made in 1792 in honour of the French Revolution

Exploring Bouches-du-Rhône and Nîmes

At the mouth of the Rhône lie the flat, wetland marshes and sand dunes of the Camargue wildlife reserve. Further inland, cities such as Aix-en-Provence, Arles and Nîmes are awash with ancient architecture. Northeast of Arles, the herb-covered chain of the Alpilles rises from the surrounding plains to the heady heights of Les Baux, and there are some stunning walks through the mountains. St-Rémy-de-Provence makes a good base for exploring the Alpilles. Popular coastal towns are Marseille and the scenic port of Cassis. A short car or boat trip away lie Les Calanques, deep, narrow inlets set between pine trees and white cliffs.

Atlantes grace the doorway of the Pavillon de Vendôme in Aix

SIGHTS AT A GLANCE

iew across the harbour of Fort St-Jean, Marseille

GETTING AROUND

If you have a car, the auto-routes are fast and bypass slow traffic in the towns. The A8 autoroute which leads along the Riviera meets the Paris–Marseille A7 Autoroute du Soleil 17 km (11 miles) west of Aix, while the A9 Languedocienne heads west through Nîmes towards Spain.

The main towns are all linked by trains and buses, though bus services tend to be poor outside towns. Arles and Aix-en-Provence make particularly good bases for getting around. Boat trips are organized from Arles and Stes-Maries-de-la-Mer in the Camargue, where a good way to see the countryside is to hire the native horses.

KEY

— Motorway

— Major road

— Secondary road

— Minor road

— Scenic route

— Main railway

— Minor railway

— Regional border

Part of the Chartreuse du Val-de-Bénédiction, Villeneuve

Villeneuve-lès-Avignon ❶

Road map B3. 🚶 *12,500.* 🚉
Avignon. 🚌 🛈 *1 pl Charles David*
(04 90 25 61 33). 🛒 *Thu & Sat.*
www.villeneuvelesavignon.fr

This town arose beside the
Rhône, opposite Avignon *(see
pp166–7),* and the connecting
bridge, Pont St-Bénézet, was
guarded by the **Tour de
Philippe le Bel**, built in 1307.
Its rooftop terrace, 176 steps
up, gives a fine panorama of
the papal city. Even better is
the view from the two giant
40-m (130-ft) round towers at
the entrance to the impressive
14th-century **Fort St-André**,
which enclosed a small town,
monastery and church.

Between these two bastions
lies the 14th-century Eglise-
Collégiale Notre-Dame. In the
Musée Pierre de Luxem-bourg
is *The Coronation of the Virgin*
(1453) by Enguerrand
Quarton, regarded as the best

work of the Avignon School.
This work was painted for the
abbot of the **Chartreuse du
Val-de-Bénédiction**, which was
founded by Innocent VI in
1356. There are three cloisters
and a chapel dedicated to St
John the Baptist decorated with
frescoes by Giovanetti da
Viterbo. The building is now
used as a cultural centre.

♣ **Fort St-André**
Tel *04 90 25 45 35.* ◯ *Apr–Sep:*
daily; Oct–Mar: Tue–Sun. ● *1 Jan,*
1 May, 1–11 Nov, 25 Dec. 🎟

🏛 **Musée Municipal Pierre de
Luxembourg**
Rue de la République. **Tel** *04 90 27*
49 66. ◯ *mid-Jun–mid-Sep: daily;*
mid-Sep–mid-Jun: Tue–Sun. ● *Feb,*
1 Jan, 1 & 11 Nov, 25 Dec. 🎟 ♿

⛪ **Chartreuse du Val-de-
Bénédiction**
Rue de la République. **Tel** *04 90 15*
24 24. ◯ *daily.* ● *1 Jan, 1 May,*
1 & 11 Nov, 25 Dec. 🎟 ♿ 🛍

Barbentane ❷

Road map B3. 🚶 *3,600.*
🚉 *Avignon, Tarascon.*
🛈 *Le Cours (04 90 90 85 86).*

Members of Avignon's Papal
court liked to build summer
houses in Barbentane, on the
slopes beside the Rhône 10
km (6 miles) south of the city.
One such was the handsome
Renaissance Maison des
Chevaliers with an arcaded
gallery, opposite the 13th- to
15th-century Notre-Dame-de-
Grace. Only the 40-m (130-ft)
Tour Anglica remains of the
town's 14th-century castle.

Just outside the medieval
quarter is the **Château de**

Barbentane, a finely decorated Italianate mansion, built
in 1674 by the Barbentane
aristocracy who still own it.

In the town is the 12th- to
13th-century **Moulin de
Mogador**, which was used as
an oil and flour mill.

♣ **Château de Barbentane**
Barbentane. **Tel** *04 90 95 51 07.*
◯ *Easter–Jun, Oct: Thu–Tue; Jul–Sep:*
daily; Nov & Mar: Sun. ● *Dec–Feb.* 🎟

Provençal doll and doll's carriage,
Château de Barbentane

Abbaye de St-Michel de Frigolet ❸

Road map B3. **Tel** *04 90 95 70 07.*
◯ *4.15pm Sun. Phone to reserve for
groups.* ♿ 🛍

The abbey is situated south of
St-Michel de Frigolet, in the
unspoiled La Montagnette
countryside. A cloister and
small abbey church date from
the 12th century, but in 1858 a
Premonstratensian abbey was
founded and one of the most
richly decorated and, indeed,
flamboyant churches of that
period was built. The whole
interior is colourfully painted,
with stars and saints on the
pillars and ceiling. After a brief
period of exile in Belgium
early this century, the monks
returned to Frigolet, and there
are now 15 of them. There is
a restaurant, accommodation
in 40 rooms and the monks
sell their deceptively potent
traditional liqueur based on
local herbs here. *Frigolet* is
Provençal for thyme.

The ceiling of the abbey church of St-Michel de Frigolet

Pont du Gard ❹

Road map A3. 🚉 Nîmes.
🛈 Route du Pont du Gard, 30210
Vers (04 66 37 50 99).

Begun around 19 BC, this
bridge is part of an aqueduct
which transported water from
a spring near Uzès to Roman
Nîmes (see pp132–3). An
underground channel, bridges
and tunnels were engineered
to carry the 20 million litre
(4.4 million gallon) daily
water supply a distance of 50
km (31 miles). The three-
tiered structure of the Pont du
Gard spans the Gardon valley
and was the tallest aqueduct
in the Roman empire. Its

The Pont du Gard, the tallest of all Roman aqueducts at 48 m (158 ft)

Trademark graffiti left by 18th-century masons on the stones

huge limestone blocks, some
as heavy as 6 tonnes, were
erected without mortar. The
water channel, covered by
stone slabs, was in the top
tier of the three. Skilfully
designed cutwaters ensured
that the bridge has resisted
many violent floods.

It is not known for certain
how long the aqueduct
continued in use but it may
still have been functioning as
late as the 9th century AD.
The adjacent road bridge was
erected in the 18th century.
The **Site du Pont du Gard** has
a museum (open daily)
tracing the aqueduct's history.

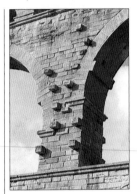

Protruding stones for supporting scaffolding during construction

THE REMAINS OF THE AQUEDUCT

Uzes

The source of water, at
Fontaine d'Eure, was only 17 m
(56 ft) higher above sea level
than the Castellum at Nîmes.

At Pont du Bornègre the aqueduct
emerged from an underground tunnel
to cross this triple-arched bridge. The
water was then channelled back into
a clearly-defined tunnel.

At Pont de la Lône an overhead
arcade carries the aqueduct for
400 m (1,320 ft). Leaks have left
large limestone incrustations in
the stonework.

Pont Roupt is a vast bridge,
over 255 m (840 ft) long, with
37 surviving arches.

D981

D3

GARRIGUES
DE PERRET

D19

Pont du Gard

The church at St Bonnet
contains some stones cut
from the aqueduct. Its
vaults imitate the arches
of the Pont du Gard.

0 kilometres   3

0 miles   3

GARRIGUES
DE REMOULINS

D986

At Sernhac two tunnels,
each about 60 m (197ft)
long, are accessible
to visitors.

PONT DU GARD   48m

275m

TO NÎMES   A9

Nîmes

Publicity poster for a Nîmes festival

A magnificent carved black bull at the end of the avenue Jean-Jaurès highlights Nîmes' passion for bullfighting. Crowds fill Les Arènes, the Roman amphitheatre, for bullfights during the three annual *ferias (see pp32–33)*. Year round, the city's biggest draw is its fine Roman architecture, and it is a great city of the arts. The city's textile industry is famous for creating denim *(de Nîmes)*, the tough material used for blue jeans and worn by the Camargue cowboys. Most shops stock Provençal fabrics *(see p221)*.

Exploring Nîmes

Roman veterans from Emperor Augustus's 31 BC Egyptian campaign introduced the city's coat of arms: a crocodile chained to a palm tree. Today, the logo is splashed on everything from bollards to road signs.

Nîmes' generous boulevards give it a wide-open feel. A renaissance of modern building, art and design, including the fine Carré d'Art, lends a touch of class. Some of the new monuments, such as the Fontaine du Crocodile in place du Marché, are becoming as well known as Nîmes' most familiar landmark, the Castellum.

The city's coat of arms: a crocodile and palm tree

Les Arènes

Bd des Arènes. **Tel** 04 66 76 72 95. ◯ daily. ● 1 Jan, 1 May, 25 Dec & on performance days. restricted
Of all the city's Roman ruins, the most dramatic is the 1st-century amphitheatre. At 130 m (427 ft) by 100 m (328 ft) and with seating for 22,000, it is marginally smaller than Arles' amphitheatre *(see p146)*. It was built as a venue for gladiatorial combat, chariot racing and waterborne battles (it could be flooded).

After the collapse of Rome in 476, it became a fortress and knights' headquarters. Until its 19th-century restoration, it was used as home to 2,000 people in slum conditions. Today it is considered to be perhaps the best preserved of all Roman amphitheatres.

Porte d'Auguste

Bd Amiral Courbet.
With a central arch 6 m (20 ft) high and 4 m (13 ft) wide, this gate was built to take horsemen and carriages, since the main road from Rome to Spain, the Domitian Way, passed through the middle of Nîmes.

An ancient inscription tells visitors that the city walls were built in 15 BC and extended for nearly 6 km (4 miles).

The Roman amphitheatre, today used for bullfights at festival times

Maison Carrée

Pl de la Maison Carrée. **Tel** 04 66 36 26 76. ◯ daily. ● 1 Jan, 1 May, 25 Dec.
The Maison Carrée ("square house") is the Roman world's best-preserved temple. Built by Augustus's son-in-law Marcus Agrippa, it is Hellenic with Corinthian columns around the main hall. Louis XIV's chief minister, Colbert, wanted it taken brick by brick to Versailles.

Carré d'Art

Pl de la Maison Carrée. 04 66 76 35 80. ◯ Tue–Sun.
On the opposite side of the square from the Maison Carrée and in stunning contrast to it, is the Carré d'Art. This modern art complex, finished in 1993, was designed by Norman Foster.

Norman Foster's Carré d'Art

Musée du Vieux Nîmes

Pl aux Herbes. **Tel** 04 66 76 73 70. ◯ Tue–Sun. ● 1 Jan, 1 May, 1 Nov, 25 Dec.
The 17th-century Bishop's Palace just east of the cathedral houses this museum. The old-fashioned interior has been beautifully restored: the summer room has Directoire and Empire-style furnishings and Old Town views. In the wardrobe is a billiard table with inlaid work by the eldest Bernassau son from Nîmes.

Musée Archéologique et Musée d'Histoire Naturelle

13 bis bd Amiral Courbet. **Tel** 04 66 76 74 54. ◯ Tue–Sun. ● 1 Jan, 1 May, 1 & 11 Nov, 25 Dec.
The ground-floor gallery of this museum has a number of pre-Roman carvings, including busts of Gallic warriors, friezes and also contemporary objects. Upstairs, Gallo-Roman tools

and household utensils give a good idea of life at the time. There is also a range of glassware and bronze objects. The pottery collection includes the pre-Roman Warrior of Grézan. The atmospheric chapel in this one-time Jesuits' College is used for temporary displays.

🏛 Musée des Beaux-Arts
Rue Cité Foulc. **Tel** 04 66 67 38 21. ◻ Tue–Sun. ⬤ 1 Jan, 1 May, 1 & 11 Nov, 25 Dec. 🈺 ♿
A diverse collection in the Fine Art Museum includes paintings by Boucher, Rubens and Watteau. The ground floor displays a large Roman mosaic, *The Marriage of Admetus*, found in 1883 in Nîmes' former covered market .

🔓 Cathédrale Notre-Dame et St-Castor
Pl aux Herbes. **Tel** 04 66 67 27 72. ◻ daily during services.
Nîmes' cathedral, in the centre of the Old Town, dates from the 11th century but was extensively rebuilt in the 19th century. The west front has a partly Romanesque frieze with scenes from the Old Testament.

⛏ Castellum
Rue de la Lampèze.
Between the Porte d'Auguste and the Tour Magne, set in the Roman wall, is the Castellum, a tower used for storing the water brought in from Uzès via the aqueduct at Pont du Gard *(see p131)*. The water was distributed in the town by means of a canal duct system.

Archaeological museum statue

🌿 Jardin de la Fontaine
Quai de la Fontaine. **Tel** 04 66 67 65 56.
The city's main park lies at the end of the wide avenue Jean-Jaurès. It was named after an underground spring harnessed in the 18th century. The park's 2nd-century Temple of Diana, part of a complex of baths, is today in ruins. Benedictine nuns lived there during the Middle Ages and converted it into a church, which was sacked in the Wars of Religion *(see pp46–7)*.
At the summit of the 114-m (374-ft) Mont Cavalier stands the 34-m (112-ft) octagonal Tour Magne. Of all the towers originally set in Nîmes' Roman

wall, this is the most remarkable. Dating from 15 BC, it is the earliest surviving Roman building in France. There are 140 steps, worth climbing for a fine view of Mont Ventoux.

L'Obéissance Récompensée by Boucher, Musée des Beaux-Arts

NÎMES

0 metres 250
0 yards 250

Key to Symbols see back flap

Aigues-Mortes ❻

A lone, sturdy sentinel set among the salt marshes of the Camargue, Aigues-Mortes ("dead waters" in Provençal) looks today much as it must have done when it was completed, around 1300. Then, however, the Rhône had not deposited the silt which now landlocks the town. Canals brought the vast stone blocks to make its walls from the quarries of Beaucaire, and the town's founder, Louis IX set sail from under the shadow of Tour de Constance on his crusade of 1248 *(see pp42–3)*. Only the Hundred Years' War saw its ramparts breached: now its gates are always open to the besieging armies of admiring visitors.

Tour de la Poudrière
was the arsenal, where weapons and gunpowder were stored.

Porte de l'Arsenal

King Louis IX
Saint Louis, as he was to become, built Aigues-Mortes as his only Mediterranean sea port. People had to be bribed to come and settle in this inhospitable spot.

Porte de la Reine
was named for Anne of Austria, who visited the town in 1622.

Tour de la Mèche
or "wick tower" held a constant flame used to light cannon fuses.

Chapelle des Pénitents Blancs

Tour des Sels

RUE DE L'ARSENAL
RUE HOCHE
RUE SARSENAL
RUE ROUGET DE L'ISLE
RUE ROGER
BOULEVARD GAMBETT
SALENGRO
RUE PAUL BERT
RUE BAUDIN
RUE

★ The Ramparts
The 1,634-m (1-mile) long walls are punctuated by ten gates, six towers, arrow slits and overhanging latrines.

Chapelle des Pénitents Gris
Built from 1676–99, this chapel is still used by an order founded in 1400. Named for their grey cowls, they walk with their white-cowled former rivals in the Palm Sunday procession.

STAR SIGHTS

★ Tour de Constance

★ The Ramparts

Porte de la Marine
This was the main portside gate. Ships were moored by the Porte des Galions, anchored to a vast metal ring known as an organeau.

VISITORS' CHECKLIST

Road map A4. 🕍 6,150. 🚌 av de la Liberté. 🚌 rte de Nîmes. 🛈 Pl St-Louis (04 66 53 73 00). 🏪 Wed, Sun. 🎵 Nuits d'Encens (Mediterranean music; Jun); Festival St-Louis (Aug). www.ot-aiguesmortes.fr

Porte des Galions

Place St-Louis
This charming, leafy square, lined with cafés, is at the heart of town life. In its centre is a bronze statue of Saint Louis, on a base carved with the prows of crusader ships.

Porte de l'Organeau

Notre-Dame des Sablons, "Our Lady of the Sands", was built before the town itself.

Tour des Bourguignons
In a bloody massacre of 1421 Gascons took the town from Burgundy. Too many to bury, salted bodies were stored here.

KEY

– – – Suggested route

0 metres   100

0 yards   100

★ Tour de Constance
This tower often held religious prisoners: first Catholic, then Calvinist, and then Huguenot women like Marie Durand, freed in 1768 after 38 years.

The Camargue ❼

Gardians look after the horses and bulls

This flat, scarcely habited land is one of Europe's major wetland regions and natural history sites. Extensive areas of salt marsh, lakes, pastures and sand dunes, covering a vast 140,000 ha (346,000 acres), provide a romantic and haunting environment for the wildlife. Native horses roam the green pastures and are ridden by the traditional cowboys of the region, the *gardians*, (see p22) who herd the black bulls. Numerous sea birds and wildfowl also occupy the region, among them flocks of greater flamingoes. North of the reserve, rice is cultivated in paddy fields. Many of the thousands of visitors confine their exploration to the road between Arles and Saintes-Maries-de-la-Mer, and miss the best of the wild flora and fauna.

Camargue Bulls
Periodically, the herds of black bulls are rounded up by the gardians *to perform in local bullfights. The larger bulls are sold to Spain.*

Camargue Horses
These hardy animals are direct descendants of pre-historic horses. The foal's coat turns white between the age of four and seven.

Parc Ornithologique du Pont-de-Gau bird reserve *(see p138)* is where most birds in the Camargue live and where, twice a year, over 350 species of migrating birds stop off on their journey north or south.

N572

D570

Le Petit Rhône

Méjanes

PLAINE DE LA CAMARGUE

PETITE CAMARGUE

D570

P

Centre de Gines

Stes-Maries-de-la-Mer

CAMARGUE BIRDS

This region is a haven for bird spotters, particularly during the spring when migrant birds visit on their journey north. Resident birds include little egrets and marsh harriers. This is the only French breeding site of the slender-billed gull, and the red-crested pochard, rarely seen in Europe, also breeds here.

Little egret (Egretta garzetta)

Slender-billed gull (Larus genei)

Marsh harrier (Circus aeruginosus)

Collared pratincole (Glareola pratincola)

Black-winged stilt (Himantopus himantopus)

Red-crested pochard (Netta rufina)

European Beavers

European beavers came close to extinction at the start of the 20th century, when they were hunted for their fur. These nocturnal animals were protected in 1905 and began to colonize the region in the 1970s.

VISITORS' CHECKLIST

Road map B4. ✈ 90 km (56 miles) east Marignane-Marseille. 🚌 🚉 av Paulin Talabot, Arles. 🛈 5 av Van Gogh, Stes-Maries-de-la-Mer (04 90 97 82 55). 🎭 Pèlerinage des Gitans (24–25 May, end Oct). **www**.camargue.fr

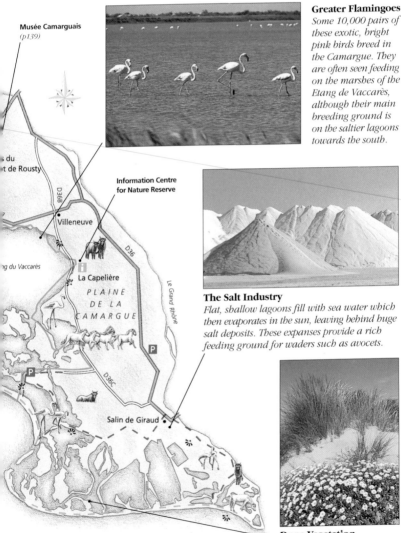

Greater Flamingoes

Some 10,000 pairs of these exotic, bright pink birds breed in the Camargue. They are often seen feeding on the marshes of the Etang de Vaccarès, although their main breeding ground is on the saltier lagoons towards the south.

Musée Camarguais
(p139)

Information Centre
for Nature Reserve

s du
t de Rousty

D368

Villeneuve

D36

g du Vaccarès

La Capelière

PLAINE
DE LA
CAMARGUE

Le Grand Rhône

P

D36C

P

Salin de Giraud

The Salt Industry

Flat, shallow lagoons fill with sea water which then evaporates in the sun, leaving behind huge salt deposits. These expanses provide a rich feeding ground for waders such as avocets.

Dune Vegetation

The sand dunes form a line between the lagoons and salt marshes and the sea. Among the many wild flowers that grow here is sea chamomile.

KEY

— Nature reserve boundary

– – Walking routes

– – Walking and cycling routes

0 kilometres   5

0 miles   5

Exploring the Camargue

Entrance to Méjanes bullring

The unique character of the Camargue has given rise to unusual traditions. The native white horses and black bulls are ranched by *manadiers* and herded, branded and tended by the region's cowboys, or *gardians*, whose small, low, whitewashed houses dot the landscape. Local bullfights are advertised in Saintes-Maries-de-la-Mer, the main tourist centre of the region and chief place to stay, also renowned for its gypsy population. It has a sandy beach and offers watersports and boat trips. Tourist offices throughout the area provide information on walks, but the best views are from the 7-km (5-mile) footway and cycle path along the Digues-de-la-Mer (sea dyke) from the town. Several sights within the Camargue have been turned into museums and exhibitions of local life and natural history. Several ranches and activity centres organize rides and riding holidays.

church, the **Musée Baroncelli** in the old town hall is devoted to zoology and archaeology.

Still in the Saintes-Maries area, 4.5 km (3 miles) north of the centre on the banks of the Etang de Ginès, lies the **Parc Ornithologique du Pont-de-Gau**, with a vast range of Camargue birdlife (*see p136*).

🏛 Musée Baroncelli
Ancien Hôtel de Ville, rue Victor Hugo.
Tel *04 90 97 87 60.* ⬜ *Apr–11 Nov: Wed–Mon alternate weeks (phone)*
The documents and artifacts relating to bull rearing and local life on display here were amassed by Marquis Folco de Baroncelli-Javon (1869–1943), a *manadier* who promoted the *gardian* life and the region's customs and traditions.

🏛 Le Centre d'Information du PNRC
Pont-de-Gau. ***Tel*** *04 90 97 86 32.* ⬜ *Apr–Sep: daily; Oct–Mar: Sat–Thu.* ● *1 Jan, 1 May, 25 Dec.*
This information centre offers wonderful views over the flat lagoon. Photographs and documents chronicle the history of the Camargue and its diverse flora and fauna.

🦅 Parc Ornithologique du Pont-de-Gau
Pont-de-Gau. ***Tel*** *04 90 97 82 62.* ⬜ *daily.* ● *25 Dec.*
Most of the birds that live in or migrate through the region are represented in this reserve. Huge aviaries house birds that might otherwise be hard to spot. Try to keep to the signposted paths to avoid damage or disturbance (*see p136*).

A bloodless Camargue bullfight in Méjanes

A place of pilgrimage

The three Marys who gave Saintes-Maries-de-la-Mer its name are Mary Magdalene, Mary Jacobea (the Virgin Mary's sister) and Mary Salome, mother of the apostles James and John. Set adrift after the Crucifixion with, among others, their servant Sara, Saint Martha and her brother Lazarus, they landed here in their boat. They built a shrine to the virgin, and while the others went to spread the word of the gospel, Mary Jacobea, Mary Salome and Sara stayed behind.

In winter, the town is an unpretentious, whitewashed, low-rise resort. It overflows during the May and October festivals, when Mary Salome and Mary Jacobea are celebrated, their statues marched

to the sea to be blessed. The larger festival is in May, when gypsies from all over the world come to pay homage to their patron saint, Sara, the richly dressed black Madonna who lies in the crypt of the 9th-century Eglise de Notre-Dame-de-la-Mer. An effigy is also paraded through the streets to the sea. Afterwards there are bullfights, horse races and flamenco dances (*see pp228–9*).

Throughout the centre of the town are cheery restaurants with checked tablecloths, and shops selling patterned skirts, shirts and scarves, lucky charms and Romany souvenirs. The prominent church is also worth visiting for the view from the rooftop walkway of its simple, fortified exterior. Just 40 m (44 yards) away from the

Honey buzzard enclosure at the Pont-de-Gau bird sanctuary

🏛 Musée Camarguais

Parc Naturel Régional de Camargue, Mas du Pont de Rousty. (On the D570, 10km south-west of Arles). **Tel** 04 90 97 10 82. ⬛ Apr–Sep: daily; Oct–Mar: Wed–Mon. ⬛ 1 Jan, 1 May, 25 Dec. ⬛ ⬛ ⬛

A traditional Provençal *mas* or farmhouse *(see pp22–23)*, that only a short time ago was part of a farm raising cattle and sheep, has been converted to accommodate a fascinating museum of the Camargue. The main part of the museum is housed in a huge sheep barn, built in 1812 and skilfully restored. Displays, including video footage and slide shows, provide an excellent introduction to traditional life in the Camargue and to the unique plant and animal life of the Camargue delta. Among the many subjects covered are

Eglise de Notre-Dame-de-la-Mer, in Saintes-Maries-de-la-Mer

the lives of the Camargue cowboys, and the *grand* and *petit* Rhône rivers which once flowed far to the east past Nîmes. Many of the displays are focused on traditional life at the time of poet and champion of the Provençal language, Frédéric Mistral, *(see p28)*, a local man who won the Nobel Prize for literature in 1904.

A signposted 3.5-km (2-mile) nature trail leads out from the museum to the Marré de la Grand Mare and back again by a pleasant circular route. Examples of traditional *mas* husbandry are marked on the way. An observation tower at the end of the walk gives great views over the surrounding countryside.

The fine Romanesque façade of the abbey church at St-Gilles-du-Gard

St-Gilles-du-Gard ❽

Road map A3. 🏠 12,200. ⬛ ℹ 1 place F Mistral (04 66 87 33 75). ⬛ Thu & Sun.

Called the "Gateway to the Camargue", St-Gilles is famous for its **Abbaye de St-Gilles.** In medieval times the abbey was vast. The building was damaged in 1562 during the Wars of Religion and all that remains are the west façade, chancel and crypt. The carved façade is the most beautiful in all Provence. It includes the first sculpture of the Passion in Christendom, from the late 12th century.

Founded by Raymond VI of Toulouse, the abbey church was the Knights of St John's first priory in Europe. It soon became a key place on the pilgrimage route to Santiago de Compostela in Spain and a port of embarkation for the Crusades *(see pp42–3)*. The crypt houses the tomb of Saint Gilles, a hermit who arrived by raft from Greece.

The belltower of the original abbey contains *La Vis*, a spiral staircase which is a masterpiece of stonemasonry.

Beaucaire ❾

Road map B3. 🏠 14,000. ⬛ Tarascon. ⬛ ℹ 24 cours Gambetta (04 66 59 26 57). ⬛ Thu & Sun.

The bullring in Beaucaire occupies the site of one of the largest fairs in Europe. Held every July for the past seven centuries, it attracted up to a

quarter of a million people. A smaller version of the fair takes place today, with a procession through the town on 21 July. It was inaugurated by Raymond VI in 1217, who enlarged the **Château de Beaucaire.**

This was later used by the French kings to look down on their Provençal neighbours across the river. It was partly dismantled on the orders of Cardinal Richelieu but the triangular keep and enough of the walls remain to indicate its impressive scale. There is a Romanesque chapel within the walls, and medieval spectacles, including frequent displays of falconry.

The **Abbaye de St-Roman** is situated 5 km (3 miles) to the northwest of Beaucaire. Dating from the 5th century, it is the only troglodyte monastery in Europe.

♦ Château de Beaucaire

Place Raymond VII. **Tel** 04 66 59 47 61. ⬛ for falconry displays only; phone to check schedule. ⬛

The unique troglodyte Abbaye de Saint-Roman near Beaucaire

The legendary Tarasque, the terror of Tarascon

Tarascon ⑩

Road map B3. 🏠 13,000. 🚉 🚌
ℹ️ 59 rue des Halles (04 90 91 03
52). 🚌 Tue & Fri. **www**.tarascon.org

The gleaming white vision of
the **Château de Tarascon** is
one of the landmarks of
the Rhône. Little is left of the
glittering court of Good King
René who finished the building
his father, Louis II of Anjou, began early in the 15th century
(see pp46–7). Following René's
death in 1480, Provence fell to
France, and the castle became
a prison until 1926. A drawbridge leads to the poultry yard
and garrison quarters. Beside
it rises the impressive main
castle, centred on a courtyard
from where two spiral staircases lead to royal apartments
and other rooms in its sturdy
towers. Prisoners' graffiti and
some painted ceiling panels
remain, but the only adorn-
ment is a handful of borrowed
17th-century tapestries which
depict the deeds of Roman
general Scipio (237–183 BC).

The **Collégiale Ste-Marthe**,
nearby has a tomb in the crypt
to the monster-taming saint.
According to legend, St Martha
(see p42) rescued the inhabitants from the Tarasque, a
man-eating monster, half lion,
half armadillo, which gave the
town its name. The event is
celebrated each June in the
Fête de la Tarasque (see p33).

In the old town is the 16th-
century Cloître des Cordeliers
where exhibitions are held.
On the arcaded Rue des
Halles is the 17th-century
town hall, with an attractively
carved façade and balcony.

The traditional life of the area
and its hand-printed fabrics is
seen in the **Musée Souleïado**.
The ancient textile industry
was revived in 1938, under the
name Souleïado, which means
"the sun passing through the
clouds" in Provençal. In the
museum are 40,000 wood-
blocks dating from the 18th
century, many of them still
used for the company's
colourful prints.

The **Maison de Tartarin** is a
museum devoted to the tall-
story telling Provençal "hero"
of three comic novels by
Alphonse Daudet (see p28).

⛪ **Château de Tarascon**
Bd du Roi René. **Tel** 04 90 91 01 93.
◻️ daily. ⬤ 1 Jan, 1 May, 1 & 11
Nov, 25 Dec. 🎟️ 📷

🏛️ **Musée Souleïado**
39 rue Proudhon. **Tel** 04 90 91 08
80. ◻️ May–Oct: daily; Nov–Apr:
Tue–Sat. ⬤ 1 Jan, 1 & 11 Nov, 25
Dec. 🎟️

🏛️ **Maison de Tartarin**
55 bis bd Itam. **Tel** 04 90 91 05 08.
◻️ mid-Mar–mid-Dec: Mon–Sat.
⬤ 1 May, 1 & 11 Nov. 🎟️

The fairy tale Château de Tarascon,
stronghold of Good King René

St-Rémy-de-Provence ⑪

Road map B3. 🏠 10,000.
🚉 Avignon. ℹ️ pl Jean-Jaurès
(04 90 92 05 22). 🚌 Wed.

St-Rémy is ideal for exploring
the Alpilles countryside which
supplies the plants for its
traditional herboristeries, or
herb shops. The **Musée des
Arômes** displays implements of
their craft and properties of the
local flora.

St-Rémy's **Eglise St-Martin**
contains an exceptional organ
which can be heard during
the summer festival "Organa",
or on Saturday recitals.

Two of the town's most
attractive 15th–16th-century
mansions are now museums.
The **Musée des Alpilles** has a
fine ethnographic collection
and the **Hôtel de Sade**, home
of the infamous Marquis' fore-
bears, contains some Roman

Herbs and spices on sale in St-Rémy
market, place de la République

remains from nearby Glanum.
The well-known 16th-century
physician and astrologer,
Nostradamus, was born in a
house in the outer wall of the
avenue Hoche, in the old
quarter of St-Rémy.

**Le Centre d'Art Présence
Van Gogh** in the 18th-century
Hôtel Estrine is a reminder of
the great artist's association
with St-Rémy. In May 1889,
after he had mutilated his ear,
he arrived at the **Clinique
St-Paul**, which is situated
between the town and the
Roman remains at Glanum.
The grounds and the 12th-
century cloisters of the clinic
can be visited, and the tourist
office gives a map of some of
the views Van Gogh painted
while he stayed here.

Just behind the clinic is Le
Mas de la Pyramide, a farm-
stead half-built into the rock,

The triumphal arch at Glanum, built in the reign of Augustus, a 15-minute walk from the centre of St-Rémy

which has remained in the same family for generations. It was formerly a Roman quarry.

The remains of the earliest Greek houses in Provence, from the 4th-century BC, are in **Glanum** *(see p40)*, a Greco-Roman town at the head of a valley in the Alpilles. Dramatic memorials, known as Les Antiques, stand on the roadside: a triumphal arch from 10 BC, celebrating Caesar's conquest of the Greeks and Gaul, and a mausoleum from about 30 BC.

🏛 Musée des Arômes
34 bd Mirabeau. **Tel** 04 90 92 48 70.
⬜ Easter–mid-Sep: daily; mid-Sep–Easter: Mon–Sat. ⬤ public hols. ⬤ ⬤

🏛 Musée des Alpilles
Place Favier. **Tel** 04 90 92 68 24.
⬜ Mar–Dec: daily. ⬤ 1 May, 25 Dec. ⬤

🏛 Hôtel de Sade
Rue du Parage. **Tel** 04 90 92 64 04.
⬜ Tue–Sun. ⬤ 1 Jan, 1 May, 1 & 11 Nov, 25 Dec. ⬤

🏛 Le Centre d'Art Présence Van Gogh
8 rue Estrine. **Tel** 04 90 92 34 72.
⬜ Tue–Sun. ⬤ Jan & Feb. ⬤ ⬤ restricted.

🏛 Clinique St-Paul
Av Vincent Van Gogh, St-Paul de Mausole. **Tel** 04 90 92 77 00.
⬜ daily. ⬤

⛪ Glanum
Rte des Baux. **Tel** 04 90 92 23 79.
⬜ daily. ⬤ 1 Jan, 1 May, 1 & 11 Nov, 25 Dec. ⬤ ⬤ ⬤

Les Alpilles ⑫

Road map B3. 🚌 *Arles, Tarascon, Salon-de-Provence.* 🚌 *Les Baux-de-Provence, St-Rémy-de-Provence, Eyguières, Eygalières.* ℹ️ *St-Rémy-de-Provence (04 90 92 05 22).*

St-Rémy-de-Provence is on the western side of the limestone massif of Les Alpilles, a 24-km (15-mile) chain between the Rhône and Durance. A high point is **La Caume**, at 387 m (1270 ft), reached from St-Rémy, just beyond Glanum.

East of St-Rémy, the road to Cavaillon runs along the north side of the massif, with a right turn to Eygalières. The painter Mario Prassinos (1916–85), whose work is displayed in Notre-Dame-de-Pitié in St-Rémy, lived here. Just beyond the village is the 12th-century Chapelle St-Sixte.

The road continues towards Orgon where there are views across the Durance Valley and the Luberon. Orgon skirts the massif on the eastern side. A right turn leads past the ruins of Castelas de Roquemartine and Eyguières, a pleasant village with a Romanesque church. It is a two-hour walk to Les Opiés, a 493-m (1,617-ft) hill crowned by a tower. This forms part of the GR6 which crosses the chain to Les Baux, one of the best walking routes in Provence. From Castelas de Roquemartine the road heads back west towards Les Baux.

The chalky massif of Les Alpilles, "Little Alps", in the heart of Provence

A late 18th-century fresco showing the Baux warriors in battle against the Saracens in 1266

Les Baux-de-Provence ⑬

Road map B3. 🚶 *460*. 🚌 ℹ️
La Maison du Roy (04 90 54 34 39).
www.lesbauxdeprovence.com

Les Baux sits on a spur of the Alpilles (*bau* in Provençal means escarpment), with views across to the Camargue (*see pp136–9*). The most dramatic fortress site in Provence, it has nearly two million visitors a year, so avoid midsummer, or go early in the morning. The pedestrianized town has a car park beside the Porte Mage gate.

When the Lords of Baux built their fine citadel here in the 10th century, they claimed one of the three wise men, King Balthazar, as ancestor and took the star of Bethlehem as their emblem. These fierce warriors originated the troubadour Courts of Love and wooed noble ladies with poetry and songs. This became the medieval convention known as courtly love and paved the way for a literary tradition.

The citadel ruins lie on the heights of the escarpment. Their entrance is via the 14th-century Tour-du-Brau, which houses the **Musée d'Histoire des Baux-de-Provence**. A plateau extends to the end of the escarpment, where there is a monument to the poet Charloun Rieu (1846–1924). In the town centre, two other museums of local interest are

Monument to poet Charloun Rieu

the **Fondation Louis Jou** and the **Musée des Santons**. Next door to the 12th-century Eglise St-Vincent is the Chapelle des Pénitents Blancs, decorated in 1974 by the local artist Yves Brayer. Just north of Les Baux lies the **Cathédrale d'Images**.

🏛 Musée d'Histoire des Baux-de-Provence
Hôtel de la Tour-du-Brau, Rue du Trenca. **Tel** 04 90 54 55 56.
⭕ *daily.* 🎫 ♿ *restricted.*
This small archaeological museum contains objects from Les Baux and its environs.

🏛 Fondation Louis Jou
Hôtel Brion, Grande Rue. **Tel** 04 90 54 34 17.
⭕ *Thu–Mon pms only.*
Medieval books are housed here, along with a collection of prints and drawings by Dürer, Goya and Jou, the local engraver after whom the museum is named.

🏛 Musée des Santons
Place Louis Jou. **Tel** 04 90 54 34 39.
⭕ *daily.*
In the 16th-century old town hall, a Provençal crib scene has been created, representing the nativity at Les Baux. Handmade clay *santons* or figurines (*see p48*), representing saints and local figures, show the evolution of Provençal costume.

🏛 Cathédrale d'Images
Route de Maillane. **Tel** 04 90 54 38 65. ⭕ *Mid-Feb–early Jan: daily.* 🎫
♿ **www**.cathedrale-images.com
Located on the D27 road to the north of Les Baux and within walking distance of the main car park in Les Baux is the Val d'Enfer or the Valley of Hell. This jagged gorge, said to be inhabited by witches and spirits, may have inspired some of Dante's poetry. It is also the site where bauxite was discovered in 1822 by the mineralogist Berthier, who named it after the town. It was in this big quarry that the

View of the citadel and village of Les Baux

Cathédrale d'Images or Picture Palace was established. The imaginative slide show is projected not only onto the white limestone walls of the natural theatre, but also the floor and ceiling, creating a three dimensional effect. The 30-minute show is renewed each year. Accompanied by captivating music, it is an extraordinary audio-visual experience.

Les Baux's Chapelle des Pénitents, next to the Eglise St-Vincent

Fontvieille ⑭

Road map B3. 👥 3,500. 🚍 🚉
🛈 5 rue Marcel Honorat (04 90 54 67 49). 🚍 Mon & Fri.

Fontvieille is an agreeable country town in the flat fruit and vegetable lands of the irrigated Baux Valley. Half-way between Arles and Les Alpilles, the town makes an excellent centre from which to explore. Until the French Revolution in

1789, the town's history was bound up with the Abbaye de Montmajour. The oratories that stand at the four corners of the small town were erected in 1721 to celebrate the end of the plague (see pp48–9).

To the south on the D33, set on a stony hill is the Moulin de Daudet and further on at Barbegal are the remarkable remains of a Roman aqueduct and a series of 4 water mills.

Abbaye de Montmajour ⑮

Road map B3. Route de Fontvieille. **Tel** 04 90 54 64 17. ☐ Apr–Sep: daily; Oct–Mar: Wed–Mon. ● 1 Jan, 1 May, 1 & 11 Nov, 25 Dec. 🎫

Standing out like Noah's ark on Mount Ararat, 5 km (3 miles) northwest of Arles, this Benedictine abbey was built in the 10th century. At the time, the site was an island refuge in marshland. The handful of monks in residence spent all their spare time draining this area of marshland between the Alpilles chain and the Rhône.

The abbey is a massive and imposing place, though all the Baroque buildings were destroyed by fire 1726 and never restored. The original church is said to have been founded by Saint Trophime as a sanctuary from the Romans. It grew rich in the Middle Ages when thousands of pilgrims arrived at Easter to purchase pardons. After 1791, the abbey was broken up by two successive

The cloisters and keep of the Abbaye de Montmajour

owners who bought it from the state. The abbey was largely restored in the 19th century.

The **Eglise Notre-Dame** is one of the largest Romanesque buildings in Provence. Below, the 12th-century crypt has been built into the sloping hill. The cloister has double pillars ornamented with beasts and lies in the shadows of the 26-m (85-ft) tower, built in the 1360s. It is worth climbing the 124 steps to the tower platform to see the stunning view across to the sea. Also carved into the hillside is the atmospheric **Chapelle de St-Pierre**. It was established at the same time as the abbey and is a primitive place of worship. There are a number of tombs in the abbey grounds, but the principal burial area is the 12th-century **Chapelle Ste-Croix**. It lies not far to the east and is built in the shape of a Greek cross.

DAUDET'S WINDMILL

The Moulin de Daudet is one of the most famous literary landmarks in France. Alphonse Daudet was born in Nîmes in 1840 and made his name in Paris. The windmill is the setting of Daudet's Letters from my Windmill, stories about Provençal life, first published in 1860 and popular ever since. He observed the local characters and wrote about their lives with irony and pathos. He never actually lived in the mill, but made imaginative use of some of the resident miller's tales. When he stayed in Fontvieille he was a guest in the 19th-century Château de Montauban. He came to find respite from the capital, but returned there in order to write his stories. The restored mill can be visited, and there is a small museum dedicated to Daudet.

Street-by-Street: Arles ⓰

Many of the tourist sites in Arles bear the stamp of
their Roman past, and all are within comfortable
walking distance of the central place de la République.
On its north side is the Hôtel de Ville, behind which is
the place du Forum. This square is the heart of modern
life in Arles. Another place to sit at a café and observe
the Arlésiens is the boulevard des Lices, where
the lively twice-weekly market is held. Some of the shops
here and in nearby rue Jean-Jaurès sell bright Provençal
fabrics. For museum-buffs, an inclusive ticket gives
access to all the museums except the Espace Van Gogh.

Les Thermes de Constantin are all that remain of Constantine's Palace, built in the 4th century AD.

Musée Réattu
This museum on the banks of the Rhône houses 18th–19th-century and modern art, including this figure of Le Griffu (1952) by Germaine Richier.

Hôtel de Ville

Museon Arlaten
The Hôtel de Laval-Castellane contains the largest folklore collection in Provence, a treasure house of local history.

★ **Eglise St-Trophime**
This fine Romanesque church has a 12th-century portal of the Last Judgment, including saints and apostles.

L'Espace Van Gogh, a cultural centre

Egyptian Obelisk
An ancient obelisk with fountains at its base (one of which is shown here) stands in the place de la République. It came from the Roman circus across the Rhône.

STAR SIGHTS
★ Les Arènes
★ Théâtre Antique
★ Eglise St-Trophime

★ Les Arènes
This is one of the largest, best-preserved Roman monuments in Provence. The top tier provides an excellent panoramic view of Arles.

VISITORS' CHECKLIST

Road map B3. 🏠 *52,000*. ✈
Nîmes-Arles-Camargue. 🚉 🚌
av P Talabot. 🛈 *esp C de Gaulle
(04 90 18 41 20).* 🛒 *Wed, Sat.*
🎭 *Feria Pascale (Easter); Fête des
Gardians (1 May); Fêtes d'Arles
(Jul). Feria des Prémices du Riz
(Sep).* **www**.ville-arles.fr

★ Théâtre Antique
Once a fortress, its stones were later used for other buildings. These last remaining columns are called the "two widows".

Notre-Dame-de-la-Major is dedicated to Saint George, patron saint of the Camargue *gardians* (cowboys).

PLACE DE LA MAJOR

Cloisters of St-Trophime
This sculpted capital is a fine example of the Romanesque beauty of the cloisters.

VAN GOGH IN ARLES

Vincent Van Gogh painted over 300 canvases in the 15 months he lived in Arles, but the town has none of his work. In belated appreciation of this lonely artist, the Hôtel-Dieu has been turned into L'Espace Van Gogh, with a library and exhibition space. Several sites are evocative of him, however; the Café Van Gogh in the place du Forum has been renovated to look as it did in his *Café du Soir*.

L'Arlésienne **by Van Gogh (1888)**

KEY

— — — Suggested route

0 metres   100

0 yards   100

Exploring Arles

The city of Arles was a Greek site expanded by the Romans into a "little Rome". Here, on the most southerly crossing point on the Rhône, they built shipyards, baths, a racetrack and an arena. Then the capital of the three Gauls – France, Spain and Britain – Arles remains one of the most distinctive towns in Provence with fine relics from its Gallo-Roman past. Cars should be parked outside the narrow lanes of the old town.

Sarcophagi on Les Alyscamps

♈ Les Arènes
Rond-point des Arènes. *Tel* 04 90 49 36 86. ☐ daily. ● 1 Jan, 1 May, 1 Nov, 25 Dec & for bullfights. 🖼

The most impressive of the surviving Roman monuments, the amphitheatre is on the east side of the old town. It was the largest of the Roman buildings in Gaul. Slightly oval, it measures 136 m (446 ft) by 107 m (351 ft) and could seat 20,000. The floors of some of the internal rooms were decorated with mosaics, the better to wash down after bloody affrays. Today both Provençal and Spanish bullfights are held regularly in the arena.

Just to the southwest of the amphitheatre is the elegant Roman **Théâtre Antique**, which has 2,000 tiered seats arranged in a hemisphere.

🏛 Musée de l'Arles Antique
Presqu'île du Cirque Romain. *Tel* 04 90 18 88 88. ☐ daily. ● 1 Jan, 1 May, 1 Nov, 25 Dec. 🖼 🅰 🄳

Opened in 1995, this museum displays ancient artifacts from Arles and Christian and pagan art. Arles became Christian after Constantine's conversion in AD 312, and fine examples of Romano-Christian sculpture are here. Among the pagan art is a copy of the Venus of Arles and Roman mosaics.

♈ Cryptoporticus
Rue Balze. ☐ daily. ● 1 Jan, 1 May, 1 Nov, 25 Dec. 🖼

These huge subterranean galleries *(see p41)*, ventilated by air shafts, were part of the forum's structure.

♈ Les Alyscamps
Av des Alyscamps. ☐ daily. 🖼 🅰

From Roman to late Medieval times, Les Alyscamps was one of the largest and the most famous cemeteries in the Western world. Romans avoided it at night, making it

Roman mosaic of *Europa and the Bull*, in the Musée de l'Arles Antique

an ideal meeting place for early Christians, led by St Trophime. Christians were often buried by the tomb of Genesius, a Roman servant and beheaded Christian martyr.

♙ Eglise St-Trophime
Place de la République. *Tel* 04 90 96 07 38. ☐ daily. 🅰

This is one of the most beautiful Romanesque churches in Provence. The portal and cloisters are exquisitely decorated with biblical scenes. St Trophime, thought to be the first bishop of Arles in the early 3rd century, appears with St Peter and St John on the carved northeast pillar.

🏛 Museon Arlaten
Hôtel Laval-Castellane, 29 rue de la République. *Tel* 04 90 93 58 11. ☐ Jul–Sep: daily; Oct–Jun: Tue–Sun. ● 1 Jan, 1 May, 1 Nov, 25 Dec. 🖼

This folklore collection includes costumes, tableaux and artifacts covering two spacious floors. A treasure trove of information about local customs, superstitions and traditions, it was founded in 1896 by the poet Mistral *(see p28)*, who refurbished the 16th-century Hôtel Laval-Castellane using his Nobel prize money.

🏛 Musée Réattu
10 rue du Grand-Prieuré. *Tel* 04 90 49 37 58. ☐ daily. ● 1 Jan, 1 May, 1 & 11 Nov, 25 Dec. 🖼

The local artist Jacques Réattu (1760–1833) and his contemporaries form the basis of this collection. A Picasso donation and a photographic display are among 20th-century works.

View of Arles from the opposite bank of the Rhône

Martigues ❼

Road map B4. 🎪 *45,000.* 🚃 🚌
🛈 *Rond-Point de l'Hôtel de Ville (04
42 42 31 10).* 🛥 *Thu & Sun.*
www.ville-martigues.fr

The Etang de Berre, situated
between Marseille and the
Camargue, has the largest
petroleum refinery industry in
France, which dominates the
landscape. However, on the
inland side of the Canal de
Caronte is the former fishing
port and artists' colony of
Martigues, which still attracts
a holiday crowd.

Martigues lies on both banks
of the canal and on the island
of Brescon, where the Pont San
Sébastien is a popular place for
artists to set up their easels.
Félix Ziem (1821–1911) was
the most ardent admirer of
this "little Venice" *(see p26);*
his paintings and works by
contemporary artists can be
viewed in the **Musée Ziem**.

🏛 **Musée Ziem**
Bd du 14 juillet. **Tel** *04 42 41 39
60.* ◻ *Jul–Aug: Wed–Mon;
Sep–Jun: Wed, Thu–Sun pms.*

**Canal San Sébastien in Martigues,
known as the Birds' Looking-Glass**

Salon-de-
Provence ❽

Road map B3. 🎪 *40,000.* 🚃 🚌
🛈 *56 cours Gimon (04 90 56 27
60).* 🛥 *Wed & Sun.*

Known for its olives (the
olive oil industry was
established in the 1400s) and
soap, Salon-de-Provence is
dominated by the castellated
Château de l'Empéri. Once
home of the archbishops of

The 12th-century Cistercian Abbaye de Silvacane

Arles, this now contains the
Musée de l'Empéri, which has
a large collection of militaria
from Louis XIV to World War I.

The military tradition in the
town is upheld by the French
Air Force officers' college, La
Patrouille Aérienne de France.
Near the château is the 13th-
century **Eglise de St-Michel**
and in the north of the old
town is the Gothic **St-Laurent**,
where the French physician
and astrologer Nostradamus is
buried. Nostradamus is Salon's
most famous citizen. Here, in
his adopted home, he wrote
Les Centuries, his book
of predictions, pub-
lished in 1555. It
was banned by the
Vatican, as it fore-
told the dimin-
ishing power of
the papacy. But
his renown was
widespread and in
1560 he was made
Charles IX's
physician.

Salon's four-day
Gospel music festival
in July echoes throughout the
town, with concerts in the
château, free street performances and song workshops.

♟ **Château de l'Empéri**
Montée du Puech. **Tel** *04 90 56 22
36.* ◻ *Wed–Mon.* ⬤ *1 Jan, 1
May, 1 Nov, 24–25 Dec, 31 Dec.* 📷

**Nostradamus, astrologer
and citizen of Salon**

Abbaye de
Silvacane ❾

Road map C3. **Tel** *04 42 50 41 69.*
◻ *Apr–Sep: daily; Oct–Mar:
Wed–Mon.* ⬤ *1 Jan, 1 May, 25
Dec.* 📷 ❚

Like her two Cistercian sisters,
Silvacane is a harmonious
12th-century monastery tucked
away in the countryside. A bus
from Aix-en-Provence runs
regularly to Roque-d'Anthéron,
the nearest village. The abbey
was founded on the site of a
Benedictine monastery,
in a clearing of a
"forest of reeds"
(silva canorum).
It adheres to the
austere Cistercian
style, with no
decoration. The
church, with nave,
two aisles and a
high, vaulted tran-
sept, is solid, bare
and echoing. The
cloisters, arcaded
like a pigeon loft,
are 13th century and the refectory 14th century. Shortly after
the refectory was built, all the
monks left and the church
served the parish. After the
Revolution, it was sold as
state property and became a
farm until transformed back
into an abbey.

Aix-en-Provence ⑳

Provence's former capital is an international students' town, with one of the region's most cosmopolitan streets of restaurants and bars, rue de la Verrerie. The university was founded by Louis II of Anjou in 1409 and flourished under his son, Good King René (see p46–7).

Another wave of prosperity transformed the city in the 17th century, when ramparts, first raised by the Romans in their town of Aquae Sextiae, were pulled down, and the mansion-lined cours Mirabeau was built. Aix's renowned fountains were added in the 18th century.

The cours Mirabeau, grandest of Aix's boulevards

Exploring Aix

North of the cours Mirabeau, sandwiched between the Cathédrale St-Sauveur and the place d'Albertas, lies the town's old quarter. Sights include the Musée des Tapisseries, housed in the former Bishop's palace, and the splendid 17th-century Hôtel de Ville. Built around a courtyard by Pierre Pavillon from 1655–1670, it stands in a square now used as a flower market. Nearby is the 16th-century clock tower.

Just outside the old town are the ancient Roman baths, the Thermes Sextius, and nearby is the 18th-century spa complex.

Aix's finest street, the cours Mirabeau, is named after the orator and revolutionary Comte de Mirabeau. At its western end is the Fontaine de la Rotonde, a cast-iron fountain built in 1860. The north side is lined with shops, pâtisseries and cafés, the most illustrious being the 18th-century Les Deux Garçons (see p219). The south side is lined with

elegant hôtels: No. 4, Hôtel de Villars (1710); No. 10, the Hôtel d'Isoard de Vauvenargues, (1710), former residence of the Marquis of Entrecasteau who murdered his wife here; No. 19, Hôtel d'Arbaud Jouques (1730); No. 20, Hôtel de Forbin (1658); and Hôtel d'Espagnet at No. 38, once home to the Duchess of Montpensier, known as "La Grande Mademoiselle", niece of Louis XIII. South of the cours Mirabeau is the Quartier Mazarin built during the time of Archbishop Michel Mazarin. Aix's first Gothic church, St-Jean-de-Malte, now houses the Musée Granet.

Pavillon de Vendôme detail

🔓 Cathédrale St-Sauveur

34 pl des Martyrs-de-la-Résistance. **Tel** 04 42 23 45 65. ☐ Mon–Sat. 🗡 for cloisters.
The cathedral at the top of the old town creaks with history. The main door has solid walnut panels sculpted by Jean Guiramand of Toulon (1504). On the right there is a fine 4th–5th-century baptistry, with a Renaissance cupola standing on 2nd-century Corinthian columns. These are from a basilica which stood here beside the Roman forum. The jewel of the church is the triptych of *The Burning Bush* (1476, see pp46–7) by Nicolas Froment (under restoration until 2004). South of the cathedral are the tiled Romanesque cloisters.

🏛 Musée des Tapisseries

28 place des Martyrs-de-la-Résistance. **Tel** 04 42 23 09 91. ☐ Wed–Mon. 🗡 31 Dec–1 Jan, 1 May, 24–25 Dec.
Apart from magnificent 17th- and 18th-century Beauvais tapestries, the museum has opera costumes and stage designs from 1948 onwards, used in the annual Festival International d'Aix (see p33).

🏛 Musée du Vieil Aix

17 rue Gaston-de-Saporta. **Tel** 04 42 21 43 55. ☐ Tue–Sun. 🔴 public hols. 🗡
This eclectic collection of local memorabilia includes furniture, marionettes, a 19th-century *crèche parlante* and figures from the Corpus Christi parade commissioned by King René.

The 17th-century Hôtel de Ville, with the flower market in front

🏛 Muséum d'Histoire Naturelle

6 rue Espariat. **Tel** 04 42 27 91 27. ☐ daily. 🔴 1 Jan, 1 May, 24–25 Dec, 31 Dec. 🗡 📷
Located in the Hôtel Boyer d'Eguilles, designed by Pierre Puget and built in 1675, the museum has some fascinating collections of mineralogy and palaeontology. Dinosaur eggs which were found locally are a high point of the exhibits.

Cézanne's studio, filled with his furniture and personal belongings

Musée Granet

13 rue Cardinale. **Tel** 04 42 38 14 70.
reopening 2006 after renovation; phone to check schedule.

The city's main museum is in an impressive 17th-century former priory of the Knights of Malta. François Granet (1775–1849) was a local painter, and bequeathed his collection of French, Italian and Flemish paintings to Aix. These include Ingres' *Portrait of Granet* and *Jupiter and Thetis*. There are also works by Granet himself and other Provençal painters, with eight canvases by Paul Cézanne, plus archaeological material from Roman Aix.

Fondation Vasarely

1 av Marcel Pagnol. **Tel** 04 42 20 01 09. Mon–Sat. 1 May, 25 Dec–1 Jan. ground floor only.

One of Aix's most distinctive landmarks, this series of black-and-white metal hexagons was designed by the king of Op Art Victor Vasarely in the mid-1970s to house his foundation. Alongside his monumental works, its exhibitions promote art in the city at a national and international level.

Atelier Paul Cézanne

9 av Paul Cézanne. **Tel** 04 42 21 06 53.
daily. 1 Jan. 1 May, 25 Dec.
www.atelier-cezanne.com

Ten minutes' walk uphill from the cathedral is the modest house of artist Paul Cézanne (see p26). The studio, designed by Cézanne himself, is much as he left it when he died in 1906. Here he painted *Les Grandes Baigneuses*, and not far from here you can see the Ste-Victoire, a favourite subject.

Pavillon de Vendôme

32 rue Célony. **Tel** 04 42 21 05 78.
Wed–Mon. 31 Dec & 1 Jan, 1 May, 24 & 25 Dec.

One of Aix's grandest houses, built for Cardinal de Vendôme in 1667 and later enlarged, the main entrance is supported by two figures of Atlantes (see p48), and the rooms are filled with Provençal furniture.

AIX-EN-PROVENCE

0 metres 500
0 yards 500
Key to Symbols see back flap

Marseille ㉑

France's premier port and oldest major city is in a surprisingly attractive setting, centred on the Vieux Port, which fishing boats enter between the guardian forts of St-Jean and St-Nicolas. On the north side are the commercial docks and the old town, rebuilt after World War II. People have lived here for 26 centuries, its mixture of cultures being so varied that Alexandre Dumas called it "the meeting place of the entire world".

The Vieux Port looking south, with Notre-Dame-de-la-Garde on high

Exploring Marseille

Inland, running from the end of the port, is La Canebière – cannabis walk – a big, bustling boulevard which stretches from former hemp fields down to the port where the hemp was made into rope.

At the top of La Canebière is the Neo-Gothic Eglise des Réformés. A left and a right turn lead to boulevard Longchamp, and a walk along its length brings you to the Palais Longchamp. This is not really a palace, but more an impressive folly in the form of a colonnade that fans out around a fountain and ends in two large wings. These wings support a natural history and a fine arts museum.

Behind the palace is the city's zoo. Beyond the grid of shopping streets to the south, the town rises towards the basilica of Notre-Dame-de-la-Garde, which provides an unparalleled view of the city.

If you visit the morning fish market on the quai des Belges, you can delight in Marseille's famed *bouillabaisse (see p207)* at one of the countless nearby fish restaurants. Just behind the quai des Belges, at the back of St-Ferréol, is the Jardin des Vestiges, where remains of the ancient Greek settlement from the 4th century BC have been recently discovered.

🏛 Vieille Charité

2 rue de la Vieille Charité. *Tel* 04 91 14 58 80. ◯ Tue–Sun. ● public hols. 🎟 🔲 📷 🔲 ♿

The old town's finest building is the Vieille Charité, a large, well-restored hospice designed by Pierre Puget (1620–94), architect to Louis XIV. Begun in 1671, its original purpose was to house rural migrants. It is centred on a beautifully proportioned chapel with an oval dome, now used as an exhibition centre. The first floor has a small but rich collection of ancient Egyptian artifacts in the Musée d'Archéologie Méditerranéenne and the second floor displays African and Oceanic art.

⛪ Cathédrale de la Major

Place de la Major. *Tel* 04 91 90 53 57. ◯ daily.

The old town descends on the west side to the Cathédrale de la Major, a Neo-Byzantine confection completed in 1893. Its crypt contains the tombs of the bishops of Marseille. Beside it, small and beautiful, is the 11th-century Ancienne Cathédrale de la Major, part of which was sacrificed in the building of the new cathedral. Inside are a reliquary altar of 1073 and a 15th-century altar.

🏛 Musée des Docks Romains

28 place Vivaux. *Tel* 04 91 91 24 62. ◯ Tue–Sun. ● public hols. 🎟

During post-war rebuilding the Roman docks were uncovered. A small museum, mainly displaying large storage urns once used for wine, grain and oil, occupies the site of the docks, now buried in the foundations of a residential block.

The Palais Longchamps, a 19th-century folly set around a fountain

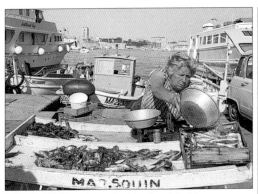

Stall at the daily fish market, on the old port's quai des Belges

🏛 Musée du Vieux Marseille

Maison Diamantée, 2 rue de la Prison. *Tel* 04 91 55 28 68. ☐ *Tue–Sun.*

The quai du Port follows the north side of the port past the 17th-century Hôtel de Ville. Behind it lies the most interesting museum of the town's history: the recently renovated Musée du Vieux Marseille, in the 16th-century Maison Diamantée. The building takes its name from the diamond-shaped stones in its façade. It houses 18th-century Provençal furniture, domestic objects and *santons*.

🏛 Musée d'Histoire de Marseille

Centre Bourse, square Belsunce. *Tel* 04 91 90 42 22. ☐ *Mon–Sat.* ● *public hols.*

In the Centre Bourse shopping centre is the Musée d'Histoire de Marseille. Reconstructions of the city at the height of the Greek period make this a good starting point for a tour. From here there is access to the Jardin des Vestiges, with remains of Greek fortifications and ancient docks dating from the 1st century AD.

🏛 Musée Cantini

19 rue Grignan. *Tel* 04 91 54 77 75. ☐ *Tue–Sun.* ● *public hols.*

The Musée Cantini is housed in the 17th-century Hôtel de Montgrand. Its collection of 20th-century art, given by the sculptor Jules Cantini, includes Fauve, Cubist and Surrealist paintings.

🏛 Musée de la Faïence

157 av Montredon. *Tel* 04 91 72 43 47. ☐ *Tue–Sun.* ● *public hols.*

Marseille's fine new ceramic museum, in the 19th-century Château Pastré, has over 1,200 items of local, national and European ceramics from Neolilithic times to today.

The imposing, heavily fortified walls of the Abbaye de St-Victor

⛪ Abbaye de St-Victor

Place St-Victor. *Tel* 04 96 11 22 60. ☐ *daily.* for crypt.

Marseille's finest piece of religious architecture is St Victor's basilica, between Notre-Dame and the port. This religious fortress belonged to one of the most powerful abbeys in Provence. It was founded in the 5th century by a monk, St Cassian, in honour of St Victor, martyred two centuries earlier, and was enlarged from the 11th to the 14th centuries.

There are crypts containing catacombs, sarcophagi and the cave of St Victor.

On 2 February each year St-Victor becomes a place of pilgrimage. Boat-shaped cakes are sold to commemorate the legendary arrival in Provence of the Stes-Maries *(see p41).*

⛪ Basilique de Notre-Dame-de-la-Garde

Rue Fort du Sanctuaire. *Tel* 04 91 13 40 80. ☐ *daily.*

The basilica of Notre-Dame-de-la-Garde, which dominates the south of the town at 155 m (500 ft), is a 19th-century Neo-Byzantine extravaganza. It is presided over by a golden Madonna on a 46-m (150-ft) bell tower. Much of the interior decoration is by the Düsseldorf School. Many come for the incomparable view over the city, while others come here to leave votive offerings.

🏛 Musée Grobet-Labadié

140 bd Longchamp. *Tel* 04 91 62 21 82. ☐ *Tue–Sun.* ● *public hols.*

To the north of the city, at the top of boulevard Longchamp, is the finest house in Marseille, with one of the most unusual interiors in the region. It was built in 1873 for a Marseille merchant, Alexandre Labadié. The house and its collection were given to the city in 1919 by his daughter, Marie-Louise.

The Musée Grobet-Labadié has a fine furniture collection, tapestries, 17th–19th century paintings, and many objects of interest, including unusual musical instruments, among them silk and ivory bagpipes.

Detail of *The Flagellation of Christ*, in the Musée Grobet-Labadié

🏛 Musée des Beaux-Arts

Palais Longchamp, 42 bd Longchamp.
Tel 04 91 14 59 30. ◯ Tue–Sun.
🔵 public hols. 🈶 🔆

The museum contains works by the city's best known sons: the sculptor, painter and architect Pierre Puget (1620–94) and the caricaturist, sculptor and painter, Daumier (1808–79). Serre's paintings of Marseille's plague in 1721 *(see pp48–9)* are housed here and there is a large collection of Flemish, Italian and French painting, including works by Rubens, Carracci, Courbet and Ingres.

The Château d'If in the bay of Marseille, a prison in reality and fiction

Le Sacrifice de Noé by Pierre Puget in the Musée des Beaux Arts

⚓ Château d'If

Tel 04 91 59 02 30. ◯ May–Aug: daily; Sep–Apr: Tue–Sun. 🈶 🔢

Fact, fiction and legend mingle in this island castle in the bay of Marseille. Until the 16th century it was a barren island, only visited by local fishermen. On a trip to Marseille in 1516, François I decided to make it a fortress. It was built in 1529, and turned into a prison in 1540 till World War I. Famous inmates have included Alexander Dumas' fictional Count of Monte Cristo, the legendary Man in the Iron Mask *(see p71)* and the real Comte de Mirabeau. In 1516, the first rhinoceros ever to set foot in Europe was brought ashore here, and drawn by Albrecht Dürer *(see p47)*.

🏢 Cité Radieuse

280 boulevard Michelet. **Tel** 04 91 16 78 00 (for guided tour information). A landmark in modern architecture, the Cité Radieuse or Radiant City was opened in 1952. This vertical, concrete construction by Le Corbusier includes shops, social clubs schools and crèches *(see p25)*.

MARSEILLE

Key to Symbols see back flap

0 metres 500
0 yards 500

Aubagne ❷❷

Road map C4. 🏘 44,000. 🚃 🚌
ℹ️ av Antide Boyer (04 42 03 49 98).
🏪 Tue, Thu, Sat & Sun.
www.aubagne.com

Marcel Pagnol's life and work is the main attraction of this unprepossessing market town. It has a tradition of making ceramics and *santons* (*see p48*). The tableaux can be seen in the Petit Monde de Marcel Pagnol display opposite the tourist office.

Just outside the town is the headquarters of the French Foreign Legion, moved here from Algeria in 1962. The headquarters has a **Musée de la Légion Etrangère** with memorabilia on display from a variety of campaigns ranging from Mexico to Indochina.

🏛 **Musée de la Légion Etrangère**
Chemin de la Thuilière. **Tel** 04 42 18 82 41. ⏰ Jun–Sep: Tue–Sun (excl Fri pm); Oct–May: Wed, Sat & Sun. ♿ restricted.

Les Calanques ❷❸

Road map C4. 🚂 Marseille. 🚌 Marseille, Cassis. 🚉 Cassis. ⛴ Cassis, Marseille. ℹ️ Cassis (04 42 01 71 17).

Between Marseille and Cassis the coast is broken up by *calanques* – enticing fjord-like inlets lying between vertical white cliffs. Continuing deep under the blue waters, they offer safe natural harbours and

Poster for Pagnol's film *Angèle*

fascinating aquatic life, with glorious views from the high clifftops (*see also pp30–1*). Their precipitous faces provide a challenge to climbers.

Access to some inlets is by boat. From Cassis, it is possible to walk to the nearest *calanque*, Port-Miou. Beyond it lies Port-Pin, with occasional pine trees and a shady beach, but the most scenic is En-Vau, which has a sandy beach and needle-like rocks rising from the sea. On the western side, the Sormiou and Morgiou inlets can be approached by road.

In 1991, a cave was found with its entrance 100 m (350 ft) beneath the sea at Sormiou. It is decorated with pictures of prehistoric animals resembling the ancient cave paintings at Lascaux in the Dordogne.

Bear in mind when visiting the area that the main car parks serving Les Calanques beaches are notorious for theft.

MARCEL PAGNOL

A plaque at No. 16 cours Barthélemy in Aubagne marks the birthplace of Pagnol, Provençal writer and film-maker. Born in 1895, his holidays were spent in the village of La Treille. His insights into rural Provence enriched tales such as *Jean de Florette* and *Manon des Sources*. The Office de Tourisme has a Circuit Marcel Pagnol, with routes and walks which take in La Treille and other sites of Pagnol's inspiration.

Cassis ❷❹

Road map C4. 🏘 8,000. 🚃 🚌
ℹ️ Le Port (04 42 01 71 17).
🏪 Wed & Fri.

A favourite summer resort of such artists as Derain, Dufy and Matisse, Cassis is a lovely little port, tucked into limestone hills. The Romans liked it, too, and built villas here, and when Marseille prospered in the 17th century a number of mansions were erected. It was also a busy, prosperous fishing centre in the 19th century, and is still known for its excellent seafood. The local delicacy is fresh sea urchins, enjoyed with a glass of Cassis' reputed AOC white wine.

There is a charming **Musée Municipal Méditerranéen**, with items dating back to the Greeks, some rescued from the seabed. It also shows Cassis to have been a substantial trading port up till World War II, when the Germans effectively demolished its fleet. There are paintings by Félix Ziem (*see p26*) and by other early 20th-century artists who were equally drawn to Cassis, like Winston Churchill, who learnt to paint here.

Apart from Les Calanques, there are three good beaches, notably the Plage de la Grande Mer. Between Cassis and La Ciotat are the red cliffs of Cap Canaille, with a 4-hour walk along the Route des Crêtes.

🏛 **Musée Municipal Méditerranéen**
Rue X-d'Authier. **Tel** 04 42 01 88 66. ⏰ Wed–Sat. ● public hols.

En-Vau, the most beautiful of Les Calanques, along the coast from Cassis

VAUCLUSE

*V*aucluse is a land of vines and lavender, truffles and melons,
which many know about through the books of the English ex-
patriate Peter Mayle, depicting village life in the Luberon, an
idyllic countryside where Picasso spent his last years. Roussillon, set
among ochre quarries, also became the topic of a book, when American
sociologist LaurenceWylie experienced village life there in the 1950s.

The jewel of Vaucluse is the fortified riverside city of Avignon, home to the popes during their "Babylonian exile" from 1309–77, and now host to one of the great music and theatre festivals of France. The popes' castle at Châteauneuf-du-Pape is now a ruin, but well worth a visit for the stupendous wines it produces. The Côtes-du-Rhône region is justly renowned, and its vineyards spread as far northeast as the slopes of the towering giant of Provence, Mont Ventoux.

The Roman legacy in Vaucluse is also remarkable. It is glimpsed in the great theatre and triumphal arch in Orange, and in the ruins of Vaison-la-Romaine which were not built over by successive civilizations. Carpentras was also a Roman town, but its claim to fame is its possession of France's oldest synagogue. The story of the Jews, who were given papal protection in Vaucluse, is one of many religious histories which can be traced through the region. Another is the Baron of Oppède's brutal crusade against the Vaudois heretics in 1545, when many villages were destroyed.

Near Oppède, at Lacoste, a path leads to the château of France's notorious libertine Marquis de Sade. Perhaps a more elevated writer was Petrarch, who lived in Fontaine-de-Vaucluse, where the Sorgue river emerges from a mysterious source.

Façade of vine-covered house at Le Bastidon, near the Luberon

◁ Fountain in village square, Châteauneuf-du-Pape

Exploring Vaucluse

Vaucluse, which takes its name from the Latin *vallis clausa* (closed valley), covers 3,540 sq km (2,200 sq miles). It is bordered by the Rhône on the west, the Durance in the south, and the foothills of the Alps to the east, and has a series of highland chains, dominated by the serene Mont Ventoux *(see p160)*. The extraordinary Dentelles pinnacles are in the west and to the south is the Vaucluse Plateau, where the river Sorgue flows in the beautiful and dramatic setting of Fontaine-de-Vaucluse.

SIGHTS AT A GLANCE

The roofs and terraces of Gordes, crowned by the church and castle

KEY

▬▬	Motorway
▬▬	Major road
▬	Secondary road
▪▪▪	Minor road
▬	Scenic route
～	Main railway
▬	Minor railway
▬▬	Regional border

Night view across the Rhône of Avignon's famous bridge and Palais des Papes

GETTING AROUND

The main highways, the A7 Autoroute du Soleil and its accompanying toll-free national road, the N7, travel down the Rhône valley to the west of the region. The main railway line follows these roads, stopping at the principal towns, and the TGV halts at Avignon. The other railway lines across Vaucluse are used for freight, so you may need to take a bus from Avignon to such places as Vaison-la-Romaine, Carpentras and Orange. Boat trips are organized on the Rhône at Avignon.

MONT VENTOUX

alaucène D974 **4**

Bédoin

D164

D974

Mormoiron D217 Sault-de-Vaucluse

zan D942

Nesques St Jean-de-Sault D943 *Plateau de Saint Christal*

Venasques D30

AUCLUSE

NTAINE-DE-UCLUSE D4 St Saturnin-lès-Apt

9 ABBAYE DE SÉNANQUE

des **13** GORDES D943

ries

Coustellet **14** ROUSSILLON

lon N100 APT **17**

Ménerbes Saignon

Lacoste N100

Bonnieux *Grand* *Luberon*

16 D943 *Mourre Nègre* *1125m*

ETIT LUBERON *Parc Naturel* D956 Digne-les-Bains

Régional

Lourmarin *de Luberon* Grambois

CADENET **18** **19** ANSOUIS A51

D973 **21** LA TOUR D'AIGUES

Durance D973

20 PERTUIS N96

0 kilometres 10 A51

0 miles 10 *Aix-en-Provence*

The Belvédère Pasteur garden in Bollène

Bollène ❶

Road map B2. 🏛 *14,500.* 🅿
🅿 ℹ *pl Reynaud de la Gardette
(04 90 40 51 44).* 🛒 *Mon.*

Despite being spread along the A7 autoroute, Bollène is pleasant, with airy boulevards and walks beside the river Lez, where there is a camping site. The narrow streets of the old quarter lead to the 11th-century **Collégiale St-Martin**, with its timber saddleback roof and Renaissance doorway. Bollène became famous in 1882, when Louis Pasteur stayed here and developed innoculation against swine fever. The **Belvédère Pasteur** garden above the town has views over the Rhône valley to the Cévennes, the Bollène hydroelectric power station and Tricastin nuclear power plant. The town hosts a world music festival during the last two weeks of July.

Just north of Bollène is the ghost village of Barri. Its troglodyte houses, some still in use at the end of the last century, proved handy hiding places in World War II.

Vaison-la-Romaine ❷

Road map B2. 🏛 *5,900.* 🚉 ℹ *pl du Chanoine Sautel (04 90 36 02 11).* 🛒 *Tue.* **www**.*vaison-la-romaine.com*

The pavement cafés in this attractive stone-and-red-roof town on the river Ouvèze are among Provence's most chic. The modern town sits beside the Roman town, opposite the hilltop Haute-Ville on the other side of the river. Vaison is a smart address for Parisians' second homes and, judging by the opulent remains left by the Romans, it has long been sought after. The Romans lived with the native Celtic Vocontii and the population was around 10,000. Two sites have been excavated, divided by the avenue Général-de-Gaulle. The upper site, known as the Puymin Quarter, has a Roman theatre, still used for Vaison's summer festival in July, centred on dance. Its stage is cut out of rock, and the theatre seats up to 4,000. Many Roman remains come from the villa of a wealthy family, the House of the Messii, and an elegant,

Mosaic in the museum at Vaison-la-Romaine

colonnaded public building, Pompey's Portico. The site is dotted with copies of original statues that are now kept in the **Musée Théo Desplans**, and include a powerful nude of Hadrian and his well-draped empress, Sabina. Many statues were designed to have their heads replaced whenever there was a change of local officials. Other remains include a communal six-seater latrine and a 3rd-century silver bust which once stood in the hall of a patrician's house in La Villasse, the district on the other side of the avenue Général-de-Gaulle.

The Haute-Ville, which artists and craftspeople helped to repopulate, is reached by means of a Roman bridge, a single 56-ft (17-m) span used for more than 2,000 years until recent devastating floods necessitated huge repairs. Entrance is via a 14th-century fortified gate. The Romanesque church, built as a **cathedral**, has 7th-century columns in the apse, and a 12th-century cloister. A walk to the summit will reveal the ruined castle the victorious Counts of Toulouse built here in 1160.

> 🏛 **Roman City**
> Fouilles de Puymin and Musée Théo Desplans, pl du Chanoine Sautel.
> **Tel** *04 90 36 02 11.* ⬤ *daily.* ⬤ *1 Jan, 25 Dec.* 🎫 🛈 🚻 👶 📷

Grounds of Roman house with 3rd-century silver bust, Vaison-la-Romaine

A Tour of the Dentelles ❸

Dentelle means "lace", and the Dentelles de
Montmirail is the name of the 15-km
(9-mile) range of hills which form a lacework
of delicate peaks. Not as high or rugged as
they initially seem, the Dentelles have good
paths and offer some of the most accessible,
enjoyable mountain walks in Provence. The
paths are bright with broom and flanked by
pines, oaks and wild almond trees. When
you have had your fill of the stunning scenery,
enjoy fine Côtes-du-Rhône wines and delicious
goat's cheese produced in the picturesque
villages tucked into the folds of the Dentelles.

Muscat grapes outside Beaumes-de-Venise

Gigondas vineyard

Vaison-la-Romaine ①
A chic town, favoured by
wealthy Parisians, Vaison
is built on separate Roman
and medieval sites. Among
its many attractions are
the cathedral with its 6th-
century sarcophagus of
healer St Quenin, and a
Romanesque chapel.

Gigondas ⑥
The local red wine
is highly regarded
and its producers
include the master-
chef Roux brothers.
The Counts of
Orange built the
14th-century
château.

Malaucène ②
This former Huguenot stronghold has a clock tower, originally
built as a watchtower during the
Wars of Religion (see pp46–7).

Le Barroux ③
Surrounded by olive
and apricot trees,
this tiny village
is overlooked by
a 12th-century
château, once a
stronghold of the lords
of Baux. It has fine views.

Vacqueyras ⑤
The home of the famous
troubadour, Raimbaud, who
died on a Crusade, this
village has a church with a
6th-century baptistry.

Beaumes-de-Venise ④
This is a town of many
restaurants, and the home of
Muscat, the town's famous
fortified sweet white dessert
wine, which can be enjoyed
with lunch or dinner.

KEY
▬▬▬ Tour route
═══ Other roads

0 kilometres 2
0 miles 2

TIPS FOR DRIVERS

Tour length: 50 km (30 miles).
Stopping off points: The hilltop
village of Crestet; Lafare, a hamlet
leading to the 627-m (2057-ft)
Rocher du Turc; and Montmirail,
a 19th-century spa resort visited
by Mistral. (See also pp250–51.)

Mont Ventoux ④

✈ Avignon. 🚶 2,600. 🚌 Orange,
Bedoin. ℹ Espace Marie-Louis
Gravier, Bedoin (04 90 65 63 95).

The "Giant of Provence" is
the dominant feature west of
the Alps, a limestone massif
which reaches 1,912m (6,242
ft). It is easy to reach the car
park at the top, unless there is
deep snow, which can last
until April. The snowline starts
at 1,300 m (4,265 ft), but the
limestone scree of its summit
forms a year-round white cap.

Until 1973 there was a motor
race on the south side of Mont
Ventoux, to the top: speeds
reached up to 145 km/h (90
mph). A car rally takes place
in Bedoin in June. The roads
have gradually improved and
the worst hairpins are now
ironed out, but the mountain
roads are often included as a
gruelling stage on the Tour de
France. Britain's cyclist Tommy
Simpson suffered a fatal heart
attack here in 1967.

It takes around five hours to
walk to the summit of Mont
Ventoux. Petrarch (see p45)
made the first recorded journey
from Malaucène on one May
dawn in 1336. As there were
no roads then, it took him a
great deal longer.

The mountain is often windy
and its name comes from the
French word (vent) for wind.

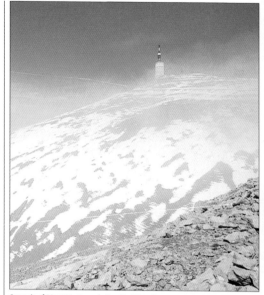

Summit of Mont Ventoux during the Mistral season

Engraving of motor rally car
ascending Mont Ventoux (1904)

When the northerly Mistral
blows, it can almost lift you out
of your boots. But the winds
dry the moisture in the sky,
painting it a deep blue colour
and leaving behind in-
credibly clear vistas.

There are three
starting points for
a walking tour of
the mountain:
Malaucène, on
the north slopes,
Bedoin to the
south and Sault
to the east. An-
other direct route for
hikers is from Brantes
on the northeast side, up the
Toulourenc valley. The first
two towns both have tourist
offices which organize guided
hikes to see the sun rise at the
summit. The 21-km (13-mile)
road from Malaucène passes

Monument to cycling hero
Tommy Simpson

the 12th-century Chapelle
Notre-Dame-du-Groseau and
the Source Vauclusienne, a
deep pool tapped for an aqueduct by the Romans. The
ski centre at Mt Serein is
based 5 km (3 miles)
from the summit.
A viewing table
at the peak helps
to discern the
Cévennes, the
Luberon and
Ste-Victoire.
Descending via
Bedoin, the
road passes the Col
des Tempêtes, known
for its stormy weather. The ski
centre of Le Chalet-Reynard is
at the junction leading to Sault
and les Gorges de la Nesque,
and St-Estève, once notorious
for racing car accidents, has
fine views over the Vaucluse.

PROVENCAL FLOWERS

Because the temperature on
Mont Ventoux drops between
the foot and the summit by
around 11˚ C (20˚ F), the vegetation alters from the lavender
and peach orchards of the plain
via the oak, beech and conifer
woodlands to the arctic flowers
towards the summit. June is the
best month for flowers.

Early purple orchid
Orchis mascula

Alpine poppy
Papaver rhaeticum

Trumpet gentian
Gentiana clusii

For hotels and restaurants in this region see pp202–203 and pp216–217

Orange ❺

Road map 2B. 🚶 28,000. 🚃 🚌
🛈 5 cours Aristide Briand (04 90 34
70 88). 🚢 Thu. www.provence-
orange.com

This historical town contains
two of the finest Roman monuments in Europe: The
Théâtre Antique d'Orange is
known for its world-famous
concerts (see pp162–3). The
Arc de Triomphe celebrates
Julius Caesar's conquest of the
Gauls and victory over the
Greek fleet. Orange is also
the centre for the Côtes-du-
Rhône vineyards and produce
such as olives, honey and
truffles. Around the 17th-
century Hôtel de Ville, streets
open on to peaceful, shady
squares with café terraces.

Side-chapel altar in the Ancienne
Cathédrale Notre-Dame, Orange

Roman Orange
When the first Roman army
attempted to conquer Gaul, it
was defeated near Orange with
a loss of 100,000 men in 105
BC. When it came back three
years later and triumphed, one
of the first monuments built to
show supremacy was the 22-m
(72-ft) Arc de Triomphe on the
via Agrippa between Arles and
Lyons, today cast to one side.

The Old Town
Old Orange is centred around
the 17th-century town hall and
**Ancienne Cathédrale Notre-
Dame**, with its crumbling
Romanesque portal, damaged
in the Wars of Religion (see
pp46–7). The theatre's wall
dominates the place des
Frères-Mounet. Louis XIV
described it as "the greatest
wall in my kingdom". There is

an excellent view of the
theatre, the city of Orange
and the Rhône plain from
Colline St-Eutrope. This is the
site of the remains of the
castle of the princes of Orange,
who gave the Dutch royal
family its title, the House of
Orange, through marriage.
The family also lent their
name to states and cities
around the world.

🏛 Arc de Triomphe
Av de l'Arc de Triomphe.
The monument has excellent
decorations devoted to war
and maritime themes. There is
a modernistic quality, particularly visible in the trophies
above the side arches. On the
east face, Gallic prisoners,
naked and in chains, broad-
cast to the world who was in
charge. Anchors and ropes
showed maritime superiority.
    When Maurice of Nassau
fortified the town in 1622 by
using Roman buildings as
quarries, the arch escaped this
fate by being incorporated into
the defensive walls as a keep.

🏛 Musée Municipal
Rue Madeleine Roch. **Tel** 04 90 51
17 60. ⬜ daily.
The exhibits found in the
courtyard and ground floor
reflect the history of Orange.
They include more than 400
marble fragments which, when
assembled, proved to be plans
of the area, based on three

Stone carving of a centaur in the
Musée Municipal, Orange

surveys dating from AD 77,
and extending from Bollène
to Auzon. Also in the museum
are portraits of members of the
Royal House of Orange and
paintings by the British artist,
Sir Frank Brangwyn (1867–
1956). One room demonstrates
how printed fabrics were made
in 18th-century Orange.

🏛 Maison J-H Fabre
Harmas de J-H Fabre.
Tel 04 90 70 00 44. ⬜ Wed–Mon.
🈚
At Sérignan-du-Comtat, 8 km
(5 miles) northeast of Orange
is L'Harmas, the estate of the
entomologist and poet Jean-
Henri Fabre (1823–1915). His
superb collection of insects
and fungi, and the glorious
surrounding botanical garden,
attract visitors from all over
the world.

Arc de Triomphe monument, representing Julius Caesar's conquests

Théâtre Antique d'Orange

Orange's Roman theatre is one of the best preserved of the entire Roman empire in Europe. It was constructed at the beginning of the Christian era against the natural height of the Colline-St-Eutrope. Its stage doors were hollow so that actors could stand in front and amplify their voices; today other acoustic touches make it ideal for concerts. In Roman times the theatre was also used for meetings and lectures. The *cavea*, or tiered semicircle, held up to 7,000 spectators, seated according to their social status. From the 16th to 19th centuries, the theatre was filled with squalid housing, traces of which can still be seen.

Awning Supports
Still visible on the exterior walls are corbels which held the huge velum-*bearing masts.*

ROMAN THEATRE

This reconstruction shows the theatre as it would have looked in Roman times. Today it owes its reputation to the exeptional state of the stage wall.

Main entrance

A canvas awning, known as a *velum*, protected the theatre-goers from sun or rain.

Night Concerts
Cultural events such as Les Chorégies d'Orange, *a festival of opera, drama and ballet, once frequented by Sarah Bernhardt, have been held here since 1869 (see p33). The theatre is also a popular rock concert venue.*

The stage curtain (*aulaeum*) was lowered to reveal the stage, rather than raised. It was operated by machinery concealed beneath the floor of the stage.

The Great Wall
Built of red limestone, this massive construction is 103 m (338 ft) long, 36 m (117 ft) high and over 1.8 m (5 ft) thick.

Emperor Augustus

This 3.5-m (11-ft) statue, with a hand raised in greeting, dominates the stage at the third level. At its base kneels a figure in breeches, possibly a defeated enemy. Other statues have been destroyed, but this copy was returned to the niche in 1951.

Side rooms, or *parascaenia*, were where actors could rest, and props be stored, when not required on stage.

Stage Wall

The inner face of the stage wall (Frons Scaenae) still bears fragments of marble friezes and mosaics. A frieze of centaurs framed the royal doorway in the centre.

Each strip of *velum* awning could be rolled individually to suit the direction of the sunlight.

Marble Columns

The stage wall had three levels, the two upper levels with 76 marble columns, of which only two remain. The wall's many surfaces broke up sound waves, so that the actors could speak without their voices having an echo.

Winched capstans held and tightened the ropes supporting the *velum*.

The Great Roman Temple

From 1925–37, excavations took place to the west of the theatre, where 22 houses had been pulled down. They unearthed a vast semicircle and ruins of a temple. Together with the theatre, they would have formed an Augusteum, an architectural unit devoted to the worship of Roman emperors.

Romanesque church at Caderousse

Caderousse ●

Road map B2. ⚌ 2,500. ⓘ La Mairie (04 90 51 90 69). ⓐ Tue.

This bankside village lies at a point where Hannibal is said to have crossed the river Rhône with his elephants on his way to Rome in 218 BC. For centuries, Caderousse has stoically endured the floods of the River Rhône, and plaques on the town hall record the high levels of floodwater. By 1856, the villagers had had enough, and erected a dyke which is still in place today. Its four entry points can close if floods should threaten again.

Caderousse has a Romanesque church, **St-Michel**, to which the Flamboyant Gothic chapel of St-Claude was added during the 16th century.

Châteauneuf-du-Pape ●

Road map B3. ⚌ 2,100. ⓘ Sorgues, then taxi. ⓘ place du Portail (04 90 83 71 08). ⓐ Fri.

The best-known of the Côtes-du-Rhône wine labels takes its name from an unassuming yellowish village on a small hill, given over to cellars and restaurants selling the products of the local growers entitled to the *appellation contrôlée*. The **Musée du Vin** traces the history and current state of the local viniculture.

At the top of the village are the ruins of the **Château des Papes**, mostly burned down in the 16th-century Wars of Religion. From the remaining walls there is a superb view of Avignon and the vineyard-lined clay fields where smooth stones deposited by the Rhône reflect the sun's heat onto 13 varieties of grapes. The château

was built in 1317 by John XXII, an Avignon pope who planted the first vineyards, but it took some 400 years for the wine's reputation to spread. Today, there are 350 Châteauneuf-du-Pape domaines. The nearby town of Pernes-les-Fontaines is known for its 40 fountains, in particular the 18th-century Fontaine du Cormoran. Until 1914, each of the fountains had an individual keeper.

🏛 **Musée du Vin**
Rte d'Avignon, Châteauneuf-du-Pape. **Tel** 04 90 83 70 07. ◯ daily. ● 1 Jan, 1 May, 25 Dec. ⓑ restricted. ◻

Carpentras ●

Road map B3. ⚌ 27,000. ⌸ ⓘ Hôtel-Dieu, place Aristide Briand (04 90 63 00 78). ⓐ Fri.

As the capital of the Comtat Venaissin, this market town is in the centre of the Côtes-du-Ventoux wine region. It has a reputation for truffles and *berlingots*, stripy caramel sweets.

Boulevards encircle the old town, but the Porte d'Orange is the only surviving part of the medieval ramparts. In the Middle Ages, the town had a large Jewish community, and their 14th-century **synagogue** is the oldest in France, now used by some 100 families. While not openly persecuted under papal rule, many Jews changed faith and entered the **Cathédrale-St-Siffrein** by its 15th-century south door, the *Porte Juive*. The cathedral is in the centre of the old town, near a smaller version of

Orange's Arc de Triomphe. In it are Provençal paintings and statues by local sculptor Jacques Bernus (1650–1728). The *Hôtel-Dieu* has a fine 18th-century pharmacy, and there are regional costumes in the **Musée Comtadin-Duplessis**.

✡ **Synagogue**
Pl Maurice Charretier. **Tel** 04 90 63 39 97. ◯ Mon–Fri. ● Jewish feast days.

⛪ **Cathédral St-Siffrein**
Pl de Gaulle. ⓑ ● Mon, Sun pm.

🏛 **Musée Comtadin-Duplessis**
234 bd Albin-Durand. **Tel** 04 90 63 04 92. ◯ Wed–Mon. ● public hols. ⓖ

Pharmacy in the 18th-century *Hôtel-Dieu* at Carpentras

Abbaye de Sénanque ●

Road map C3. **Tel** 04 90 72 05 72. ◯ Feb–mid-Nov: Mon–Sat & Sun pm; mid-Nov–Jan: pms only, by guided tour. ⓖ ◻ ⓑ www.senanque.fr

The beautifully sited Abbaye de Sénanque, surrounded by a tranquil sea of lavender, is best approached from Gordes (see p169). Its monks are often to be seen in the fields.

Like the other abbeys that make up the Cistercian triumvirate in Provence (see p43), Sénanque is harmonious and

Châteauneuf-du-Pape vineyards

unadorned. It was founded in 1148 by an abbott and 12 monks, and the building of the serene north-facing abbey church started 12 years later.

Some roofs of the building are still tiled with limestone slates called *lauzes*, also used for making traditional stone dwellings known as bories *(see p169)*. The abbey's simply designed interior has stone walls, plain windows and a barrel-vaulted ceiling.

Sénanque reached its zenith in the early 13th century, when the abbey owned several local farms. But new riches brought corruption in the 14th century, and by the 17th century, only two monks remained. In 1854 it was restored and housed Cistercian monks, some of whom remained there from 1926 to 1969. Then a wealthy industrialist formed the *Association des Amis de Sénanque* to restore the abbey. The monks have been living there since 1988, and some of their home produce is for sale.

Fontaine-de-Vaucluse, where the Sorgue river begins

Abbaye de Sénanque with lavender

Fontaine-de-Vaucluse ❿

Road map B3. 🚶 580. 🚌 *Avignon.* ℹ️ *chemin de la Fontaine (04 90 20 32 22).*

The source of the Sorgue river is one of the natural wonders of Provence. It begins underground, with tributaries that drain the Vaucluse plateau, an area of around 2,000 sq km (800 sq miles). In the closed valley above the town, water erupts from an unfathomable depth to develop into a fully fledged river. Beside the river is the **Moulin à Papier Vallis Clausa**, which produces handmade paper using the same method as in the 15th century. It now sells maps, prints and lampshades.

The underground museum, the **Eco-Musée du Gouffre**, features a speleologist's findings over 30 years of exploring Sorgue's dams, caves and waterfalls. The **Musée d'Histoire 1939–1945**, traces the fate of the Resistance during WWII and daily life under Occupation. The **Musée Pétrarque** was the house where the poet lived for 16 years, and wrote of his unrequited love for Laura of Avignon.

🏭 **Moulin à Papier Vallis Clausa**
Chemin du Gouffre. **Tel** *04 90 20 34 14.* ◻ *daily.* ⬤ *1 Jan, 25 Dec.* ♿

🏛 **Eco-Musée du Gouffre (Musée de Spéléologie)**
Chemin du Gouffre. **Tel** *04 90 20 34 13.* ◻ *Feb–15 Nov: daily.* 📷 ♿ 🚻 ✒️

🏛 **Musée d'Histoire 1939–45**
Chemin de la Fontaine. **Tel** *04 90 20 24 00.* ◻ *Apr–Oct: Wed–Mon; Nov–Dec & Mar: Sat–Sun.* ⬤ *Jan, Feb, 1 May, 25 Dec.* 📷 ♿

🏛 **Musée Pétrarque**
Rive gauche de la Sorgue. **Tel** *04 90 20 37 20.* ◻ *Apr–Oct: Wed–Mon.* 📷

L'Isle-sur-la-Sorgue ⓫

Road map B3. 🚶 18,000. 🚌 🚉 ℹ️ *pl de la Liberté (04 90 38 04 78).* 🛒 *Thu & Sun (antiques and flea).*

This attractive town is a major haunt for antique hunters at weekends. It lies on the river Sorgue which once powered 70 watermills that pressed grain and oil. Today, nine idle wheels remain. The town's 17th-century **Notre-Dame-des-Anges** is ornate inside. The tourist office is in an 18th-century granary, and the Hôpital, also 18th century, has a collection of Moustiers pottery jars in its pharmacy.

Water wheel near place Gambetta, l'Isle-sur-la-Sorgue

Street-by-Street: Avignon ⑫

St Jerome, Petit Palais

Bordered to the north and west by the Rhône, the medieval city of Avignon is the chief city of Vaucluse and gateway to Provence. Its walls cover nearly 4.5 km (3 miles) and are punctuated by 39 towers and seven gates. Within the walls thrives a culturally rich city with its own opera house, university, several foreign language schools and numerous theatre companies. The streets and squares are often filled with buskers, and the Avignon festival in July, which includes theatre, mime and cabaret, has now become a major international event.

Chapelle St-Nicolas, named after the patron saint of bargemen, is a 16th-century building on a 13th-century base. Entrance is via Tour du Châtelet.

Porte du Rhône

★ Pont St-Bénézet
Begun in 1177 by shepherd boy Bénézet, this bridge is the subject of the famous rhyme Sur le Pont d'Avignon.

Conservatoire de Musique
The façade of this former mint, the Hôtel des Monnaies (1619), bears the arms of Cardinal Borghese.

RUE FER
RUE DE LIMAS
RUE GRANDE FUSTERIE
RUE DES GROTTES
RUE DE LA BALANCE
RUE ST-ETIENNE
RUE PETITE FUSTERIE
RUE RACINE
PLACE DE L'HORLOGE

Place de l'Horloge
The main square was laid out in the 15th century and is named after the Gothic clock tower above the town hall. Many of today's buildings date from the 19th century.

KEY

– – – Suggested route

0 metres   100
0 yards   100

Musée du Petit Palais
*The former episcopal offices house
a museum of medieval and
Renaissance Italian paintings
and French works by the
Avignon School, including
this 1457 Vierge de Pitié.*

VISITORS' CHECKLIST

Road map B3. 🏛 90,000. ✈
8 km (5 miles) Avignon-Caumont.
🚉 🚍 bvd St-Roch. ℹ 41
cours Jean-Jaurès. (04 32 74 32
74). 🛒 Tue–Sun. 🎭 Le Festival
d'Avignon (see p33).
www.ot-avignon.fr

Rocher des Doms
*These hillside gardens behind
Notre-Dame-des-Doms are the
site of earliest settlement.*

★ Palais des Papes
*Popes ruling in the 14th century built this
grand, fortress-like palace (see pp44–5). The
Chambre du Pape, here, has exquisite tiles.*

Eglise St-Pierre
*This church was built during
the 14th to early 16th centuries. The doors on its west
façade were carved in 1551
by Antoine Valard. Inside is
a fine 15th-century pulpit.*

STAR SIGHTS

★ Palais des Papes

★ Pont St-Bénézet

Exploring Avignon

Massive ramparts enclose one of the most fascinating towns in southern France. A quick stroll reveals *trompe l'oeil* windows and mansions such as King René's house in the rue du Roi-René. This street leads to the rue des Teinturiers, named after local dyers and textile-makers, where a bridge for pedestrians crosses the river Sorgue to the 16th-century Chapelle des Pénitents Gris.

Palais des Papes in Avignon glimpsed across the river Rhône

♣ Palais des Papes
Pl du Palais. **Tel** 04 90 27 50 00.
◯ *daily (times vary).* 🖼 🏛 🖼 🖼 🖼
These buildings *(see pp44–5)* give an idea of the grand life under the seven French popes who built a miniature Vatican during their rule here, lasting from 1309–77. They owned their own mint, baked a vast number of loaves every day, and fortified themselves against the French.

Entrance is by means of the Porte des Champeaux, beneath the twin pencil-shaped turrets of the flamboyant Palais Neuf (1342–52), built by Clement VI, which extends south from the solid Palais Vieux (1334–42) of Benoit XII. In the new palace, the main courtyard, La Cour d'Honneur, is the grand central setting for the summer festival *(see p229)*. La Chambre du Pape in the Tour des Anges opposite the entrance has exquisite tiles, and there are fine 14th-century deer-hunting scenes painted by Matteo Giovanetti and others in the adjoining Chambre du Cerf.

The Palais Vieux has two square defence towers. The

Bird tile in the Chambre du Pape

larger rooms around it include the 45-m (148-ft) banqueting hall, Le Grand Tinel, and La Salle du Consistoire, centre of courtly activity, where pictures of all the popes are displayed. The chapel beside it has exquisite frescoes painted by Giovanetti between 1346 and 1348.

⛪ Cathédrale Notre-Dame-des-Doms
Pl du Palais. **Tel** 04 90 86 81 01. ◯ *Apr–Nov: daily.*
This building beside the Palais des Papes was begun in the 12th century. Since then it has been damaged and rebuilt several times. A gilded Madonna was added on to the tower as recently as the 19th century, and the original 6th-century altar is now located in the Chapelle St-Roch, where two popes are entombed.

🏛 Musée du Petit Palais
Pl du Palais. **Tel** 04 90 86 44 58.
◯ *Wed–Mon.* ● *1 Jan, 1 May, 14 Jul, 1 Nov, 25 Dec.* 🖼 🏛
Set around an arcaded courtyard, the "little palace", built in 1318, was modified in 1474 to suit Michelangelo's patron and nemesis, Cardinal Rovere,

later Pope Julius II. It became a museum in 1958, and houses Avignon's medieval collection, which includes works by Simone Martini and Botticelli, as well as frescoes and sculptures from the Avignon School, and many French and Italian religious paintings.

🏛 Musée Lapidaire
27 rue de la République. **Tel** 04 90 86 33 84. ◯ *Wed–Mon.* ● *1 Jan, 1 May, 25 Dec.* 🖼
Once a 17th-century Baroque Jesuit college, the museum has Celtic-Ligurian, Egyptian, Gallic and Roman artifacts, including masks from Vaison-la-Romaine and a 2nd-century Tarasque monster *(see p158)*.

🏛 Musée Calvet
65 rue Joseph Vernet. **Tel** 04 90 86 33 84. ◯ *Wed–Mon.* ● *1 Jan, 1 May, 25 Dec.* 🖼 🖼 *restricted.*
This evocative museum was visited by the French writer Stendhal, who left his inscription behind. Currently undergoing enlargement to permit the permanent display of many of the museum's treasures at present stored in their vaults, the highlight is undoubtedly the 19th–20th century collection, with works by Soutine, Manet, Dufy, Gleizes and Marie Laurencin.

🏛 Fondation Angladon-Dubrujeaud
5 rue Laboureur. **Tel** 04 90 82 29 03. ◯ *Wed–Sun, pm only.* 🖼 🖼
This museum cleverly combines modern technology with the intimacy of a private home for displaying this outstanding private collection of 18th–20th-century works of art.

🏛 Collection Lambert
Hôtel de Caumont, 5 rue Violette. **Tel** 04 90 16 56 20. ◯ *Tue–Sun.* ● *1 May.* 🖼 🖼 🖼 🏛
Avignon's latest 'museum' is in an elegant 18th-century mansion, next to the new School of Art. It has been completely overhauled to house the outstanding collection of contemporary art on loan to the city for 20 years from gallery-owner Yvon Lambert. The collection was started in the 1960s, and represents all the major art movements since then.

Gordes ❸

Road map C3. 🏛 *2,000.* 🛈 *Le Château (04 90 72 02 75).* 🚍 *Tue.* **www**.gordes-village.com

Expensive restaurants and hotels provide a clue to the popularity of this hilltop village, which spills down in terraces from a Renaissance château and the church of St-Firmin. Its impressive position is the main attraction, although its vaulted, arcaded medieval lanes are also alluring. The village has been popular with artists ever since the academic Cubist painter André Lhote began visiting in 1938.

The **Château de Gordes** was built in the 16th century on the site of a 12th-century fortress. One of the château's best features is an ornate 16th-century fireplace in the great hall on the first floor, decorated with shells, flowers and pilasters. In the entrance there is an attractive Renaissance door. The building was rented and restored by the Hungarian-born Op Art painter Victor Vasarely (1908–97), and once housed a museum of his abstract works.

The newly-opened 17th-century Caves du Palais St-Firmin are worth visiting, if only to see the impressive old stone olive press.

Just outside Gordes is the **Village des Bories** (*see box*), now a museum of rural life.

⛪ **Château de Gordes**
Tel 04 90 72 02 75. ⭘ *daily.* ● *1 Jan, 25 Dec.* 📷

⛪ **Village des Bories**
Rte de Cavaillon. *Tel* 04 90 72 03 48. ⭘ *daily.* ● *1 Jan, 25 Dec.* 📷 ♿ *restr.*

BORIES

The ancient dwellings known as *bories* were domed drystone buildings made from *lauzes* (limestone slabs), with walls up to 1.5 m (4 ft) thick. They dated from 2,000 BC and were regularly rebuilt, using ancient methods, until the last century when they were abandoned. Around 3,000 bories are still standing, many in fields where they were used for shelter or storing implements. Twenty have been restored in the Village des Bories, outside Gordes.

Roussillon ❹

Road map C3. 🏛 *1,200.* 🛈 *pl de la Poste (04 90 05 60 25).* 🚍 *Thu.*

The deep ochres used in the construction of this hilltop community are stunning. No other village looks so warm and rich, so harmonious and inviting. Its hues come from at least 17 shades of ochre discovered in and around the village, notably in the dramatic former quarries along the Sentier des Ochres. The quarries are to the east of the village, a 45-minute round trip from the information office. The Conservatoire des Ochres et Pigment Appliqués in the old factory (*open daily in summer*), is worth visiting. It displays a huge collection of natural pigments, and runs day courses on the subject.

A superb panorama to the north can be seen from the Castrum, the viewing table beside the church, above the tables with umbrellas in the main square.

Before its recent housing boom, Roussillon was a typical Provençal backwater. During the early 1950s, an American sociologist, Laurence Wylie, moved to Roussillon, spent a year there with his family and wrote a book about village life, *Un Village du Vaucluse*. He concluded that Roussillon was a solidly "hard-working, productive community" for all its feuds and tensions. Playwright Samuel Beckett lived here in WWII, but his impression was much less generous.

The hilltop village of Gordes, spilling down in terraces

Triumphal arch behind Cavaillon

Cavaillon ⑮

Road map B3. 🏘 *25,000.* 🚉 🚌
ℹ️ *pl François Tourel (04 90 71 32 01).*
🗓 *Mon.* **www**.cavaillon-luberon.com

Perhaps the best place to get
your bearings is the viewing
table outside the **Chapelle St-
Jacques** at the top of the town,
which renders the Luberon
range in perspective against
Mont Ventoux and the Alpilles
chain. In closer proximity are
the acres of fruit and vegetable
plots, for Cavaillon is France's
largest market garden, synonymous especially with melons.
Its local market competes with
the one in Apt for renown as
the most important in Vaucluse.

Colline St-Jacques was the
site of the pre-Roman settlement that, under Rome, was
moved down from its heights
and prospered. There is a 1st-
century Roman arch in place
Duclos nearby. Roman finds
have been collected in the
Musée Archéologique
in the Grand Rue, which leads
north from the church, a former cathedral dedicated to
its 6th-century bishop, Saint
Véran. The synagogue in rue
Hébraïque dates from 1772,
although there has been one
on this site ever since the 14th
century. A small museum, the
Musée Juif Comtadin, commemorates its history.

🏛 **Musée Archéologique**
Hôtel Dieu, Porte d'Avignon.
Tel *04 90 76 00 34.* 🗓 *Jun–Oct:
Wed–Mon.* 🖼

🏛 **Musée Juif Comtadin**
Rue Hébraïque. **Tel** *04 90 76 00 34.*
🗓 *Oct–Mar: Mon, Wed–Fri; Apr–
Sep: Wed–Mon.* ⚫ *1 Jan, 1 May,
25 Dec.* 🖼

A Tour of the Petit Luberon ⑯

The Parc Naturel Régional covers 1,200 sq km (463 sq
miles) of a limestone mountain range running east
from Cavaillon towards Manosque in the Alpes-de-
Haute-Provence. It embraces about 50 communities
and a past peppered with such infamous figures as
the Baron of Oppède and the Marquis de Sade. An unspoiled area, it is ideal for walking. Its two main centres
are Apt and Lourmarin. The D943 in the Lourmarin
Coomb valley divides the park: the Grand Luberon
(see p172) is to the east; and to the west is the Petit
Luberon, a land of limestone cliffs, hidden corries and
cedar woods, with most
towns and villages to the
north side of the range.

Oppède-le-Vieux ①
The dominating ruined castle belonged to Jean Maynier, Baron of
Oppède, whose bloody crusade
against the Luberon Vaudois in
1545 destroyed 11 villages.

AVIGNON

CAVAILLON

Cedar Forest Botanical Trail,
Bonnieux

| 0 kilometres | 2 |
| 0 miles | 2 |

KEY

▬▬▬ Tour route

═══ Other roads

LUBERON WILDLIFE

The Parc Naturel Régional is rich
in flora and fauna. The central
massif is wild and exposed on
the north side, sheltered and
more cultivated in the south. A
wide range of habitats exist in
a landscape of white chalk and
red ochre cliffs, cedar forests,
moorlands and river-hewn
gorges. Information is available
from La Maison du Parc in Apt
(see p172) which publishes
suggested walks and tours.

Monkey orchid (Orcis
simia) *is found on the
sunny, chalky grasslands.*

The rugged peaks of the Petit Luberon

Tour length: 40 km (25 miles).
Stopping-off points: Ménerbes
has several cafés, Bonnieux is good
for lunch and the Cedar Forest has
attractive picnic spots. Lourmarin,
where Albert Camus lived and was
buried, is handy for the Petit and
Grand Luberon. All these villages
are small, and quickly fill with
cars, so you may have to walk
some distance, and even climb to
castle heights. (See also pp250–1.)

Ménerbes ②
At the foot of this stronghold of
16th-century Calvinists is the
Musée du Tire-Bouchon, a fascinating collection of corkscrews,
dating from the 17th century.

Bonnieux ④
The Musée de la Boulangerie
gives a history of bread making.
From here the two-hour Cedar
Forest Botanical Trail is a
pleasant, scenic walk.

Lacoste ③
Little remains of the Marquis
de Sade's château. Arrested
for corrupt practices in 1778,
he spent 12 years in prison
writing up his experiences.

D188
②
Abbaye St-Hilaire
D109
③
④
D3
D36
D943

MONTAGNE DU LUBERON

Lourmarin ⑤
The Countess of Agoult, whose family
owned the village château, bore the
composer Franz Liszt (1811-86) three
children: one married Richard Wagner.

⑤

AIX-EN-PROVENCE

Wild boar (Sus scrofa, *known
as* sanglier *in French) is a hunt-
er's prize and a chef's delight.*

Eagle owl (*Bubo bubo, known
as* dugas *in Provençal) is judged
Europe's largest owl.*

Beaver (*Castor fiber, known as*
castor *in French) builds dams
on the Calavon and Durance.*

GRAND LUBERON

This spectacular range of mountains to the east of the Lourmarin Coomb rises as high as 1,125 m (3,690 ft) at Mourre Nègre. The fine view at the summit must be appreciated on foot, and takes several hours from where you leave the car at Auribeau. The area is outstandingly beautiful and ideal to escape from the crowds. The panorama from the top takes in Digne, the Lure mountain and Durance valley, the Apt basin, l'Etang de Berre and Mont Ventoux.

Apt ⑰

Road map C3. 🚗 *11,500*. 🚌
🚆 *Avignon*. 🚶 *20 av Philippe de Girard (04 90 74 03 18)*. 🛒 *Tue & Sat*.

Apt is the northern entry to the Parc Naturel Régional du Luberon *(see pp170–71)*. The Maison du Parc, a restored 17th-century mansion, provides a full introduction to the area, with details of walks, *gîtes d'étapes* and flora and fauna. It also has a **Musée de la Paléontologie**, with fascinating examples of fossils found in the Luberon.

The busy old town of Apt has a square for playing *boules*, fountains and plane trees. Surrounded by cherry orchards, it claims to be the world capital of crystallized fruit. The **Musée de l'Aventure Industrielle** explains how the production of crystallized fruits and earthenware pottery combined with the extraction of ochre to bring prosperity to Apt in the 18th and 19th centuries. The town is also famous for truffles and lavender essence. The Saturday market offers a wide range of Provençal delicacies as well as entertainment, including jazz, barrel organ music and some stand-up comedy. Excursions can be made to the *Colorado de Rustrel*, the best ochre quarry site by the River Dôa, to the northeast.

The medieval **Cathédrale Ste-Anne** lies at the heart of Apt's old town. Legend has it that the veil of St Anne was brought back from Palestine and hidden in the cathedral by Auspice, who is thought to have been Apt's first bishop. Each July her festival is celebrated, with a procession through the town. The Royal Chapel commemorates Anne of Austria. She paid a pilgrimage to Apt to pray for fertility and contributed the funds to finish the chapel, which was finally completed around 1669–70.

Inside the sacristy is the treasury containing the saint's shroud, and an 11th-century Arabic standard from the First Crusade (1096–9). In the apse is a 15th–16th-century window which depicts the tree of Jesse. Not far away is the 17th-century Hôtel d'Albertas.

14th-century priest's embroidery

The items displayed in the **Musée Archéologique** are a treasure trove of prehistoric flints, stone implements, Gallo-Roman carvings, jewellery and mosaics from that period. The second floor shows local ceramics, such as the work of Apt ceramicist Léon Sagy (1865–1939).

🔱 Cathédrale St-Anne
Rue St-Anne. **Tel** 04 90 74 36 60.
🕐 Tue–Sun.

🏛 Musée de la Paléontologie
Maison du Parc, 60 place Jean-Jaurès.
Tel 04 90 04 42 00. 🕐 Mon–Sat.
⬤ Oct–Mar: Sat, public hols. 🖼

🏛 Musée de l'Aventure Industrielle
Pl du Pastal. **Tel** 04 90 74 95 30.
🕐 Wed–Sat. ⬤ public hols. 🖼

🏛 Musée Archéologique
27 rue de l'Amphithéâtre. **Tel** 04 90 74 78 45. 🕐 Jun–Sep: Sun pm–Mon, Wed–Sat; Oct–May: Mon, Wed–Fri pms & Sat. ⬤ public hols. 🖼

Jam label illustrating traditional produce of Apt

For hotels and restaurants in this region see pp202–203 and pp216–217

Cadenet 18

Road map C3. 4,000.
Avignon. 11 pl du Tambour
d'Arcole (04 90 68 38 21). Mon
& Sat (marché paysan, May–Oct).

Tucked underneath the hills in the Durance valley, Cadenet has 11th-century castle ruins and a 14th-century church with a fine square bell tower. Its font is made from a Roman sarcophagus. In the main square, which is used as the *marché paysan* (farmers' market), is a statue of the town's heroic drummer boy, André Estienne, who beat such a raucous tattoo in the battle for Arcole Bridge in 1796 that the enemy thought they could hear gunfire, and retreated.

Drummer boy in
Cadenet town square

Ansouis 19

Road map C3. 1,000. pl du
Château (04 90 09 86 98).
Thu, Sun. www.ansouis.fr

One of the most remarkable things about the Renaissance **Château d'Ansouis** is that it has been owned by the Sabran family since 1160. Theirs is a proven pedigree: in the 13th century, Gersende de Sabran and Raymond Bérenger IV's four daughters became queens of France, England, Romania and Naples respectively. In 1298, Elzéar de Sabran married Delphine de Puy, a descendant of the

Viscount of Marseille. But she had already resolved to become a nun, so agreed to the marriage, but not to its consummation. Both were canonized in 1369. The castle's original keep and two of its four towers are still visible. It has a grand staircase and a guard room with 17th- to 19th-century armour. Its gardens include the Renaissance Garden of Eden, built on the former cemetery. The **Musée Extraordinaire de Georges Mazoyer** has an individual mix of the artist's work, Provençal furniture and a recreated underwater cave, all in 15th-century cellars.

♣ **Château d'Ansouis**
Tel 04 90 09 82 70. for guided
tours Easter–Oct: daily pms only;
Nov–Easter hols: Thu–Mon pms.
Dec–Jan.

🏛 **Musée Extraordinaire de Georges Mazoyer**
Rue du Vieux Moulin. **Tel** 04 90 09
82 64. daily pm only.

Pertuis 20

Road map C3. 18,000.
Le Donjon, pl Mirabeau (04 90 79 15
56). Wed & Sat (marché paysan), Fri.

Once the capital of the Pays d'Aigues, present-day Pertuis is a quiet town, whose rich and fertile surrounding area was gradually taken over by

Aix-en-Provence. Pertuis was the birthplace of the philandering Count of Mirabeau's father, and the 13th-century clock tower is to be found in place Mirabeau.

The **Eglise St-Nicolas**, rebuilt in Gothic style in the 16th century, has a 16th-century triptych and two 17th-century marble statues. To the southwest is the battlemented 14th-century **Tour St Jacques**.

Triumphal arch entrance to La
Tour d'Aigues' Renaissance château

La Tour d'Aigues 21

Road map C3. 3,800. to
Pertuis. Château de la Tour
d'Aigues (04 90 07 50 29). Tue.

Nestling beside the Luberon, and surrounded by vineyards and orchards, this town takes its name from a 10th-century tower. The 16th-century castle completes the triumvirate of Renaissance châteaux in the Luberon (the others are Lourmarin and Ansouis). Built on the foundations of a medieval castle by Baron de Cental, its massive portal is based on the Roman arch at Orange (*see p161*). The castle was damaged in the French Revolution (1789 –94), but has been partially restored. Its cellars house two museums, one on ceramics, the other on local architecture – both tell the region's story.

🏛 **Salle de l'Habitat Rural en Pays d'Aigues et Musée des Faïences et des Céramiques**
Caves du Château, La Tour
d'Aigues. **Tel** 04 90 07 50 33.
daily. Sep–Jun: Tue pm &
Sat–Sun am; 25 Dec, 1 Jan.

Duchess's bedroom in the Château d'Ansouis

ALPES-DE-HAUTE-PROVENCE

*I*n this, the most undiscovered region of Provence, the air is clearer than anywhere else in France, which is why it was the chosen site for France's most important observatory. But the terrain and the weather conditions can be severe. Inaccessibility to areas has restricted development and the traditional, rural way of life is still followed.

Irrigation has helped to improve some corners of this mountainous land. The Valensole plain is now the most important lavender producing area of France. Peaches, apples and pears have been planted in orchards only recently irrigated by the Durance, the region's main river, which has been tamed by dams and a hydro-electric power scheme. These advances have created employment and helped bring prosperity to the region. Another modern development is the Cadarache nuclear research centre, situated just outside Manosque. The town's population has grown rapidly to 20,300 inhabitants, overtaking the region's capital, Digne-les-Bains. Famous for its lavender and healthy living, Digne is a handsome spa town that has attracted visitors for more than a century and now hopes to enhance its appeal through its devotion to sculpture, which fills the streets.

The region's history and architecture have also been greatly influenced by the terrain and climate. Strategically positioned citadels crown mountain towns such as Sisteron, which was won over by Napoleon in 1815, and the frontier town of Entrevaux. The design of towns and buildings has remained practical, in keeping with the harsh winter and strong Mistral winds. Undoubtedly, the beauty of the region is seen in the high lakes and mountains, the glacial valleys and the colourful fields of Alpine flowers.

Bundles of cut lavender drying in fields near the Gorges du Verdon

◁ Olive groves on the hills outside the fortified town of Entrevaux

Exploring Alpes-de-Haute-Provence

This remote and rugged area in the north of Provence covers 6,944 sq km (2,697 sq miles) of mountainous landscape. Its main artery is the Durance river which is dotted with dams, gorges and lakes – a haven for mountaineers and canoeists. One tributary is the Verdon, which runs through the stunning Gorges du Verdon, Europe's answer to the Grand Canyon. The scenery becomes wilder and more rugged in the northeast, with Mont Pelat at the heart of the Parc National du Mercantour. Further south lie the plains of Valensole, which colour the landscape in July when the abundant lavender blossoms.

Fields of lavender on the Valensole plains

SIGHTS AT A GLANCE

KEY

═══	Motorway
───	Major road
┄┄┄	Minor road
───	Scenic route
───	Minor railway
▬▬▬	International border
▬▬▬	Regional border
△	Summit

A quiet Provençal-style bar in the mountain town of Castellane, situated in the picturesque old quarter

0 kilometres   10

0 miles   10

GETTING AROUND

The Durance river provides the point of entry into the region. The A51 autoroute from Aix-en-Provence follows the river to Sisteron and on to La Saulce, just short of Gap. National roads continue to follow the Durance, to Lac de Serre-Ponçon in the north, then east along the Ubaye to Barcelonnette. The the region's capital, Digne-les-Bains, is well-connected by national roads, but otherwise there are only minor roads. The region's railway line also follows the Durance, connecting Sisteron and Manosque with Aix.

The dramatic Rocher de la Baume, just outside the town of Sisteron

Sisteron ❶

Road map D2. 7,500.
Hôtel de Ville, pl de la République
(04 92 61 12 03). Wed & Sat.

Approaching Sisteron from
the north or south, it is easy
to see its strategic importance.
The town calls itself the "gateway to Provence", sitting in a
narrow valley on the left bank
of the Durance river, surrounded by olive groves. It is a
lively town, protected by the
most impressive fortifications
in Provence. However, it has
suffered for its ideal military
position, most recently in heavy
Allied bombardment in 1944.

The **citadelle**, originally built
in the 12th century, dominates
the town and gives superb
views down over the Durance.
These defences, though incom-
plete, are a solid assembly of
keep, dungeon, chapel, towers
and ramparts, and offer a fine
setting for the Nuits de la
Citadelle, the summer festival
of music, theatre and dance.
The cathedral in the main
square, **Notre-Dame des
Pommiers**, is an example of
the Provençal Romanesque

A traditional Provençal farmhouse just outside the village of Seyne

school, dating from 1160. At
its east end, the 17th-century
Chapelle des Visitandines,
houses the new **Musée Terre
et Temps**. To the right of the
church, follow signs to the Old
Town, where small boutiques,
cafés and bars line the narrow
alleyways called *andrônes*.
Rocher de la Baume on the
opposite bank is a popular
practice spot for mountaineers.

♣ **La Citadelle**
04200 Sisteron. **Tel** 04 92 61 27
57. ☐ Apr–11 Nov: daily.

Seyne ❷

Road map D2. 1,200.
place d'Armes (04 92 35 11 00).
Tue & Fri.

The small mountain village of
Seyne dominates the Vallée de
la Blanche, sitting 1,210 m
(3,970 ft) above sea level.
Horses and mules graze in the
nearby fields, and there is a
celebrated annual horse and
mule fair. Beside the main road
is **Notre-Dame de Nazareth**, a
13th-century Romanesque
church with Gothic portals,
sundial and large rose window.
The path by the church leads
up to the **citadelle**, built by
Vauban in 1693, which encloses
the still-standing 12th-century
watchtower. The town is also
a centre for winter sports, with
facilities nearby at St-Jean, Le
Grand Puy and Chabanon.

Barcelonnette ❸

Road map E2. 3,500.
place Frédéric Mistral (04 92 81
04 71). Wed & Sat.

In the remote Ubaye Valley,
surrounded by a demi-halo of
snowy peaks, lies Provence's
northernmost town. It is a flat,
open town of cobbled streets,
smart cafés and restaurants and
quaint gift shops, selling specialities such as raspberry and
juniper liqueurs. The town was
named in 1231 by its founder
Raymond-Bérenger V, Count
of Barcelona and Provence,
whose great-grandfather of the
same name married into the
House of Provence in 1112.

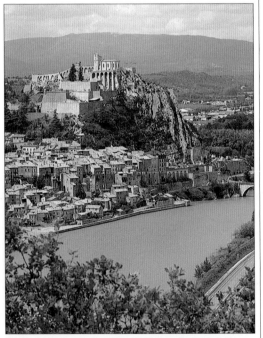

Sisteron citadel, strategically positioned high above the Durance valley

NAPOLEON IN PROVENCE

In his bid to regain power after his exile on Elba, Napoleon knew his only chance of success was to win over Sisteron. On 1 March, 1815, he secretly sailed from the island of Elba, landing at Golfe-Juan with 1,026 soldiers.

He hastily started his journey to Paris via Grenoble, making his first stop at Grasse, where the people shut their doors against h im. Abandoning carriages, cannon and horses, Napoleon and his troops scrambled along mule-tracks and across difficult terrain, surmounting summits of more than 3,000 ft (1,000 m). At Digne, he lunched at the Hôtel du Petit Paris before spending the night at Malijai château where he waited for news of the royalist stronghold of Sisteron. He was in luck. The arsenal was empty and he entered the town on 5 March – a plaque on rue du Jeu-de-Paume honours the event. The people were, at last, beginning to warm to him.

The dramatic *Napoleon Crossing the Alps*, painted by Jacques Louis David in 1800

One of the distinctive residential villas in Barcelonnette

The town's Alpine setting gives it a Swiss flavour; it also has Mexican spice. The Arnaud brothers, whose business in Barcelonnette was failing, emigrated to Mexico and made their fortune. Others followed, and on their return in the early 20th century, they built grand villas which encircle the town.

Housed in one of the villas is the **Musée de la Vallée**, where the Mexican connection is explained through illustrations and costumes. There are four other branches of this museum in the Ubaye valley, at St-Paul, Jauziers, Pontis and Le Lauzet.

In summer there is an information point here for the Parc National du Mercantour. The park stretches along the Italian border and straddles the Alpes

Maritimes region in the south (*see p97*). It is a haven for birds, wildlife and fauna, with two major archaeological sites.

🏛 **Musée de la Vallée**
10 av de la Libération. **Tel** 04 92 81 27 15. ◯ Wed, Thu & Sat pm; Jul–Aug: daily (school hols same: pms); Sep–Jun: Wed, Thu, Fri & Sat pms. 🖼

Mont Pelat ❹

🚉 Digne-les-Bains, Thorame-Verdon. 🚌 Colmars, Allos. 🛈 place du Presbytère, Allos (04 92 83 02 81).

This is the loftiest peak in the Provençal Alps, rising to a height of 3,050 m (10,017 ft) and all around are mountains and breathtaking passes, some

of them closed by snow until June. Among them are the Col de Cayolle (2,327 m/7,717 ft) on the D2202 to the east, and the hair-raising Col d'Allos (2,250 m/7,380 ft) on the D908 to the west. South of Mont Pelat, in the heart of the Parc National du Mercantour, is the beautiful 50-ha (124-acre) Lac d'Allos. It is the largest natural lake in Europe at this altitude. The setting is idyllic, ringed by snowy mountains, its crystal-clear waters swimming with trout and char. Another record-breaker is Cime de la Bonette, on the D64 northeast of Mont Pelat, at 2,862 m (9,390 ft) the highest pass in Europe. It has what is perhaps the most magnificent view in all this abundant mountain scenery.

Cime de la Bonette, the highest mountain pass in Europe

Colmars ❺

Road map 2E. 400. 🚌 ❶
Ancienne Auberge Fleurie (04 92 83 41 92). 🚋 *Tue & Fri (Jun–Sep).*

Colmars is an unusually complete fortified town, nestling between two medieval forts. You can walk along the 12-m (40-ft) ramparts, which look across oak-planked roofs, patched in places with sheet steel. The town is named after the hill on which it is built, *collis Martis*, where the Romans built a temple to the god Mars. Vauban, the military engineer, designed its lasting look. On the north side, an alley leads to the 17th-century **Fort de Savoie**, a fine example of military architecture. From the Porte de France a path leads to the Fort de France.

Situated among wooded hills Colmars is popular in summer, when time is spent relaxing on wooden balconies (*soleillades, lit*, sun-traps), or strolling along alpine paths, soaking up the beautiful views. Signposts lead from the town to the Cascade de la Lance, a waterfall half-an-hour's walk away.

♦ **Fort de Savoie**
04370 Colmars. **Tel** *04 92 83 41 92.*
⬜ *Sep– Jul by appointment only; Jul–Aug: daily.* 🗹 🗹 *obligatory.*

Digne-les-Bains ❻

Road map 2D. 17,700. 🚉 🚌 ❶
pl du Tampinet (04 92 36 62 62). 🚋
Wed & Sat. **www.ot-dignelesbains.fr**

The capital of the region has been a spa town since Roman times, primed by seven hot springs. It still attracts those seeking various cures, who visit the Etablissement Thermal, a short drive southeast of the town. Health seems to radiate from Digne's airy streets, particularly from the boulevard Gassendi, named after the local mathematician and astronomer Pierre Gassendi (1592–1655). This is where the town's four-day lavender

The fortified town of Colmars, flanked by two compact forts

carnival rolls out in August *(see p229)*, for Digne styles itself the *"capitale de la Lavande"*. In recent years, the town has promoted itself as an important centre for modern sculpture, which liberally furnishes the town.

The **Musée Départemental** is found in the old town hospice and houses 16th–19th-century French, Italian and Dutch paintings, a collection of contemporary art and 19th-century scientific instruments. Among portraits of Digne's famous is Alexandra David-Néel, one of Europe's most intrepid travellers, who died in 1969 aged 101. Her house, *Samten-Dzong* (fortress of meditation) is now the **Fondation Alexandra David-Néel** and includes a Tibetan centre and a museum. At the north end of

the boulevard Gassendi is the 19th-century **Grande Fontaine** and just beyond this lies the oldest part of Digne-les-Bains, now a residential suburb. The most impressive architectural site is the cathedral of **Notre-Dame-du-Bourg**. It is the largest Romanesque church in Haute Provence, built 1200–1330.

The **Jardin Botanique des Cordeliers**, an enchanting walled garden in a converted convent, houses a large and varied collection of plants and herbs with medicinal qualities.

🏛 **Musée Départemental**
64 bd Gassendi. **Tel** *04 92 31 45 29.* ⬜ *Wed–Mon.* ⬛ *public hols*
🗹 ⬛ ⬛

🏛 **Fondation Alexandra David-Néel**
27 av Maréchal Juin. **Tel** *04 92 31 32 38.* ⬜ *daily.* 🗹 *4 per day (3 from Oct–Jun).* ⬛

🌸 **Jardin Botanique des Cordeliers**
Couvent des Cordeliers, Collège Maria Borrély. **Tel** *04 92 31 59 59.*
⬜ *Apr–Oct: Tue–Sat.* ⬛ *public hols.* ⬛

Street sculpture in Digne

Les Pénitents des Mées **7**

The curiously-shaped Pénitents des Mées, dominating the area

Road map 3D. ✈ *Marseille.* 🚉 *St-Auban.* 🚌 *Les Mées.* 🛈 *21 bd de la République. (04 92 34 36 38) pms.*

One of the most spectacular geological features in the region is Les Pénitents des Mées, a serried rank of columnar rocks more than 100 m (300 ft) high and over a mile (2 km) long. The strange rock formation is said to be a cowled procession of banished monks. In local mythology, monks from the mountain of Lure took a fancy to some Moorish beauties, captured by a lord during the time of the Saracen invasion in the 6th century. Saint Donat, a hermit who inhabited a nearby cave, punished their effrontery by turning them into stone.

The small village of Les Mées is tucked away at the north end. Walk up to the chapel of St-Roch for a clear view of the rocks' strange formation of millions of pebbles and stones.

Lurs **8**

Road map 3D. 🚶 *320.* 🚉 *La Brillane.* 🛈 *04700 Lurs (04 92 79 10 20) pms.*

The Bishops of Sisteron and the Princes of Lurs were given ownership of the fortified town of Lurs in the 9th century, under the command

of Charlemagne. Earlier this century, the small town was virtually abandoned, and was only repopulated after World War II, mainly by printers and graphic artists, who keep their trade in the forefront of events with an annual competition.

The narrow streets of the old town, entered through the Porte d'Horloge, are held in by the medieval ramparts. North of the restored Château of the Bishop-Princes is the beginning of the 300-m (900-ft) **Promenade des Evêques** (Bishops' walk), lined with 15 oratories leading to the chapel of Notre-Dame-de-Vie. It is worth visiting purely for the stupendous views over the sea of poppy fields and olive groves of the Durance valley.

Head north out of Lurs on the N96, to the 12th-century **Prieuré de Ganagobie**. The church contains beautifully restored red-, black- and white-tiled mosaics, inspired by oriental and Byzantine design and imagery. Offices are held several times a day by the monks – visitors may attend.

🏠 **Prieuré de Ganagobie**
N96, 04310. **Tel** *04 92 68 00 04.*
◯ *Tue–Sat pms, & Sun.* 🏠

Floor mosaic of the church of the 12th-century Prieuré de Ganagobie

---

LE TRAIN DES PIGNES

An enjoyable day out is to be found on the Chemin de Fer de Provence, a short railway line that runs from Digne-les-Bains to Nice. It is the remaining part of a network that was designed to link the Côte d'Azur with the Alps, built between 1891 and 1911. Today the Train des Pignes, a diesel train, usually with two carriages, runs four times a day throughout the year. It is an active and popular service, used by locals going about their daily business as much as by tourists. It rattles along the single track at a fair pace, rolling by the white waters of

the Asse de Moriez and thundering over 16 viaducts, 15 bridges and through 25 tunnels.

The train journey is an excellent way of seeing the surrounding countryside, although the ride can be bumpy at times. The most scenic parts are in uninhabited countryside, for instance between St-André-les-Alps and Annot, where the grés d'Annot can be seen clearly *(see p187)*. The journey takes about 3 hours each way and can be broken en route. Entrevaux *(see p187)* is a good place to stop, half-way between the two towns.

The vaulted scriptorium of the Couvent des Cordeliers in Forcalquier

Forcalquier ❾

Road map C3. 👥 *4,300.* 🚌 🚉 *4 pl du Bourguet (04 92 75 10 02).* 🛒 *Mon.* **www**.forcalquier.com

Crowned by a ruined castle and domed chapel of the 19th-century Notre-Dame-de-Provence, Forcalquier is an intriguing shadow of its former self. Its heart lies in the old town, redolent of its days as a state and capital of the region.

Streets that once rang with trade and troubadours are now silent, although the weekly market is a lively affair, filled with lavender and honey stalls and local artists and artisans selling their wares.

There are some fine façades in the old town, but only one remaining gate, the Porte des Cordeliers. The **Couvent des Cordeliers** nearby dates from 1236 and is where the local lords have been entombed. The carefully restored cloisters, library, scriptorium and refectory can all be visited. The **Observatoire de Haute Provence** to the south of the town was sited here after a study in the 1930s to find the town with the cleanest air. The Centre d'Astronomie nearby is a must for star-gazers.

⛪ Couvent des Cordeliers
Bd des Martyres. **Tel** 04 92 75 10 02. 🕐 *Jul & Aug: daily.* 📷 🎫 *obligatory: 3 per day.*

⛪ Observatoire de Haute Provence
St-Michel l'Observatoire. **Tel** 04 92 70 64 00. 🕐 *Wed pm.* 📷 🎫 *only.*

Manosque ❿

Road map C3. 👥 *20,300.* 🚌 🚉 🚉 *pl du Docteur Joubert (04 92 72 16 00).* 🛒 *Sat.* **www**.ville-manosque.fr

France's national nuclear research centre, Cadarache, has brought prosperity to Manosque, an industrial town which has sprawled beyond its original hill site above the Durance. The centre has 13th- and 14th-century gates, Porte Soubeyrand and Porte Saunerie. The perfume shop in rue Grande was once the atelier of writer Jean Giono's father *(see p28).* The **Centre Jean Giono** tells the story of his life. The town's adoptive son is the painter Jean Carzou, who decorated the interior of the **Couvent de la Présentation** with apocalyptic allegories of modern life.

⛪ Centre Jean Giono
3 bd Elémir Bourges. **Tel** 04 92 70 54 54. 🕐 *Oct–Jun: Tue–Fri; Jul–Sep: daily.* 📷 ⬤ *public hols.*

⛪ Couvent de la Présentation – Fondation Carzou
9 bd Elémir Bourges. **Tel** 04 92 87 40 49. 🕐 *Jul–May: Wed–Sat pms; Jun: Tue–Sat pms.* ⬤ *23 Dec–3 Jan.*

Gréoux-les-Bains ⓫

Road map D3. 👥 *2,000.* 🚌 🚉 *5 av des Marronniers (04 92 78 01 08).* 🛒 *Tue & Thu.*

The cleansing thermal waters of Gréoux-les-Bains have been enjoyed since antiquity, when baths were built by the Romans in the 1st century AD. The waters can still be enjoyed at the Etablissement Thermal, on the east side of the village, on Avenue du Verdon, where bubbling, sulphurous water arrives at the rate of 100,000 litres (22,000 gallons) an hour.

Like most spa towns, Gréoux flourished in the 19th-century and has retained a restful air.

LAVENDER AND LAVENDIN

The famous flower of Provence colours the Plateau de Valensole every July. Lavender began to be cultivated in the region in the 19th century and provides the world with around 80 per cent of its needs. Harvesting continues until September and is mostly mechanized although, in some areas, it is still collected in cloth sacks slung over the back. After two or three days' drying it is sent to a distillery.

These days the cultivation of a hybrid called lavendin has overtaken traditional lavender. Lavender is now used mainly for perfumes and cosmetics, lavendin for soaps.

Harvesting the abundant lavender in Haute Provence

The sweeping fields of the Plateau de Valensole, one of the largest lavender-growing areas of Provence

A restored castle ruin of the Templars is on a high spot and an open-air theatre is in the grounds. The **Crèche de Haute Provence** in Gréoux is well worth a visit for its display of a clay village with *santons* and *son-et-lumière* shows.

Crèche de Hte Provence
36 av des Alpes. *Tel* 04 92 77 61 08. ⬜ Mar–Dec: Tue–Sun 🖾 🕭

Corinthian columns front the Gallo-Roman baths in Gréoux-les-Bains

Valensole ⑫

Road map D3. 🏚 2,200. 🛈 pl des Héros de la Résistance (04 92 74 90 02). 🖃 Sat.

This is the centre of France's most important lavender-growing area. It sits on the edge of the Valensole plains with a sturdy-towered Gothic church at its height. Admiral Villeneuve was born here in 1763, the unsuccessful adversary of Admiral Nelson at the Battle of Trafalgar. Signs for locally made lavender honey are everywhere and just outside the town is the **Musée**

Vivant de l'Abeille. This is an interactive museum explaining the intriguing life of the honey bee, with informative demonstrations, photographs and videos. In the summer, you can visit the beehives and see the beekeepers at work.

Musée Vivant de l'Abeille
Rte de Manosque. *Tel* 04 92 74 85 28. ⬜ Tue–Sat. ● public hols. 🖾 🕭

Riez ⑬

Road map D3. 🏚 1,700. 🚌 🛈 4 allée Louis Gardiol (04 92 77 99 09). 🖃 Wed & Sat. www.ville-riez.fr

At the edge of the sweeping Valensole plateau is this unspoiled village, filled with small shops selling ceramics and traditional *santons*, honey and lavender. Its grander past is reflected in the Renaissance façades of the houses and mansions in the old town. This is entered through the late-13th-century Porte Aiguyère, which leads on to the peaceful, tree-

lined Grand'Rue, with the finest examples of Renaissance architecture at numbers 27 and 29.

The most unusual site is the remains of the 1st-century AD Roman temple dedicated to Apollo. It stands out of time and place, in the middle of a field by the river Colostre; this was the original site of the town where the Roman colony, *Reia Apollinaris,* lived. On the other side of the river is a rare example of Merovingian architecture, a small baptistry dating from the 5th century.

In the tourist office is the small **Musée Nature en Provence**, which traces the geological history of Provence, with an exhibition of over 3,000 fossils, minerals and rocks. The highlight of the museum is a copy of a remarkably preserved fossil of a wader bird dating back 35 million years.

Musée Nature en Provence
4 allée Louis Gardiol. *Tel* 04 92 77 99 09. ⬜ Jul–mid-Sep: daily; mid-Sep–Jun: Mon–Sat. ● Sun pm, publ hols. 🖾

Fossil of a wader bird, housed in the Musée Nature en Provence in Riez

Tour of the Gorges du Verdon ⓮

The breathtaking chasm of the Gorges du Verdon is one of the most spectacular natural phenomena in France. The Verdon river, a tributary of the Durance, cuts into the rock up to 700 m (2,300 ft) deep. A tour of the gorges takes at least a day and this circular route encompasses its most striking features. At its east and west points are the historic towns of Castellane, the natural entry point to the gorges, and Moustiers-Ste-Marie. Parts of the tour are particularly mountainous, so drivers must be aware of hairpin bends and narrow roads with sheer drops. Weather conditions can also be hazardous and roads can be icy until late spring.

Hikers in one of the deep gorges

Moustiers-Ste-Marie ④
Set on craggy heights, the town is famed for its *faïence (p186).*

Flowered-façade in Moustiers

Aiguines ③
The beautifully restored 17th-century château crowns the small village, with fine views down to the Lac de Ste-Croix.

KEY

▬▬▬	Tour route
-----	Other roads
❋	Viewpoint

0 kilometres   2
0 miles   2

TIPS FOR DRIVERS

Tour length: 113 km (72 miles).
Stopping-off points: La Palud-sur-Verdon has several cafés and Moustiers-Ste-Marie is a good place to stop for lunch. For an overnight stop, there are hotels and camp sites in the town of Castellane. (See also pp250–1.)

The azure-blue waters of the enormous Lac de Ste-Croix

OUTDOOR ACTIVITIES

The Verdon gorges have offered fantastic opportunities for the adventurous since Isadore Blanc (1875–1932) made the first complete exploration in 1905. Today's activities include hiking, climbing, canoeing and white-water rafting *(see pp226–7)*. Boating needs to be supervised as the river is not always navigable and the powerful water flow can change dramatically.

White-water rafting down the fast-flowing Verdon river

Gorge explorer, Isadore Blanc

Point Sublime ⑥
This is one of the best viewing points. Signposted walks lead down to the canyon floor, but a torch is required to walk through the long tunnels.

Castellane ①
An ancient clock tower and gate remain in the Old Town of Castellane, a popular tourist centre *(p186)*.

La Palud-sur-Verdon ⑤
Organized walking excursions start at the village of La Palud, the so-called capital of the Gorges.

Rougon

Trigance

View of Pont de Tusset

Pont de l'Artuby ②
Park at either end of the 100-m (328-ft) bridge, which spans the Artuby river, and marvel at the superb views. It is also a favourite spot for bungee jumping.

Stunning view across the meandering river Verdon

Moustiers-Ste-Marie ⓯

Road map 3D. 🏘 *630.* 🚌 🛈 *Hôtel Dieu, rue de la Bourgade (04 92 74 67 84).* 🛒 *Fri am.*
www.ville-moustiers-sainte-marie.fr

The setting of the town of Moustiers is stunning, high on the edge of a ravine, beneath craggy rocks. Situated in the town centre is the parish church, with a three-storey Romanesque belfry. Above it, a path meanders up to the 12th-century chapel of Notre-Dame-de-Beauvoir. The view across to the Gorges du Verdon (*see pp184–85*) is magnificent.

A heavy iron chain, 227 m (745 ft) in length, is suspended above the ravine. Hanging from the centre is a five-pointed, golden star. Although it was renewed in 1957, it is said to date back to the 13th century, when the chevalier Blacas hoisted it up in thanks for his release from captivity during the Seventh Crusade of St Louis (*see p42*).

Moustiers is a popular tourist town, the streets crowded in summer. This is due to its setting and its ceramics. The original Moustiers ware is housed in the **Musée de la Faïence**. Modern reproductions can be bought in the town. The new **Musée de la Préhistoire** in Quinson, 40 km (25 miles) south, is a must.

🏛 Musée de la Faïence
Moustiers-Ste-Marie. **Tel** *04 92 74 61 64.* ◻ *Apr–Oct: Wed–Mon; Nov–Mar: Sat–Sun pms only; school hols: Wed–Mon pms only.* ◼ *Jan.* 🖼

Notre-Dame-du-Roc chapel, perched high above the town of Castellane

Castellane ⓰

Road map 3D. 🏘 *1,500.* 🚌 🛈 *rue Nationale (04 92 83 61 14).* 🛒 *Wed & Sat.* www.castellane.org

This is one of the main centres for the Gorges du Verdon, surrounded by campsites and caravans. Tourists squeeze into the town centre in summer and, in the evenings, fill the cafés after a day's hiking, climbing, canoeing and white-water rafting. It is a well-sited town, beneath an impressive 180-m (600-ft) slab of grey rock. On top of this, dominating the skyline, is the chapel of **Notre-Dame-du-Roc**, built in 1703. A strenuous, 30-minute walk from behind the parish church to the top is rewarded with superb views.

Castellane was once a sturdy fortress and repelled invasion several times. The lifting of the siege by the Huguenots in 1586 is commemorated every year with firecrackers at the Fête des Pétardiers (last Sat in Jan).

The town's fortifications were completely rebuilt in the 14th century after most of the town, dating from Roman times, crumbled and slipped into the Verdon valley. Most social activity takes place in the main square, place Marcel-Sauvaire, which is lined with small hotels that have catered for generations of visitors.

All that remains of the ramparts is the Tour Pentagonal and a small section of the old wall, which lie just beyond the 12th-century St-Victor church, on the way up to the chapel.

MOUSTIERS WARE

The most important period of Moustiers faïence was from its inception in 1679 until the late 18th century, when a dozen factories were producing this highly-glazed ware. Decline followed and production came to a standstill in 1874, until it was revived in 1925 by Marcel Provence. He chose to follow traditional methods, and output has continued ever since.

The distinctive glaze of Moustiers faïence was first established in the late 17th century by Antoine Clérissy, a monk from Faenza in Italy. The first pieces to be fired had a luminous blue glaze and were decorated with figurative scenes, often copied from engravings of hunting or mythological subjects. In 1738, Spanish glazes were introduced and brightly coloured floral and fauna designs were used.

A number of potters continue the tradition, with varying degrees of quality, and can be seen at work in their *ateliers*.

A tureen in Moustiers' highly glazed faïence ware

The narrow streets of Moustiersy

St-André-les-Alpes ⓱

Road map 3D. 🏠 *850.* 🚌 🚉
ℹ️ *place Marcel Pastorelli (04 92 89 02 39).* 🛒 *Wed & Sat.*

Lying at the north end of the Lac de Castillon, where the river Isolde meets the river Verdon, is St-André. It is a popular summer holiday and leisure centre, scattered around the sandy flats on the lakeside. The lake is man-made, formed by damming the river by the 90-m (295-ft) Barrage de Castillon and is a haven for swimming and watersports.

Inland, the scenery is just as picturesque, surrounded by lavender fields and orchards. Hang-gliding is so popular in the area that one of the local producers advertises its wine as "the wine of eagles".

Annot ⓲

Road map 3E. 🏠 *1,000.* 🚌
ℹ️ *bvd Saint-Pierre (04 92 83 23 03).* 🛒 *Tue.* **www**.annot.fr

The town of Annot, on the Train des Pignes railway line *(see p181)*, has a distinct Alpine feel. Annot lies in the the Vaïre valley, crisscrossed by icy waters streaming down from the mountains. The surrounding scenery however, is a more unfamiliar pattern of jagged rocks and deep caves.

Vast sandstone boulders, known as the *grès d'Annot*, are strewn around the town, and local builders have con-

The steep path of zigzag ramps leading to the citadel of Entrevaux

structed houses against these haphazard rocks, using their sheer faces as outside walls. The *vieille ville* lies behind the main road, where there is a Romanesque church. The tall buildings that line the narrow streets have retained some of their original 15th- to 18th-century carved stone lintels.

Most Sundays in summer, a 1909 Belle Epoque steam train chugs its way from Puget-Théniers to Annot, a pleasant way for visitors to enjoy the unspoiled countryside.

Entrevaux ⓳

Road map 3E. 🏠 *800.* 🚉 🚌
ℹ️ *Porte Royale (04 93 05 46 73).* 🛒 *Fri.*

It is clear to see why Entrevaux is called a "fairytale town", as you cross the drawbridge and enter through the Porte Royale. The dramatic entrance is flanked by twin towers, the Porte de France and the Porte d'Italie, and from here you enter the Ville Forte. A good time to visit is early-August, when the town holds its biennial music festival *(see p33)*. The next is in 2004.

Fortified in 1690 by the military engineer Vauban (1633–1707), Entrevaux became one of the strongest military sites on the Franco-Savoy border. Even the 17th-century cathedral was skilfully incorporated into the turreted ramparts.

Unlike most military strongholds, the citadel was not built on top of a hill, but strategically placed on a rocky outcrop. A steep, zigzag track leads to the citadel, 135 m (440 ft) above the village. The 20-minute climb to the top, past basking lizards, should not be made in the midday heat.

Houses in the town of Annot built against huge sandstone rocks

TRAVELLERS' NEEDS

WHERE TO STAY

The diversity of Provence is reflected in the wide range of hotels it has to offer. Accommodation varies from luxurious palaces like the Carlton in Cannes to simple country cottages where a warm welcome, peaceful setting and often excellent cuisine are more customary than mod cons.

A broad range of hotels from all price categories has been selected across the length and breadth

Négresco doorman

of Provence. The hotel listings on pages 194–203 are arranged by *département* and town according to price. They have been selected for offering interesting accommodation and good value for money. Self-catering holidays are a popular and inexpensive option and on pages 192-3 information is given on renting a rural home or *gîte*, and camping, as well as how to find B&Bs and youth hostels in the area.

WHERE TO LOOK

There is no shortage of hotels in Provence and the Côte d'Azur. Ever since the crusades of the Middle Ages, the medieval villages and ports have accommodated travellers, to varying degrees of luxury.

Some of the most attractive and best value coastal accommodation is found along the shores of the Var between Toulon and St-Tropez. The glamour and glitz come further east – the coast from Fréjus to Menton is predictably extravagant, but you can find accommodation to suit all budgets and tastes, from the exclusive Eden Roc, favourite of filmstars on Cap d'Antibes, to the 15th-century town house of the Hôtel des Arcades in Biot.

Inland, the major towns and cities of Provence offer a good variety of hotels, from the luxurious mansions of Aix-en-Provence and Arles to the more simple hostelries of the Luberon and the Var. Most villages offer at least one small hotel. Pleasant surprises are to be found – the dreamy ideal of a converted farmhouse or medieval priory lost in the midst of vibrant lavender fields is very much a reality if you know where to look.

If you are seeking tranquillity, travel north to the wilds of Haute Provence where several châteaux and *relais de poste* (post-houses and coaching inns) provide excellent accommodation and regional cuisine in rustic surroundings.

Those seeking a country idyll should head to the hills and valleys of the Central Var, the Luberon National Park or the foothills of Mont Ventoux. More refined bases include the university town of Aix, the papal capital of Avignon or the Roman town of Arles. Much-maligned Marseille does in fact make an exciting, cosmopolitan base, offering excellent hotels and restaurants.

HOTEL PRICES

Single occupancy rates are usually the same as two sharing – prices are normally per room, not per person. Tax and service are included in the price, with the exception of full board (*pension*) and half board (*demi-pension*), and rates posted are exclusive of breakfast. You are not required to take breakfast and should stipulate if you want it.

Rooms with a shower tend to be 20 per cent cheaper than those with a bath. In more remote areas, half board may

The palatial Hôtel Carlton in Cannes (see p195)

be obligatory and is often necessary in places where the hotel has the only restaurant. In high season, popular coastal hotels may give preference to visitors who want half board.

Prices drop considerably in Provence in low season (Oct–Mar). Many hotels close for five months of the year, reopening for Easter. During festivals *(see pp32-5 & pp228-9)*, prices can rival high-season tariffs. In low season, discount packages are common along the coast. It is worth checking with travel agents or contacting the hotels directly as many of the biggest and most famous hotels offer dramatic discounts – even the palaces of the Riviera need to fill their rooms in winter.

The elegant reception area of the Grand Hôtel du Cap-Ferrat *(see p196)*

Hôtel de Paris entrance *(see p196)*

HOTEL GRADINGS

French hotels are classified by the tourist authorities into five categories: one to four stars, plus a four-star deluxe rating. A few very basic places are unclassified. These ratings give an indication of the level of facilities you can expect but offer little idea of cleanliness, ambience or friendliness of the owners. Some of the most charming hotels are blessed with few stars, while the higher ratings often turn out to be impersonal business hotels.

FACILITIES AND MEALS

Facilities will vary greatly depending on the location and rating of each hotel. In remoter areas most hotels have adjoining restaurants, and nearly all feature a breakfast room or terrace. Many three-star hotels have swimming pools which can be a godsend in the summer. Parking is readily available at country hotels. Some city hotels have underground or guarded parking – in the larger cities like Marseille and Nice this is becoming a necessity as car crime is an increasing problem. Most hotels will have telephones in the bedrooms. Televisions are rarer, especially outside towns. Double beds *(grands lits)* are common, but it is advisable to specify you want one.

Many Provençal hotels are converted buildings and, while this adds a definite charm, it can mean enduring eccentric plumbing, erratic electricity and ceilings that go bump in the night. Some hotels are near a main road or town square – choosing a room at the back is usually all that is required for a peaceful night.

Many hotels use the time-honoured French bolster – a long cushion which many find uncomfortable – if you desire a pillow, ask for *un oreiller*. You have to ask specifically for a room with a bath or toilet – a *cabinet de toilette* simply has a basin and bidet.

Traditional French breakfasts are common in Provence and in summer are often enjoyed outside. Evening meals are served daily until about 9pm, except Sunday when dining rooms are often closed – check before you arrive. Check-out time is about noon – if you stay any longer you will have to pay for an extra day.

BOOKING

In high season it is imperative to book well in advance, especially for any popular coastal hotels. During peak season, proprietors may ask for a deposit. Tourist offices *(see p237)* are useful if you want personal descriptions and recommendations of places. Tourist offices will also book for you. Outside peak season (Jun–Sep) you may be able to turn up on the day, but it is always wise to phone ahead to make sure the establishment is open.

The exclusive Eden Roc *(see p195)*

CHILDREN

Families with young children can often share a room at no extra cost, since prices are per room and not per person. Few hotels will refuse children although some insist they must be well behaved. Numerous country hotels boast modern annexes with bungalow apartments specifically designed for visiting families, often only a few steps away from the swimming pool.

One of the many typical Provence château-hotels

THE CLASSIC FAMILY HOTEL

If you are travelling on a budget, the friendly, family-run hotel is ideal. These establishments are found in virtually every village and the atmosphere is extremely informal, with children, cats and dogs running in and out. It is likely to be the focal point of the village, with the dining room and bar open to non-residents.

The annual *Logis de France* guide, available from the **French Government Tourist Office**, lists these one- and two-star restaurants-with-rooms *(auberges)*, often specializing in regional cuisine. Most are basic roadside inns, with only a few listed in the main towns and cities, but off the beaten track you can find charming converted farmhouses and inexpensive seaside hotels.

THE MODERN CHAIN HOTEL

Outside the main motorway routes there are few chain hotels in Provence. For those wishing to break their journey or seeking inexpensive accommodation on the outskirts of towns, the chains **Campanile, Formule 1** and **Ibis** offer modern and comfortable rooms. They are a safe and practical bet if nothing else is available, and can be booked directly over the phone by credit card. However, they do lack the charm and intimacy of an authentic Provençal hotel. Often you can find accommodation in the town itself or the surrounding countryside for an equivalent price, albeit with a less sanitized decor.

Other modern chains are geared to the business traveller and are found in most major towns. **Sofitel, Novotel** and **Mercure** all have hotels in Aix, Nice, Marseille and Avignon. For more information, phone the French Government Tourist Office.

DIRECTORY

CHAIN HOTELS

Campanile
Tel 01 64 62 46 46 Paris.
www.envergure.fr

Formule 1
Tel 020-8507 0789 (UK, for brochure).
Tel 0892 685 685 France.
www.hotelformule1.com

Ibis, Novotel, Sofitel, Mercure
Tel 020-8283 4500 UK.
Tel 01 60 87 90 90 Paris.
www.accorhotels.com

SELF-CATERING/ BED AND BREAKFAST

Maison des Gîtes de France
59 rue St Lazare, 75009 Paris. *Tel 01 49 70 75 75.*
Fax 01 42 81 28 53.
www.gites-de-france.fr

Brittany Ferries
For brochure with gîtes.
Tel (08705) 360360 UK.
www.brittany-ferries.co.uk

HOSTELS

CROUS
39 av G Bernanos, 75005 Paris.
Tel 01 40 51 55 55.

FUAJ (Fédération Unie des Auberges de Jeunesse)
9 rue Brantôme, 75003 Paris. *Tel 01 48 04 70 40.*
Fax 01 42 77 03 29.
www.iyhf.org

YHA (Youth Hostel Association, UK)
Trevelyan House, Dimple Rd, Matlock, Derbyshire BE4 3YH.
Tel (01629) 592 600.
Fax (01629) 592 702.
www.yha.org.uk

American Youth Hostel Association
8401 Colesville Road, Suite 600, Silver Spring, MD 20910.
Tel (301) 495 1240.
www.hiayh.org

CAMPING

Camping and Caravaning Club
Tel (02476) 694995.
Fax (02476) 694886.
www.campingand caravanningclub.co.uk

Eurocamp UK
Tel (08703) 338 338.
Fax (01606) 787 036.
www.eurocamp.co.uk

Fédération Française de Camping-Caravaning
78 rue de Rivoli, 75004 Paris. *Tel 01 42 72 84 08.*
Fax 01 42 72 70 21.

National Campers and Hikers Association (US)
Tel (716) 668-6242.
www.fcrv.org

DISABLED TRAVELLERS

APF
17 bd Auguste Blanqui, 75013 Paris. *Tel 01 40 78 69 90.* **www**.apf.asso.fr

GIHP

10 rue Georges de Porto-Riche, 75014 Paris.
Tel 01 43 95 66 36.
Fax 01 45 40 40 26.

Mobility International USA
45 W Broadway, Eugene, Oregon 97401.
Tel (541) 343 1284.
www.miusa.org

Holiday Care
7th floor Sunley House, 4 Bedford Park, Croydon, Surrey CRO 2AP.
Tel (0845) 124 9971.
www.holidaycare.org.uk

FURTHER INFORMATION

French Government Tourist Office
UK: 178 Piccadilly, London W1J 9AL.
Tel (09068) 244 123.
Fax (020) 7493 6594.
US: 444 Madison Ave, New York, NY 10022.
Tel (410) 286 8310.
www.franceguide.com

BED AND BREAKFAST

In rural areas, some cottages, farms and private houses offer bed and breakfast. These *chambres d'hôtes* come in all shapes and sizes and will provide dinner on request. They are listed separately in tourist office brochures and many are inspected and registered by the **Gîtes de France** organization; look out for their distinctive green and yellow *chambres d'hôtes* road signs. Departmental brochures are available from the Paris office and the website has a useful online research and reservation facility.

Gîtes de France road sign

HOSTELS

For the single traveller this is the cheapest, and often the most convivial, accommodation option. A membership card from your national **Youth Hostel Association** is required, or an *Ajiste* card, which you can obtain from French hostels. In summer, you can stay in vacated university residences; contact **CROUS**, the Centre Régional des Oeuvres Universitaires. For the regions' main youth hostels see p245.

SELF-CATERING

Provence is a popular self-catering destination and many companies specialize in renting anything from rural farm cottages to beach apartments. One of the best organizations is **Gîtes de France**, with its headquarters **Maison des Gîtes de France** in Paris, which provides detailed lists of accommodation to rent by the week in each *département*.

Often the owners live nearby and are always welcoming, but rarely speak much English. Don't expect luxury from your *gîte* as facilities are basic, but it is a great way to get a better insight into real Provençal life.

CAMPING

Long a popular pastime in Provence, camping remains an invitingly cheap and atmospheric way of seeing the area. Facilities vary, from a basic one-star farm or vineyard site to the camping metropolises of the Riviera, complete with water fun parks and satellite TV. **Eurocamp** specializes in family holidays. Luxury tents are pre-assembled at the campsite of your choice and everything is ready on arrival. Organized children's entertainment and baby-sitting are available on site. Some campsites will not accept visitors unless they have a special *camping carnet*, available from the AA, RAC and clubs such as the **Fédération Française de Camping-Caravaning.**

DISABLED TRAVELLERS

Due to the venerable design of most Provençal hotels, few are able to offer unrestricted wheelchair access. Larger hotels have lifts and hotel staff will go out of their way to aid disabled guests. The **Association des Paralysés de France (APF)** publishes a guide to accessible accommodation.

Other useful sources of information are the **Groupement pour l'Insertion des Personnes Handicappés Physiques (GIHP)** and **Holidaycare**, who publish a guide to France listing specialised tour operators for disabled travellers.

USING THE LISTINGS

The hotels on pages 194–203 are listed according to area and price category. The symbols summarize the facilities at each hotel.

📇 no credit cards
🛗 lift
🍴 restaurant in hotel
🏊 hotel swimming pool or beach
🧒 children's facilities
🏋 fitness facilities
🗔 air-conditioning in all rooms

Price categories for a standard double room (not per person) with shower for one night, including tax and service, but not breakfast:

€ Under 90 euros
€€ 90–140 euros
€€€ 140–180 euros
€€€€ 180–260 euros
€€€€€ Over 260 euros

Camping in Provence, a popular accommodation alternative

Choosing a Hotel

These hotels have been selected across a wide price range for their good value, excellent facilities, and location. This chart lists the hotels by area in the same order as the rest of the guide. Within each area, entries are listed alphabetically within each price category, from the least expensive to the most expensive.

PRICE CATEGORIES
For a standard double room (not per person) with shower for one night, including tax and service, but not breakfast:
€ under 90 euros
€€ 90–140 euros
€€€ 140–180 euros
€€€€ 180–260 euros
€€€€€ over 260 euros

THE RIVIERA AND THE ALPES MARITIMES

ANTIBES L'Auberge Provençale
€
61 pl Nationale, 06600 **Tel** *04 93 34 13 24* **Fax** *04 93 34 89 88* **Rooms** *7*
Road map *E3*

A large town house under the spreading plane trees of the town's bustling main square. Despite its location in one of the Riviera's trendiest spots, this *auberge* creates the atmosphere of an old-fashioned inn. Has spacious and clean rooms furnished with rustic furniture and canopied beds. Excellent value for money. **www.aubergeprovencale.com**

ANTIBES Mas Djoliba
€€
29 av Provence, 06600 **Tel** *04 93 34 02 48* **Fax** *04 93 34 05 81* **Rooms** *13*
Road map *E3*

Mas Djoliba is an old-fashioned farmhouse set among lots of greenery, in a location that is a convenient distance from old Antibes and the beaches. A low-rise property with palm trees around its pool-terrace. It is surprisingly good value for money. Closed end Oct–beg Feb. **www.hotel-djoliba.com**

BEAULIEU SUR MER Le Select Hôtel
€
1 Pl Charles-de-Gaulle, 06310 **Tel** *04 93 01 05 42* **Fax** *04 93 01 34 30* **Rooms** *19*
Road map *E3*

An affordable option for Riviera budget travellers, the Select is situated close to the station and offers simple rooms and a *pension* atmosphere. Ask for a room overlooking the square, as those at the rear can be stuffy. Not ideal for families with children, but a good choice for an overnight stay.

BEAULIEU SUR MER Hôtel Métropole
 €€€€€
15 boulevard Maréchal Leclerc, 06310 **Tel** *04 93 01 00 08* **Fax** *04 93 01 18 51* **Rooms** *39*
Road map *E3*

Part of the prestigious Relais et Châteaux consortium, the Métropole exudes grandeur and an air of luxury. Fabulous sea views, manicured lawns shaded by palm trees, a gourmet restaurant and a gorgeous heated sea-water pool are accompanied by ultramodern facilities. The ultimate spot in Beaulieu for a romantic break. **www.le-metropole.com**

BIOT Hôtel des Arcades
€
16 pl des Arcades, 06410 **Tel** *04 93 65 01 04* **Fax** *04 93 65 01 05* **Rooms** *10*
Road map *E3*

This 15th-century inn is a haven of tranquillity in the quiet place des Arcades. The bedrooms are small (some might say poky), but atmospheric. Top-floor rooms have terraces with views over the hills to the sea. The hotel bar also serves as a breakfast room and restaurant. **www.cote.azur.fr/hotel-arcades-des-biot_151.htm**

BIOT Domaine du Jas
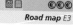 €€€
625 route de la Mer, 06410 **Tel** *04 93 65 50 50* **Fax** *04 93 65 02 01* **Rooms** *16*
Road map *E3*

Just outside Biot, this hotel seems much more luxurious than its three-star rating would lead the visitor to expect. A terrace pool (heated all summer) is shaded by palms and oleanders. The rooms are well equipped with WiFi access and there's a free private garage. No restaurant, but snack meals are available on demand all day. **www.domainedujas.com**

CANNES Hôtel des Allées
€
6 rue Emile Negrin, 06400 **Tel** *04 93 39 53 90* **Fax** *04 93 99 43 25* **Rooms** *18*
Road map *E4*

For those without money to burn, the small and friendly Hôtel des Allées is definitely the best value in Cannes. This centrally-located hotel sits on a quiet side-street, just at a short distance from la Croisette. Some rooms have balconies with a sea view. **www.hotel-des-allees.com**

CANNES Hôtel Molière
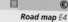 €€
5–7 rue Molière, 06400 **Tel** *04 93 38 16 16* **Fax** *04 93 68 29 57* **Rooms** *24*
Road map *E4*

This 19th-century building is just minutes away from la Croisette, Cannes' sea-front esplanade. Bright and comfortable rooms and balconies overlook an attractive garden, which compensates for the absence of a swimming pool. Very good value and much in demand, so book well in advance. **www.hotel-moliere.com**

CANNES Hôtel Splendid
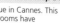 €€
4–6 rue Felix Faure, 06400 **Tel** *04 97 06 22 22* **Fax** *04 93 99 55 02* **Rooms** *62*
Road map *E4*

For those whose budget will not stretch to the magnificent Carlton, this white wedding cake of a hotel with its Belle Epoque frontage is a superb alternative. Fantastic views of the yacht harbour from the rooftop restaurant. Some sea-facing rooms have great balconies. Good service and a warm, friendly atmosphere. **www.splendid-hotel-cannes.fr**

Key to Symbols *see back cover flap*

CANNES Eden Hôtel 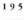 €€€

133 rue d'Antibes, 06400 **Tel** *04 93 68 78 00* **Fax** *04 93 68 78 01* **Rooms** *42*   **Road map** E4

This new hotel is bright and furnished in the trendiest possible style, with a hint of 1960s retro complementing modern touches. Close to the town's fashionable shopping streets, its facilities will include an outdoor and indoor heated pool, whirlpool, massage room and fitness centre by mid 2006. **www.eden-hotel-cannes.com**

CANNES Carlton Inter-Continental €€€€€

58 la Croisette, 06400 **Tel** *04 93 06 40 06* **Fax** *04 93 06 40 25* **Rooms** *338*   **Road map** E4

The grandest of the grand hotels, this is where the stars come to stay. There is a long waiting list for reservations during the Cannes Film Festival. It is worth paying a premium for rooms amid Art Deco surroundings that offer a view of the sea and the private beach with its loungers and parasols. **www.cannes.intercontinental.com**

CAP D'ANTIBES Villa Val des Roses €€

6 chemin des Lauriers, 06160 **Tel** *06 85 06 06 29* **Fax** *04 92 93 97 24* **Rooms** *4*   **Road map** E3

An Art Deco villa that harks back to the 1920s, Val des Roses is quite close to the Mediterranean and the beach. The swimming pool has a sea view and is shaded by palm trees. Rooms are individually designed and although there is no restaurant, the breakfast bar offers lavish salads and snacks. **www.val-des-roses.com**

CAP D'ANTIBES La Gardiole et La Garoupe €€€

60-74 chemin de la Garoupe, 06160 **Tel** *04 92 93 33 33* **Fax** *04 92 67 61 87* **Rooms** *40*   **Road map** E3

Pines and cypresses surround the 1920s buildings of this affordable hotel, at least by Cap d'Antibes standards. Beamed ceilings and whitewashed walls perpetuate the rural image. Light and airy bedrooms vary in price according to size. There's a shady terrace, and the restaurant serves Provençal cuisine. **www.hotel-lagaroupe-gardiole.com**

CAP D'ANTIBES Hôtel du Cap – Eden-Roc €€€€€

Boulevard Kennedy, 06601 **Tel** *04 93 61 39 01* **Fax** *04 93 67 76 04* **Rooms** *120*   **Road map** E3

Built in 1870, this ultimate Antibes palace is a hideaway for the rich and famous, who arrive by private yacht at the hotel's own jetty. Features luxury suites or apartments and seaside cabanas. Also offers a huge heated sea-water pool, superb food, obsequious service, and cutting edge facilities. **www.edenroc-hotel.fr**

EZE Hermitage du Col d'Eze 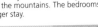 €

Grande Corniche, 06360 **Tel** *04 93 41 00 68* **Fax** *04 93 41 24 05* **Rooms** *32*   **Road map** F3

Probably the best value for money in expensive Eze, although the price includes compulsory half board in July and August. The location, a short distance from Eze, is hard to beat, with its fine views of the mountains. The bedrooms have been recently renovated and this is a good choice for an overnight halt or a longer stay.

EZE Les Terrasses d'Eze €€€€

Route de la Turbie, 06360 **Tel** *04 92 41 55 55* **Fax** *04 92 41 55 10* **Rooms** *81*   **Road map** F3

Contrasting with most of Eze's hotels that are housed in medieval buildings, Les Terrasses is a striking piece of modern architecture with superb sea views. The large, light and airy rooms have private balconies. The restaurant has both indoor and outdoor seating. **www.terrasses-eze.com**

EZE Château Eza €€€€€

Rue de la Pise, 06360 **Tel** *04 93 41 12 24* **Fax** *04 93 41 16 64* **Rooms** *7*   **Road map** F3

This building is a collection of medieval houses perched high at the summit of Eze's "eagle's nest". Once home to Sweden's Prince William, it has been converted into a luxury hotel, with elegant rooms and breathtaking views from its terraces. The hotel also boasts an award-winning restaurant and a private beach. **www.chateaueza.com**

JUAN-LES-PINS Eden Hotel €

16 av Louis Gallet, 06160 **Tel** *04 93 61 05 20* **Fax** *04 93 92 05 31* **Rooms** *17*   **Road map** E3

It's hard to find a better budget option than the Eden in Juan-les-Pins. This 1930s building has a certain slightly faded charm, with unpretentious rooms and a location close to the beach, that makes up for its lack of a pool. Although there is no full-service restaurant, breakfast is served on a pleasant terrace.

JUAN-LES-PINS Hôtel des Mimosas €€

Rue Pauline, 06160 **Tel** *04 93 61 04 16* **Fax** *04 93 92 06 46* **Rooms** *34*   **Road map** E3

Palm trees surround this gracious hotel, built at the turn-of-the-19th-century, offering character and style at a reasonable rate. The cool, comfortable rooms are simply furnished. Request a room with a balcony overlooking the swimming pool, or on the ground floor; the ones facing outward can be a little noisy.

MENTON Hôtel le Dauphin €

28 av Général de Gaulle, 06500 **Tel** *04 93 35 76 37* **Fax** *04 93 35 31 74* **Rooms** *28*   **Road map** F3

This modern hotel offers affordable comfort. Ask for a sea-facing room as those overlooking the avenue can be noisy. There's no full-service restaurant, but light snacks are on offer. With the eating places on the Menton seafront just a few steps away, this is no hardship. Sound-proof rooms are available for musicians. **www.hotel-ledauphin.com**

MENTON Hôtel Aiglon €€

7 av de la Madone, 06500 **Tel** *04 93 57 55 55* **Fax** *04 93 35 92 39* **Rooms** *28*   **Road map** F3

Not far from the seafront, the comfortable Aiglon has a heated swimming pool and a luxuriant garden. Housed in a charming 19th-century town house, it has a well-regarded restaurant with tables on a terrace shaded by palms. Although not the cheapest place to stay in Menton, it offers a lot for the price. **www.hotelaiglon.net**

MONACO Hôtel Alexandra
35 boulevard Princesse Charlotte, 98000 **Tel** *00 377 93 50 63 13* **Rooms** *56*

€€€

Road map *F3*

Proving that not all hotels in Monaco have to be costly, Hôtel Alexandra conceals comfortable bedrooms behind its grandiose Belle Epoque façade. Perhaps not ideal for a long stay, but good for a weekend break. To make up for the lack of a restaurant, breakfast is delivered to your room each morning. **www.monaco-hotel.com/montecarlo/alexandra/**

MONACO Columbus
23 av des Papalins, 98000 **Tel** *00 377 92 05 90 00* **Fax** *00 377 92 05 91 67* **Rooms** *153*

€€€€€

Road map *F3*

This newish arrival on the Monegasque hotel scene is in the trendy Fontvielle quarter. The look is modern, with dark stone and polished metal. Cutting-edge rooms with facilities such as broadband access. There's no pool, but a state-of-the-art fitness centre and an excellent restaurant and cigar bar are sure to impress. **www.columbushotels.com**

MONACO Hôtel de Paris
Pl du Casino, 98000 **Tel** *00 377 98 06 25 25* **Fax** *00 377 92 16 38 50* **Rooms** *191*

€€€€€

Road map *F3*

The opulent Hôtel de Paris has been the flagship of Monaco's grand hotels for more than a century. Features magnificent facilities, flawless service, fine dining and a location next to the casino. The celebrity guest list includes Queen Victoria and other crowned heads of Europe, to film stars and other bigwigs. **www.sbm.mc**

MONACO L'Hermitage
Square Beaumarchais, 98000 **Tel** *00 377 98 06 25 25* **Fax** *00 377 92 16 38 52* **Rooms** *280*

€€€€€

Road map *F3*

This cream-coloured Belle Epoque palace is one of the grandest hotels in Europe and a Monaco landmark, with its glass-domed Winter Garden foyer, lavish restaurant and marble terrace. Huge, opulent rooms have lots of luxury trimmings. This is the place to stay if you have just made a fortune at the Monte Carlo casino. **www.sbm.mc**

NICE La Belle Meunière
21 av Durante, 06000 **Tel** *04 93 88 66 15* **Fax** *04 93 82 51 76* **Rooms** *17*

€

Road map *F3*

This unpretentious hotel has comfortable and relatively quiet rooms, but few other facilities. However, it is conveniently located and has its own parking facilities – extremely useful in Nice, where this is at a premium and theft from cars is common. Few hotels in Nice offering this level of comfort in this price range.

NICE Le Petit Palais
17 av Emile Bieckert, 06000 **Tel** *04 93 62 19 11* **Fax** *04 93 62 53 60* **Rooms** *25*

€€

Road map *F3*

A 19th-century villa and once home to renowned film personality Sacha Guitry, this quiet hotel on the Cimiez slopes offers attractive views over the tiled rooftops and narrow streets of the Old Town and the Promenade des Anglais. Despite its lack of a restaurant, pool or garden, it is an affordable base for a short break in Nice.

NICE La Pérouse
11 quai Rauba Capeu, 06300 **Tel** *04 93 63 34 63* **Fax** *04 93 62 59 41* **Rooms** *58*

€€€€

Road map *F3*

Located at the eastern end of the Baie des Anges, this cliff-top hotel has the best views in Nice. The panorama from its windows has inspired painters such as Matisse and Dufy. The sea-facing rooms have small terraces and in summer, the restaurant provides outdoor seating beneath lemon trees. **www.hroy.com**

NICE Le Négresco
37 promenade des Anglais, 06000 **Tel** *04 93 16 64 00* **Fax** *04 93 88 35 68* **Rooms** *121*

€€€€€

Road map *F3*

The Négresco is the grande dame of Riviera hotels and has been a landmark on the Promenade des Anglais since it opened in 1913. Hosts a seemingly endless list of rich and famous guests. Superb decoration featuring works of art, flawless service and modern facilities make this one of the world's greatest hotels. **www.hotel-negresco-nice.com/**

ST-JEAN-CAP-FERRAT La Fregate
11 ave Denis Séméria, 06230 **Tel** *04 93 76 04 51* **Fax** *04 93 76 14 93* **Rooms** *10*

€

Road map *F3*

This is a family-run hotel with simply-decorated rooms on a small street near the harbour. There is no restaurant (apart from a small breakfast room) but there are lots of places to eat and drink nearby. Definitely the best place to stay in if you are exploring Provence on a tight budget or just passing through.

ST-JEAN-CAP-FERRAT Clair Logis
12 av Centrale, 06230 **Tel** *04 93 76 51 81* **Fax** *04 93 76 51 82* **Rooms** *18*

€€

Road map *F3*

This villa, set in a large, lush garden, is very good value and has, over the years, attracted a list of famous guests, including former French president Général de Gaulle. The rooms are comfortable in a slightly old-fashioned way, with smaller, more modern rooms in the annexe. There is no pool, but the beach is not far away. **www.hotel-clair-logis.fr**

ST-JEAN-CAP-FERRAT Grand Hôtel du Cap Ferrat
Boulevard du Général de Gaulle, 06230 **Tel** *04 93 76 50 50* **Fax** *04 93 76 0452* **Rooms** *44*

€€€€€

Road map *F3*

Located at the southern tip of Cap Ferrat, this is one of the world's most expensive hotels. Its grand Mediterranean-style rooms are set in tropical garden surroundings. A funicular railway transports guests to and from the Olympic-sized, landscaped sea-water pool, where Charlie Chaplin taught his children how to swim. **www.grand-hotel-cap-ferrat.com**

ST-JEAN-CAP-FERRAT La Voile d'Or
Port de St-Jean, 06230 **Tel** *04 93 01 13 13* **Fax** *04 93 76 11 17* **Rooms** *45*

€€€€€

Road map *F3*

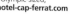

Not quite the most expensive hotel in St-Jean, but not cheap either, La Voile d'Or is worth every cent. The bedrooms are immaculate, there are two pools and views of the yacht harbour and the coast. The restaurant has a delightful terrace and a menu that emphasizes the classic French culinary tradition. **www.lavoiledor.fr**

Key to Price Guide *see p194* **Key to Symbols** *see back cover flap*

ST-PAUL Hôtel "Les Messugues"

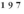

Domaine des Gardettes, route Fondation Maeght, 06570 **Tel** *0493 32 53 32* **Rooms** *15*   **Road map** *E3*

This charming hotel is the perfect base for exploring the St-Paul region. Set in tranquil surroundings outside the walls of St-Paul-de-Vence, this 1930s villa is a piece of history in its own right. The doors to each bedroom come from a 19th-century prison. Parking is available. Also has a pretty pool. **www.messugues.com**

ST-PAUL-DE-VENCE Hostellerie des Remparts

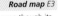

72 rue Grande, 06570 **Tel** *04 93 32 09 88* **Fax** *04 93 32 06 91* **Rooms** *9*   **Road map** *E3*

In the heart of this picturesque *village perché*, the Hostellerie des Remparts offers modern comforts within a medieval setting. The bedrooms are furnished with antiques, and all of them have marvellous views. The village is car-free and the car park is some distance away, so this is not a good place for those with mobility difficulties.

VENCE Mas de Vence

539 av Emile Hugues, 06140 **Tel** *04 93 58 06 16* **Fax** *04 93 24 04 21* **Rooms** *40*   **Road map** *E3*

This medium-sized, modern establishment may not appeal to those looking for somewhere quaint, even though its architecture and colours are in keeping with Provençal tradition. It has excellent facilities, including air-conditioned, sound-insulated rooms, a small garden and a terrace-restaurant beside the swimming pool. **www.azurline.com**

VENCE La Roseraie

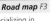

51 av Henri Giraud, 06140 **Tel** *04 93 58 02 20* **Fax** *04 93 58 99 31* **Rooms** *12*   **Road map** *E3*

Colourful Provençal fabrics and furniture adorn the lovingly-decorated bedrooms of this smart Belle Epoque town house, which has become Vence's most sought-after boutique hotel by far. It requires reservations months or even years in advance. Palm trees and magnolias shade the enticing garden, where breakfast is served.

VILLEFRANCHE Hôtel Versailles

7 boulevard Princesse Grace, 06230 **Tel** *04 93 76 52 52* **Fax** *04 93 01 97 48* **Rooms** *46*   **Road map** *F3*

This modern hotel has enough facilities for a longer stay, including a swimming pool, a restaurant specializing in Provençal cuisine and bedrooms with great views. Perhaps the only drawback is its location on a busy thoroughfare. However, this makes the hotel easy to find. It also offers secure parking. **www.hotelversailles.com**

VILLEFRANCHE Hôtel Welcome

1 Quai Amiral Courbet, 06230 **Tel** *04 93 76 27 62* **Fax** *04 93 76 27 66* **Rooms** *36*   **Road map** *F3*

This ochre-painted hotel has a certain period charm and great views of the sea and the port of Villefranche. Most rooms have balconies or terraces. Ask for a room overlooking the bay, as the view from those facing the town is less attractive. Artist Jean Cocteau stayed here while painting the Chapel of St Peter nearby. **www.welcomehotel.com**

THE VAR AND THE ILES D'HYERES

BORMES-LES-MIMOSAS Le Bellevue

Pl Gambetta, 83230 **Tel** *04 94 71 15 15* **Fax** *04 94 05 96 04* **Rooms** *12*   **Road map** *D4*

This family-run hotel has spacious bedrooms, with wrought-iron balconies offering stunning views of the terracotta-tiled rooftops and out across to the Iles de Porquerolles. Room 10 is the largest, with en suite facilities and double French windows, shaded by two large palm trees. The beach is only 3 km (2 miles) away. **www.bellevuebormes.fr.st**

BORMES-LES-MIMOSAS Le Grand Hôtel

167 route de Baguier, 83230 **Tel** *04 94 71 23 72* **Fax** *04 94 71 51 20* **Rooms** *52*   **Road map** *D4*

This hotel is aptly named, with its grand location in the Massif des Maures, high above the Mediterranean. Its decor is a slightly faded Belle Epoque style of the 1900s. The beautiful rooms (some with balconies), spectacular setting, sun-soaked terrace and friendly service go a long way in making it a memorable stay. **www.augrandhotel.com**

COGOLIN Au Coq Hôtel

Pl de la Mairie, 83310 **Tel** *04 94 54 13 71* **Fax** *04 94 54 03 06* **Rooms** *24*   **Road map** *E4*

Set in the centre of a bustling village, this lovely pink hotel is a short distance from St-Tropez and the beaches of Cavalaire, yet distant enough to avoid the brashness of these resorts. The rooms are comfortable and spacious, and there's a lovely terrace garden in which to sunbathe.

COLLOBRIERES Hôtel des Maures

19 boulevard Lazare-Carnot, 83310 **Tel** *04 94 48 07 10* **Fax** *04 94 48 02 73* **Rooms** *10*   **Road map** *D4*

This small and simple family-run affair is great value for money. The hotel has a highly popular restaurant, which serves traditional Provençal food. Although the rooms are not en suite, there are bathrooms on each floor. A good option for budget travellers.

FAYENCE Hôtel la Sousto

4 rue du Paty, 83440 **Tel** *04 94 76 02 16* **Rooms** *6*   **Road map** *E3*

A charming, small hotel in the centre of a typical Provençal village. The rooms have basic cooking facilities allowing for a self-catering holiday. Some of them have terraces looking out on to the bougainvillea-clad walls or the valley beyond. An ideal base for walking and hiking in the surrounding countryside.

FAYENCE Moulin de la Camandoule

Chemin de Notre-Dame des Cyprès, 83440 **Tel** *04 94 76 00 84* **Fax** *04 94 76 10 40* **Rooms** *E3*   **Road map** *E3*   €€

A converted 15th-century olive mill is the setting for this peaceful hotel in a valley beneath the village of Fayence. The machinery that was originally used to press the olives can still be seen here. The restaurant serves delicious traditional Provençal dishes, and there's a terraced garden to soak up the sun. **www.camandoule.com**

FOX-AMPHOUX Auberge du Vieux Fox

Pl de l'Eglise, 83670 **Tel** *04 94 80 71 69* **Fax** *04 94 80 78 38* **Rooms** *8*   **Road map** *D4*   €€

A former staging post for the Knights Templar in the Middle Ages, this hotel has retained many of its medieval features, which more than compensate for the small rooms. The restaurant's excellent food, served in a rustic dining room, draws locals from miles around. There's also a terrace with parasols to enjoy the views.

FREJUS Hôtel Arena

145 rue Général de Gaulle, 83600 **Tel** *04 94 17 09 40* **Fax** *04 94 52 01 52* **Rooms** *36*   **Road map** *E4*   €€

A real taste of Provence can be found here in both the decor – warm bright colours evoking the sea, wooden furniture and mosaic tiles – and in the fine restaurant. The rooms look out over lovely patios, and the garden is landscaped with palm trees, oleander and geraniums. The restaurant serves top-class Provençal cuisine. **www.arena-hotel.com**

GRIMAUD VILLAGE Côteau Fleuri

Pl des Pénitents, 83310 **Tel** *04 94 43 20 17* **Fax** *04 94 43 33 42* **Rooms** *14*   **Road map** *E4*   €€

Panoramic views of the Massif des Maures are amongst the many attractions of this grey-stone inn on the side of a hill. The restaurant boasts a huge fireplace and in summer, food is served on the lovely flower-filled terrace. The speciality is fish and other local seasonal ingredients. **www.coteaufleuri.fr**

GRIMAUD VILLAGE Hôtel la Pierrerie

Quartier du Grand Pont, 83310 **Tel** *04 934 43 24 60* **Fax** *04 94 43 24 78* **Rooms** *14*   **Road map** *E4*   €€

A quiet alternative to the flashy resort of St-Tropez, which it overlooks from its hilltop location, this three-star hotel is housed in a collection of old farm buildings surrounding the outdoor pool. It is landscaped with cypress and palm trees. The rooms are sparsely decorated in Provençal style, but are spacious and welcoming. **www.lapierrerie.com**

HYERES Hôtel du Soleil

Rue du Rempart, 83400 **Tel** *04 94 65 16 26* **Fax** *04 94 35 46 00* **Rooms** *22*   **Road map** *D4*   €

A charming ivy-clad old house, perched on a hill high above this pretty medieval town. Some rooms have panoramic sea views; others are set in the eaves of the house, but all are tradtionally furnished. There's also a sunny terrace with parasoled tables. **www.hotel-du-soleil.fr**

ILE DE PORQUEROLLES Auberge des Glycines

Pl d'Armes, 83400 **Tel** *04 94 58 30 36* **Fax** *04 94 58 35 22* **Rooms** *11*   **Road map** *D5*   €€

Situated in the heart of the village, near the pier and the church, this is a wonderful island getaway. The rooms are decorated with sweeping curtains and antique furniture, as is the dining room, which also boasts a large open fire. Enjoy breakfast and dinner on the shaded patio. Half board accommodation is available. **www.aubergedesglycines.net**

ILE DE PORT-CROS Le Manoir d'Hélène

Port-Cros, 83400 **Tel** *04 94 05 90 52* **Fax** *04 94 05 90 89* **Rooms** *22*   **Road map** *D5*   €€€€

A hotel situated on this island paradise is a rarity. Le Manoir d'Hélène is a simple, yet seductive 19th-century manor house, offering a warm welcome and delicious food, served among groves of eucalyptus trees. Offers only half board accommodation, but with food this good, that's certainly not a problem.

LA CADIERE D'AZUR Hostellerie Bérard

Rue Gabriel-Péri, 83740 **Tel** *04 94 90 11 43* **Fax** *04 94 90 01 94* **Rooms** *38*   **Road map** *C4*   €€

This 11th-century convent is now an attractive inn, with a heated outdoor pool, a shady terrace, lovely gardens and a well-respected restaurant. The rooms, cells of former nuns, are comfortable and spacious, despite their austere look. The hotel also offers courses in cooking, wine-tasting and watercolour painting. **www.hotel-berard.com**

LE LAVANDOU Hôtel le Rabelais

Rue Rabelais, 83980 **Tel** *04 94 71 00 56* **Fax** *04 94 71 82 55* **Rooms** *20*   **Road map** *D4*   €

This seafront hotel has brightly-decorated, sun-drenched rooms, even if some of them are a bit on the small side. There's also a pretty flower-filled terrace from which you can watch all the bustling portside activity. Breakfast is served on the terrace in summer. The beach is nearby. **www.le-rabelais.fr**

LES ARCS SUR ARGENS Logis du Guetteur

Pl du Château, 83460 **Tel** *04 94 99 51 10* **Fax** *04 94 99 51 29* **Rooms** *13*   **Road map** *D4*   €€€

The hotel forms part of an 11th-century castle overlooking this small village. The medieval atmosphere is sustained in the sturdy stonework and wooden doors. The rooms, however, have all modern amenities and comforts. The dining room is evocatively set in the basement. The ramparts provide superb views. **www.logisduguetteur.com**

SEILLANS Hôtel des Deux Rocs

Pl Font d'Amont, 83440 **Tel** *04 94 76 87 32* **Fax** *04 94 76 88 68* **Rooms** *14*   **Road map** *E3*   €

This 18th-century Provençal mansion on the peaceful village square has both a strong family atmosphere and good Mediterranean cuisine. Some bedrooms are smaller and darker than others – those at the front of the building are the biggest, brightest and best. In summer, meals are served beside the square's fountain. **www.hoteldeuxrocs.com**

Key to Price Guide *see p194* **Key to Symbols** *see back cover flap*

ST-TROPEZ Lou Cagnard

Av Paul Roussel, 83990 **Tel** *04 94 97 04 24* **Fax** *04 94 97 09 44* **Rooms** *19*   **Road map** *E4*

The bedrooms in this hotel, in an old town house, have been recently smartened up. There is no air conditioning, and the rooms facing the street are noisy. Make advance reservations for a room overlooking the small garden with mulberry trees. The hotel is only a minute's walk away from the lively square, place des Lices. **www.hotel-lou-cagnard.com**

ST-TROPEZ Hôtel Mouillage

Port du Pilon, 83990 **Tel** *04 94 97 53 19* **Fax** *04 94 97 50 31* **Rooms** *12*   **Road map** *E4*

This tiny hotel is a real find, with bedrooms that juxtapose traditional Provençal fabrics and paintwork with eclectic furnishings from North Africa, India and Bali. It even has a pool and the service is excellent. A romantic hideaway, it is also a comfortable place to spend a night or two while touring. Parking is available. **www.hotelmouillage.fr**

ST-TROPEZ Le Yaca

1 boulevard Aumale, 83990 **Tel** *04 94 55 81 00* **Fax** *04 94 97 58 50* **Rooms** *28*   **Road map** *E4*

Three 18th-century houses that once attracted a range of Impressionist painters, have been converted into a lovely hotel. A favourite among the rich and famous for many years. The rooms, decorated with antiques and wooden beams, provide great views. The restaurant serves excellent Italian cuisine. **www.hotel-le-yaca.fr/**

ST-TROPEZ Le Byblos

Av Paul Signac, 83990 **Tel** *04 94 56 68 00* **Fax** *04 94 56 68 01* **Rooms** *59*   **Road map** *E4*

This is the height of glamour for those with an unlimited budget. A luxurious complex of brightly-coloured houses sets the tone at the Mediterranean's most famous resort. The sumptuous bedrooms will make you feel like a Hollywood star. In addition, there is a beauty salon and spa treatments. **www.byblos.com**

TOULON Hôtel Mercure

Pl Besagne, 83000 **Tel** *04 98 00 81 00* **Fax** *04 94 41 57 51* **Rooms** *139*   **Road map** *D4*

Next door to the Palais des Congrès and close to the harbour, this chain hotel has been brightly decorated to reflect the warm colours of the Mediterranean. Palm trees and stained-glass windows add to the uniqueness of the spacious restaurant, which serves traditional Mediterranean fare. **www.accorhotels.com**

TOURTOUR L'Auberge St-Pierre

St-Pierre, 83690 **Tel** *04 94 50 00 50* **Fax** *04 94 70 59 04* **Rooms** *16*   **Road map** *D4*

Situated in a converted 16th-century farmhouse, this hotel makes for a tranquil stay. A trickling fountain graces the dining room, while the terrace offers wonderful views across the Haut Var. A fully-functioning farm still surrounds the hotel. Rooms have balconies looking out over the countryside. **www.guideprovence.com/hotel/saint-pierre**

TOURTOUR La Bastide de Tourtour

Montée St Denis, 83690 **Tel** *04 98 10 54 20* **Fax** *04 94 70 54 90* **Rooms** *25*   **Road map** *D4*

Located just outside the village, this ancient converted complex has panoramic views of the pine forests of the Haut Var. Some of the rooms have balconies that also offer sweeping views. The restaurant is set in a vaulted room and serves classical French cuisine. Along with the pool, the hotel also has tennis courts. **www.verdon.net**

BOUCHES-DU-RHONE AND NIMES

AIX-EN-PROVENCE Le Prieuré

458 route de Sisteron RN 96, 13100 **Tel** *04 42 21 05 23* **Fax** *04 42 21 60 56* **Rooms** *22*   **Road map** *C4*

Bedrooms in this converted 17th-century priory, in a quiet suburb of Aix, are comfortable. Ask for one overlooking the pond, which ripples with fish, and the stretching alleys of plane trees in formal gardens designed by Le Nôtre. In summer, breakfast is served on a sunny terrace. A pleasant hotel at an affordable price. **http://hotel.leprieure.free.fr/**

AIX-EN-PROVENCE Saint Christophe

2 av Victor-Hugo, 13090 **Tel** *04 42 26 01 24* **Fax** *04 42 38 53 17* **Rooms** *56*   **Road map** *C4*

Fantastic value for money, this superb town house hotel has bedrooms with all modern facilities. Book in advance to secure a room with a balcony. The hotel is decorated in Art Deco style, and has a bustling old-fashioned brasserie on the ground floor. **www.francemarket.com/stchristophe**

AIX-EN-PROVENCE Hôtel des Augustins

3 rue Masse, 13100 **Tel** *04 42 27 28 59* **Fax** *04 42 26 74 87* **Rooms** *29*   **Road map** *C4*

A converted 12th-century convent, with the reception housed in a chapel. Large, comfortable rooms in traditional Provençal style make the Hôtel des Augustins a haven of peace in the heart of Aix. The surprising absence of a restaurant is no real handicap with so many places to eat nearby. **www.hotel-augustins.com**

ARLES Hôtel Calendal

5 rue Porte de Laure, 13200 **Tel** *04 90 96 11 89* **Fax** *04 90 96 05 84* **Rooms** *35*   **Road map** *B3*

This good-value hotel in the historic centre of Arles, close to the Roman arena, has a mix of small rooms and large bedrooms – all charmingly decorated. A few have balconies with views of the arena or the Roman theatre. Breakfast is served in a garden shaded by palm trees. Original photographs grace the public areas. **www.lecalendal.com**

ARLES Hôtel d'Arlatan
26 rue du Sauvage, 13200 **Tel** *04 90 93 56 66* **Fax** *04 90 49 68 45* **Rooms** *47*   €€

Road map *B3*

This 16th-century town residence of the Comtes d'Arlatan is one of the most beautiful historic hotels in the region. Glass panels in the salon floor offer glimpses of fourth-century Roman foundations. There's a walled garden and a stone terrace for breakfast in summer. Antiques and curios furnish individually-decorated bedrooms. **www.hotel-arlatan.fr**

ARLES Hôtel Mireille
Rine droite Trinquetaille, 13200 **Tel** *04 90 93 70 74* **Fax** *04 90 93 87 28* **Rooms** *34*   €€

Road map *B3*

A tree-shaded terrace pool, a fine restaurant and colourful bedrooms make this hotel, on the right bank of the Rhône, an attractive place to stay. Trinquetaille itself is a rather bland suburb, but is easy to locate for those travelling by car. The hotel has parking space. The core of historic Arles is easily accessible. **www.hotel-mireille.com**

ARLES Nord Pinus
14 Pl du Forum, 13200 **Tel** *04 90 93 44 44* **Fax** *04 90 93 34 00* **Rooms** *26*   €€€€

Road map *B3*

Overlooking the central square, where van Gogh painted the Café de Nuit, this historic Arles landmark has accommodated luminaries such as Mistral, Picasso and Cocteau. A national monument, it offers comfortable rooms, and contemporary art, old photographs and large mirrors in the public areas. **www.nord-pinus.com**

CASSIS Le Clos des Arômes
10 rue Abbé Paul Mouton, 13260 **Tel** *04 42 01 71 84* **Fax** *04 42 01 31 76* **Rooms** *14*   €

Road map *C4*

This peaceful hotel in a sensitively-refurbished Cassis house stands amid a garden overflowing with flowers and greenery. Le Clos des Aromes is extremely good value for money, and is much in demand. Book well in advance, especially for stays in July and August.

CASSIS Les Jardins de Cassis
Rue A Favier, 13260 **Tel** *04 42 01 84 45* **Fax** *04 42 01 32 38* **Rooms** *36*   €€

Road map *C4*

The most pleasant place to stay in the picturesque port of Cassis. The bedrooms, housed in a cluster of small pastel-coloured buildings, are well thought-out. The pool is set amid a garden of lemon trees and bougainvillea. The restaurant (open from June to September) serves a Mediterranean lunch around the pool. **www.hotel-lesjardinsde-cassis.com**

FONTVIEILLE La Régalido
Av F Mistral, 13990 **Tel** *04 90 54 60 22* **Fax** *04 90 54 64 29* **Rooms** *15*   €€

Road map *B3*

Housed in a converted olive oil mill, in the centre of sleepy Fontvieille, La Régalido is a luxurious and welcoming hotel, with tastefully-decorated and inviting rooms and a delightful flower garden with palm and fig trees. The restaurant has a pretty terrace for alfresco dining, and the menu features Provençal cuisine at its best. **www.francemarket.com**

LES-BAUX-DE-PROVENCE L'Hostellerie de la Reine Jeanne
Grande rue, 13520 **Tel** *04 90 54 32 06* **Fax** *04 90 54 32 33* **Rooms** *10*   €

Road map *B3*

This old house is set in the centre of one of Provence's most charming and popular villages. Offers attractive, individually-decorated and simply furnished rooms. Extremely well-priced, the hotel provides a panoramic view of the village and the valley. Not ideal for small children. Parking is always a challenge here. **www.la-reinejeanne.com**

LES-BAUX-DE-PROVENCE Auberge de la Benvengudo
Vallon de l'Arcoule, 13520 **Tel** *04 90 54 32 54* **Fax** *04 90 54 42 58* **Rooms** *23*   €€€

Road map *B3*

This attractive former country house, with its ivy-clad walls, is one of the most charming places to stay on the fringes of the Bouches-du-Rhône. Has comfortable, lavishly-decorated bedrooms, a large garden, swimming pool and tennis court. The restaurant serves regional cuisine. **www.benvengudo.com**

MARSEILLE Hôtel Péron
119 corniche Kennedy, 13007 **Tel** *04 91 31 01 41* **Fax** *04 91 59 42 01* **Rooms** *28*   €

Road map *C4*

Although this hotel's modern exterior may lack character, its bedrooms and bathrooms are a riot of 1960s kitsch, with costumed dolls and mural paintings evoking the different regions of France. Reserve a room in the front for a sea-facing balcony and double glazing. **http://hotel-peron.com**

MARSEILLE Saint-Ferreol Hotel
19 rue Pisancon, 13000 **Tel** *04 91 33 12 21* **Fax** *04 91 54 29 97* **Rooms** *12*   €

Road map *C4*

Located near the Vieux Port, this small, modern hotel has an air of glamour. The rooms are on the smaller side, but well equipped and thoughtfully designed. Most have double glazing (essential in noisy Marseille) and some have whirlpool baths. The bedrooms are named after artists with Provençal connections. **www.hotel-stferreol.com**

MARSEILLE Hôtel Mercure Beauvau
4 rue Beauvau, 13001 **Tel** *04 91 54 91 00* **Fax** *04 91 54 15 76* **Rooms** *73*   €€€€

Road map *C4*

Built almost a century ago and renovated in 2004, this elegant hotel is part of the Mercure chain of four-star hotels. It is located next to the Vieux Port, its fish market and the bustle of Marseille's most famous street, La Canebière. Rooms are air conditioned and sound-proofed. The only drawback is the absence of a pool. **www.accor-hotels.com**

MAUSSANE-LES-ALPILLES L'Oustaloun
Pl de l'Eglise, 13520 **Tel** *04 90 54 32 19* **Fax** *04 90 54 45 57* **Rooms** *9*   €

Road map *B3*

This small town is less crowded with visitors in summer than tourist hotspots such as Les Baux. L'Oustaloun is a tiny hostelry on its main square. Situated within a restored 16th-century town house, the rooms are pleasingly simple. Meals are served in a cool, vaulted dining room, which is a welcome escape from the summer heat. **www.loustaloun.com**

Key to Price Guide *see p194* **Key to Symbols** *see back cover flap*

NIMES Hôtel Kyriad Nîmes Centre

10 rue Roussy, 30000 **Tel** *04 66 76 16 20* **Fax** *04 66 67 65 99* **Rooms** *28* **Road map** *A3*

A recently-renovated hotel located on a quiet street in the centre of the city, near the cathedral. Set in an old converted house, the colourful public spaces have a unique bullfighting theme. The rooms are individually decorated and the top-floor rooms have patios and views over the city's rooftops. **www.hotel-kyriad-nimes.com**

NIMES L'Orangerie

755 rue Tour de l'Evèque, 30000 **Tel** *04 66 84 50 57* **Fax** *04 66 29 44 55* **Rooms** *36* **Road map** *A3*

A modern, but appealing hotel, with the advantage of its own swimming pool. Decorated with the bright colours of the Mediterranean, some of the rooms have balconies, while others have whirlpool baths. The restaurant is highly rated, serving local produce prepared with flair, but is non-smoking only. **www.orangerie.fr**

NIMES New Hotel de la Baume

21 rue Nationale, 30000 **Tel** *04 66 76 28 42* **Fax** *04 66 76 28 45* **Rooms** *34* **Road map** *A3*

Located in the heart of Nîmes' Old Town, boasts a spectacular central staircase and open courtyard, preserved from the 17th century, when this was a private home. The rooms are spacious, decorated in a mixture of traditional features and modern style. **www.new-hotel.com**

NIMES Imperator Concorde

Quai de la Fontaine, 30900 **Tel** *04 66 21 90 30* **Fax** *04 66 67 70 25* **Rooms** *60* **Road map** *A3*

This charming hotel dates back to the 1930s, when its guests included such celebrities as Ernest Hemingway and Ava Gardner. It has all the facilities one would expect from a four-star member of the prestigious Concorde group, including an outstanding restaurant and a pretty courtyard. **www.concorde-hotels.com**

SAINTES-MARIES-DE-LA-MER Hôtel de Cacharel

Route de Cacharel, 13460 **Tel** *04 90 97 95 44* **Fax** *04 90 97 87 97* **Rooms** *15* **Road map** *B4*

This historic ranch in the heart of the Camargue marshland, was once home to *gardians*, the cowboys that worked the land of this region. Today, this hotel is particularly popular with equestrians for its riding facilities. Although there's no restaurant, the hotel provides meat and cheese platters on request. **www.hotel-cacharel.com**

SAINTES-MARIES-DE-LA-MER Mas de la Fouque

Route du Petit Rhône, 13460 **Tel** *04 90 97 81 02* **Fax** *04 90 97 96 84* **Rooms** *19* **Road map** *B4*

You get what you pay for at the Camargue's most luxurious hotel. The bedrooms have terraces overlooking the lagoon, while the dining room looks out over the park. Tennis courts, mini-golf facilities and a stable of the region's famous white horses are also available. There's even a heliport if you really want to arrive in style. **www.masdelafouque.com**

SALON-DE-PROVENCE L'Abbaye de Ste-Croix

Route de Val de Cuech, 13300 **Tel** *04 90 56 24 55* **Fax** *04 90 56 31 12* **Rooms** *21* **Road map** *B3*

This picturesque hotel is housed in a converted 12th-century abbey. The rooms, which were originally monks' cells, are decorated in a rustic style. The breathtaking views of the surrounding area can be enjoyed from a shaded terrace around the pool. The restaurant prides itself on its local cuisine. **www.relaischateaux.com/saintecroix**

ST-REMY-DE-PROVENCE Hôtel l'Amandiere

Av Théodore–Aubanel, 13210 **Tel** *04 90 92 41 00* **Fax** *04 90 92 48 38* **Rooms** *26* **Road map** *B3*

A peaceful retreat outside the main town, surrounded by a pretty garden. There's a rustic feel all around, from the decor of the rooms to the traditional masonry of the hotel and the gardens surrounding the pool. Nearby is the Alpilles canal, which offers the ideal opportunity for leisurely strolls and summer picnics. **http://Perso.wanadoo.fr/hotel.amandiere**

ST-REMY-DE-PROVENCE Le Mas des Carassins

1 chemin Gaulois, 13210 **Tel** *04 90 92 15 48* **Fax** *04 90 92 63 47* **Rooms** *14* **Road map** *B3*

This typical Provençal farmhouse is outside the main town, picturesquely set amid lavender fields and olive groves. The building has been renovated with great care and retains its traditional feel. The open-air swimming pool is a welcome feature in the summer months. The restaurant is open thrice a week, only to hotel guests. **www.hoteldescarassins.com**

ST-REMY-DE-PROVENCE L'Hôtel des Ateliers de l'Image

36 boulevard Victor Hugo, 13210 **Tel** *04 90 92 51 50* **Fax** *04 90 92 43 52* **Rooms** *32* **Road map** *B3*

Set in a former music hall, this contemporary hotel has a photography theme. The rooms and hallways are decorated with exhibitions of photos, and a developing lab allows eager guests to print their own images. The restaurant menu combines French classics with Japanese cuisine. **www.hotelphoto.com**

ST-REMY-DE-PROVENCE Domaine de Valmouriane

Petite route des Baux, 13210 **Tel** *04 90 92 44 62* **Fax** *04 90 92 37 32* **Rooms** *11* **Road map** *B3*

A beautiful and luxurious converted 18th-century farmhouse, surrounded by pine forests and vineyards. The rooms are decorated with Provençal fabrics, and offer sumptuous marble bathrooms. The restaurant serves local cuisine beneath a vaulted ceiling. There's an open fire in the bar, and a shaded terrace beside the pool. **www.valmouriane.com**

VILLENEUVE-LES-AVIGNON Hôtel de l'Atelier

5 rue de la Foire, 30400 **Tel** *04 90 25 01 84* **Fax** *04 90 25 80 06* **Rooms** *23* **Road map** *B3*

A 16th-century house is the setting for this quiet, peaceful hotel. The public and guest rooms are dominated by antique furniture, art works and original wooden beams. There's a beautiful stone fireplace in the hotel lounge. The roof terrace has both sunny and shaded areas, filled with the fragrance of its blooming flower pots. **www.hoteldelatelier.com**

VILLENEUVE-LES-AVIGNON La Magnaneraie   €€€

37 rue Camp de Bataille, 30400   **Tel** *04 90 25 11 11*   **Fax** *04 90 25 46 37*   **Rooms** *29*   **Road map** *B3*

Used to breed silkworms in the 15th-century, this hotel is now a refined, tranquil place to stay. Anitique furniture adorns the rooms, some of which have patios reached through sun-drenched French doors. The restaurant is decorated with frescoes and there are options for outdoor eating in the lovely gardens. **www.hostellerie-la-magnaneraie.com**

VAUCLUSE

AVIGNON Hôtel le Splendid   €

17 rue Agricol Perdiguier, 84000   **Tel** *04 90 86 14 46*   **Fax** *04 90 85 38 55*   **Rooms** *17*   **Road map** *B3*

A good-value option in the heart of the old quarter. Offers comfortable, brightly-decorated, rooms, with overtones of Provençal style chintz. Opposite the hotel is the cloister of St Martial church, which has a beautiful garden and fountain. Ask for rooms overlooking the street for a superb view of the gardens. **www.avignon-splendid-hotel.com**

AVIGNON Hôtel Mignon   €

12 rue Joseph-Vernet, 84000   **Tel** *04 90 82 17 30*   **Fax** *04 90 825 78 46*   **Rooms** *16*   **Road map** *B3*

This one-star hotel offers excellent value in, what is otherwise, a pricey town. All the rooms are en suite and have colour TVs, and there are Internet and email facilities in the reception area. The old-fashioned decor is fittingly Provençal, with matching bedspreads and curtains. A Continental breakfast is included in the price. **www.hotel-mignon.com**

AVIGNON Hôtel d'Europe   €€€€

14 pl Crillon, 84000   **Tel** *04 90 14 76 76*   **Fax** *04 90 14 76 71*   **Rooms** *41*   **Road map** *B3*

One of Avignon's finest hotels, dating back to the 16th century – Napolean is said to have stayed here. The top-floor rooms offer views of the Palais des Papes, which is beautifully floodlit at night. The restaurant serves top-class cuisine and wines. Sounds of a trickling fountain in the garden enhance the peaceful atmosphere. **www.hotel-d-europe.fr**

AVIGNON La Mirande   €€€€€

4 pl de la Mirande, 84000   **Tel** *04 90 14 20 20*   **Fax** *04 90 86 26 85*   **Rooms** *19*   **Road map** *B3*

Set in the shadow of the grand Palais des Papes, this is without doubt the best place to stay in town. What was once a cardinal's mansion, has now been renovated in 18th-century style. The restaurant is one of the finest in the region, with a beautiful Baroque interior and an outside area surrounded by trees and aromatic plants. **www.la-mirande.fr**

GORDES Le Mas de Romarins   €€

Route de Sénanque, 84220   **Tel** *04 90 72 12 13*   **Fax** *04 90 72 13 13*   **Rooms** *12*   **Road map** *C3*

An 18th-century country house has been renovated to create this comfortable and peaceful three-star hotel. Traditional features include stone fires and bathrooms decorated with ceramic Provençal tiles. There's a pretty terrace where guests can enjoy breakfast. The pool is bordered by flower beds. **www.hoteldesromarins.com**

LE BARROUX Hôtel les Géraniums   €

Pl de la Croix, 84330   **Tel** *04 90 62 41 08*   **Fax** *04 90 62 56 48*   **Rooms** *22*   **Road map** *B2*

Set in an ancient house in one of the region's famous "perched villages", the rooms at this hotel are expectedly rustic, but comfortable. There is also a modern annexe, with slightly larger rooms. The restaurant, with original woodwork decor and a pleasant terrace, serves traditional Provençal dishes. **www.avignon-et-provence.com/hotels/les-geraniums/gb**

LE BARROUX Hostellerie Francois Joseph   €€

Chemin de Rabassières, 84330   **Tel** *02 90 62 52 78*   **Fax** *02 90 62 33 54*   **Rooms** *12*   **Road map** *B2*

Two traditional farmhouses, tucked away in a garden with spectacular views of the countryside, have been converted into rooms and apartments with their own cooking facilities. There are also two cottages in the grounds with private gardens. Breakfast is served on the veranda or the patio. Closed November to March. **www.hotel-francois-joseph.com**

LOURMARIN Hostellerie le Paradou   €€

Combe de Lourmarin D943/Route d'Apt, 84160   **Tel** *04 90 68 04 05*   **Fax** *04 90 08 54 94*   **Rooms** *9*   **Road map** *C3*

This hotel has a breathtaking setting alongside the Lourmarin gorges, surrounded by a shady park and close to the river bank. The restaurant prides itself on Provençal cooking with a sophisticated touch. Meals are served on the terrace in summer and in front of an open fire in winter. **www.leparadou-lacascade.com**

LOURMARIN Auberge de la Fenière   €€€

Route de Cadenet, 84160   **Tel** *04 90 68 11 79*   **Fax** *04 90 68 18 60*   **Rooms** *9*   **Road map** *C3*

A haven in the heart of the Grand Luberon region, known for its abundant wildlife and superb views. The rooms are decorated along the theme of arts and crafts such as the Painter's Room, filled with canvases and the Bastketweaver's Room, decorated with wickerwork. The grounds have two gypsy caravans as well. **www.reinesammut.com**

LOURMARIN Le Moulin de Lourmarin   €€€€€

Rue Temple, 84160   **Tel** *04 90 68 06 69*   **Fax** *04 90 68 31 76*   **Rooms** *19*   **Road map** *C3*

This hotel preserves the original millstones from its days as an olive oil mill, and boasts a two-star Michelin restaurant with four luscious menus *(see p217)*. The rooms are located within the stone walls of the 300-year old mill. Not, perhaps, an ideal place for a long holiday, but good for savouring a meal and staying overnight. **www.moulindelourmarin.com**

Key to Price Guide *see p194*   **Key to Symbols** *see back cover flap*

PERNES-LES-FONTAINES Mas de la Bonoty

Chemin de la Bonoty, 84210 **Tel** *04 90 61 61 09* **Fax** *04 90 61 35 14* **Rooms** *8* **Road map** *B3*

This renovated 17th-century farmhouse is surrounded by fragrant lavender fields and olive groves. The rooms are decorated in a rustic way, although they are equipped with modern features. The dining room beautifully preserves its original stonework and wooden beams. Also offers striking views of Mont Ventoux. **www.bonoty.com**

ROUSSILLON Le Mas de Garrigon

€€

Route de St-Saturnin d'Apt, 84220 **Tel** *04 90 05 63 22* **Fax** *04 90 05 70 01* **Rooms** *9* **Road map** *C3*

A peaceful farmhouse located amid pine forests. Everything here is designed for refined tastes, including the classical music, which plays in the public lounges in the evenings. The brightly-coloured rooms follow themes of artists or writers who contributed to Provence. **www.masdegarrigon-provence.com**

SEGURET Domaine de Cabasse

€€

Route de Sablet, 84110 **Tel** *04 90 46 91 12* **Fax** *04 90 46 94 01* **Rooms** *13* **Road map** *B2*

This hotel is part of a working vineyard, and wine tastings for guests are part of the appeal. The rooms are comfortable and clean, if a little sparse, and the swimming pool adds to the relaxing atmosphere. The restaurant is highly rated with lots of local produce and the wine list is, of course, excellent. **www.domaine-de-cabasse.fr**

SEGURET La Table du Comtat

 €€€

Le Village, 84110 **Tel** *04 90 46 91 49* **Fax** *04 90 46 94 27* **Rooms** *8* **Road map** *B2*

A stone house dating back to the 14th century, situated at the top of the medieval village. Offers wide-reaching views of the plains, particularly from the dining terrace. The staff are friendly and helpful, advising on activities within the area such as hiking or bike rides. The restaurant has a first-class reputation. **http://perso.wanadoo.fr/table.comtat/etablis.htm**

VAISON-LA-ROMAINE Le Beffroi

€€

Rue de l'Evêché, 84110 **Tel** *04 90 36 04 71* **Fax** *04 90 36 24 78* **Rooms** *22* **Road map** *B2*

This has been an inn since the 16th century. Although the guest rooms now have all the modern fittings one would desire, the public rooms retain a period feel with antique furniture and chandeliers. There is a garden and a terrace where you can dine in summer. The town's château is only a few steps away. **www.le-beffroi.com**

ALPES-DE-HAUTE-PROVENCE

CASTELLANE Nouvel Hôtel du Commerce

 €

Pl de l'église, 04120 **Tel** *04 92 83 61 00* **Fax** *04 92 83 72 82* **Rooms** *35* **Road map** *D3*

A good place to stay for a night or two in a picturesque town, that makes a good base for exploring. Rooms look out over the market square or over the crag that surmounts Castellane. The bedrooms are prettily decorated, well equipped and immaculately clean. The dining room veranda is a lovely, airy spot in the heat of summer. **www.hotel-fradet.com**

CHATEAU-ARNOUX La Bonne Etape

€€€€

Chemin du Lac, 04160 **Tel** *04 92 64 00 09* **Fax** *04 92 64 37 36* **Rooms** *11* **Road map** *D2*

This renovated 18th-century building is run by a family that takes great pride in its service. The rooms are stunningly decorated with antiques, but each has its own individual feel. The restaurant has a well-deserved reputation for excellence in serving classic French cuisine amid elegant surroundings. **www.bonneetape.com**

FORCALQUIER Hostellerie des Deux Lions

 €

11 pl du Bourguet, 04300 **Tel** *04 92 75 25 30* **Fax** *04 92 75 06 41* **Rooms** *13* **Road map** *C3*

Right on the corner of the town's main square, the Deux Lions' central position has secured its role as a staging post since the 17th century. The rooms are spacious and nicely decorated; those at the front are protected from street noise with double glazing.

MOUSTIERS-STE-MARIE La Bonne Auberge

€

Rue Principale "Le Village", 04360 **Tel** *04 92 74 66 18* **Fax** *04 92 74 65 11* **Rooms** *19* **Road map** *D3*

Refurbished recently, this hotel offers great value for money in terms of scenery and facilities. Within walking distance of Moustiers' restaurants and cafés, it is also a short drive from the breathtaking Verdon canyon. Bedrooms are light and simple, the cooking is tasty and the swimming pool is a welcome bonus.

MOUSTIERS-STE-MARIE La Bastide de Moustiers

 €€€€

Chemin de Quinson, 04360 **Tel** *04 92 70 47 47* **Fax** *04 92 70 47 48* **Rooms** *12* **Road map** *D3*

Housed in a 17th-century building, this hotel offers the latest facilities within its venerable exteriors. The Provençal buildings are surrounded by a gorgeous garden and the hotel has sweeping views of the surrounding mountains. The restaurant has a good wine list. Special rooms are available for disabled people. **www.bastide-moustiers.com**

REILLANNE Auberge de Reillanne

€

D214 Le Pigonnier, 04110 **Tel** *04 92 76 45 95* **Fax** *04 92 76 45 95* **Rooms** *6* **Road map** *C3*

This large and charming mansion (a converted fortified manor) in the Luberon region is surrounded by a vast garden. The living rooms and other public areas are lined with bookshelves, while the comfortable rooms are rustic with a mishmash of country furniture and textured fabrics. The restaurant offers good French country cooking.

RESTAURANTS, CAFES AND BARS

One of the joys of this sun-drenched region is the abundance of fresh, enticing food on offer. The coast of Provence is famous for its seafood restaurants – these are best in the coastal towns of Marseille and Nice, but generally do not come cheap.

For traditional Provençal fare, it is advisable to head inland to the villages of the Var and northern Vaucluse. In the valleys of Haute Provence, the cuisine is more simple, but delicious – local game and the much-loved truffle

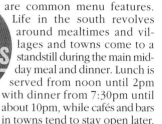

Les Routiers road sign

are common menu features. Life in the south revolves around mealtimes and villages and towns come to a standstill during the main midday meal and dinner. Lunch is served from noon until 2pm with dinner from 7:30pm until about 10pm, while cafés and bars in towns tend to stay open later, especially in high season *(see pp218–19)*. The restaurants on pages 210–17 have been carefully selected for their excellence of food, decor and ambience, covering all price ranges.

TYPES OF RESTAURANT

In the country, you may eat at a *ferme auberge*, a small, basic inn attached to a farm or wine estate. Here you will enjoy good, inexpensive meals, often made with fresh farm produce, eaten with the host's family as part of your room and board. Many country restaurants are attached to hotels but serve a predominantly non-residential clientele. These establishments are good value for money and are often the focus of local social activity.

In towns, there is the usual mixture of Americanized fast food joints and more traditional French restaurants. The larger towns such as Aix, Nice and Avignon provide a wide range of restaurants, including some of the best outside Paris.

For those on the move, look out for the distinctive red and blue Les Routiers sign – this is a long established organization that recommends anything from large family restaurants to

smaller brasseries, serving good quality, inexpensive food in a friendly, relaxed atmosphere.

In Provence, as in the rest of France, the decor of a restaurant is very much secondary to the quality of the food. This said, there are many places that offer charming medieval interiors or superb views.

In spite of recent legislation requiring restaurants to provide their clientele with a non-smoking section, a laissez-faire attitude prevails. If you are sensitive to smoke, ask for a table near the window or door.

HOW MUCH TO PAY

Prices in Provence are generally lower than those in urban France. Most restaurants offer fixed-price menus which are invariably better value than à la carte. Lunch is always good value – you can enjoy a large repast with wine for under 12€. Inland you can dine very well for under 30€ a head while, on the coast, the

Les Deux Garçons in Aix (see p219)

profusion of restaurants means that prices are kept competitively lower. In the deluxe dining rooms of the Côte d'Azur and the Riviera, you can expect to spend at least 61€ a head, although the food will usually be of outstanding quality.

Restaurants are obliged by law to post menu prices outside. These generally include service, but a tip is expected for good service – up to five per cent of the bill. The most widely accepted credit card is Visa, linked to the French Carte Bleue. American Express is becoming increasingly popular, as is the case with Diners Club. Traveller's cheques are virtually unheard of for settling bills.

MAKING RESERVATIONS

For the up-market palaces of the Côte d'Azur and Riviera, reservations are often mandatory. In season, it may be necessary to reserve a table in

Relaxing in the popular Café de Paris in St-Tropez (p218–19)

the smallest restaurants. In rural areas it is normally possible to find a table – the owner will simply add one to the terrace or extend his or her establishment further into the street.

DRESS CODE

The French are generally well-turned out, even when dressed casually, and visitors should aim for the same level of presentable comfort when eating out. Beach clothes are not acceptable, except in cafés and bars. The listings on pages 210–15 indicate which restaurants require formal dress.

READING THE MENU

Menus usually comprise three courses. The waiter will take your choice of *entrée* (first course) and main course. Dessert is ordered afterwards. More expensive menus are often four courses, with cheese eaten before the dessert, while some country restaurants serve six course extravaganzas, which can take several hours to eat.

The *entrée* usually includes salads, pâté, Provençal soups and often shellfish. Main dishes are predominantly a choice of lamb, chicken or fish – game is widely available in season.

Coffee is always served after, not with, dessert – you will need to specify whether you want it *au lait* (with milk).

The elegant Colombe d'Or restaurant in St-Paul-de-Vence *(see p212)*

Breakfast for two in a local café

CHOICE OF WINE

Wine is so much a part of everyday life in Provence that you will find a good range at even the smallest establishments *(see pp208–9)*. The price may be off-putting as all restaurants put a large mark-up on wine (up to 300 per cent).

Most wine is produced locally and usually served in carafes. Ordering a *demi* (50 cl) or *quart* (25 cl) is an inexpensive way of sampling the region's finest wines. French law divides the country's wines into four classes, in ascending order of quality: Vin de Table, Vin de Pays, Vin Délimité de Qualité Supérieure (VDQS) and Appellation d'Origine Contrôlée (AOC). If in doubt, order the house wine *(la réserve)* – few owners will risk their reputation on an inferior quality wine as this is their personal choice.

VEGETARIAN FOOD

Uniquely vegetarian restaurants are hard to find, as this concept has largely yet to filter down to the carnivorous South. Most establishments will offer salads, omelettes or soup, or dishes from the *entrée* menu. Some can rustle up a concoction of Provençal vegetables if given warning.

CHILDREN

Meals in Provence are very much a family affair and children are welcome in most places. However, special facilities like high chairs or baby seats are rarely provided. More and more establishments have a children's menu and many will be happy to provide smaller dishes at reduced rates.

SERVICE

As eating is a leisurely pastime in France, service can be slow. In small restaurants do not expect rapid attention: there may be only one waiter and dishes are cooked to order.

WHEELCHAIR ACCESS

Wheelchair access to many restaurants is restricted. In summer, this will be less of a problem at establishments with outside terraces; even so, when booking ahead, ask for a conveniently situated table.

USING THE LISTINGS

Key to the symbols in the listings on pages 210–17.

 no credit cards

 wheelchair access

 caters for children

 jacket and tie required

 outdoor eating

Price categories for a three-course evening meal for one, including a half-bottle of house wine, cover charge, tax and service:

€ Under 30 euros

€€ 30–45 euros

€€€ 45–60 euros

€€€€ 60–90 euros

€€€€€ Over 90 euros

The Flavours of Provence

The cooking of Provence is known as *cuisine du soleil* ("the cuisine of the sun") with good reason. Famous for its abundance of glorious, sun-ripe fruit and vegetables, it is also healthy with plenty of fresh fish and seafood and fine-quality, lean meat from mountain pastures. Cheeses tend to be made with goats' milk. Good produce is enhanced by key ingredients: olive oil, garlic and aromatic herbs. Local markets are a colourful feast of seasonal produce: tomatoes, aubergines (eggplants), peppers and courgettes (zucchini), and freshly picked cherries, melons, lemons and figs. Most of all, though, Provence is the land of olives and of rich green olive oil.

Olives and olive oil

Scented, sun-ripened Cavaillon melons in a Provençal market

VEGETABLES

In Provençal cooking, vegetables play a leading role. They may be served raw as crudités with *aioli* (garlic mayonnaise) or *tapenade* (puréed anchovies, olives and capers). Tomatoes and courgettes (zucchini) are often stuffed in the Niçois style, with minced meat, rice and herbs. Small violet arti-

chokes come with a sauce of lemon and butter, or sautéed with bacon. A favourite soup is the robust *pistou*, beans and vegetables laced with a pungent sauce of basil, pine nuts and garlic. *Ratatouille* is a fragrant stew of vegetables cooked with olive oil, garlic and herbs. Popular salads include *salade niçoise* and *mesclun*, a regional mixture of leaves, including rocket, lamb's lettuce, dandelion leaves and chervil.

MEDITERRANEAN FISH

The fish of the Mediterranean is highly prized, culminating in the famous *bouillabaisse*. A wide range of fish is caught, including rockfish, *rascasse* (scorpion fish), red mullet, sea bream, john dory, monkfish and squid. Around Nice, the main catch is sardines and anchovies. Most are best enjoyed simply grilled with herbs, like the classic *loup* (sea bass) with

Lobster　Mussels　Prawns (shrimp)　Sea bass　Monkfish　Squid　Clam

Selection of Mediterranean seafood available in Provence

PROVENCAL DISHES AND SPECIALITIES

Provence has produced several renowned dishes, of which *Bouillabaisse* is the most famous. The ingredients of this fish stew vary from place to place, though Marseille claims the original recipe. A variety of local seafood (always including *rascasse*, or scorpion fish) is cooked in stock with tomatoes and saffron. The fish liquor is traditionally served first, with croûtons spread with *rouille*, a spicy mayonnaise, and the fish served afterwards. Once a fishermen's supper, it is now a luxury item you may need to order 24 hours in advance. A simpler version is *bourride*, a garlicky fish soup. Rich red wine stews, known as *daubes*, are another speciality, usually made with beef, but sometimes tuna or calamari. Other classics include *ratatouille* and *salade niçoise*.

Fresh figs

Bouillabaisse *Fish often found in this Provençal classic includes monkfish, snapper and conger eel.*

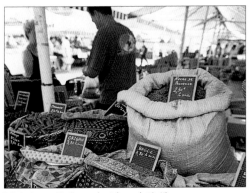
Dried spices and herbs on sale at the market in Nice

fennel. Seafood includes mussels *(moules)*, tiny crabs, giant prawns *(gambas)* and sea urchins *(oursins)*. Look out for trout from the Alpine streams north of Nice and freshwater eels in the Camargue. Popular fish dishes include *soupe de poissons* (fish soup), octopus cooked provençal style with white wine, tomatoes and herbs, and the famous *brandade de morue*, a speciality of Nîmes, a purée of salt cod, cream, potatoes and olive oil.

MEAT AND GAME

Lamb is the most popular meat, especially that of Sisteron, where it is grazed on high mountain pastures, resulting in delicately herb-flavoured flesh. Beef is most often served as a *daube*, named after the pot-bellied

terracotta dish *(daubière)* in which it is gently cooked for hours. Another speciality is *boeuf gardien*, the bull's-meat stew of the Camargue, served with nutty local red rice. Game from the mountains and woods includes wild rabbit, hare and wild

Display of the famous and delicious *saussicons d'Arles*

boar. Regional *charcuterie* features *caillettes* (cakes of chopped pork and liver with spinach and juniper berries) and the *saucisson* of Arles, once made from donkey but now usually pork and beef.

FRUIT AND HONEY

Elaborate desserts are rare, since there is so much sweet ripe fruit for the picking. Cavaillon melons are among the best in France, and the famous lemons of Menton are celebrated in an annual festival. Candied fruit has been produced in Apt since the Middle Ages. Local honeys are scented with chestnut, lavender or rosemary.

ON THE MENU

Beignets des fleurs de courgette Courgette (zucchini) flower fritters.

Fougasse Flat olive oil bread often studded with olives.

Ratatouille Stew of aubergine (eggplant), tomatoes, courgettes (zucchini) and peppers.

Salade Niçoise Lettuce with hard-boiled egg, olives, green beans, tomatoes and anchovies.

Socca Chickpea (garbanzo) pancakes, a speciality of Nice.

Tarte Tropezienne, St-Tropez's indulgent sponge cake stuffed with *crème patissière*.

Tourte des blettes Pie of chard, raisins and pine kernels.

Artichauts à la barigoule *Small violet artichokes are stuffed with bacon and vegetables, cooked in wine.*

Loup au fenouil *A sea bass is stuffed with fennel twigs and baked with white wine or grilled over more twigs.*

Boeuf en daube *Beef is marinated in red wine, onions and garlic, then stewed with orange peel and tomato.*

What to Drink in Provence

The region covered by this book could not encompass a more varied and enticing range of wines. To the north, the stony, heat-baked soil of the southern Rhône nurtures intense, spicy red wines, the best of which is Châteauneuf-du-Pape. In the south, the Mediterranean coast produces a range of lighter, fresh and fruity whites and rosés, as well as some delicious red wines. Especially good are the dry white wines of seaside Cassis and reds or rosés from the tiny fine wine pocket of Bandol. In the past, some Provençal wines had a reputation for not "travelling" well, but the introduction of modern wine-making techniques and more suitable grape varieties are fast improving quality. Here, we suggest a selection of wines to look out for on local menus.

Two bottle styles distinctive of the region's wines

WHITE WINES

The Rhône produces several fine, rich, buttery whites from grapes such as Viognier. The more accessible, and less expensive, alternatives listed below are perfect with the region's delicious seafood.

RECOMMENDED WHITES

- *Clos Ste-Magdeleine*
  Cassis
- *Châteaux Val Joanis*
  Côtes du Luberon
- *Domaine St-André-de-Figuière*
  Côtes de Provence
- *Domaines Gavoty*
  Côtes de Provence

A fine white Châteauneuf-du-Pape

White Côtes-du-Rhône

ORANGE • Gigondas
• Beaumes-de-Venise
Lirac • Châteauneuf-du-Pape
Tavel •
• AVIGNON
• NIMES
• Les Baux-de-Provence
• ARLES
Rhône
AIX-EN-PROVENCE
• Palette
MARSEILLE
Cassis
Ban

ROSE WINES

Provençal rosé is no longer just a sweetish aperitif wine in a skittle-shaped bottle. Grape varieties like Syrah give a full flavour and more body. Tavel is a typical example – dry and weighty enough to accompany Provençal flavourings such as garlic and herbs. Bandol's *vin gris* is also highly regarded.

RECOMMENDED ROSES

- *Château Romassan*
  Bandol
- *Commanderie de Bargemone*
  Côtes de Provence
- *Commanderie de Peyrassol*
  Côtes de Provence
- *Domaine la Forcadière*
  Tavel
- *Domaines Gavoty*
  Côtes de Provence

WINE AREAS OF PROVENCE

Wine-producing areas are concentrated in the southwest of the region, where vineyards cluster on the rocky hillsides (*côtes*). Les Arcs is a good base for a Côtes de Provence wine tour (*see pp108–9*).

Pale rosé *(gris)* from Bandol

Terraced vineyards on the coast above Cassis

RED WINES

At its best, Châteauneuf-du-Pape produces heady, intense wines to accompany the most robust meat dishes. Bandol also makes superb, long-lived red wines. For a lighter alternative, choose a Provençal or Côtes-du-Rhône red. Wines from one of the named Rhône villages should be of superior quality – or seek out reds from reliable producers in, for example, Les Baux-de-Provence, or the Côtes du Luberon.

Fine red wine from Les Baux

A jewel in Côtes du Luberon's crown

A spicy Châteauneuf-du-Pape

RECOMMENDED REDS

- *Château de Beaucastel*
  Châteauneuf-du-Pape
- *Château du Trignon*
  Sablet, Côtes-du-Rhône
- *Château Val Joanis*
  Côtes du Luberon
- *Domaine de Pibarnon*
  Bandol
- *Domaine des Alysses*
  Coteaux Varois
- *Domaine Font de Michelle*
  Châteauneuf-du-Pape
- *Domaine Tempier*
  Bandol

The grape harvest for Côtes de Provence red wine

KEY TO WINE AREAS

- Bandol & Côtes de Provence
- Bellet
- Cassis
- Costières du Gard
- Coteaux d'Aix-en-Provence
- Coteaux de Pierrevert
- Coteaux Varois
- Côtes de Provence
- Côtes de Ventoux
- Côtes du Luberon
- Côtes-du-Rhône

A light Muscat de Beaumes-de-Venise

FORTIFIED WINES

Despite the misleading name, *vins doux naturels* (naturally sweet wines) are sweet wines fortified with spirit. They are delicious as a chilled apéritif, with desserts or instead of an after-dinner liqueur. Most are based on the exotically scented Muscat grape, and range from cloyingly sweet to lusciously fragrant. An unusual alternative is red Rasteau, a port-like wine based on the Grenache grape.

Typical Muscat bottle shape

The stony, sun-reflecting soil of the Rhône valley

Choosing a Restaurant

The restaurants in this section have been selected for their excellent food, decor and ambience. Within each area, entries are listed alphabetically within each price category, from the least to the most expensive. For *Flavours of Provence* see pages 206–7 and details of *Cafés, Bars and Casual Eating* are on pages 218–9.

PRICE CATEGORIES
For a three-course evening meal for one, including a half bottle of house wine, cover charge, tax and service:
€ under 30 euros
€€ 30–45 euros
€€€ 45–60 euros
€€€€ 60–90 euros
€€€€€ over 90 euros

THE RIVIERA AND THE ALPES MARITIMES

BAR-SUR-LOUP L'Ecole des Filles
€€
380 av Amirale de Grasse, 06620 **Tel** 04 93 09 40 20 **Fax** 04 93 42 43 97   **Road map** E3

Situated in a former village school, this restaurant is perennially popular with locals. The food and decor are Provençal in flavour and style. There's a sunny terrace for the summer months. The restaurant offers à la carte and fixed-price menus. Non-smoking tables available. Closed Mon, Tue.

BIOT Les Terraillers
€€€€
11 route Chemin Neuf, 06410 **Tel** 04 93 65 01 59 **Fax** 04 93 65 13 78

This sophisticated restaurant serves rich dishes, flavoured with truffles and the herbs of surrounding hills. The *foie gras* escalope is not to be missed, and the lamb is a culinary triumph. The wine list highlights some of the better *vins de pays* of the Provençal vineyards. Closed Wed, Thu.

CAGNES-SUR-MER Fleur de Sel
€
85 Montée de la Bourgade, 06800 **Tel** 04 93 20 33 33 **Fax** 04 93 20 33 33   **Road map** E3

A delightful restaurant serving unpretentious cooking at affordable prices (especially when you choose from the set menus). The surroundings are rustic and the restaurant is in the heart of the village of Haut de Cagnes. There is an adequate choice of wines. Closed Wed, Thu lunch.

CAGNES-SUR-MER Le Cagnard
€€€€€
45 rue Sous-Barri, Haut de Cagnes, 06800 **Tel** 04 93 20 73 21 **Fax** 04 93 22 06 39   **Road map** E3

The outstanding Cagnard has an epicurean menu with truffles, pigeon languoistine and more, all perfectly prepared and immaculately presented in the surroundings of a 14th-century mansion. Some of the best Provence and Gard wines accompany the menu. Part of the Relais et Châteaux group. Closed Mon, Tue, Thu lunch.

CANNES Au Bec Fin
€
12 rue 24 Aout, 06400 **Tel** 04 93 38 35 86   **Road map** E4

Great value for money in what is generally a pricey destination. Among its specialities of delicious yet simply prepared dishes are sauerkraut and a range of grilled Mediterranian fish. The staff are friendly and the place is always busy, but it's usually possible to get a table without booking in advance. Closed Sun.

CANNES La Mère Besson
€
13 rue de Frères-Pradignac, 06400 **Tel** 04 93 39 59 24   **Road map** E4

Unlike so much of Cannes, which buzzes with energy year-round, this is a great place to relax, away from the hustle and bustle. The food is simple Provençal classics – try the *aïoli* (garlic mayonnaise) with snails, or the very traditional *estouffade* (stew). Closed Sun.

CANNES Le Comptoir des Vins
€
13 boulevard de la Republique, 06400 **Tel** 04 93 68 13 26 **Fax** 04 93 68 52 51   **Road map** E4

This wine-cellar restaurant does things a little differently – you choose your wine first, then decide what to eat with it. The wine list is extensive but need not break your budget. The food is hearty and simple. Surprisingly, this is more of a lunch-time place than a nightspot. Closed Mon–Wed dinner, Sun.

CANNES Royal Gray
€€
38 rue des Serbes, 06400 **Tel** 04 92 99 79 60 **Fax** 04 923 99 26 10   **Road map** E4

It's difficult to eat more lavishly than in the surroundings of the Royal Gray, where diners can expect some of the finest cooking in Cannes at a surprisingly affordable price and with courteous service. The accent is on Provençal flavours and Mediterranean seafood, accompanied by an extensive wine list.

CANNES La Palme d'Or
€€€€€
73 la Croisette, 06400 **Tel** 04 92 98 74 14 **Fax** 04 93 39 03 38   **Road map** E4

Children are not barred from this restaurant of the stars, nor is it essential to wear a tie, but diners who are not dressed to impress may feel self-conscious here. The food is superb, with fresh seafood and a costly and impressive wine list. La Palme d'Or is the restaurant of the Hôtel Martinez. Booking is essential. Closed Sun, Mon.

Key to Symbols *see back cover flap*

EZE Troubadour
Rue du Brec, 06360 **Tel** *04 93 41 19 03*   **Road map** F3

This restaurant, serving lunch and dinner can only be reached on foot. Its three small dining rooms, tucked away inside medieval walls, offer a respite from the summer sun. The set menus and à la carte options are inspired by classic Provençal cooking. Closed Sun, Mon; end-Jun–mid-Jul; mid-Nov–mid-Dec.

GRASSE Bastide St Antoine
48 av H. Dunant, 06130 **Tel** *04 93 70 94 94* **Fax** *04 93 70 94 95*   **Road map** E3

Jacques Chibois's restaurant is attached to his delightful boutique-hotel in Grasse's quartier St-Antoine, close to the town centre. The menu will excite lovers of inventive French cuisine, with duckling, truffles, and an inventive approach to vegetables. The excellent wine list is mainly Provençal.

JUAN-LES-PINS Les Pêcheurs
10 boulevard Maréchal Juin Cap d'Antibes, 06160 **Tel** *04 92 93 13 30* **Fax** *04 92 93 15 04*   **Road map** E4

The Hôtel Juana recently exchanged its celebrated rooftop restaurant for this wonderful place, fondly referred to as the "gastronomic cruise ship". Indulge in the Grilled Royal Sea-Bass with preserved lemons, marinated Provençal vegetables and basil. Open for lunch and dinner except Tuesdays and Wednesdays. Closed Tue, Wed; Jul, Aug lunch.

MENTON A'Braïjade Meridionale
66 rue Longue, 06500 **Tel** *04 93 35 65 65* **Fax** *04 93 35 65 65*   **Road map** C4

The menu here has a near-obsession with lemon-flavoured dishes with a hint of North Africa such as lemon-marinaded brochettes, lemons stuffed with tuna, eggs, olives, capers and aïoli, lemon-grilled chicken and lamb paprika. Closed Sep–Jun Tue, Wed; Jul, Aug lunch.

MENTON Auberge Pierrot-Pierrette
Pl de l'Eglise, 06500 **Tel** *04 93 35 79 76* **Fax** *04 93 35 79 76*   **Road map** F3

Located on a hill 5 km (3 miles) from the town of Menton, this restaurant has a true rural feel and a friendly atmosphere. It also has wonderful views from its outside terrace. The food is uncompromisingly fresh and the bill of fare changes with the seasons. Dishes may include *écrevisses* (shrimps) and duck a l'orange.

MONACO Zebra Square
10 av Princesse Grace, 98000 **Tel** *00 377 99 99 25 50* **Fax** *00 377 99 99 25 60*   **Road map** F3

This trendy restaurant, an off-shoot of one of Paris's smartest hotel-restaurants, lives up to its name – with zebra stripes everywhere. The multi-cultural menu features grills, seafood and fusion recipes at reasonable prices. With terrace tables in the sun right on the sea, it's the best choice in Monaco for lunch or dinner.

MONACO Bar et Boeuf
Av Princesse Grace, 98000 **Tel** *00 377 92 16 60 60* **Fax** *0 377 92 16 60 61*   **Road map** F3

Another Alain Ducasse masterpiece, the cutting-edge interior of this restaurant has been designed by Philippe Starck. The restaurant's theme is surf and turf as seen in its name – *bar* is a kind of sea bass; *boeuf* is beef. Some dishes are also influenced by Far Eastern flavours. Closed mid-May–mid-Sep lunch.

MONACO Le Louis XV
Pl du Casino, 98000 **Tel** *00 377 98 06 88 64* **Fax** *00 377 98 06 59 07*   **Road map** F3

The kitchen is run by the renowned masterchef Alain Ducasse. Edward VII was a regular in his day and it was during his visit that the classic *crêpe suzette* (pancake flambéed with orange liqueur) was created, named after his mistress. Divine food and exceptional wine list. Closed Tue, Wed.

MOUGINS Resto des Arts
Rue du Maréchal-Foch, 06250 **Tel** *04 93 75 60 03*   **Road map** E3

A simple restaurant with a family feel, and serving equally simple but excellent local cuisine. Fixed-price menus are great value for money, particularly at lunch time, but there is an à la carte menu as well. Specialities include *daube provençale* (beef stew) and *petits farcis* (whole tomatoes stuffed with minced meat, vegetable and garlic).

MOUGINS Le Moulin de Mougins
Notre-Dame-de-Vie, route départementale 3, 06250 **Tel** *04 93 75 78 24* **Fax** *04 93 90 18 55*   **Road map** E3

Alain Llorca's Michelin-starred restaurant is 2.5 km (1.5 miles) from Mougins. Booking is essential, especially in high season. A great venue for a special treat, with its cuisine leaning towards innovative seafood. The wines include some of the best of Provence. Modern sculptures adorn the garden terrace. Closed Mon.

NICE L'Acchiardo
38 rue Droite, 06000 **Tel** *04 93 85 51 16*   **Road map** F3

Set in the heart of Nice's Old Town, this is probably the most authentic bar and restaurant in the city, always buzzing with locals. Many people consider the fish soup to be the best there is, but all the cooking is delicious. The wines are served directly from the barrel. The restaurant only accepts cash payments. Closed Sun, Sat dinner.

NICE Le Boccaccio
7 rue Masséna, 06000 **Tel** *04 93 87 71 76* **Fax** *04 93 82 09 06*   **Road map** F3

One of the best places for seafood in Nice, the centrally-located Boccaccio is on a bustling, car-free street. The imaginative interior has stained-glass windows and tables spread out over several floors. The bill of fare features excellent fresh fish dishes, prepared tastefully. The set menu offers value for money. Closed Mon, Sat dinner.

NICE Le Chantecler

37 promenade des Anglais, 06000 **Tel** *04 93 16 64 00* **Fax** *04 93 88 35 68*   **Road map** *F3*

A thriving 19th-century establishment that still retains its high standards and reputation. Decorated with artworks and tapestries, it has a Regency feel to it. Although there are a variety of fixed-price menus, the menu Chantecler is highly recommended for its four exceptional courses. The restaurant owns two Michelin stars.

PEILLON Auberge de la Madone

Peillon village, 06440 **Tel** *04 93 79 91 17* **Fax** *04 93 79 99 36*   **Road map** *F3*

A restaurant specializing in vegetarian cuisine is an unusual find in France, but this is one that's continually popular. Try the *tourton des pénitents* (vegetable pie with almonds). The terrace is surrounded by olive trees and offers great views out over the valley. Closed Wed, Thu lunch.

ROQUEBRUNE-CAP-MARTIN Les Deux Frères

Pl des Deux Frères, 06190 **Tel** *04 93 28 99 00* **Fax** *04 93 28 99 10*   **Road map** *F3*

Provençal cooking, with an emphasis on lamb and duck can be savoured here. The restaurant is housed in a former school, and on warmer days, tables are placed on the square so diners can watch the world go by and enjoy the views down to Monaco and the Mediterranean. Closed Mon, Tue lunch; mid-Jun–mid-Sep.

ST-JEAN-CAP-FERRAT Le Pirate

Nouveau Port, 06230 **Tel** *04 93 76 12 97*   **Road map** *F3*

Overlooking the picturesque port, this family-run restaurant specializes in fish and seafood. Choose from dishes such as monkfish and lobster with garlic mayonnaise or *bouillabaisse*, a rich soup-cum-stew of mixed fish, including mussels, prawns and lobster. The fixed-price menus are excellent value for money.

ST-MARTIN-VESUBIE La Bonne Auberge

Allee de Verdun, 06450 **Tel** *04 93 03 20 49* **Fax** *04 93 03 20 69*   **Road map** *E2*

The restaurant of this old stone-built inn, set among a spectacular landscape, has tables on a leafy outdoor terrace. The menu is well-priced and offers an array of well-made local dishes and regional wines. It's a popular spot for lunch, so booking is advisable. The two-star hotel rooms are simple, clean and medium priced.

ST-PAUL-DE-VENCE La Colombe d'Or

Pl du Général de Gaulle, 06570 **Tel** *04 93 32 80 02* **Fax** *04 93 32 77 78*   **Road map** *E3*

This is one of the most famous and atmospheric restaurants in Provence and is still frequented by the rich and famous as it was at the time when Impressionist painters paid for meals with their artworks. The walls are lined with original Picassos and Matisses. The cooking is traditional yet inventive.

ST-TROPEZ L'Echalotte

35 rue Allard, 84100 **Tel** *04 94 54 83 26* **Fax** *04 94 54 83 26*   **Road map** *E4*

This up-to-the-minute restaurant, with its elegant, honey-coloured façade, is a favourite with those in the know in St-Tropez. The food is traditional and is reputed to be consistently delicious. Grilled steak with shallots is the restaurant's signature dish. The menu also includes Provençal stalwarts such as stuffed courgettes (zucchini). Closed Thu.

TOUET-SUR-VAR Auberge des Chasseurs

Av Général de Gaulle, 06710 **Tel** *04 93 05 71 11* **Fax** *04 93 05 71 11*   **Road map** *E3*

The cosy interior of this family inn, located in the scenic valley of the Var, is warmed by a big open fire in winter and on cooler evenings, while in warmer months, there are tables outside amid shade and greenery. The menu is traditional fare and the adequate wine list is modestly priced. Check before going, since closing times vary throughout the year.

VENCE Auberge des Seigneurs

Pl du Frêne, 06140 **Tel** *04 93 58 04 24* **Fax** *04 93 24 08 01*   **Road map** *E3*

This inn, housed in a wing of a castle, has hosted artists, aristocrats and crowned heads. Works of local painters adorn the dining room. The menu is mainly Provençal, with dishes such as spit-roasted lamb and grilled fresh fish. The wide wine list is moderately priced. Closed Mon, Tue–Thu lunch.

VENCE L'Armoise

9 pl de Peyra, 06140 **Tel** *04 93 58 19 29*   **Road map** *E3*

Andre Valentine specializes in fish dishes in this restaurant, but the menu changes every week and there is at least one meat dish. The piece de resistance is the *marmite* (stew) of fish and vegetables with a crayfish sauce. The roasted scallops, prawn and *bouillabaisse* are marvellous too. Closed Sun dinner, Mon lunch, Tue lunch.

VENCE Jacques Maximin

689 chemin de la Gaude, 06140 **Tel** *04 93 58 90 75* **Fax** *04 93 58 22 86*   **Road map** *E3*

It is worth making a pilgrimage to Vence to eat at this restaurant. Specialities include roast duck in garlic and *poivrade*, roast monkfish and other innovative dishes that draw their inspiration from the seas and slopes of Provence. The dining room has some fine works of art. Reservations essential. Closing times vary.

VILLEFRANCHE L'Oursin Bleu

11 quai Courbet, 06230 **Tel** *04 93 01 90 12* **Fax** *04 93 01 80 45*   **Road map** *F3*

A bubbling aquarium in the foyer hints that the accent is on fresh fish here. The location is delightful – the quayside of a lively yacht and fishing harbour, with tables under umbrellas on the terrace. The dining room is decorated with maritime memorabilia. Ideal for a long, lazy summer lunch. Closed Tue; mid-Jun–mid-Feb.

Key to Price Guide *see p210* **Key to Symbols** *see back cover flap*

VILLEFRANCHE Le Carpaccio

Promenade des Marinières, 06230 **Tel** *04 93 01 72 97* **Fax** *04 93 01 97 34*   **Road map** *F3*

Book ahead in summer for a table on the terrace of this restaurant with its spectacular views across the bay to St-Jean-Cap-Ferrat. The view is on show in winter too, thanks to the big-picture windows. Seafood, pizzas from the wood-fired oven and other dishes complement the signature dish, carpaccio (thinly sliced raw beef).

THE VAR AND THE ILES D'HYERES

COLLOBRIERES La Petite Fontaine

1 pl de la République, 83610 **Tel** *04 94 48 00 12* **Fax** *04 94 48 03 03*   **Road map** *D4*

This restaurant is in the centre of Collobrières, a scenic hill village. The menu includes chicken and garlic fricassée, rabbit with fresh herbs, duck with wild mushrooms. The wines come from the local wine cooperative, by the glass or by the carafe. Closed Mon, Sun dinner; Feb; second week Sep.

FAYENCE Le Castellaras

Route de Seillans, 83440 **Tel** *04 94 76 13 80* **Fax** *04 94 84 17 50*   **Road map** *E3*

Only 4 km (2.5 miles) from the centre of Fayence, Le Castellaras merits a special journey for a range of dishes: lamb fillet with tarragon sauce, scampi marinated in olive oil, lemon and tarragon, polenta in truffle oil. The wine list is drawn from the Côtes de Provence vineyards. Closed Mon, Tue (except Jul, Aug).

FAYENCE Le France

1 grand rue du Château, 83440 **Tel** *04 94 76 00 84*   **Road map** *E3*

A grand family dining room with a terrace makes this a pleasant place to stop for lunch. Choose from set menus, à la carte, or a more ambitious one that includes Provençal wild boar and long roasted lamb with garlic. The extensive wine list is affordable. Closed Mon, Sat lunch, Sun dinner.

ILE DE PORQUEROLLES Mas du Langoustier

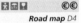

Ile de Porquerolles Ouest, 83400 **Tel** *04 94 58 30 09* **Fax** *04 94 58 36 02*   **Road map** *D5*

An appropriately fishy menu at this restaurant includes John Dory roasted with sea urchin roe, grilled red mullet, and other dishes such as wild mushrooms and *foie gras*, complemented by Provençal wines. Diners are driven from the port to this hotel-restaurant, close to the western tip of the picturesque island.

LA CADIERE D'AZUR Hostellerie Bérard

Rue Gabriel-Péri, 83740 **Tel** *04 94 90 11 43* **Fax** *04 94 90 01 94*   **Road map** *D4*

This hotel-restaurant in the converted buildings of an 11th-century convent has a fine view over the Bandol vineyards. Owner and chef René Bérard does marvellous things with fish and shellfish, including a sublime saffron-flavoured mussel soup. Bandol wines complement his excellent cooking. Closed Mon lunch, Sat lunch.

LA GARDE-FREINET Hôtel la Sarrazine

Route Nationale 98, 83680 **Tel** *04 94 55 59 60* **Fax** *04 94 55 59 60*   **Road map** *E4*

This attractively located restaurant has a fire roaring on cooler evenings and prettily-arranged flowers adorning its tables outside in summer. The affordable Provençal menu includes dishes such as rabbit with polenta and honey and red mullet fillets with ratatouille and *tapenade*.

LA MOLE Auberge de la Môle

Av Gabriel Peri, 83740 **Tel** *04 94 49 57 01*   **Road map** *D4*

This intimate restaurant, tucked away in the square of the tiny village of La Môle, has a pleasant bar in the front, while the atmospheric restaurant is at the rear of the building. Regional fare characterizes the excellent menu – duck, lamb, terrines, salads, and a good cheese board. Closed Mon.

ST-TROPEZ Le Bistrot Saint Tropez

3 pl des Lices, 83990 **Tel** *04 94 97 11 33*   **Road map** *E4*

This trendy brasserie's interior has low lighting and cleverly-placed gold mirrors, while the terrace looks over the pretty place des Lice. The cuisine has a "world food" influence, but French favourites such as scrambled eggs and truffles and lamb chops with *câpres* (mushrooms) can still be savoured.

ST-TROPEZ La Pesquière/Le Mazagran

1 rue des Remparts, 83990 **Tel** *04 94 97 05 92* **Fax** *04 94 97 05 92*   **Road map** *E4*

Twin, family-run restaurants on either side of the central place de la Ponche, with great views over the bay to Ste-Maxime. The seafood salad is superb as are the grilled and stuffed sardines with anchovies and olives, the *calamari à la Provençale* and the *aïoli* and fresh pasta. Relish a warm apple tart or *Tropézienne* to finish.

ST-TROPEZ Leï Mouscardins

10 rue Portalet, 83990 **Tel** *04 94 97 29 00* **Fax** *04 94 97 76 39*   **Road map** *E4*

This restaurant's picturesque location beside the Tour de la Portalet is one of its main selling points. Another is an imaginative menu with signature dishes such as soup of almond milk and green olives, and an array of dishes inspired by local traditions, combined with modern influences. The wine list is strong on regional vintages. Closed lunch.

TOULON La Chamade

25 rue Denfert Rochereau, 83000 **Tel** *04 94 92 28 58* **Fax** *049 4 92 28 58*   **Road map** *D4*

Renowned for a menu that has remained unchanged for years (and why change a winning formula?), La Chamade features dishes such as *foie gras* roasted with potatoes, sea bass, roasted figs, dates with gentian. The single fixed-price menu offers a choice of three appetizers, main courses and desserts. Closed Sun, Sat lunch.

BOUCHES-DU-RHONE AND NIMES

AIGUES-MORTES Le Café des Bouzigues

7 rue Pasteur, 30220 **Tel** *04 66 53 93 95*   **Road map** *A4*

With more than 60 covers indoors and on a large patio, it's easy to find a table at this bistro, a relatively affordable place in pricey Aigues-Mortes. The Mediterranean menu includes regional seafood and reasonably-priced wines. Lamb and aubergine (eggplant) tian and peach salad are among the outstanding dishes.

AIGUES-MORTES Les Enganettes

12 rue Marceau, 30220 **Tel** *04 66 53 69 11*   **Road map** *A4*

With tables on the pavement and in a more secluded inner courtyard, Les Enganettes serves an array of Mediterranean, Camarguais, Spanish, Italian and Moroccan-influenced dishes. The set menus and à la carte dishes are good value. There are musical evenings with live piano.

AIX-EN-PROVENCE Brasserie Leopold

2 av Victor-Hugo, 13090 **Tel** *04 42 26 01 24* **Fax** *04 42 38 53 17*   **Road map** *C4*

A classic brasserie with dozens of tables on the ground floor of the comfortable Hotel Saint-Christophe. A great place for a full-scale meal, a snack or just a drink, with tables on the pavement as well as inside. Strong on regional cuisine and traditional brasserie fare, with few concessions to trendy modern cooking.

AIX-EN-PROVENCE Mas d'Entremont

Route des Platriéres, 13090 **Tel** *04 42 17 42 42* **Fax** *04 42 21 15 83*   **Road map** *C4*

The food here is typically Provençal, with lots of meat and fish, while the list of Provençal wines is good, if not outstanding. In summer, eat outdoors on a terrace overlooking the gardens, while in cooler weather, sit in the indoor dining room, where huge picture windows open onto the surrounding park.

AIX-EN-PROVENCE L'Aixquis

22 rue Leydet, 13100 **Tel** *04 42 27 17 41* **Fax** *04 42 93 10 61*   **Road map** *C4*

A variety of dishes and a good wine list have made this one of Aix's most popular eating places. Chef Benoit Strohm is known for his signature dishes such as rabbit marinated in sage, fresh tomatoes and basil or ratatouille. The salon is decorated with colourful murals. Closed Sun, Mon dinner.

AIX-EN-PROVENCE Relais Sainte-Victoire

Route Nationale 7, Beaurecueil, 13100 **Tel** *04 42 66 94 98* **Fax** *04 42 66 85 96*   **Road map** *C4*

Book in advance for a table on the terrace of this country inn at Beaurecueil at the foot of Mont Sainte-Victoire. Fresh Provençal produce is prepared with a modern approach in dishes such as honey-glazed lamb and grilled sardines with sun-dried tomatoes. Closed Mon, Fri lunch, Sun dinner

AIX-EN-PROVENCE Le Clos de la Violette

10 av de la Violette, 13100 **Tel** *04 42 23 30 71* **Fax** *04 42 21 93 03*   **Road map** *C4*

An elegant address in a chic mansion, standing in its own gardens makes this an ideal place for a romantic evening. Though perhaps not for small children. People do dress up a little here. The extensive wine list is strong on local and Provençal wines. The à la carte is Provençal with a modern edge.

ARLES La Gueule du Loup

39 rue des Arènes, 13200 **Tel** *04 90 96 96 69* **Fax** *04 90 96 96 69*   **Road map** *B3*

La Gueule du Loup ("the Wolf's Maw") is a lot more welcoming than its ferocious name implies. The menu is well-priced and changes almost everyday. Prompt service and a good choice of wines. Not for gourmets looking for cutting-edge cuisine, but brilliant at what it does – exquisite Provençal fare. Closed Sun, Mon lunch.

ARLES Vitamine

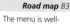

16 rue du Dr Fanton, 13200 **Tel** *04 90 93 77 36*   **Road map** *B3*

Provence is notably short on havens for vegetarians; the colourful little Vitamine being an honourable exception. More than 50 salads and pasta dishes to choose from, along with fresh fruit and vegetable juices and herbal teas. It fills up quickly, so come early for lunch or dinner. Takeaway meals are available. Vitamine is also child-friendly. Closed Sun.

ARLES Lou Marques

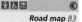

9 Boulevard Lices, 13200 **Tel** *04 90 52 52 52* **Fax** *04 90 52 52 53*   **Road map** *B3*

Lou Marques – the restaurant of the venerable Hôtel Jules César – is one of the best places to eat in Arles, with a central location, a nice terrace and a bill of fare that concentrates on classic Provençal dishes. The surroundings are dignified, as the hotel and restaurant are housed in a former convent. Closed Mon lunch, Sat lunch.

Key to Price Guide *see p210* **Key to Symbols** *see back cover flap*

CARRY-LE-ROUET L'Escale

Promenade du Port, 13620 **Tel** *04 42 45 00 47* **Fax** *04 42 44 52 03* **Road map** *C4*

Inventive fish dishes such as sautéed sea urchin with apples are the keynotes of this restaurant. Tables on the terrace overlook the small port of Carry, set among parasol pines on the Côte Bleue. In cooler weather, the indoor dining room, painted in warm tones, is cosy. Book at weekends.

DIGNE LES BAINS Le Grand Paris

19 boulevard Thiers, 04000 **Tel** *04 92 31 11 15* **Fax** *04 92 32 32 82* **Road map** *D2*

In the dignified surroundings of Digne's best hotel, this is also the town's best restaurant, with a menu that leans towards traditional dishes such as fillet of lamb and roasted duck breast with shallots. Adventurous gourmets may find the menu a little unimaginative, but the quality and quantity are unchallengeable and the wine list is great.

LES-BAUX-DE-PROVENCE Hostellerie de la Reine Jeanne

Grande Rue, 13520 **Tel** *0490 54 32 06* **Fax** *04 90 54 40 46* **Road map** *B3*

This restaurant, part of a small hotel on Les Baux's bustling main street, is surprisingly cheap and cheerful in this busy tourist spot. It serves reasonably-priced dishes, prepared according to what is fresh and good each day. Regular features include traditional fare, with leeks and olives and tender baby lamb in garlic. It also has an inexpensive list of wines.

LES-BAUX-DE-PROVENCE L'Oustau de Baumanière

Route Départementale 27, Le Val d'Enfer, 13520 **Tel** *04 90 54 33 07* **Fax** *04 90 54 40 46* **Road map** *B3*

This superb restaurant rates two Michelin stars and has a dazzling menu and a stellar wine list, along with lovely surroundings and magnificent views of the valley. Jean-André Charial's cuisine mixes traditional Provençal influences with the best of nouvelle cuisine to create a memorable dining experience.

MARSEILLE Chez Madie (Les Galinettes)

138 quai du Port, 13000 **Tel** *04 91 90 40 87* **Road map** *C4*

A Marseille institution for generations (now in the hands of the eponymous founder's granddaughter), this quayside haven is perhaps the most authentic restaurant in Marseilles. *Bouillabaisse, bourride* and other fish dishes are complemented by tripe and pigs' trotters. Not suitable for vegetarians or children.

MARSEILLE Les Arcenaulx

25 cours d'Estienne d'Orves, 13000 **Tel** *04 91 59 80 49* **Road map** *C4*

In the former warehouse district north of the Vieux Port, now the hub of the city's nightlife, Les Arcenaulx occupies the premises of a 17th-century bookseller-publisher. A great place to start or end an evening's bar-hopping. Dishes include rabbit and sardine and ginger paté. Closed Sun.

MARSEILLE L'Epuisette

Vallon des Auffes, 13007 **Tel** *04 91 52 17 82* **Fax** *04 91 59 18 80* **Road map** *C4*

Painted in Mediterranean blue and white, L'Epuisette wins favour for an excellent seafood menu featuring grilled John Dory, seasonal lobster ravioli and truffle risotto. The wine list includes Cassis and Côteaux d'Aix-en-Provence. Reservations recommended. Closed Sun, Mon; Aug.

MARSEILLE Le Miramar

12 quai du Port, 13002 Marseille **Tel** *04 91 91 10 40* **Fax** *04 91 56 64 31* **Road map** *C4*

One of the best places to sample the fine seafood and *bouillabaisse*. Marseille's trademark dish is prepared by chef Christian Buffa at his restaurant located beside the old port. Tables are much in demand and booking at least 48 hours in advance is mandatory. In summer, choose a table on the quayside terrace. Closed Sun, Mon.

MARSEILLE Le Petit Nice Passédat

160 corniche Kennedy, anse de Maldorme, 13000 **Tel** *04 91 59 25 92* **Fax** *04 91 59 28 08* **Road map** *C4*

Housed in the Belle Epoque villa of the Passédat Hotel, this restaurant has wonderful views of the Mediterranean. The menu is strong on seafood and features lobster terrine, rock lobsters with hazelnut sauce, and crab in ginger. The wine list is extensive. Closed Sun, Mon.

NIMES Au Flan Coco

31 rue du Mûrier, 30000 **Tel** *04 66 21 84 81* **Road map** *A3*

An informal and affordable spot in Nîmes, with tables on the pavement on sunny days and good regional cooking prepared by a team of *traiteurs*, who use fresh ingredients and prepare your meal while you watch. The shop next door, under the same management, also sells delicious takeaway meals – ideal for picnics. Closed Sun.

NIMES Enclos de la Fontaine

Quai de la Fontaine, 30000 **Tel** *04 66 21 90 30* **Fax** *04 66 67 70 25* **Road map** *A3*

L'Enclos de la Fontaine, the pleasantly-modern restaurant of the classic Imperator Concorde hotel, is probably Nîmes' finest establishment. Despite that, it is affordable. The fare is both classical and inventive, with traditional dishes and newer options such as veal with fresh fig fritters. Book in advance for a table in the courtyard in summer.

NIMES Au Plaisirs des Halles

4 rue Littré, 30000 **Tel** *04 66 36 01 02* **Fax** *04 66 36 08 00* **Road map** *A3*

With a particularly good regional wine list from the Languedoc, Corbières, Minervois, Provence and Herault, Au Plaisirs des Halles is decorated on clean, modern lines. Its patio is a very pleasant place to eat on a sunny afternoon or summer evening. Closed Sun, Mon; two weeks end-Oct–early Nov.

PARADOU–MAUSSANE-LES-ALPILLES Bistrot de La Petite France

Av Vallée des Baux, 13000 **Tel** *04 90 54 41 91* **Fax** *04 90 54 52 50* — **Road map** *B3*

This small restaurant, on the D 17, running west to Fontvieille, can be a stopover between Les Baux and Arles. It has a fine wine list, dishes such as pig's trotters with morel mushrooms, *foie gras* and truffles on two menus of seasonal regional dishes. There is even a menu for juniors. Closed Wed, Thu lunch; Nov.

ST-REMY-DE-PROVENCE Le Jardin de Frédéric

8 boulevard Gambetta, 13210 **Tel** *04 90 92 27 76* — **Road map** *B3*

This affordable, family-run restaurant has pleasant surroundings. The imaginative menu including rack of Sisteron lamb in garlic sauce, sea bass in basil, cod soufflé flavoured with saffron, and delicious desserts. In summer, there are tables outside the pretty green-painted villa that houses the restaurant. Closed Wed, Thu lunch.

VAUCLUSE

AVIGNON La Fourchette

17 rue Racine, 84000 **Tel** *04 90 85 20 93* **Fax** *04 90 85 57 60* — **Road map** *B3*

Much loved locally, La Fourchette is a quirky little eating place. Antique forks and festival posters adorn the walls. The menu is traditional, with a modern take on dishes such as duck breast in garlic and a vegetable crêpe (pancake) or grilled sea bass. It has an excellent choice of cheeses. Booking is mandatory. Closed Sat, Sun.

AVIGNON Le Petit Bedon

70 rue Joseph-Vernet, 84000 **Tel** *04 90 82 33 98* — **Road map** *B3*

This restaurant, just inside the walls of Avignon's old quarter, has a high reputation for poached vegetables with tapenade and pistou, *bourride de loup* (sea bass), and courgette (zucchini) purée with garlic. An amiable atmosphere and a decent list of mainly Provençal wines. Closed Sun, Mon.

AVIGNON Hiély-Lucullus

5 rue de la République, 84000 **Tel** *04 90 86 17 07* **Fax** *04 90 86 32 38* — **Road map** *B3*

Located inside a medieval building, this old-fashioned, bourgeois restaurant has a history of catering to the gourmands of Avignon. It's decorated in Belle Epoque style (though it dates only from the 1930s). The menu concentrates on classics such as *foie gras* flan with morels. Closed Tue, Wed.

AVIGNON Christian Etienne

10 rue Mons, 84000 **Tel** *04 90 86 16 50* **Fax** *04 90 86 67 09* — **Road map** *B3*

The wine list is strong on Provençal and Burgundy vintages and the location in the medieval heart of Avignon, close to the Palais des Papes, is hard to beat. The food is equally unbeatable in this restaurant, with seasonal menus that emphasize local produce. Choose from set menus or à la carte. Closed Sun, Mon (except in July).

AVIGNON La Mirande

4 pl de la Mirande, 84000 **Tel** *04 90 14 20 20* **Fax** *04 90 86 26 85* — **Road map** *B3*

One of the best places to eat in Avignon, with tables beneath olive trees and the floodlit walls of the Palais des Papes or indoors in a grand dining room (once a cardinal's palace). The extensive menu is dazzling, the wine list equally so, and the staff are friendly. For a special night out; book in advance. Closed Tue, Wed.

CARPENTRAS Chez Serge

90 rue Cottier, 84200 **Tel** *04 90 63 21 24* **Fax** *04 90 63 21 24* — **Road map** *B3*

A surprising discovery in sleepy Carpentras, the style and menus of Chez Serge reflect a mix of old and new. It is family-friendly (highchairs available). The excellent pizzas will please young eaters, plus there's some imaginative fare, such as Armenian grilled platters and lamb, chicken and duck. The wine list is extensive, including some from Italy and California.

CAVAILLON Restaurant Prévot

353 av de Verdun, 84300 **Tel** *04 90 71 32 43* **Fax** *04 90 71 97 05* — **Road map** *B3*

A gastronomic treat in the heart of the pretty market-town of Cavaillon. Chef Jean-Jacques Prévot is mad about melons – his restaurant has them as a decorative motif and there's an entire set menu dedicated to the gourd family. The melon and scallops is recommended. There's a good selection of wines as well. Closed Sun, Mon.

CHATEAUNEUF-DU-PAPE La Mère Germaine

3 rue Commandant Lemaitre, 84230 **Tel** *04 90 83 54 37* **Fax** *04 90 83 50 27* — **Road map** *B3*

Surrounded by vineyards, this restaurant has an outstanding list of regional wines. The cooking is classic Provençal, servings are generous and although not cheap, La Mère Germaine offers value for money. Service is friendly and efficient. Go for lunch to make the most of the excellent view. Closed Tue, Wed, Sun dinner.

CHATEAUNEUF-DU-PAPE Le Pistou

15 rue Joseph Ducos, 84230 **Tel** *04 90 83 71 75* — **Road map** *B3*

A good choice for those visiting Châteauneuf-du-Pape on a smaller budget. This bistro serves traditional staples and varying daily specials. Located in a quiet lane close to the medieval castle, its farmhouse-style decor is unassuming, but service is friendly and prompt. It also offers takeaway meals. Closed Sun dinner.

Key to Price Guide *see p210* **Key to Symbols** *see back cover flap*

GIGONDAS Les Florets

Route des Dentelles, 84190 **Tel** *04 90 65 85 46* **Fax** *04 90 65 88 42*   **Road map** *B2*

This hotel-restaurant provides fine views of the Dentelles de Montmirail from its outdoor terrace. The seating here and in the indoor restaurant is limited, so arrive early or book ahead. Well-presented regional cooking is complemented by the fine wines of the Gigondas region. Closed Mon dinner, Tue, Wed.

LOURMARIN Moulin de Lourmarin

Rue du Temple, 84160 **Tel** *04 90 68 06 69* **Fax** *04 90 68 31 76*   **Road map** *C3*

Two Michelin stars keep this hotel-restaurant *(see p202),* located in a former olive press, ahead of the local competition. Book in advance, especially during the Cannes Film Festival. Dishes include truffles *en croûte* and roasted venision; there's even a cake trolley. Closed Tue, Wed lunch, Thu lunch.

ORANGE Le Yaca

24 pl Silvain, 84100 **Tel** *04 90 34 70 03*   **Road map** *B2*

With a vaulted stone dining room and outdoor tables in summer, Le Yaca, next to Orange's ancient Roman theatre, is a great place for delicious and inexpensive meals. Enjoy generous helpings of dishes such as leg of lamb with a cheese crust, olive purée, and a rich chicken liver terrine. Closed Tue dinner, Wed.

SEGURET La Table du Comtat

Le Village, 84110 **Tel** *04 90 46 91 49* **Fax** *04 90 46 94 27*   **Road map** *B2*

This hotel-restaurant has wonderful views of the Dentelles and the surrounding countryside from its terrace. The menu includes such delights as truffles, pigeon, wild boar and other game. The fine wine cellar has excellent Côtes-du-Rhône and other vintages. Also a comfortable place for a short stay *(see p203).* Closed Tue lunch.

SERIGNAN DU COMTAT Le Pre du Moulin

Route de Sainte-Cécile des Vignes, 84830 **Tel** *04 90 70 14 55* **Fax** *04 90 70 05 62*   **Road map** *B2*

Master chef Pascal Alonzo prepares delicacies such as truffle ravioli with artichokes and roast Remuzat lamb in this comfortable hotel-restaurant on a popular countryside wine-tasting route. The wine list is packed with big Côtes-du-Rhône and Gigondas vintages. Closed Mon, Sun dinner.

ALPES-DE-HAUTE-PROVENCE

CASTELLANE Auberge du Teillon

La Garde Route Napoléon, 04120 **Tel** *04 92 83 60 88*   **Road map** *D3*

This pleasant country inn, a short distance from the tourist hotspot of Castellane, offers an unpretentious bill of fare that changes seasonally. Traditional dishes are prepared with fresh ingredients. The specialities include hand-smoked "Norway" salmon and home-made *foie gras.* Closed Sun, Mon dinner, Tue lunch.

CHATEAU-ARNOUX La Bonne Etape

Chemin du Lac, 04160 **Tel** *04 92 64 00 09* **Fax** *04 92 64 37 36*   **Road map** *D3*

La Bonne Etape is the only real reason to stop in this nondescript market-town. This charming inn has an array of dishes and specializes in fresh local produce, especially lamb. The extensive wine list features vintages from almost every region in France. The dining room is decorated with paintings and tapestries.

DIGNE-LES-BAINS L'Origan

6 rue du pied de Ville, 04000 **Tel** *04 92 31 62 13* **Fax** *04 92 31 62 13*   **Road map** *D2*

This restaurant is a good place for lunch, dinner or even an overnight stop. The surroundings are unpretentious, but Chef Philippe Cochet's menu is imaginative, featuring dishes some may find challenging, such as pig's feet and tripe, as well as truffles and good fish dishes. Closed Sun; Christmas; last two weeks Feb.

MANOSQUE Restaurant Dominique Bucaille

43 boulevard Tilleuls, 04100 **Tel** *04 92 72 32 28* **Fax** *04 92 72 32 28*   **Road map** *C3*

Dominique Bucaille specializes in variations on traditional cuisines and many dishes use the delicious potatoes for which this area is well known. Lamb from the mountain pastures of Haute Provence also features strongly, accompanied by wines from the Luberon and Provence. Closed Sun, Wed dinner.

MANOSQUE Hostellerie de la Fuste

Route de Valensole, 04210 **Tel** *04 92 72 05 95* **Fax** *04 92 72 92 93*   **Road map** *C3*

An elegant country inn, 6.5 km (4 miles) from Manosque and well worth the journey. The menu features local produce and its own home-grown vegetables, served on a terrace shaded by 300-year-old plane trees. Fish and meat dominate the menu and there's a good choice of cheeses and desserts. Closed Sun dinner, Mon lunch.

MOUSTIERS-STE-MARIE La Treille Muscate

Pl de l'Eglise, 04360 **Tel** *04 92 74 64 31* **Fax** *04 92 74 63 52*   **Road map** *D3*

Enjoy excellent fare such as a pistou of vegetables in this lovely bistro located in the main square of one of the region's prettiest villages. It overlooks a swift-flowing stream and has tables on the terrace. With a choice of set menus and a decent wine list, it's a great venue for a relaxed alfresco lunch. Closed Wed.

Cafés, Bars and Casual Eating

In rural areas the world over the local bar is the centre of village life, and nowhere is this more true than in Provence. Everywhere you go you will find lively watering holes, often with outside terraces or gardens. Most bars and cafés double as lunchtime restaurants, serving straightforward daily specials at reasonable prices. Snacks are not really a part of French life but nearly all bars will make you a traditional *baguette* sandwich or a *croque monsieur* (toasted ham and cheese sandwich). Drinking is a subject close to Provençal hearts – *pastis*, the aniseed spirit synonymous with Marseille, is the region's lifeblood. In many country towns, you will see the locals sitting outside sipping *pastis* from the early morning onwards, along with strong black coffee. Lunchtime tipples include ice-cold rosé, the perfect accompaniment to a sun-filled day.

CAFÉS

There is little distinction between cafés and bars in Provence and most serve alcohol all day. In the country, village cafés will often close around 8pm. In larger towns, many places stay open much later – popular Marseillais and Niçois bars close when the last person leaves. Many stay open all night, serving breakfast to the diehards as dawn breaks. A lot of cafés are also *tabacs* (tobacconists) selling cigarettes, tobacco, sweets and stamps.

While most Provençal cafés are simple places, where decor is restricted to the local fire brigade calendar and fashion to a hunting jacket and boots, there are several stylish exceptions. No visit to Aix is complete without an hour or two spent sipping coffee on the cours Mirabeau, one of the places in Provence to see and be seen. On the Côte d'Azur, chic cafés abound. In Cannes the **Brasserie Carlton** is the place to spot film stars during the festival. In Nice, the cafés on the cours Saleya are the hub of day and nightlife, while Monaco boasts the crème de la crème, the **Café de Paris**.

WHAT TO EAT

Most Provençal cafés serve breakfast although, in village establishments, this will just be a couple of slices of *baguette* and coffee. More elaborate affairs are served in towns, with fresh orange juice, hot croissants and jam. Café lunches usually include a *plat du jour* (dish of the day) and a dessert, along with a quarter litre of wine. These can be great bargains, costing little more than 10€. For more basic lunches, sandwiches, omelettes and salads can be ordered. Evening meals are usually the reserve of restaurants, although in rural areas, the local bar will also serve dinner, normally a varient on the lunchtime menu.

WHAT TO DRINK

Since Roman days, when the legionnaires introduced wine to the region, drinking has been a favoured pastime in Provence. Cold beer seems to surpass the fruit of the vine in the hearts of most farmers, as village bars are filled with locals downing *pressions* (half-pint glasses of beer). More potent tipples include *pastis*, a 90 per cent proof nectar flavoured with aniseed, vanilla and cinnamon, and *marc*, a brandy distilled from any available fruits. Soft drinks such as *un diabolo* (fruit syrup mixed with lemonade) and *orange pressée* (freshly squeezed orange juice) are also popular. As in most Mediterranean lands, coffee is a way of life – *un café* is a cup of strong and black expresso. If you want white coffee, ask for *un café crème*. For filter or instant coffee order *un café filtre* or *un café américain*. Tea will always be served black unless you ask for milk or lemon. Herbal teas are also available, known as *tisanes* or *infusions*.

BARS

In most towns you will find a handful of bars that only serve beer and miscellaneous alcohol, rather than the more diverse range offered by cafés. These bars are lively in true Mediterranean style. Student centres such as Nice, Marseille and Aix contain British-style pubs, offering a large selection of European bottled and draught beer. Some have live bands, such as **Wayne's Bar, De Klomp,** and **O'Hara's** in Nice.

More upmarket bars are found in the plush hotels of the Côte d'Azur. Here, in Belle Epoque splendour, you can sip champagne listening to jazz piano, string quartets or opera singers. Among the most impressive are the bars of the Carlton and Martinez hotels in Cannes, Le Négresco in Nice, **Somerset Maugham** at the Grand Hôtel in St-Jean-Cap-Ferrat and the Hermitage in Monte-Carlo (*see* Where to Stay, pp194–203).

PICNIC AND TAKE-AWAY FOOD

You are never far from food in Provence. The traditional street food of Provence is the *pan bagnat*, a thick bun filled with crisp salade Niçoise and doused in olive oil. Pizza is a local favourite, and every small town has its pizza van, where your choice is cooked to order. A particularly Provençal form of pizza is *pissaladière*, an onion pizza coated with anchovies and olives. In Nice, the number one snack is *socca*, thick crêpes made from chick-pea flour (*see pp206–7*).

The French love picnics and the Provençaux are no exception. French alfresco eating is complex – families set out tables, chairs, barbecues and portable fridges. To service this penchant for portable food, Provençal villages have specialist shops offering ready-to-eat food. *Boulangeries* and *pâtisseries* serve everything from fresh croissants to quiches and a dazzling array of cakes and tarts. Nearly all *pâtisseries* provide freshly made *baguette* sandwiches.

In the main towns, specialist butchers called *traîteurs* provide ready-made dishes, such as salads, cold meats and roast chicken, sold in cartons according to weight. **Au Flan Coco** in Nîmes and **Bataille** in Marseille are fine examples. Most supermarkets also have similar delicatessen counters. *Charcuteries* specialize in pork dishes, particularly pâtés and sausages. For traditional spicy sausages much prized in the Camargue, head to the **Dorel et Milhau** in Arles.

The best place to buy picnic food is the local market. Every town in Provence has its market, some daily, like Aix-en-Provence, some just once or twice a week. No Provençal picnic is complete without

French bread – the *baguette* is the mainstay of the country and Provence is no exception. The only difference is that the region boasts numerous local breads, incorporating traditional ingredients. *Pain aux olives* is found almost everywhere, often in the form of *fougasse*, a flat, lattice-like loaf. Alternatively, this may contain anchovies (*pain aux anchois*), or spinach (*pain aux épinards*) and there is a sweet version flavoured with almonds. Wholemeal or brown bread is an anathema to the traditional Provençaux, although many bakeries now produce it – ask for *pain aux céréales*. The nearest to healthy bread is *pain de campagne*, a sturdier *baguette* made with unrefined white flour. One of

the finest *boulangeries* in the region is **Le Four à Bois**, in the old quarter of Nice, where the same recipes have been used for generations.

Boulangeries are found in every village and usually have a good selection of *pâtisseries*, cakes and tarts. Provençal ingredients are combined to make these delights, such as honey, almonds and fruit – try those at **Béchard** in Aix-en-Provence. For those with an even sweeter tooth, these same ingredients are used in the handmade chocolates and candied fruit. *Calissons* (an almond-paste sweet) and *suce-miel* (honey-based candy) are very popular. Two of the best shops are **Puyricard** in Aix and **Auer** in Nice.

DIRECTORY

CAFES

Aix-en-Provence
Brasserie des Deux Garçons
53 cours Mirabeau.
Tel 04 42 26 00 51.

Cannes
Brasserie Carlton
58 la Croisette.
Tel 04 93 06 40 06.

Eze
Château Eza Salon de Thé
Rue de la Pise.
Tel 04 93 41 12 24.

Monaco
Café de Paris
Le Casino, place du Casino.
Tel 00 377 92 16 20 20.

Nice
Le Grand Café de Turin
5 place Garibaldi.
Tel 04 93 62 29 52.

Nîmes
Le Café Olive
22 boulevard Victor Hugo.
Tel 04 66 67 89 10.

St-Paul-de-Vence
Café de la Place
Place du Général de Gaulle.
Tel 04 93 32 80 03.

St-Tropez
Café des Arts
Place des Lices.
Tel 04 94 97 02 25.

Le Café de Paris
15 Quai de Suffren.
Tel 04 94 97 00 56.

Senequier
Quai Jean Jaurès.
Tel 04 94 97 00 90.

BARS AND PUBS

Aix-en-Provence
Le Bistro Aixois
37 Cours Sextius.
Tel 04 42 27 50 10.

Avignon
Pub Z
58 rue de la Bonneterie.
Tel 04 90 85 42 84.

Cannes
Le Zanzibar
85 rue Félix-Faure.
Tel 04 93 39 30 75.

Juan-les-Pins
Xtrême Café
6 rue Aubernon.
Tel 04 93 34 03 90.

Pam-Pam
137 boulevard Wilson.
Tel 04 93 61 11 05.

Marseille
Le Bar de la Marine
15 quai de Rive Neuve.
Tel 04 91 54 95 42.

La Part des Anges
33 rue Sainte.
Tel 04 91 33 55 70.

Monaco
Bar du Soleil
Le Casino, terrace du Casino.
Tel 00 377 92 16 63 59.

Flashman's
7 avenue Princesse Alice.
Tel 00 377 93 30 09 03.

Nice
Wayne's Bar
15 rue de la Préfecture.
Tel 04 93 13 46 99.

De Klomp
8 rue Mascoinat.
Tel 04 93 92 42 85.

O'Hara's
22 rue Droite.
Tel 04 93 80 43 22.

Les Trois Diables
2 cours Saleya.
Tel 04 93 62 47 00.

Nîmes
La Petite Bourse
2 boulevard Victor Hugo.
Tel 04 66 67 44 31.

St-Jean-Cap-Ferrat
Somerset Maugham
Grand Hôtel de Cap-Ferrat,
71 boulevard du Général de Gaulle.
Tel 04 93 76 50 50.

Villefranche
Le Cosmo Bar
Quai Courbet.
Tel 04 93 01 84 05.

PICNIC AND TAKE-AWAY FOOD

Aix-en-Provence
Béchard
12 cours Mirabeau.

Puyricard
7 Rue Rifle-rafle.

Arles
Dorel et Milhau
11 rue Réattu.

Marseille
Bataille
18 rue Fontange.

Le Four des Navettes
136 rue Sainte.

Nice
Le Four à Bois
35 rue Droite.

Auer
7 rue St-François-de-Paule.

Nîmes
Au Flan Coco
31 rue du Mûrier d'Espagne.

SHOPS AND MARKETS

Shopping in Provence is one of life's great delights. Even the tiniest village may be home to a craftsman potter or painter, or you may arrive on market day to find regional produce – artichokes, asparagus, wild mushrooms – still fresh with the dew from the surrounding fields. Larger towns are packed with individual boutiques selling anything from dried flowers to chic baby clothes, and the fashion-conscious will always be

Provençal olive oil

able to find an avenue or two of famous names in which to window-shop. If the idea of cramming fresh foodstuffs into your luggage to take back home proves too daunting, Provence has perfected the fine art of packaging its produce, with the bottles, jars and boxes often works of art in themselves. This section provides guidelines on opening hours and the range of goods with a Provençal flavour to be found in the many stores and markets.

OPENING HOURS

Food shops open at around 7am and close at noon for lunch, a break which may last for up to three hours in Provence. After lunch most stay open until 7pm, sometimes even later in big towns such as Nice and Marseille. Bakers often stay open until 1pm or later, serving tasty lunchtime snacks. Most supermarkets and hypermarkets stay open throughout lunchtimes.

Non-food shops are open 9am–7pm Mon–Sat, but some may close for lunch. Many are closed on Monday mornings.

Food shops and newsagents open on Sunday mornings but almost every shop is closed on Sunday afternoon. Small shops may close for one day a week out of high season.

LARGER SHOPS

Hypermarkets *(hypermarchés* or *grandes surfaces)* can be found on the outskirts of every sizeable town: look out for the signs indicating the *Centre Commercial.* Among the largest are Casino, Auchan and Carrefour. Discount petrol is usually sold: you may have to pay in cash.

Department stores, or *grands magasins,* including Monoprix and Prisunic, are usually found in town centres. More up-market stores such as Printemps and Galeries Lafayette are found both in towns and at out-of-town complexes.

Sweetly-scented dried flowers in a St-Tropez shop window

SPECIALIST SHOPS

One of the great pleasures of shopping in Provence is that specialist food shops still flourish despite the new large supermarkets. The bread shop *(boulangerie)* is usually combined with the *pâtisserie* selling cakes and pastries. The cheesemonger *(fromagerie)* may also be combined with a shop selling other dairy produce *(laiterie),* but the *boucherie* (butcher) and the *charcuterie* (delicatessen) tend to be separate shops.

A *traiteur* sells prepared foods. For dry goods and general groceries, you need an *épicerie.* Cleaning products and household goods are sold at a *droguerie* and hardware at a *quincaillerie.* Booksellers *(librairies)* in the main towns sometimes sell English books. For addresses, see page 243.

A Provençal olive merchant and his wares

MARKETS

This guide gives the market days for every town featured. To find out where the market is, ask a passer-by for *le marché.* Markets are morning affairs, when the produce is super-fresh – by noon the stall-holders will already be packing up and the best bargains will have been sold out hours ago. By French law, price tags must state the origin of all produce: *du pays* means local.

Les marchés de Provence were immortalized in song by Gilbert Bécaud, and rightly so. In a country famed for its markets, these are among the best. Some are renowned – cours Saleya *(see p84)* in Nice and the food and flower markets of Aix *(see p148),* for example, should not be missed. Others take more searching out, such as the truffle markets of the Var. Try Aups *(see p104)* on a Thursday during truffle season, from November to February.

The flower, fruit and vegetable market in cours Saleya, Nice

Bags of dried herbs on display in the market of St-Rémy-de-Provence

REGIONAL SPECIALITIES

The sunshine of Provence is captured in its distinctive, vividly coloured fabrics, known as *indiennes*. Many shops sell them by the metre; others, such as **Les Textiles Mistral** and **Souleïado** also make them into soft furnishings, cowboy shirts and boxer shorts.

Throughout Provence, working olive mills churn out rich, pungent oil, which is also used to make the chunky blocks of soap, *savon de Marseille*. Tins and jars of olives, often scented with *herbes de Provence*, are widely available, as are bags of the herbs themselves. Bags of lavender, and honey from its pollen, are regional specialities; local flowers appear in other forms too, from dried arrangements to scented oils, or perfumes from Grasse *(see p67)*.

Traditional sweets *(confiseries)* abound, using regional fruits and nuts: almond *calissons* from Aix, fruity *berlingots* from Carpentras and candied *fruits confits* are just a few.

LOCAL WINES

Provence is not one of the great wine regions of the world, but its many vineyards *(see pp208–9)* produce a wide range of pleasant wines and you will see plenty of signs inviting you to a *dégustation* (tasting). You will usually be expected to buy at least one bottle. Wine co-operatives sell the wines of numerous smaller producers. Here you can buy wine in five- and ten-litre containers

Liquorice-flavoured aperitif from Marseille

(en vrac). This wine is "duty free" but, with vineyards such as Châteauneuf-du-Pape and Beaumes-de-Venise, wise buyers will drink *en vrac* on holiday and pick up bargains in fine wine to bring home.

Marseille's aperitif *pastis* is an evocative, if acquired, taste.

Works by local artists sold on the harbour at St-Tropez

ARTS AND CRAFTS

Many of the crafts now flourishing in Provence are traditional ones that had almost died out 50 years ago. The potters of Vallauris owe the revival in their fortunes to Picasso *(see pp72–3)* but, more often, it is the interest of visitors that keeps a craft alive. From the little pottery *santons* of Marseille to the flutes and tambourines of Barjols, there is plenty of choice for gifts and mementos. Many towns have unique specialities. Biot is famous for its bubbly glassware, Cogolin for pipes and carpets and Salernes for hexagonal terracotta tiles.

What to Buy in Provence

Best buys to be found in Provence are those that reflect the character of the region – its geographical blessings of bountiful produce and its historic traditions of arts and crafts. While the chic boutiques of St-Tropez or Cannes may rival Paris in predicting the latest fashion trend, your souvenirs of Provence should be far more timeless. The evocative scents, colours and flavours they offer will help to keep your holiday memories alive throughout the darkest winter months, and longer – at least until your next visit.

Lavender, one of the
perfumes of Provence

THE SCENTS OF PROVENCE

Provençal lavender is used to perfume a wide range of goods, but most popular are pretty fabric bags full of the dried flowers. Bath times can be heady with the scent of local flowers and herbs, captured in delightful bottles, and Marseille's famous olive oil soaps.

Olive oil savons de Marseille

Orange water
from Vallauris

Linden-scented
bubble bath

Dried lavender, packed
in Provençal fabrics

Mallow-scented
bubble bath

Glassware

Glassblowing is a modern Provençal craft. At Biot (see p74) you can watch glassblowers at work, as well as buy examples of their art to take home.

Pottery

Look for traditional tiles, cookware and storage jars made from terre rouge, *formal china of Moustiers* faïence *(see p186) or art-works of* grès *clay.*

Terracotta Santons

Provençal Christmas cribs are peopled with these gaily painted traditional figures. Most crafts shops offer a good choice of characters.

Olive Wood

*As rich in colour and texture as its oil, the
wood of the olive can be sculpted into works
of art or turned into practical kitchenware.*

Hunting Knives

*The huntsmen's shops of Provence are an
unexpected source for the perfect picnic or
kitchen knife, safe yet razor sharp.*

Provençal Fabrics

*Using patterns and colours dating back for
centuries, these traditional prints are sold by
the metre or made up into fashionable items.*

THE FLAVOURS OF PROVENCE

No-one should leave Provence
without at least a jar of olives
or a bottle of olive oil, but consider also easy-to-pack tins, jars
and boxes of preserved fruits,
scented honey or savoury purées –
prettily packaged, they make ideal gifts.

Almond sweetmeats, the
speciality of Aix-en-Provence

Crystallized chestnuts
or *marrons glacés*

Goat's milk cheese,
wrapped in chestnut
leaves

A spicy garnish for
fish soups

Green olives with
Provençal herbs

Virgin olive oil

Puréed salt cod or
brandade de morue

Almond and
orange conserve

Lavender honey and
hazelnut *confit*

ENTERTAINMENT IN PROVENCE

There once was a time when Provence was seen as a cultural backwater, where nothing much happened except wine harvests and Mistral gales. In recent years, however, the region has been transformed and barely a month goes by without some major festival *(see pp32–35 & pp228–9)*. Concerts take place all year round, with first-class opera in Marseille, St-Tropez and Nice and rock con-

Actor at the Avignon festival

certs at Toulon. Nightlife tends to be restricted to the coastal resorts, like Juan-les-Pins and St-Tropez where clubs and bars stay open all night. In winter, things are quieter, but the small bars of Marseille and Nice remain open and full of life. Provence's most common entertainment is free – locals spend much of their time enjoying the fresh air, walking and playing *pétanque,* or Provençal bowls.

PRACTICAL INFORMATION

Information about what's on in Provence tends to be fairly localized, with tourist offices providing listings of various events. Most large towns publish a weekly paper which give outlines of the best of each week's events and are available from the main newsagents.

BUYING TICKETS

Depending on the event, most tickets can be bought at the door, but for blockbuster concerts, particularly during the summer months, it is best to reserve in advance. Tickets can be purchased at the **FNAC** chains in major towns, or at the **Virgin Megastore** in Marseille.

Theatre box-offices are open from approximately 11am–7pm seven days a week and most will accept credit card bookings over the telephone.

If you haven't booked in advance, tickets to popular concerts can be bought from touts at the venue doors on

the night – these will be more expensive than the set price. Be warned that cases of counterfeit tickets are not uncommon.

OPERA AND CLASSICAL MUSIC

Music is everywhere in Provence, from small village churches to the Belle Epoque opera houses of Marseille, Toulon and Nice. The **Opéra de Nice** is recognized as one of the best in France and there is usually no problem getting tickets. The orchestra from Monte-Carlo plays with the world's most illustrious conductors. A number of classical and jazz festivals are held throughout the summer in Toulon and attract many top orchestras and performers.

Every year on 21 June, the Fête de la Musique is held in Provence, and throughout France. Amateur and professional musicians alike set up their stages in villages

Classical cello

and towns and perform. The best way to enjoy this is to walk around and try and take in as many different "concerts". The range of genres is very impressive, from accordion music, full orchestras, one-man rap artists to electro.

ROCK AND JAZZ

Once a rock and pop desert, Provence is now enjoying something of a renaissance with Toulon's **Zenith-Oméga**, a main venue on most major world tours. For really big stadium shows, such as U2 and The Rolling Stones, Marseille's soccer stadium, **Stade-Vélodrome**, is preferred. The **Nice Jazz Festival** in the arena of Cimiez *(see p84)* is one of the world's best. It was here that Miles Davis gave one of his last performances among the Roman walls and olive groves. In recent years, top names have been favouring the **Jazz à Juan** festival in Juan-les-Pins, which has seen Ray Charles and the jazz debut of violinist Nigel Kennedy.

THEATRE

Going to the theatre in Provence can be as formal or relaxed as you choose. A trip to one of the larger theatres can involve dressing up, making special *souper* (late dinner) reservations at a nearby restaurant specializing in theatre-goers, and quaffing exorbitantly priced cham-

Miles Davis playing at the Nice Festival du Jazz in the arena of Cimiez

pagne during the interval. On the other hand, a trip to one of the smaller-scale theatres can be about casual dress, cheap ticckets and becoming totally absorbed in the show because of the intimacy and immediacy of the venue.

Marseille is the centre of theatre in Provence and boasts one of France's top theatrical companies, the **Théâtre National de la Criée.** Various smaller companies stage some of the most innovative plays in Europe, many of which end up in Paris. Avignon is also famous for its **Théâtre des Carmes,** the main venue for the **Festival d'Avignon** *(see p229).* There is also a "fringe" festival, the **Avignon Public Off,** with its own directors and box office.

The Open Tennis Championships in Monte-Carlo

SPECTATOR SPORTS

With its superb weather and glamorous reputation, the regions of Provence and the Côte d'Azur are ideal venues for some of France's top sporting events. The gruelling Tour de France passes through the region each July, while the Monte-Carlo and Nice tennis tournaments attract top players. The Grand Prix at Monaco *(see p32)* at the end of May is one of the highlights of the Formula 1 motor racing season. Horseracing enthusiasts can visit the race track at Cagnes-sur-Mer between December and March.

Provence boasts two of the top soccer teams in France – *Olympique de Marseille* and *Monaco,* known as the

millionaires' club. Rugby is becoming increasingly popular in Provence, with top-class clubs in Nice and Toulon.

DANCE

Marseille's eclectic mixture of nationalities and styles has led to highly original and powerful productions. Com-

View over the harbour in Monaco to the glittering casino

panies such as the **Bernadines** sometimes take their productions to Paris. The National Ballet Company is based at the Ecole de Danse in Marseille. The new **Centre National Chorégraphie** in Aix-en-Provence is an exciting addition to the dance scene.

GAMBLING

The Riviera is famed for its opulent casinos. If you are 18 and over you can play in most resorts. Monaco has the coast's most popular casino – **Le Casino** – where you have to pay an entrance fee and show an ID card before you start gambling. Other casinos worth visiting for architecture and atmosphere are Cannes' **Casino Croisette** and **Casino Ruhl** in Nice. If you are not a high-roller, there is always the dazzling array of slot-machines, ever ready to take your coins.

BULLFIGHTING

Perhaps the most dramatic sporting occasions in Provence are the annual *ferias* or bullfighting festivals. The traditional bullfight of Provence is the *course à la cocarde,* which starts with an *abrivado* when the bulls are chased through the town to the local arena. The bull enters the ring with a red *cocarde* or rosette tied to its horns, which the *razeteurs* or matadors try to snatch, providing riveting but goreless entertainment. At the end of the season the bullfighter with the most rosettes receives fame and adulation, as well as cash.

Increasingly, bullfights will end in death in the full-blooded Spanish-style *corrida,* but this is usually in the main arenas in Nîmes and Arles *(see p32),* and will always be advertised first. In one session there are usually six bullfights, of which two may be advertised as *mise à mort* (to the death).

Bullfighting poster for the 1992 Nîmes *feria* by Francis Bacon

CINEMA

It was in the small port of La Ciotat that Louis Lumière shot the world's first motion picture, and Marcel Pagnol laid the foundations for modern French cinema from his studios in Marseille. *La Septième Art*, as the French refer to film, reveals the respect with which the genre is held. The French are supportive of local, independent cinemans and every small town has its cinema. So when visiting the cinema, try to avoid the behemoths of UGC and Gaumont and instead head to a tiny *salle de cinéma*. If your language skills won't stretch to seeing a French film while in Provence, be sure to catch the V.O. *(Version Original)* of any other language films, which will be screend in the film's original language. V.F. *(Version Française)* denotes a dubbed screening in French.

Another thing to bear in mind is the French attitude to snacking. Essentially it is only acceptable for children, and even then only at a designated time after school. While French cinemas do have concession stands selling popcorn and sweets, it is only the foreigners who can be heard munching throughout the tense parts of the film. On the other hand, some French cinemas have bars and restaurants attached, so that film goers can dissect the movie over a meal.

As the fame of Cannes *(see p68)* reflects, film festivals are taken seriously by the French. Cannes itself is a maelstrom of media hype, old-school glamour and shiny new cash. It is an amazing experience if you can get tickets to any of the films or parties, but these are notoriously difficult to get as they are by invitation only.

DISCOTHEQUES AND NIGHTCLUBS

During the summer, the main towns of Provence boogie all night. The music is far from trend-setting, usually following styles set the previous year in New York and London, but the dancers are chic and the prices high. A handful of clubs such as **Jimmy'Z** in Monaco and **Les Caves du Roy** in St-Tropez cater for the jet-set, while those like **Whisky à Gogo** in Juan-les-Pins and **Le Blitz** in Cannes serve a much younger crowd. The dress code is usually smart and trainers are almost always forbidden.

DIRECTORY

BUYING TICKETS

FNAC
Avignon
19 rue de la République.
Tel 04 90 14 35 37.
www.fnac.com

Marseille
Centre Commercial Bourse.
Tel 04 91 39 94 00.

Nice
30 avenue Jean Médecin.
Tel 04 92 17 77 77.

Virgin Megastore
Marseille
75 rue St-Ferréol.
Tel 04 91 55 55 00.
www.virgin.fr

OPERA AND CLASSICAL MUSIC

Aix-en-Provence
Aix en Musique
3 place John Rewald.
Tel 04 42 21 69 69.

Marseille
Opéra Municipal
2 rue Molière.
Tel 04 91 55 11 10.

Nice
CEDAC de Cimiez
49 av de la Marne.
Tel 04 93 53 85 95.

Forum Nice Nord
10 bd Comte de Falicon.
Tel 04 93 84 24 37.

Opéra de Nice
4 rue St-François-
de-Paule.
Tel 04 92 17 40 00.

Toulon - Ollioules
CNCDC Châteauvallon
Tel 04 94 22 74 00.
@resa@chateauvalllon.com

Festival de Musique Classique
Tel 04 94 18 53 00.

Opéra de Toulon
Pl Victor Hugo.
Tel 04 94 92 70 78.

ROCK AND JAZZ MUSIC

Aix-en-Provence
Hot Brass Club
1857 chemin
d'Eguilles-Célony.
Tel 04 42 21 05 57.

Juan-les-Pins
Festival du Jazz
Office de Tourisme,
11 pl de Gaulle, Antibes.
Tel 04 92 90 53 00.
www.antibesjuanles
pins.com

Marseille
Espace Julien
39 cours Julien.
Tel 04 91 24 34 14.

L'Intermédiaire
63 pl Jean-Jaurès.
Tel 04 91 47 01 25.

Le Pelle-Mêle
8 place Huiles.
Tel 04 91 54 85 26.

Stade Vélodrome
Allées Ray-Grassi.
Tel 04 91 29 14 50.

Nice
Bar des Oiseaux
5 rue St-Vincent
(jazz and café
-théâtre).
Tel 04 93 80 27 33.

Festival du Jazz
5 promenade des
Anglais.
Tel 08 92 70 74 07.

Toulon
Zenith-Oméga
Bd Commandant
Nicolas.
Tel 04 94 22 66 77.

Le Scat
11 rue de la
Verrerie.
Tel 04 42 23 00 23.

THEATRE

Avignon
Avignon Public Off
BP 5, 75521 Paris
Cedex 11
Tel 01 48 05 01 19.
www.avignon-off.org

Festival d'Avignon
Espace St-Louis,
20 rue Portail Baguier.
Tel 04 90 27 66 50.
www.festival-avignon.
com

Théâtre des Carmes
6 place des Carmes.
Tel 04 90 82 20 47.

Théâtre National de la Criée
30 quai de Rive-Neuve.
Tel 04 91 54 70 54.

Marseille
Théâtre du Merlan
Avenue Raimu.
Tel 04 91 11 19 30.

Nice
Théâtre de l'Alphabet
10 bd Carabacel.
Tel 04 93 13 08 88.

Théâtre de la Semeuse
Rue du Château.
Tel 04 93 92 85 08.
www.nicejazzfest.com

DIRECTORY

SPECTATOR SPORTS

Marseille
ASPTT Tennis
La Fouragère
38 avenue
Van Gogh
Tel 04 91 93 43 43.
www.asptt-marseille.
org

Olympique de Marseille
3 Boulevard
Michelet
13008 Marseille
Tel 04 9176 59 09.
www.olympiqude
marseille.com

Monaco
Grand Prix
Automobile
Club de Monaco
Tel 07 93 15 26 00.
www.fia.com

Nice
League de la Côte d'Azur
66 route de Grenoble,
Tel 04 97 25 76 80.

Tour de France
www.letour.fr

DANCE

Aix-en-Provence
Centre National Chorégraphie
Rue des Alumettes.
Tel 04 42 93 81 81.

Marseille
Bernardines
17 bd Garibaldi.
Tel 04 91 24 30 40.

GAMBLING

Cannes
Casino Croisette
Palais des Festivals.
Tel 04 92 98 78 00.

Monaco
Le Casino
Place du Casino.
Tel 00 377 93 30 56 78.

Nice
Casino Ruhl
1 promenade des
Anglais.
Tel 04 97 03 12 22.

BULLFIGHTING

Arles
Arènes d'Arles
Rond-point des
Arènes.
Tel 04 90 96 03 70.

Nîmes
Les Arènes
Blvd des Arènes.
Tel 04 66 76 72 77.

CINEMA

Aix-en-Provence
Le Mazarin
6 rue Laroque.
04 42 26 99 85.

Avignon
Utopia Cinéma
4 rue des Escaliers
Sainte Anne.
Tel 04 90 82 65 36.
www.cinemas-utopia.org

Cannes
Cannes Film Festival
www.festival–cannes.fr

Marseille
Cinéma Chambord
283 avenue du Prado
04 91 25 71 11.

Monte Carlo
Le Sporting d'hiver
Place du Casino.
00 377 93 30 81 08.

Nice
Cinémathèque
3 esplanade Kennedy.
Tel 04 92 04 06 66.

Mercury
Cinéma
16 place Garibaldi.
Tel 04 93 55 37 81.

Nîmes
Le Sémaphore
25a rue Porte de
France.
04 66 67 88 04.

DISCOTHEQUES AND NIGHTCLUBS

Aix-en-Provence
Le Mistral
3 rue Frédéric Mistral.
Tel 04 42 38 16 49.

Avignon
Les Ambassadeurs Club
27 rue Bancasse.
Tel 04 90 86 31 55.

Cannes
Le Blitz
22 rue Macé.
Tel 04 93 39 05 25.

Disco 7
7 rue Rouguière.
Tel 04 93 39 10 36.

Jimmy'Z
Casino Croisette,
Palais des Festivals.
Tel 04 92 98 78 78.

Hyères
Le Fou du Roi
Casino des Palmiers, 1
avenue Ambroise
Thomas.
Tel 04 94 12 80 80.

Le Rêve
9 avenue Badine.
Tel 04 94 58 00 07.

Juan-les-Pins
Le Village Voom Voom
1 boulevard de la Pinède.
Tel 04 92 93 90 00.

Whisky à Gogo
Rue Jacques Leonetti.
Tel 04 93 61 26 40.

Marseille
Le Circus
5 rue du Chantier.
Tel 04 91 33 77 22.

Monaco
Jimmy'Z
26 avenue Princesse
Grace.
Tel 00 377 92 16 22 77.

Le Tiffany's
3 av Spélugues.
Tel 00 377 93 50 53 13.

Nice
Le Grand Escurial
29 rue Alphonse Karr.
Tel 04 93 82 37 66.

St-Raphaël
La Réserve
promenade René Coty.
Tel 04 94 95 02 20.

St-Tropez
Les Caves du Roy
Palace de la Côte d'Azur,
avenue Paul Signac.
Tel 04 94 97 16 02.

Papagayo
Résidence du Port.
Tel 04 94 97 07 56.

Festivals in Provence

Festivals in Provence are very much part of the way of life. They are not staged purely for the benefit of visitors and tourism, but more to continue the seasonal celebrations that are deeply rooted in tradition. Many *fêtes* are based on pagan rites while others are celebrations of historic occasions – only a few have been hijacked by fun-loving holiday-makers on the coast. Here is a selection of the best festivals from each of the *départements*.

One of the spectacular floats in the procession at the Nice Carnival

THE RIVIERA AND THE ALPES MARITIMES

The brilliant explosion of fireworks at the Carnaval de Nice above the Baie des Anges is one of the most popular images of Nice *(see pp84–5)*. It is the largest pre-Lent carnival in France, and crescendos on Shrove Tuesday with fireworks and the immolation of King Carnival, *Sa Majesté Carnaval.*

Carnival festivities, held in all Catholic countries, are based on the pagan celebrations of the death of winter and the birth of spring and life. It is a time of feasting (*mardi gras* means "fat Tuesday") before the fasting of Lent (*carne vale* is Latin for "farewell to meat").

Festivities begin three weeks before Mardi Gras, when the king is wheeled out into the streets. During the two weekends between then and his departure, the colourful, flower-decked floats of the procession parade along the 2-km (1-mile) route round Jardin Albert I, amid confetti battles, bands and mounted escorts.

Carnival characters in the streets of Nice

By the 19th century, the Nice Carnival had developed into little more than a chalk and flour battle. The floats did not appear until 1873, inspired by the local artist, Alexis Mossa, who also resurrected the figure of King Carnival. Since then, great effort and time has been put into making the costumes.

Meanwhile, the whole town is *en fête*, and parties and balls are held in hotels and public venues all night long. Visitors should book well in advance to secure accommodation.

THE VAR AND THE ILES D'HYERES

A number of festivals in the region feature the firing of muskets, reminiscent of ancient witch-scaring rites. Spectacular volleys are set off into the air in St-Tropez *(see pp118–19)* for the biannual *bravade*, commemorating two significant events.

The first one takes place on May 16 and 17 and is a religious procession devoted to the town's patron, Saint Torpès, He was a Roman soldier in the service of the emperor, Nero. In AD 68, Torpès converted to Christianity and was martyred by decapitation. His body was placed in a boat along with a hungry dog and a cockerel. Miraculously, the saint's body was untouched. The vessel was washed up onto the shores of southern France, on the spot where St-Tropez stands today.

The May *bravade* honours his arrival. Celebrations begin with the blessing of a lance by the town's priest in the Eglise de St-Tropez. From here, the saint's gilded wooden bust is taken and carried around the flag-decked town in a terrific flurry of musket volleys. The procession winds down to the beach, and the sea is blessed for safely conveying the saint.

The second *bravade* takes place on 15 June and is honoured with earth-shattering fusillades and military parades. It marks the anniversary of the day in 1637, when the local militia saw off a Spanish fleet, about 22 vessels strong, after an attempt to capture four ships of the Royal French fleet.

La bravade procession in St-Tropez, honouring the town's patron saint

BOUCHES-DU-RHONE AND NIMES

Europe's largest Romany festival, the Pèlerinage des Gitans in Saintes-Maries-de-la-Mer *(see p138)*, is a simple yet very moving occasion. At the end of May, usually 24–26, Romanies from all over the continent gather to pay their

Procession of the saints down to the sea in Saintes-Maries-de-la-Mer

respects to the patron saint of gypsies, Saint Sarah, known as the Black Madonna. This takes place in the picturesque town of Saintes-Maries-de-la-Mer.

The pilgrimage is a colourful occasion, brightened by traditional Arlesian costumes and *gardian* cowboys. The object of their veneration is Saint Sarah, the Ethiopian servant. As legend has it, she arrived on the shores of the Camargue by boat. Also on board was Mary Magdalene, and the saints Mary Jacobea (sister of the Virgin Mary) and the elderly Mary Salome (mother of the apostles Saint James and Saint John). Sarah and the Marys decided to stay in the town and they built an oratory on which the fortified church of Notre-Dame-de-la-Mer was built. The saints started to preach the gospel and the town became known as the "Mecca of Provence".

Saint Sarah stands serene and excessively robed in the crypt. On the two nights and days of celebration in May, she is remembered with a Mass and all-night vigil. The next day, the statues on the saints are borne down to the sea where the Camargue cowboys take their horses, neck-deep, into the water and the Bishop of Arles blesses the sea.

After the statues have been returned to the church, the great folk festival begins, with rodeos, bull-running, horse racing, Arletan dancing and all manner of entertainment. The *gardians* return for a smaller celebration of Mary Salome in October, when there is a procession around the church.

VAUCLUSE

The Papal city of Avignon *(see pp166–8)* is a splendid setting for the foremost arts festival in Provence, the Festival d'Avignon. Theatre, music, dance and film are all covered in the month-long programme which runs from July to early August. More than a quarter of a million visitors travel to Avignon every year to attend the largest arts festival in France. It is advisable to reserve hotels and tickets in advance to avoid disappointment *(see pp226–7 for reservations)*.

The festival was established in 1947 by the late Jean Vilar whose aim was to bring theatre to the masses. He devised a number of productions to be staged in the courtyard of the Papal Palace and his Théâtre National Populair still performs every year. Other venues include the theatres and cinemas, where films are shown all day, the opera house and churches.

Since the 1960s, the fringe-style Avignon Public Off, brings some 520 events to over 100 venues including many specially set-up theatres. Amateur performers can be seen for free in the main square outside the opera, the place de l'Horloge.

ALPES-DE-HAUTE-PROVENCE

Provence's most particular flower has its festival, the Corso de la Lavande, in the mountain spa town of Digne-les-Bains *(see p180)*.

The colourful event, which lasts for four days, takes place in August and celebrates the harvesting of the crop. There are jars and pots of honey and all kinds of lavender produce for sale in the town, and events centre on the main street, boulevard Gassendi. The climax of the festival comes on the last day when the flower-decked floats, representing a variety of themes, parade through the streets, accompanied by music, dancing and cheering. Preceding the floats is a municipal truck spraying the roads with litres of lavender water leaving the whole town heady with the distinctive, sweet perfume.

Lavender from the festival in Digne

Lively street performers at the summer Festival d'Avignon

SPECIALIST HOLIDAYS AND OUTDOOR ACTIVITIES

Everything is on offer from sun and sea bathing to skiing and extreme sports in this extraordinarily varied region of France. Watersports are extremely popular and sailing boats can be rented in most towns. For windsurfing, the experienced will head for Brutal Beach, just west of Toulon, although boards can be rented at most coastal resorts. Some of the best diving in the whole of the

Windsurfing in Provence

Mediterranean is around the Iles d'Hyères. There are also plenty of opportunities for canoeing and white-water rafting in the Verdon and Gard inland. Opportunities for walking, cycling, mountain-biking and horse riding are endless. The Féderation Française de la Randonnée Pédestre publishes the widely-available *Topo Guides*, which give descriptions of the tracks with details of overnight stops and transport.

ARTS AND CRAFTS

The **French Institute** is a good resource for courses in learning French combined with other activities. Students can undertake a French-speaking holiday by working part time on the restoration of historic sites with **Union Rempart** (Union pour la Réhabilitation et Entretien des Monuments et du Patrimoine Artistique).

You can also learn sculpting on a weekend course in a beautiful rural setting. Contact **Provence Verte** for details.

Several specialist tour operators organize dedicated painting holidays. For information, contact the **Maison de la France** tourist board.

COOKERY COURSES

An extensive range of gastronomic courses providing training in regional or classical cuisine is available. These courses are often combined

with visits to markets to learn how to source the best ingredients. The **Hostellerie Bérard** in La Cadière d'Azur runs excellent cookery courses and workshops.

Olive oil is the lifeblood of Mediterranean cuisine and many olive oil producers offer visits to their *moulins*, such as **Château Virant** in Lançon de Provence. The Olive Tree route in Canton de Levens takes you to see oil presses in action.

For lovers of figs, the family-run specialist, **Les Figuières du Mas de Luquet**, is the perfect place to learn about this delicious delicacy.

LAVENDER FIELDS AND VINEYARDS

The regions most associated with the growing and processing of lavender are around Le Mont Ventoux, the Lubéron and the Provençal Drôme. **Musée de la Lavende**, located in Lagarde d'Apt, organizes guided walking tours of a lavender field.

There are also plenty of opportunities in the whole of the region for *dégustations*. If you are looking to combine a trip to Les-Baux-de-Provence, Les Alpilles or St Rémy-de-Provence with a visit to vineyards, contact the **Syndicat des Vignerons des Baux-de-Provence**. For wines of the Lubéron, contact the **Syndicat Général des Vignerons du Lubéron**.

A cookery course in progress at Hostellerie Bérard

PERFUMERY AND AROMATHERAPY COURSES

In Grasse, perfume initiation courses allow perfume lovers to create their own *eau de toilette* with the help of a "master perfumer". These courses are available at **Le Studio des Fragrances** at Galimard. The **Tarinologie Workshop** at Molinard also offers courses. The other major perfumery is **Fragonard**, where aroma-synergy workshops are on offer. These courses allow participants to learn the virtues and benefits of plants and essential oils. Lessons are given by professional aromatherapists and plant experts.

EXTREME SPORTS

The exciting new sport of snow-kiting is skiing with a stunt kite to help with the jumps. Join the best snow-kiters on the Col du Lautaret between the Grave, the Meije peak and Serre Chevalier. For an even more extreme sport, try a different kind of diving –

Beautiful, aromatic lavender fields in Châteauneuf-du-Pape

A game of *boules* in full swing, this is still a favourite pastime in the region

under ice. Other favourite sports include paragliding (*parapente*) and hang gliding (*deltaplane*). For more information, contact the **Fédération Française de Vol Libre**. Gliding (*vol à voile*) is popular in the southern regions where the climate is warm and the thermals are so good. For details of gliding clubs, contact the **Fédération Française de Vol à Voile**.

BIRD-WATCHING

The Camargue is a twitcher's paradise. The information centre at the **Parc Naturel Regional de Camargue** provides detailed information on bird-watching. It also organizes walks within the area and has a glassed-in section, where it is possible to observe birds through binoculars. For more information contact the tourist board in Arles (*see pp144-6*) or the tourist office in Stes Maries de la Mer (*see p137*).

BOULES/PETANQUE

An emblem of Provençal life, this favourite game of the local men is rarely played by women. Somewhat similar to bowls, it is played with small metal balls on any dusty ground surface. Although the rules are simple, it can be very competitve with a touch of ferocity, making it interesting to watch.

CANOEING

Canoeing is popular in the huge Lac de Ste-Croix in the National Regional Park of Verdon. The most famous route is the 24 km (15 miles) paddle down the Gorges du

Verdon from Carrejuan Bridge to Lac de Ste Croix, which usually takes two days to cover. La Palud sur Verdon is the best base for whitewater rafting and kayaking on the rapids. For less challenging canoeing, try the River Sorgue, starting from the base of the high cliffs of Fontaine-de-Vaucluse. For more information, contact the **Fédération Française de Canoë-Kayak**.

CANYONING

The Grand Canyon du Verdon, Europe's largest canyon, can be visited by raft or on foot. It has now become a centre for adventure sports. The **Castellane Tourist Office** provides lists of companies offering canyoning, rafting and other outdoor trails.

FISHING

Bee-eater, common in Provence

Fishing is a highly popular sport on permitted lakes and rivers. Local tourist offices and fishing shops can help you obtain a licence. You can experience bountiful sea-fishing in the Mediterranean, with catches that include bass, sardines, grey mullet, and crustaceans, such as crayfish and lobster. Night-fishing is becoming increasingly popular too.

GOLF AND TENNIS

There's a great variety of golf in the area, from high-altitude courses to links facing the sea, or clinging to the fringes of cliffs. Overall, there are around 30 courses, mainly in the Bouches-du-Rhône and the Var and of these, over 20 are

18-hole courses. Some of the best are located at the Frégate course, St Cyr, St Raphaël's Golf de l'Esterel and, close to Avignon, the Golf de Châteteaublanc. Most offer lessons provided by resident experts.

The Provence Golf Pass gives access to 13 courses in the five departments, including five green fees. For golf addicts and occasional golfers alike, this is an excellent way to sample the courses available. For comprehensive information, contact the **Provence-Alpes-Côte d'Azur Regional Tourist Board** or the **Fédération Française de Golf**, which can supply a list of courses in France.

Most of the resorts and towns have their own tennis courts that are open to the public. Many of these are traditional Mediterranean clay courts.

Tennis lovers converge at Monte Carlo in April, when the International Tennis Championships come here for the Monte Carlo Open tournament.

Canoeing in the Gorges du Verdon, an exhilarating experience

HORSE RIDING

Although the wetland area of Camargue is famous for its hardy white horses, said to be direct descendants of pre-historic horses (*see p136*), the whole region – from coast to mountain to rural areas – is extremely popular with horse lovers. For a detailed list of pony-trekking and riding opportunities, contact the **Ligue Régionale de Provence de Sports Equestres**.

NATURISM

The largest and oldest naturist colony in the region is the easternmost of the Hyères islands, the Ile du Levant. It covers half the stretch of the 8 km (5 miles) long island. For more information on baring it all, contact the **Fédération Française de Naturisme**.

SKIING

The most important skiing areas are in the Maritime Alps, at the meeting point of the Alps and Provence. The main resorts, Auron, Isola 2000 and Valberg (*see p96*) are only a few hours from the coast, making it entirely possible to combine skiing and beach pleasures in a single day. In the north of the region in the Alpes de Haute-Provence are the ski resorts of Pra Loup and Chabanon. For more information, contact the **Fédération Française de Ski** in Annecy or the **Fédération Française de la Montagne et de l'Escalade**.

SPA BREAKS

Set in the hilltop village of Gordes, one of France's prettiest villages, is the newly-opened Daniel Jouvance spa, **La Bastide de Gordes**. It is undoubtedly an ideal spot for relaxing breaks.

In the picturesque, gastronomic village of Mougins, **Le Mas Candille** is an elegant, individual hotel, complemented by a Japanese-style Shiseido spa. For the ultimate in luxury, visit the **Thalazur** spa in Antibes.

WALKING, CLIMBING AND CYCLING

Long-distance walking and climbing trails are known as Grandes Randonées (GR) and shorter trails as Petites Randonées (PR). Some trails are also open to mountain bikes and horses.

Parc Naturel Régional du Lubéron offers some excellent cycling and walking trails. The information centre, **Maison du Parc**, provides a list of hikers' accommodation and details of two dozen walking trails. The Camargue has many trails and walking paths. "Sentier Littoral", a splendid coastal path from St-Tropez, covers 35 km (22 miles) to Cavalaire. You can even break the journey at Ramatuelle. An excellent French book, *Promenez-vous à Pied – Le Golfe de St-Tropez* has details of 26 walks in the area.

Perhaps the most spectacular trail in the whole of Provence is the GR 9, which crosses the Lubéron range and the Monts du Vaucluse.

For tough rock climbing, try the Buoux cliffs in the Lubéron, or one of the 933 routes in the Gorges du Verdon. The creeks, *calanques*, between Cassis and Marseille are utterly picturesque. Easier ascents can be found in the Dentelles de Montmirail, despite the craggy rock faces. The area boasts excellent vineyards, such as Gigondas, Vacqueyras and Beaumes-de-Venise in which to enjoy a *dégustation* after a climb.

Comité Departemental de la Randonnée Pédestre in Cagnes-sur-Mer, is equipped with detailed information. For details of trails in the region, contact the **Fédération Française de Randonnée Pédestre**.

Cycling tours of the lush green Lubéron in Vaucluse are great for people of all ages. In the upper Var, Figanières is famous for mountain-biking, while the Alps of Haute-Provence boast around 1,500 km (900 miles) of marked tracks. For detailed information, contact the **Fédération Française de Cyclisme**.

WATER SPORTS

Most coastal resorts have excellent facilities for both experienced and amateur sailors. Iles d'Hyères has some top-class sailing schools, in the tiny island of Bendor and the Porquerolles, the largest of the French Riviera islands.

For windsurfing, the reliable winds of the Bouches-du-Rhône and the Var make for favourable conditions. Other good locations include the Camargue, where the lively Mistral wind blows, at Port St-Louis and Les Saintes-Maries-de-la-Mer. The windsurfing regatta in St-Tropez in July is a particularly glamorous event, which is always exciting and very well-attended.

Scuba diving is popular, thanks to sparkling water, an ample sprinkling of underwater wrecks and a wealth of marine life. It is especially good in Marseille and the Iles d'Hyères and Cavalaire. The little island of Port-Cros has a special underwater "Discovery Trail". St-Raphaël is also a leading diving centre, with several World War II shipwrecks off the coast.

For more on scuba diving, contact the **Fédération Française d'Etudes et de Sports Sous-Marins** in Marseille.

The most picturesque stretch of the Rhône passes through Avignon and Arles, otherwise known as the "Cities of Art and History", and the Camargue – home to wild horses, bulls and flamingos. Several companies organize boat trips or river cruises in floating hotels. For details, contact the tourist information centres in Avignon, Arles, Les St Maries-de-la-Mer or Port St Louis du Rhône.

The *calanques* can be visited by boats from Marseille and Cassis. Contact **Les Amis de Calanques** for more details.

Many beaches are privately owned and entry is by fee. Catamarans, dinghies, water-skiing and surfing equipment are all on offer.

For detailed information, contact the national sailing school, **Fédération Française de Voile**.

DIRECTORY

ARTS AND CRAFTS

French Institute
17 Queensberry Place,
London SW7 2DT.
Tel 020 7073 1370.
www.institut-
francais.org.uk

Maison de la France
178 Piccadilly, London W1J
9AL. *Tel 090 68 244 123.*
www.franceguide.com

Provence Verte
Office de Tourisme,
83170 Brignoles.
Tel 04 94 72 04 21.
www.la-provence-
verte.net

Union Rempart
1 rue des Guillemites,
75004 Paris.
Tel 01 42 71 96 55.
www.rempart.com

COOKERY

Château Virant
Route de St Chamas,
13680 Lançon de
Provence.
Tel 04 90 42 44 47.
www.chateauvirant.com

Hostellerie Bérard
83740 La Cadière d'Azur.
Tel 04 94 90 11 43.
www.hotel-berard.com

**Les Figuières du
Mas de Luquet**
Chemin du Mas de la
Musique, Mas de Luquet,
13690 Graveson.
Tel 04 90 95 72 03.
www.lesfiguieres.com

LAVENDER FIELDS
AND VINEYARDS

**Syndicat des
Vignerons des
Baux-de-Provence**
Chateau de Romanin,
13210 Saint-Remy-de-
Provence.
Tel 04 90 92 45 87.

**Syndicat Général
des Vignerons du
Lubéron**
Château de la Tour
d'Aigues, 84240
La Tour d'Aigues.
Tel 04 90 07 34 40.
www.vins-cotes-
luberon.com

**Musée de la
Lavande**
Route de Gordes, Lagarde
d'Apt. *Tel 04 90 76 91 23.*
www.museedelalavande.
com.

PERFUMERY AND
AROMATHERAPY

Fragonard
Boulevard Fragonard,
06130 Grasse.
Tel 04 93 36 44 65.
www.fragonard.com

**Le Studio des
Fragrances**
73 route de Cannes,
06130 Grasse.
Tel 04 93 09 20 00.
www.galimard.com

**Tarinologie
Workshop**
60 Boulevard Victor Hugo,
06130 Grasse.
Tel 04 93 36 01 62.
www.molinard.com

EXTREME SPORTS

**Fédération
Française de Vol
Libre**
4 rue de Suisse, 06000
Nice. *Tel 04 97 03 82 82.*
www.ffvl.fr

**Fédération
Française de Vol à
Voile**
29 rue de Sèvres,
75006 Paris.
Tel 01 45 44 04 78.
www.ffvv.org

BIRD-WATCHING

**Parc Naturel
Regional de
Çamargue**
Pont du Gau, 13460
Saintes-Maries-de-la-Mer.
Tel 04 90 97 86 32.
www.parc-camargue.fr

CANOEING

**Fédération
Française de
Canoe-Kayak**
87 Quai de la Marne,
94340 Joinville-le-Point.
Tel 01 45 11 08 50.
www.ffck.org

CANYONING

**Castellane Tourist
Office**
Rue Nationale, Castellane.
Tel 04 92 83 61 14.
www.castellane.org

GOLF AND TENNIS

**Fédération
Française de Golf**
68 rue Anatole France,
92300, Levallois Perret.
Tel 01 41 49 77 00.
www.ffg.org

**Provence-Alpes-
Côte d'Azur
Regional Tourist
Board**
Régis Gaguère, Marseille.
Tel 04 91 56 47 25.
www.crt-paca.fr

HORSE RIDING

**Ligue Régionale de
Provence de Sports
Equestres**
298 avenue du club
Hippique,13090 Aix-en-
Provence.
Tel 04 42 20 88 02.

NATURISM

**Fédération
Française de
Naturisme**
65 rue de Tocqueville,
75017 Paris.
Tel 01 47 64 32 82.
www.ffn-naturisme.com

SKIING

**Fédération
Française de la
Montagne et de
l'Escalade**
8 quai de la Marne, 75019
Paris. *Tel 01 40 18 75 50.*
www.ffme.fr

**Fédération
Française de Ski**
50, Avenue des
Marquisats, Annecy.
Tel 04 50 51 40 34.
www.ffs.fr

SPA BREAKS

La Bastide de Gordes
Le Village, 84220 Gordes.
www.bastide-de-
gordes.com

Le Mas Candille
Boulevard Clément
Rebuffet, 06250 Mougins.
Tel 04 92 28 43 52.
www.lemascandille.com

Hôtel Thalazur 770
Chemin des Moyennes
Bréguières 06600 Antibes.
Tel 04 92 91 82 00.

WALKING,
CLIMBING AND
CYCLING

**Comité
Departemental de
la Randonnée
Pédestre**
4 avenue de Verdun,
Cagnes-sur-Mer.
Tel 04 93 20 74 73.
www.cdrp06.org

**Fédération
Française de
Cyclisme**
12 rue Louis Bertrand,
94100, Ivry-sur-Seine.
Tel 01 56 20 88 88.
www.ffc.fr

**Fédération
Française de
Randonnée
Pédestre**
14 rue Riquet, 75019 Paris.
Tel 01 44 89 93 93.
www.ffrandonnee.fr

**Maison
du Parc**
60, Place Jean Jaurès.
Tel 04 90 04 42 00.

WATER SPORTS

**Fédération
Française d'Etudes
et de Sports Sous-
Marins**
24 Quai Rive-Neuve,
Marseille.
Tel 04 91 33 99 31.
www.ffessm.fr

**Fédération
Française de Voile**
17, rue Henri Bocquillon,
75015 Paris.
Tel 01 40 60 37 00.
www.ffv.fr

**Les Amis de
Calanques**
6 Place de la Liberté,
La Ciotat.
Tel 04 42 83 54 50.

SURVIVAL GUIDE

PRACTICAL INFORMATION

In Provence, as elsewhere in France, the peak holiday period is from mid-June to the end of August. The coast is particularly busy during this period. Since the beginning of the century, famous Hollywood names have flocked to the region's beaches, followed by the masses, and so the summer holiday industry was born. Today, although sometimes expensive compared to other French regions, Provence offers accommodation ranging from top hotels to small camp sites. There are activities to suit all tastes, from skiing

National logo for tourist information

in winter to sun and sand in summer. It has some of the world's best modern art collections, fine Roman ruins, ancient festivals, excellent food and wine and breathtaking scenery. Tourist offices are invaluable for providing local information and advice about where to stay. The main branches are listed opposite *(see also Where to Stay p192)*. The pace of life in Provence is very relaxed, with no trade between noon and 3pm. So be patient, and note their old maxim: "Slow in the mornings, and not too fast in the afternoons."

Enjoying the beach in Nice

WHEN TO GO

During high season in Provence, local businesses in tourist areas can make their whole year's profit. Along the coastal roads, camp sites, restaurants and hotels can be crowded, and prices can rise by as much as 30 per cent. French school holidays run from the first week in July to the first week in September. To avoid the crowds, head for the hills of the Var and Vaucluse or the wilds of upper Provence.

Provence is at its best in May and September, when the weather is still hot, but crowds are at their smallest. Flowers bloom in May, and grapes are harvested in September. The winter months can also offer some stunning sunny days, but beware of the bitterly cold Mistral wind that can mercilessly sweep

the region. Skiing is possible between mid-November and the start of April *(see p96)*.

Most attractions stay open all year, although hours may shorten out of season. Many towns time their festivals in order to attract off-season tourists – from the Nice carnival to the Lemon festival in Menton.

TOURIST INFORMATION

Most big towns have either a *Syndicat d'initiative* or an *Office de Tourisme*, while in smaller villages, the town hall provides details. Tourist offices will supply free maps, accommodation information (which can include booking hotels) and festival timings. You can also obtain details in advance from French government tourist offices before leaving your own country.

OPENING TIMES

This guide shows opening times for each of the sights listed. Most businesses open from 8 or 9am until noon, and from 2 or 3pm until 6pm. Banks are open from 8:30am–noon and 1:30–4:30pm, Monday to Friday. The lunch break is sacred throughout the region, although larger department stores, supermarkets, tourist offices and some sights may remain open all the time.

Restaurants are often closed two days a week, normally Monday and Tuesday.

Off season, much of seaside Provence closes down. Be sure to telephone ahead to check what is open, as many hotels and restaurants may shut for several months of the year. Transport services may also be restricted out of season.

Tourist information office at Villecroze

Entertainment at Avignon festival

SIGHTSEEING

In France, many museums close for lunch – normal opening hours are from 9am–noon and 2–5:30pm. These times tend to vary according to season. Generally, museums are open for longer hours from May to September. They also usually close one day a week: national museums on Mondays and municipal museums on Tuesdays. Many museums also close throughout the month of November.

Museum admission charges range from 1.5€ to 8€. Passes for more than one museum or monument are rare. National museums are free the first Sunday of each month.

Provençal museum tickets

Normally, you will need to buy separate tickets for each sight within a town. One of the few exceptions to this rule is Arles, which offers a discounted pass allowing entry to the majority of its museums. There are usually some discounts available for students who have ISIC cards, and for anyone aged under 18 and over 65. Most museums offer free or discounted entry for everyone on Sundays.

While churches normally offer free admission, small charges may be levied for those who wish to visit cloisters and chapels.

Sign for a tobacconist

DISABLED ACCESS

The nature of Provence's old, narrow streets and ancient architecture can make it a difficult area for disabled travellers to get around. Wheelchair access is often limited and many hotels and restaurants are poorly equipped. But the newer museums offer special services and facilities for disabled visitors. For more information about facilities before departure, contact:

Nice
Association HORUS (Society for the Blind), Ecole Olympus, 31 bd Stalingrad, 06300. **Tel** 04 93 89 77 75.
@ horus-ccnv@wanadoo.fr
Groupement pour l'Insertion des Personnes Handicapées Physiques (GIHP). **Tel** 04 93 26 44 24.

Paris
Groupement pour l'Insertion des Personnes Handicapées Physiques (GIHP), 10 rue Georges de Porto-Riche, 75014. **Tel** 01 41 83 15 15.

ENTERTAINMENT INFORMATION

There are several sources of entertainment information in Provence. The large English-speaking community has its own radio station and newspaper. Riviera Radio, which broadcasts from Monte-Carlo in English, is a mini-BBC for the south of France, found on 106.3 FM and 106.5 FM. The *Riviera Reporter* is an English-language magazine which comes out 6 times a year and informs on local issues and events. Local French papers can also provide details of festivals, sporting events and the weather. *Le Provençal* serves western Provence, and *Nice Matin* and its derivatives cover eastern Provence. Most cities have their own publications listing events. Tourist offices usually provide this information too. Some tobacconists, or *tabacs*, sell newspapers and magazines.

Personal Security and Health

On the whole, Provence is a safe place for visitors. As in all Mediterranean countries it is necessary to take precautions, especially in the larger cities. Extra caution is required along the Côte d'Azur, especially in Nice, which has a higher crime rate than Marseille. Rural areas, however, are usually very safe. Car crime is prevalent along the coast – so never leave valuables in a vehicle. In Nice and Marseille, it is wise to avoid bands of innocent-looking children who may in fact be skilled in the art of pickpocketing. Consular offices can be a good source of help in an emergency *(see p239)*.

Policeman   Fireman

PERSONAL PROPERTY

Take great care of your personal property at all times. In big cities, try not to carry valuables with you. You should always make sure you are covered by adequate insurance. Choose travellers' cheques as the safest form of money.

Pickpockets are a problem in the tourist meccas of the Côte d'Azur and in towns such as Avignon and Marseille. In Nice, bag snatching is becoming a threat (more so than in Marseille), but mugging is still far from common. Try not to park your car in remote areas, and use underground or covered car parking where possible. In towns,

the multi-storey car parks are kept under surveillance by video cameras. Parking there will remove the risk of being towed away to a police pound, which is a greater everyday threat than most car crime.

Avoid taking valuables to the beach, or keep them with you. It is not advisable to sleep on beaches: robberies and attacks have been known to occur.

In the event of a theft, go to the nearest police station, or *gendarmerie*, taking identity papers (and vehicle papers, if relevant). The report process (a *PV* or *procès-verbal*) may

take time, but you will need a police statement for any insurance claim. If your passport is stolen, contact the police and your nearest consulate.

PERSONAL SAFETY

Any criminal incident, however minor, is distressing to deal with. Some train routes, for example the Marseille–Barcelona line and also the Marseille–Ventimiglia, have dubious reputations. Keep the compartment door closed and valuables close to you. Vehicles have been reported vandalized on motorail trains.

In recent summers, road pirates have operated, ramming tourist cars on motorways to make them stop. There are police stations at almost all of the motorway exits. If in trouble, keep on until the next exit.

LEGAL ASSISTANCE

If your insurance policy is comprehensive, including a service in France such as Europ Assistance or Mondial Assistance, they will be able to help with legal advice on claims, such as accident procedure. If not, you should call your nearest consulate office.

INTERPRETERS

If you are in a situation that requires an interpreter, contact **Société Française des Traducteurs Professionnels** *(see pp239 & 243)*.

Ambulance

Fire engine

Police car

OUTDOOR HAZARDS

Forest fires are a major risk in Provence. Every summer thousands of hectares are destroyed in this way. High winds and dry forests mean fire spreads rapidly, so be vigilant with cigarette butts. Camp fires are banned in the region. If you do witness a fire, contact the emergency services at once and keep well away: fire direction can change in an instant.

The Mediterranean is safe for swimming, although currents can be strong off Cap d'Antibes and the Camargue. Pollution is a minor problem around some of the major ports, although some beaches display European blue flags as a sign of cleanliness.

Fire hazard poster

If you go out walking in the mountains, beware that weather conditions can change very quickly. In winter, it is best to advise local authorities of your projected route. In summer, pack warm clothes and some provisions in case of sudden storms. Altitude sickness can occur in the southern Alps, so go up slowly, pausing regularly to acclimatize.

In the mountains behind Nice and Cannes, you may see a plain, grey-brown Montpellier snake. Despite its size (it grows to around 1.5 m/5 ft), it is very shy and will probably flee. Vipers also live in the region.

During the hunting season – from September to February, particularly Sundays – dress in brightly-coloured clothes when out walking. Signs on trees usually denote hunting areas.

MEDICAL TREATMENT

All European Union nationals are entitled to French Social Security coverage, but treatment must be paid for in cash and hospital rates can vary. Reimbursements may be received if you have obtained a European Health Insurance Card in the UK before travel. The process for claims can be complicated so it is best to purchase your own insurance.

Pharmacists can diagnose and suggest treatments. They can be recognized by the green cross outside.

DIRECTORY

EMERGENCY NUMBERS

Centre Anti-Poison (Marseille)
Tel 04 91 75 25 25

Fire (Sapeurs Pompiers)
Tel 18

Police (Gendarmerie)
Tel 17

Ambulance (SAMU)
Tel 15

TRANSLATION SERVICES

Société Française des Traducteurs Professionnels
Tel 01 48 78 43 32
www.www.sft.fr

HOSPITAL EMERGENCIES

Avignon
Hôpital Général Henri Duffaut,
305 rue Raoul Follereau.
Tel 04 32 75 33 33
Fax 04 42 16 11 62.
www.aixenprovencetourism.com

Marseille
La Conception,
147 boulevard Baille.
Tel 04 91 38 30 00

Nice
Hôpital St-Roch,
5 rue Pierre-Devoluy
Tel 04 92 03 77 77

CONSULATES

Australia
4 rue Jean Rey,
75015 Paris.
Tel 01 40 59 33 00.
www.austgov.fr

Ireland
152 Bld John Kennedy,
Cap d'Antibes.
Tel 04 93 61 50 63

UK
24 avenue du Prado, Marseille
Tel 04 91 15 72 10.
www.amb-grandebretagne.fr

USA
12 bd Paul Peytral,
Marseille.
Tel 04 91 54 92 00
www.amb-usa.fr
7 av Gustave V, Nice
Tel 04 93 88 89 55

PUBLIC TOILETS IN PROVENCE

Modern automatic toilets are now found in many towns in Provence. Do not let children under 10 use these on their own as the automatic cleaning function can be dangerous. The best alternative is to use the toilets in the cafés or restaurants where you are a customer, or go to a large department store. Traditional *pissoirs* and keyhole toilets, still found in more rural areas, are not always very clean. Toilet facilities are provided on the *autoroute* at drive-in rest areas every 20 km (12 miles).

1 Put the amount indicated in the slot.

2 Press the button to open sliding door.

3 The light shows vacant or engaged.

Banking and Local Currency

In Provence, as elsewhere in France, the banks usually offer the best rates of exchange, along with American Express and Thomas Cook. Privately-owned *bureaux de change* are common in tourist areas, especially along the coast, but tend to have more variable rates. Take care to check the commission and minimum charges before completing a transaction. Travellers' cheques are the safest form of money. Credit cards can be used to draw money from automatic teller machines, but check the charges levied by your credit card company for this service.

Bureau de change sign

BANKING HOURS

Banks in big towns usually open from 8:30am–noon and from 1:30–4:30pm, Monday to Friday. Over public holiday weekends, they are often closed from Friday noon until Tuesday morning.

USING BANKS

There is no limit to the amount of money you may bring into France, but if you want to take back more than 7,500€ to the UK, you should declare it on arrival. It is wise to carry large sums in the form of travellers' cheques.

Most banks have a *bureau de change,* offering the best exchange rates but also charging commission. Outside Paris, independent *bureaux de change* are rare, except in major railway stations and some hotels and shops. Even in remoter areas, many banks now have automatic teller machines (ATMs) that take cards in the Visa/Carte Bleue or Eurocard/Mastercard groups. To take out money, you need to tap in a PIN code. Instructions are usually given in French, English and German. ATMs may run out of notes before the weekend. Users can withdraw up to 300€ each day on Visa at the foreign counter of any bank that displays the Visa sign. Do not forget that you will need to show your passport.

TRAVELLERS' CHEQUES AND CREDIT CARDS

Travellers' cheques can be obtained from American Express, Thomas Cook or your bank. American Express cheques are widely accepted in France, and if they are exchanged at an Amex office no commission is charged.

The most common credit cards in France, accepted even at motorway tolls, are Carte Bleue /Visa and Eurocard / Mastercard. Many Provençal businesses do not accept the American Express card.

French credit cards are now "smart cards", meaning they contain a microchip capable of storing data – the *puce*. Retailers have machines which read both new smart cards and older magnetic strips. If your conventional card cannot be read in the smart card slot, you will be told you have a *puce morte*. Persuade the cashier to swipe the card through the magnetic reader *(bande magnétique)*. You may also have to tap in your PIN code and press the green key (*validez*) on a small keypad.

CONVERSION CHART

The following chart is a rough guide to equivalent currency values, rounded up or down for ease of use.

EUROS	FRANCS
1	6.5
5	33
10	65
20	130
25	165
50	330
75	495
100	650
125	820
150	980
175	1145

DIRECTORY

BUREAUX DE CHANGE

Cannes
Azuréenne de Change, 17 rue Maréchal Foch.
Tel 04 93 39 34 37

American Express
1bis rue Notre-Dame.
Tel 04 93 99 05 45

Marseille
Change de la Canebière, 39 la Canebière. *Tel* 04 91 13 71 26

Monaco
Compagnie Monégasque de Change, av de la Quarantaine.
Tel (00 377) 93 25 02 50

Nice
Office Provençal, 17 av Thiers.
Tel 04 93 88 56 80

FOREIGN BANKS

Cannes
Barclays
8 rue Frédéric Amouretti.
Tel 04 92 99 68 00

Lloyds
130 rue d'Antibes.
Tel 04 92 98 35 00

Marseille
Barclays
34 la Canebière. *Tel* 04 91 13 61 61

Monaco
American Express
5bis ave Princesse Alice.
Tel (00 377) 97 97 32 30
Barclays
31 av de la Costa.
Tel (00 377) 93 15 35 35

Lloyds
11 bd des Moulins.
Tel (00 377) 92 16 58 58

Nice
American Express
11 promenade des Anglais.
Tel 04 93 16 53 53.

Barclays
2 rue A Karr. *Tel* 04 93 82 68 00

LOST CARDS AND TRAVELLERS CHEQUES

Visa/Mastercard/Carte Bleue.
Tel 0892 705 705
American Express (Cards)
📠 01 47 77 70 00
American Express (Cheques)
Freecall *Tel* 0800 90 86 00 *(from France only).*

THE EURO

The Euro (€), the single European currency, is now operational in 12 of the 25 member states of the EU. Austria, Belgium, Finland, France, Germany, Greece, Ireland, Italy, Luxembourg, Netherlands, Portugal and Spain all chose to join the new currency; Denmark, the UK and Sweden chose to stay out, with an option to review their decision. France's Overseas Departments (Réunion etc) also all now use the euro. Euro notes are identical throughout all 12 countries, bearing architectural drawings of fictitious monuments. The coins, however, have one side identical (the value side), and one side unique to each country. Both notes and coins are valid and interchangeable within each of the 12 countries.

Bank Notes
Euro bank notes have seven denominations. The 5€ note (grey in colour) is the smallest, followed by the 10€ note (pink), 20€ note (blue), 50€ note (orange), 100€ note (green), 200€ note (yellow) and 500€ note (purple). All notes show the stars of the European Union.

5 euros

10 euros

20 euros

50 euros

100 euros

200 euros

500 euros

2 euros

1 euro

50 cents

20 cents

10 cents

Coins
The euro has eight coin denominations: 1€ and 2€; 50 cents, 20 cents, 10 cents, 5 cents, 2 cents and 1 cent. The 1€ and 2€ coins are both silver and gold in colour. The 50-, 20- and 10-cent coins are gold. The 5-, 2- and 1-cent coins are bronze.

5 cents

2 cents

1 cent

Communications

Sign for public telephone

French telecommunications are among the most advanced in the world. The main telephone company is called France Télécom, while postal services are run by La Poste. Public telephones are fairly widespread throughout Provence. Most take a telephone card *(télécarte),* available from local shops. Post offices, or *bureaux de postes,* are identified by the blue-on-yellow La Poste sign. La Poste was formerly known as the PTT, so road signs may indicate PTT. Foreign newspapers are available in most large towns, and an English-language radio station and newspaper operate on the Côte d'Azur.

Mail boxes throughout France are a distinctive yellow

USING A PHONECARD TELEPHONE

1 Lift the receiver and wait for the dialling tone.

2 Insert the *télécarte* with the arrow side facing up.

3 The screen displays the number of units still available, then gives you instructions to key in the phone number.

4 Key in the phone number and wait to be connected.

5 If you want to make another call, do not replace the receiver, simply press the green follow-on call button.

6 Replace receiver after the call. When card re-emerges, remove it.

French phonecards

TELEPHONING IN FRANCE

Nearly all French public phone boxes now take telephone cards *(télécartes)* and credit cards. Coin telephones have virtually disappeared except in some cafés. Telephone cards are sold in units of 50 or 120 and are easy to use. They can be purchased at post offices, *tabacs* (tobacconists), some newsagents and supermarkets.

Home Direct calling service, or *pays direct,* lets you make the call via an operator in your country, paying with a telephone chargecard, credit card or by reversing charges. In some cases, you can also call a third country (with AT & T for example). Reverse charge calls are known as PCV. Most phone boxes can receive incoming calls – the box telephone number is displayed above the telephone unit. Main post offices offer long distance calling facilities from booths *(cabines).* You then pay at the cashier. This is much cheaper than hotels for international calls – hotels tend to add a large surcharge. The Minitel electronic telephone directory can be used free in post offices *(see* How to Key in to Minitel*).*

MOBILE PHONES

Most new mobile phones brought from another European or Mediterranean country can be used in France. Alert your network that you plan to use it abroad so that they can enable it. However, US-based mobiles need to be "triple-band" to be used in France. International calls on mobile phones are expensive.

SENDING A LETTER

Postage stamps *(timbres)* are sold singly or in *carnets* of ten. Common postage stamps are also sold at *tabacs.*

Post office hours vary. The minimum hours are around 9am to 5pm from Monday to Friday with a two-hour lunch break from noon to 2pm. On Saturdays they are open from 9am until noon. In some larger towns, the main post office may remain open every week-day from 8am until 7pm.

Letters and parcels can be sent worldwide (although delivery times may take longer than you are used to). Letters are dropped into yellow mail boxes which often have three slots – one for the town you are in; one for the surrounding *département* (Provence is divided into five *départements,* listed under *Postcodes,* right); and one for other destinations *(autres destinations).*

For a small fee you can also receive or send mail care of post offices *(poste restante).* It is wise to underline the surname, as French officials sometimes assume the first name is the family name.

POSTCODES

All French addresses have five-digit postcodes. The first two digits represent the region's *département*. If 000 follows, this indicates the main town. The last two digits of the Marseille postcodes indicate the city's *arrondissements*.

Département Codes

Alpes-de-Haute-Provence	04
Alpes Maritimes	06
Bouches-du-Rhône	13
Var	83
Vaucluse	84

OTHER SERVICES

At post offices you can also consult the telephone directories *(annuaires)*, buy phonecards, send or receive money orders *(mandats)* and telephone all over the world. You can also make use of the fax and telex services. A huge amount of information is available when you use the Minitel electronic directory, which is rapidly replacing paper directories. This can be used free of charge at many post offices.

FOREIGN NEWSPAPERS

English-language papers which can be bought on the day of publication are the *Financial Times*, the *Guardian* and the *International Herald Tribune*, with its digest of North American news and sport. In Nice, English newspapers such as *The Times*, the *Daily Telegraph* and the *Daily Mail* are often available for sale on the same day at the airport. Most other English newspapers as well as Swiss,

Italian, German and Spanish titles, are sold the day after issue. *The News* is a monthly newspaper devoted to France. The English-speaking population of Provence has its own radio station and newspaper which provides local information. *(See Entertainment Information, p237).*

A range of newspapers available in Provence

TELEVISION AND RADIO

The subscription channel Canal+ broadcasts ABC American evening news at 7am daily. Sky News and CNN are available in many hotels. The Franco-German channel ARTE broadcasts programmes and films from all over the world, often in the original language with French subtitles. Listings indicate *vo or vf (version originale, version française)* for non-French films.

Riviera Radio broadcasts in English throughout the South of France on 106.3 and 106.5 FM stereo from Monte-Carlo. It offers news in English from the BBC and 24-hour music and current affairs, which includes BBC World Service programmes. *France Musique* is France's round-the-clock classical music station (92.2 FM in Nice and 94.7 in Marseille). *France Info* is a national rolling news station (105.2–105.8 FM).

ENGLISH-LANGUAGE BOOKSHOPS

Aix-en-Provence

Paradox, 15 rue du 4 Septembre.
Tel 04 42 26 47 99.

Cannes

Cannes English Bookshop,
11 rue Bivouac Napoléon.
Tel 04 93 99 40 08.

Marseille

Lamy, 26 rue Paradis.
Tel 04 91 33 57 05.

Monaco

Scruples, 9 rue Princesse Caroline.
Tel (00 377) 93 50 43 52.

Nice

The Cat's Whiskers,
30 rue Lamartine.
Tel 04 93 80 02 66.

Villeneuve-lès-Avignon

Centre Franco-Américain
de Provence,
10 montée de la Tour.
Tel 04 90 25 93 23.

USEFUL DIALLING CODES

- All Provence numbers start with 04. Ile de France is 01; the northwest is 02; the northeast 03; and the southwest 05.
- All Monaco numbers are prefixed 00 377 when calling from outside the Principality.
- For **operator service**, dial 12.
- For **Home Direct**, dial 0800 99, wait for tone, then dial 00.
- To make direct **international calls**, dial 00 first.
- The **country codes** for the following are: Australia: 61; Canada and USA: 1; Eire: 353; New Zealand: 64; UK: 44. Always omit the initial 0 of the country's area code.
- For all **telegrams**, dial 3655.

HOW TO KEY IN TO MINITEL

Minitel provides a vast range of services through a screen and keyboard connected to the telephone line. To use the system, press the telephone symbol and enter the Minitel number and code. For directory information, press the telephone symbol and key in 11. When beeping starts, press *Connexion/Fin*. Specify the service or name of supplier required. Enter town or area and press *Envoi* to start. To disconnect, press *Veille* or *Connexion/Fin*. Charges are displayed on the screen.

CUSTOMS AND IMMIGRATION

Currently there are no visa requirements for European Union nationals or for tourists from the United States, Canada, Australia or New Zealand staying in France for under three months. After that, a *carte de séjour* is required. Visitors coming from other countries should ask for visa information from the French authorities in their own country before departure.

TAX-FREE GOODS

If you are resident outside the EU you can reclaim the sales tax TVA (VAT) that you pay on French goods if you spend more than 175 in one shop, obtain a *bordereau de vente à l'exportation* (an export sales form) and take your purchases out of the EU within three months. The form should be signed by the retailer and yourself. Hand it in to customs when leaving the EU and the refund will be sent on to you.

Exceptions for *détaxe* rebate are food and drink, medicines, tobacco, cars and motorbikes.

DUTY-PAID LIMITS

There are no longer any restrictions on the quantities of duty-paid and VAT-paid goods you are allowed to take from one European Union country to another, as long as they are for your own use and not for resale. You may be asked to prove goods are for your personal use if they exceed the suggested amounts: 10 litres of spirits, 90 litres of wine, 110 litres of beer and 800 cigarettes.

DUTY-FREE LIMITS

For travel within the EU duty free was abolished in June 1999. For non-EU nationals arriving in the EU the following may be imported: up to 2 litres of wine, and a litre of sprits or 2 litres of drink less than 22° proof; 50g of perfume; 500g of coffee; 100g of tea; and up to 200 cigarettes. Visitors under 17 may not import or export duty-free tobacco or alcohol, even as gifts.

COUNTERFEITS

It is illegal to import, export or even to possess certain counterfeit goods in France.

Locally purchased regional wine, on which duty has been paid

IMPORTING OTHER GOODS

In general, personal goods (such as a car or a bicycle) may be imported to France duty-free and without any paperwork as long as they are obviously for personal use and not for resale. The brochure called *Voyagez en Toute Liberté* clarifies this and is available

Paris perfumes, available tax-free

from the **Centre des Renseignements des Douanes**. Customs offices can also give advice and information, but it is likely to be in French. Special rules apply, both within and without the EU, for the import and export of plants, animals, medicines, weapons and art objects. Consult your own, or French, customs.

ETIQUETTE

In all your dealings with customs, in duty-free shops, and in businesses outside the airport, remember: the people of Provence are traditionally welcoming but the French rituals of politeness apply in Provence more than anywhere. When introduced to someone, it is correct to shake hands. In shops, be prepared to say *bonjour* before asking what you want, then *merci* when you receive your change and *au revoir, bonne journée* when you depart. The usual greeting among friends of either sex is generally two or three kisses on the cheek.

While the larger tourist resorts can appear to be impersonal, in the smaller communities, any efforts by English speakers to make enthusiastic use of their French and to show a real interest in the area will be met with encouragement.

Student travellers and locals converse in the Old Town of Nice

STUDENT INFORMATION

Students with a valid International Student Identification Card (ISIC card) benefit from discounts of between 25 and 50 per cent at museums, theatres, cinemas and at many of the public monuments when you produce the card. The region's principal university is Aix-en-Provence/Marseille, and the campuses are shared between the two cities. Other large universities are located in Avignon and Nice. The BIJ and CRIJ (the Bureau Information Jeunesse/Centre Régional Information Jeunesse) in each town both provide a great deal of information about student life, and contain a list of inexpensive accommodation.

International Student Identity Card

PROVENCE TIME

Provence is one hour ahead of Greenwich Mean Time (GMT). It is in the same time zone as Italy, Spain and other western European countries. There are some standard time differences between Provence and other major cities of the world, which can vary according to local summer alterations to the time. These changes are as follows: for London: minus 1 hour from GMT; New York: minus 6 hours; Dallas: minus 7 hours; Los Angeles: minus 9 hours; Perth: plus 7 hours; Sydney: plus 9 hours; Auckland: plus 11 hours; and Tokyo: plus 8 hours.

The French use the 24-hour military clock (am and pm are not used): after midday, just continue counting 13, 14 and so on to provide the 24-hour clock time. For example, 1pm = 13:00.

ELECTRICAL ADAPTORS

The voltage in France is 220 volts. Plugs have two small round pins; the heavier-duty installations have two large round pins. Some of the up-market hotels offer built-in adaptors – for shavers only. Multi-adaptors, useful because they have both large and small pins, can be bought at most airports before departure, and standard adaptors purchased from department stores.

French two-pin electrical plug

RELIGIOUS SERVICES

Provence is a strong Catholic region, with many religious festivals and services dating back 500 years. Immigrants have brought religious diversification. Regular services in English are held at the Anglican churches in Nice and Marseille.

CONVERSION CHART

Imperial to metric
1 inch = 2.54 centimetres
1 foot = 30 centimetres
1 mile = 1.6 kilometres
1 ounce = 28 grams
1 pound = 454 grams
1 pint (UK) = 0.6 litre
1 gallon (UK) = 4.6 litres

Metric to imperial
1 millimetre = 0.04 inch
1 centimetre = 0.4 inch
1 metre = 3 feet 3 inches
1 kilometre = 0.6 mile
1 gram = 0.04 ounce
1 kilogram = 2.2 pounds
1 litre = 1.8 pints

DIRECTORY

CUSTOMS INFORMATION

Centre des Renseignements des Douanes
84 rue d'Hauteville, 75010 Paris.
Tel 0825 308 263.
www.douane.gouv.fr

Nice
18 rue Tonduti de l'Escarène.
Tel 04 93 13 78 13.

Marseille
48 av R.Schuman.
Tel 04 91 14 14 91.

STUDENT INFORMATION

Aix-en-Provence
BIJ, 37 bis bd Aristide-Briand.
Tel 04 42 91 98 00.

Marseille
CRIJ, 96 la Canebière.
Tel 04 91 24 33 50.

Nice
CRIJ, 19 rue Gioffredo.
Tel 04 93 80 93 93.

YOUTH HOSTELS

Aix
3 av Marcel Pagnol, Jas de Bouffan.
Tel 04 42 20 15 99.

Avignon
(Villeneuve-lès-Avignon)
7 bis chemin de la Justice.
Tel 04 90 25 46 20.

Marseille
Château de Bois-Luzy, Allée des Primevères.
Tel 04 91 49 06 18.

Quartier Bonneveine, impasse du Dr Bonfils.
Tel 04 91 17 63 30.

Nice
Route Forestière du Mt Alban.
Tel 04 93 89 23 64.

Clairvallon, 26 av Scudéri.
Tel 04 93 81 27 63.

Fontaine de Vaucluse
La Vignasse.
Tel 04 90 20 31 65.

PLACES OF WORSHIP

Catholic
Cathédrale Sainte-Réparate
Pl Rossetti, Nice.
Tel 04 93 62 34 40.

Basilique Notre-Dame de la Garde
Rue Fort du Sanctuaire, Marseille.
Tel 04 91 13 40 80.

Anglican
Nice Anglican Church
11 rue de la Buffa, Nice.
Tel 04 93 87 19 83.
www.anglican-nice.com

Eglise Anglicane de Marseille
4 rue de Belloi, Marseille.
Tel 04 91 90 18 81.

Jewish
Grande Synagogue
7 rue G Deloye, Nice.
Tel 04 93 92 11 38.

Temple Israëlite de Sainte Marguerite (Algerian)
205 bd Ste Marguerite, Marseille.
Tel 04 91 75 63 50.

Islamic
Mosque de la Capelette
68 rue Alfred Curtel, Marseille.
Tel 04 91 25 95 57.

TRAVEL INFORMATION

Situated at the crossroads between France, Spain and Italy, Provence is well served by international motorway and rail links. Nice airport is the most modern and the busiest of French airports outside Paris, handling 4 million visitors annually. Marseille airport also welcomes daily direct flights from major European cities, as well as weekly direct flights from New York. For travelling across France, the TGV train is swift *(see p248)*, while the motorail journey from channel ports takes 12 hours but is effortless and dispenses with motorway tolls. The motorways are excellent, but can become crowded in mid-summer.

Air France
Boeing 737

ARRIVING BY AIR

The two main airports in Provence are comfortably modern – Marseille, Marignane, and Nice, Côte d'Azur, which has recently enjoyed a face-lift. **Marseille Provence** has two terminals with national and international flights. It serves mainly business travellers and is more expensive to fly to, but is handy for destinations that are right in the centre of Provence, such as Avignon and Aix-en-Provence.

Airport taxis to the centre of Marseille cost around 35€ (43€ at night and on Sundays). There is also an airport bus to the main train station in Marseille (St-Charles) every 20 minutes. Car hire companies at the airport include Avis, Budget, Citer, Ada, Europcar and Hertz.

Nice, **Côte d'Azur** has two terminals. The east terminal (one) takes international flights and some domestic flights on French carriers (Air Littoral and TAT). Check with your travel agent to make sure which terminal you will be using. The west terminal (two) serves domestic flights only. Taxis to the centre cost 22–25€. Airport buses run to the Gare Routière station every 10 minutes, and bus No. 99 goes to Gare SNCF every 30 minutes. There are buses to Cannes every half hour and to Monaco and Menton every hour. Heli-Inter offers helicopter transits every 20 minutes to Monte-Carlo, and several times a day to St-Tropez during the summer season. The car hire companies at Nice airport include Ada, Avis, Budget, Europcar and Hertz.

There are three other airports within Provence which operate international flights: Montpellier, Nîmes and Toulon.

AIRPORT INFORMATION

Avignon-Caumont
Tel 04 90 81 51 51.
Airport to city 10 km (6 miles).
Taxi 20€.

Marseille Provence
Tel 04 42 14 14 14.
Airport to city 25 km (17 miles).
Shuttle bus 10€, taxi 35€.

Montpellier Méditerranée
Tel 04 67 20 85 85.
Airport to city 7 km (4 miles).
Shuttle bus 5€, taxi 12–15€.

Nice, Côte d'Azur
Tel 0820 423 333.
Airport to city 6 km (4 miles).
Shuttle bus 4€, taxi 22€.

Nîmes/Arles/Camargue
Tel 04 66 70 49 49.
Airport to city 8 km (5 miles).
Shuttle bus 5€, taxi 20€.

Toulon-Hyères
Tel 08 25 01 83 83.
Airport to city 23 km (15 miles).
Shuttle bus 10€, taxi 40€.

The main international terminal at Nice, Côte d'Azur airport

AIRLINE DETAILS

Provence is perhaps the most easily accessible place by air in France after Paris. The vast majority of large European cities have direct daily flights. The British carriers – British Airways, Buzz, Easyjet and British Midland – all run daily flights that depart for Nice from London Heathrow, London Gatwick, Luton or Stansted. Ryanair also has daily flights to southern France (03 44 11 41 41). The French national airline, Air France, has daily flights to and from Nice to Britain, Spain, Germany, Italy (via Lyon), North Africa and the Middle East (via Paris). Air Lib Express has frequent flights between Paris and Provence.

There is a daily Delta flight scheduled from Nice to New York and also from New York to Nice (Apr–Oct).

From all other international departure points it is necessary to change planes in Paris to reach Provence. There are no direct flights from New Zealand, but Lufthansa has flights from most major French cities, via Frankfurt, to Auckland.

Departure hall at Marseille airport

AIRLINE TELEPHONE NUMBERS

Air Canada
France *Tel 0825 880 881.*
www.aircanada.ca

Air France
France *Tel 0845 084 5111.*
www.airfrance.com

British Airways
France *Tel 0825 825 400.*
UK *Tel 0845 77 333 77.*
US *Tel 1-800-247 9297.*
www.britishairways.com

British Midland
Paris *Tel 01 48 62 55 65.*
UK *Tel 0870 6070 555.*
www.flybmi.com

Delta
Freecall (France) *Tel 0800 354 080.*
Freecall (US) *Tel 0800 241 4141.*
www.delta.com

Easyjet
France *Tel 0825 082 508.*
UK *Tel 0870 600 0000.*
www.easyjet.com

Ryan Air
Paris *Tel 08 92 55 56 66.*
www.ryanair.com

FARES AND DEALS

Airline fares to Provence are at their highest over the Easter period and in the peak season in July and August.

For flights only, Apex fares from London Heathrow are relatively inexpensive but they have to be booked well in advance. They cannot be changed or cancelled without a penalty and contain minimum and maximum stay clauses.

There are many flight deals to Nice both out of season and during the summer when the charter companies operate. Look around for the best offers at reputable discount agencies.

DISCOUNT TRAVEL AGENCIES

Aix
Usit Connections
7 cours Sextius. *Tel 04 42 93 48 48.*

Marseille
Voyages Wasteels
67 la Canebière. *Tel 08 25 88 70 46.*

UK
Trailfinders
215 Kensington High St, London
W8 6BD. *Tel 020 7937 5400.*
www.trailfinders.com

US
Council Travel
205 East 42nd Street,
New York, NY 10017.
Tel (212) 822 2700.

Nouvelles Frontières
6 East 46th Street, New York,
NY 10016. *Tel (212) 986 6006.*
www.nouvelles-frontieres.com

FLY-DRIVE AND FLY-RAIL PACKAGE HOLIDAYS

Air France and the French railways offer combined fares for flight and train. You fly into Paris and then catch the train south. Good deals are available for the main destinations such as Avignon, Arles and Marseille.

There are also companies offering tailor-made package holidays in Provence, with flight, car hire and accommodation included in the cost.

TAILOR-MADE PACKAGE HOLIDAYS

Allez France Holidays (UK)
27–31 West St, Storrington RH20 4DZ.
Tel 01903-748 155.
www.allezfrance.com

Can Be Done Ltd
(for travellers with disabilities)
11 Woodcock Hill, Harrow HA3 0PX.
Tel 020-8907 2400.
www.canbedone.co.uk

France Your Way (US)
4218 SW Raymond St, Seattle, WA
98136. Freecall. *Tel 877 374 4648.*

FLIGHT TIMES

On long-haul flights you will need to change planes in Paris or London. Approximate flight times from major cities are as follows:

London: 1 hour, 55 minutes.
Dublin: 2 hours, 20 minutes.
Toronto: 9 hours.
New York: 8 hours.
Sydney: 26 hours.

Getting Around by Train

SNCF logo

Travelling to Provence by train is fast and efficient. The French state railway, Société Nationale des Chemins de Fer **(SNCF)**, is one of Europe's best equipped and most comfortable. The train journey from Paris to Avignon is almost as quick as by air – the TGV (Train à Grande Vitesse) takes only 4 hours. With the Channel Tunnel open, travel to Provence from the UK is faster than before, though much of this route is not high speed.

MAIN ROUTES

The main train routes to Provence from Northern Europe pass through Lille and Paris. In Paris you may have to transfer to the Gare de Lyon – the main Paris station serving the south of France. Tickets from London to Nice, Avignon and Marseille, on the chunnel, hovercraft or ferry, are all available from the **Rail Europe** office in London. The Channel Tunnel connects at Lille with TGVs to the rest of France. Sea passengers arriving at Calais can catch the train to Lilles and from here there is a daily sleeper to Nice.

From southern Europe, trains run to Marseille from Barcelona in Spain (6½ hours) and Genoa in Italy (3 hours).

Within Provence and the Côte d'Azur, the coastal route between Nice and Marseille is often crowded, so it is best to reserve tickets in advance on this and other *Grandes Lignes*. In the Var and Haute Provence, railway lines are scarce, but SNCF run bus services. The private rail service **Chemins de Fer de Provence** runs the Train des Pignes *(see p181)*, a 151-km (90-mile) ride from Nice, through the scenic Var valley.

BOOKING FROM ABROAD

Bookings by post, telephone, fax or internet, for all tickets to and within France can be made in the UK and US through Rail Europe. Rail Europe also has information on prices and departure times. Reservations made abroad can be difficult to change once in France – you may have to pay for another reservation, or claim a refund on your return.

BOOKING IN FRANCE

Ticket counters at all the stations are computerized. There are also automatic ticket and reservation machines (with English instructions) on the concourse of main stations. If you have a credit card with a PIN number, you can check times and fares and make reservations using the Minitel

system *(see p243)*. For travel by TGV, a reservation is compulsory but can be made as little as five minutes before the train leaves. Costs rise considerably at peak times. The new international ticket and reservation system at Lille Europe station is connected by computer to most European travel agents and stations, allowing direct booking on services throughout the continent and the UK.

Automatic ticket machine

FARES AND BOOKING

TGVs have two price levels for 2nd class, normal and peak, and a single level for 1st class. The cost of the obligatory seat reservation is included in the ticket price. Tickets for other trains can be subject to a supplement and

Paris to Marseille now takes just three hours by TGV

THE TGV TRAIN

Trains à Grande Vitesse, or high-speed trains, travel at up to 300 km/hr (185 mph). There are five versions of TGV serving all areas of France and some European destinations. The Eurostar links Paris and London, the Thalys runs to Brussels. The new TGV Méditerranée to Provence leaves from Paris Gare de Lyon. Other TGVs leave from Grenoble, Geneva and Lausanne. The trains' speed, comfort and reliability make them relatively expensive. Always reserve a seat.

do not include the reservation charge of 3 .

Discounts of 25 per cent are available for people travelling with children (*Découverte Enfant+*), for young people (*Découverte 12–25*), for the over-60s (*Découverte Senior*), for two people travelling together (*Découverte à Deux*), for return trips including a Saturday night (*Découverte Sejour*) and for advance booking (*Découverte J8* and *Découverte J30*).

For those spending a bit more time on French railways, the SNCF issues a *Carte Enfant+* and a *Carte Senior* giving reductions of up to 50 per cent.

Rail passes bought outside the country for use in France include Eurodomino tickets which allow three, five or ten days' travel a month (with a reduction for those under 26). Inter-Rail cards allow unlimited travel in European countries excluding the one of issue. Eurail passes are available to non-European residents and, in North America, France Railpass offers yet more permutations.

A high-speed silver TGV or Train à Grande Vitesse

TYPES OF TRAIN

Not all trains in France are TGVs. *Train Rapide National* (TRN), still known as Corail, are less swift, but serve more stations and more routes. *Train Express Regional* (TER),

often only a carriage or two long, serve local routes. The overnight train from London to Nice is a *train auto couchette* (sleeper) service only. You must buy a *couchette* or berth, a fold-down bunk in a compartment of four or six. It is best to keep valuables with you. A compartment with twin berth and private washroom is a more expensive option. Not all trains contain restaurant cars or bars, even on long journeys. Check timetables for details. All TGVs have bars with light meals, and you can reserve an at-seat meal service in advance in first class.

Other services offered by SNCF include reserving a car, taxi, bike or hotel room at your station of arrival.

Rail traveller with luggage trolley

TIMES AND PENALTIES

Timetables change twice yearly and leaflets for main routes are free. The Provence-Alpes-Côte d'Azur region has an all-inclusive Transports Express Régionaux timetable, which includes coach travel.

You must time-punch your ticket in the orange machine at the platform entrance or pay a penalty on the train. Trains in France are very rarely late.

MOTORAIL

Eurotunnel rail shuttles vehicles between Folkstone and Calais (35 minutes). **Motorail** services carry cars, motorbikes and passengers overnight from Calais, Dieppe, Lille and Paris to Provence. The journey from the channel ports takes 12 hours 30 minutes, and is not cheap, but is a practical, stress-free way to avoid the long drive south. The service runs to Avignon, Marseille and Nice and seasonally to Fréjus/St-Raphaël. Debate always reigns on the merits and costs of road versus rail, but ultimately it comes down to personal choice.

DIRECTORY

INFORMATION AND RESERVATIONS

Eurostar
London Waterloo International
Waterloo Station,
Waterloo Rd,
London SE1 7LT
Tel 08705 186 186
www.eurostar.com

Paris Gare du Nord
rue de Dunkerque,
75010 Paris
Tel 08 92 35 35 39.
www.eurostar.com

Eurotunnel
(Off junction 11a, M20,
Folkestone)
Tel 08705 35 35 35
France *Tel* 08 10 63 03 04
www.eurotunnel.com

Rail Europe
179 Piccadilly,
London
W1V 0BA
Tel 08705 848 848.
www.raileurope.co.uk

Rail Europe USA
226–230 West Chester Park,
White Plains, NY 10604.
Tel 888 4387 245
(freephone in US).
www.raileurope.com

Inter-Rail Bookings
TGV
Tel 08 92 35 35 35.
SNCF
Tel 01 53 90 20 20
www.sncf.fr

Motorail
197 Piccadilly,
London
W1V 0BA
UK *Tel* 08702 415 415
www.raileurope.co.uk
France *Tel* 08 92 35 35 35

PRIVATE RAILWAY

Chemins de Fer de Provence
Tel 04 97 03 80 80.
www.trainprovence.com

Getting Around by Road

France is a motorist's paradise and the main route to Provence is via an excellent, if expensive, autoroute (motorway) network. Provence is ideal for touring, with some of the most beautiful road routes in the world, including the stunning Grande Corniche above Nice, and the hilltop lanes of the Luberon *(see pp170–71)*. Popular routes, especially the motorway and coastal roads along the Côte d'Azur, can be busy in high season.

For the truly adventurous, the Route Napoléon leads from Grenoble south across the Alps to Digne, and continues to Grasse. From Grasse, take the scenic D3 then D2210 for Nice and environs, or carry on into Cannes.

Three of the most widely used car rental firms in France

GETTING TO PROVENCE

If you are taking your own car to Provence, it is advisable to obtain a green card (a free extension of an existing policy from some insurers). Without it you are covered third party only in France, regardless of whether you have comprehensive cover in your own country. The AA, RAC and Europ Assistance have special policies. It is compulsory to take your car's original registration document, a current insurance certificate and a valid driving licence. A sticker showing the country of registration should be displayed close to the rear number plate. The headlights of right-hand drive cars must be adjusted – kits are available at most ports.

The quickest route south is the Autoroute du Soleil, the A6 motorway from Paris to Lyon, followed by the A7 to Marseille. Travellers from the UK and northern Europe will have difficulty avoiding Paris. Motorways skirt the city centre, leading from the northern A1 to the southern A6. If you can, avoid the Paris rush hour.

From Spain, the A8 motorway leads directly to Marseille and goes on to Nice and Italy.

In high season, the motorways get very crowded and if you have time it may be worth taking more minor (and attractive) roads. Try turning off the main road at Montélimar to travel to the Luberon via Nyons and Vaison-la-Romaine. Or exit at Avignon, and head into the Luberon and on to Var.

CAR RENTAL

It is worth contacting a number of car-rental firms before you go, as there are numerous special offers for cars pre-paid in the UK and USA. In France, **Rent A Car** is good value.

Fly-drive options work well for small groups. SNCF offers train and car-rental deals with collection from main stations.

For more than three weeks, the best option is the short-term purchase and buy back service (TT leasing) offered by Citroën, Peugeot and Renault from Nice airport.

USING THE AUTOROUTE TOLL

When you join an autoroute, collect a ticket from the machine. This identifies your starting point on the autoroute. You do not pay until you reach an exit toll. You are charged according to the distance travelled and the type of vehicle used.

Motorway Sign
These signs indicate the name and distance to the next toll booth. They are usually blue and white; some show the tariff rates for cars, motorbikes, trucks and caravans.

Tollbooth with Attendant
When you hand in your ticket at a staffed tollbooth, the attendant will tell you the cost of your journey on the autoroute and the price will be displayed. You can pay with coins, notes or credit cards. A receipt is issued on request.

Automatic Machine
On reaching the exit toll, insert your ticket into the machine and the price of your journey is displayed in euros. You can pay either with coins or by credit card. The machine will give change and can issue a receipt.

RULES OF THE ROAD

Remember to drive on the right. The *priorité à droite* rule applies, meaning that you must give way to any vehicle coming out of a side turning on the right, unless otherwise signposted. However, the *priorité à droite* rule no longer applies at roundabouts, meaning you have to give way to cars already on the roundabout. Flashing headlights mean the driver is claiming right of way.

Seatbelts are compulsory for front and back seats. Overtaking when there is a single solid centre line is heavily penalized.

SPEED LIMITS AND FINES

The speed limits in Provence are as follows:
• **Motorways** 130 km/hr (80 mph)
• **Dual carriageways** 110 km/hr (68 mph); 50 km/hr (30 mph) in towns
• **Other roads** 90 km/hr (56 mph).

Instant fines are issued for speeding and drink-driving.

The A6 from Paris to Lyon is the quickest route south

FAST THROUGH ROUTES

There are three main motorways in Provence: the A7 from Lyon to Marseille, the A9 from Orange to Barcelona, and the A8 from Marseille to Menton. The new A54 cuts across the Camargue from Aix-en-Provence via Arles to Nîmes. The A8 is the most expensive stretch of toll motorway in France, but allows you to drive from Nice to Aix-en-Provence in under two hours.

No entry for any vehicles

Sign indicating one-way system

VOUS N'AVEZ PAS LA PRIORITÉ

Give way at roundabout

Right of way ends, give way to right

COUNTRY ROUTES

One of the pleasures of touring Provence is turning off the main routes onto small country roads. The RN and D (*Route Nationale* and *Départmentale*) roads are a good alternative to motorways. *Bison futée* ("crafty bison") signs indicate alternative routes to avoid heavy traffic, and are especially helpful during the French holiday periods, appropriately known as the *grands départs*. The worst weekends are in mid-July, and at the beginning and end of August when French holidays start and finish.

MAPS

The best general map of Provence is the Michelin yellow map No. 245, at a scale of 1:200,000. **IGN** (Institut Géographique National) maps are more detailed. Town plans are usually provided free by tourist offices. In large towns you may need a more detailed map, published by Michelin or **Plans-Guides Blay-Foldex**. In the UK, **Stanfords** is famous for its range of maps.

Some of the national and regional maps available

DIRECTORY

CAR RENTAL

Ada
Nice **Tel** 04 93 16 03 23.
Marseille **Tel** 04 91 21 62 16.

Avis
UK **Tel** 0870 6060 100.
US **Tel** (1) (880) 331 1212.
France **Tel** 0820 05 05 05.

Budget
UK **Tel** 0800 181 181.
US **Tel** (1) (880) 527 0700.
France **Tel** 0825 352 352

Europcar
UK **Tel** 01132 422 233.
Marseille **Tel** 04 91 99 09 32.

Hertz
UK **Tel** 0870 844 8844.
US **Tel** (1) (880) 654 3131.
France **Tel** 0825 861 861.

Rent A Car
France **Tel** 0836 694 695.
Nice **Tel** 04 93 88 69 69.

TT LEASING

Nice Airport
TT Car Transit/pick up point only
Tel 04 93 21 39 74.

Rest of France
Reservations **Tel** 01 40 71 72 40.

TRAFFIC INFORMATION

CRIR
Tel 08 26 02 20 22

Autoroute ESCOTA
24hr: **Tel** 04 93 49 33 33.

MAPS

Espace IGN
107 rue de la Boétie,
75008 Paris.
Tel 01 43 98 80 00.

Plans-Guides Blay-Foldex
40-48 rue des Meuniers,
93108 Montreuil.
Tel 01 49 88 92 10.

BUS AND COACH COMPANIES

Eurolines
London Victoria Coach Station.
UK **Tel** 020-7730 8235.
France **Tel** 08 92 69 52 52.
www.eurolines.fr

Intercars
Gare Routière, 5 bd Jean Jaurès,
Nice. **Tel** 04 93 80 08 70.
www.intercars.fr

PARKING

Parking in the big towns, particularly along the coast, is strictly regulated. If you are illegally parked, you may be towed away instantly to the police pound to face a fine of up to 152 . Most Provençal towns now have pay and display machines *(horodateurs)*. Many places offer free parking from noon to 2pm – ticket machines automatically allow for this. Parking is often time limited. Even if you are legally parked, you may find yourself hemmed in when you return: the French usually honk their horns to attract the guilty party.

An *horodateur*, or pay-and-display machine

PETROL

Petrol is relatively expensive in France, especially on autoroutes. Large super-markets and hypermarkets sell petrol at a discount. A map issued by French Government Tourist offices *(see p237)* indicates the cheaper petrol stations situated up to 2 km (just over a mile) from motor-way exits. Unleaded petrol is found in most stations. Diesel is also common and is the cheapest fuel in France, thanks to lobbying by truck drivers. LPG gas is available, often on motorways. A map of locations can be obtained from any LPG station in France.

Mountain bikes are ideal for exploring the Provençal countryside

CYCLING

Cycling is one of the most pleasant ways to see Provence. Although the French are cycling enthusiasts, at the moment there are few cycle lanes in towns in Provence. However, some towns, such as Arles, Avignon and Nîmes, have specified cycle routes. You can take bikes on certain trains – check the timetable first for the bike symbol. You can also hire bicycles at a num-ber of stations. Rental shops are common, especially in the Luberon and in towns around the Camargue, which rent out mountain bikes *(VTT)*. Bicycle theft is common along the Côte d'Azur – make sure you are fully insured before you go.

A taxi meter showing a 2-euro fare, or *prix à payer*

TAXIS

Prices vary from one part of Provence to another. The charges are predictably highest along the Côte d'Azur, where prices of 30 for a 20-minute ride are not uncommon. Else-where the pick-up charge is usually around 2 , and 0.60 or more for every kilometre.

An extra charge will be made for any luggage. All taxis must use a meter, or a *compteur*. Hailing a taxi is not customary in Provence – you must go to a taxi rank or book by phone.

HITCHHIKING

Hitchhiking is possible in France, although officially it is frowned upon. You are not supposed to hitch on the motorways and if you do will be cautioned by the police. Allostop-Provoya can put you in touch with cars heading south from Paris, and for region to region lifts: **Tel** *01 53 20 42 42.*

COACH AND BUS TRAVEL

Coach travel used to be the cheapest way of getting to Provence, but reductions in air fares have now made it a less competitive option. The jour-ney time to Nice from London with **Eurolines** takes almost 24 hours, compared to a 2-hour flight. Coaches depart twice a week in the summer from London to St-Raphaël and Nice, and twice a week all year to Avignon and Marseille. **Intercars'** services also leave from Madrid, Spain to Nice, and from Portugal (Porto, Lisbon, Faro) to Nice and Marseille. A 32-hour service departs from Nice and Marseille to Tangiers.

Big towns have a bus station but, otherwise, the bus services are surprisingly limited. SNCF runs bus services in northern Provence, and private com-panies run along the major motorways between towns and on some minor routes, such as the coastal road between Toulon and St-Tropez *(see also p251)*. Local bus services are notoriously erratic.

Eurolines long-haul coach

Travelling by Boat

There are few more enticing sights than the glittering Mediterranean of the southern Provençal coast. Almost every city along this stretch of water has a port with boats for hire. Ferry and boat companies operating to offshore islands are easy to find, and there are trips to Corsica from Marseille and Nice throughout the year. For water-lovers, **Kuoni** tour operators offer cruises. The other main waterways in Provence are the Rhône and Durance rivers. Houseboat and barge holidays tend to centre on the Rhône and Camargue, and there are a number of river Rhône sightseeing tours.

Sailing out of a rocky inlet on the Provençal coast

MEDITERRANEAN PORTS

Car ferries depart all year round from Marseille and Nice to Corsica (Bastia, Ajaccio and Ile Rousse), operated by **SNCM Ferryterranée**. Summer ferries run from Marseille to Propriano, and from Toulon to Ajaccio, Bastia and Propriano, often crossing overnight. SNCM has one or two weekly sailings from Marseille and Toulon to Sardinia. There are crossings to North Africa every week from Marseille to Tunis or Algiers, and to Oran weekly in high season.

Regular ferries and boats to nearby islands operate from Bandol to the Ile de Bendor; from Tour Fondu to Porquerolles; and from Port d'Hyères and Le Lavandou to Le Levant and Port-Cros.

CRUISES AND RIVER TRIPS

The Mediterranean is famous as a cruise destination, and numerous companies operate on the south coast of France, stopping at St-Tropez, Villefranche and Monaco. **Crown Blue Line** has a good range of

boats for hire for weekly river trips. Day cruises to the Iles d'Hyères sail from Quai Stalingrad at Toulon.

Some of the smaller, local boats moored in St-Tropez

Les Grands Bateaux de Provence offer trips to Arles, and **La Camargue au Fil de l'Eau** runs daily cruises in a converted *péniche* – a traditional river cargo boat. **Mireio** runs dinner, dance or lunch cruises from Avignon to Arles. Barge or houseboat holidays can be planned and booked by **Rive de France**.

SAILING

Over 70 ports along the Provence coastline welcome yachts, and mooring charges vary. The Côte d'Azur ports are particularly expensive. Contact the **Fédération Française de Voile** for information on sailing clubs and where to hire boats.

DIRECTORY

CAR FERRY

SNCM Ferryterranée
Marseille **Tel** 08 90 64 00 95.
www.sncm.fr

CRUISES & RIVER TRIPS

Crown Blue Line
2 quai du Canal, 30800 Saint-Gilles.
Tel 04 66 87 79 15.

Les Grands Bateaux de Provence
Avignon. **Tel** 04 90 85 62 25.

La Camargue au Fil de l'Eau
30220 Aigues-Mortes.
Tel 04 66 53 79 47.

Kuoni
www.kuoni.co.uk

Mireio
Avignon. **Tel** 04 90 85 62 25.

Rive de France
Boulogne. **Tel** 01 41 86 01 02.

SAILING

Fédération Française de Voile
Tel 01 40 60 37 00.
www.ffvoile.org

A privately owned motorboat from Cannes

General Index

Acknowledgments

Dorling Kindersley would like to thank the following people whose contributions and assistance have made the preparation of this book possible.

Main Contributor

Roger Williams is a writer and editor who was for many years associated with the *Sunday Times* magazine. He has written two novels and a number of guide books, on places ranging from Barcelona to the Baltic States, and was a contributor to *Over Europe*, the first aerial record of the united continent. He visits France regularly, and has been writing about Provence for more than 30 years.

Contributors

Adele Evans, John Flower, Robin Gauldie, Jim Keeble, Anthony Rose, Martin Walters.

Additional Photography

Demetrio Carrasco, Andy Crawford, Lisa Cupolo, Nick Goodall, Steve Gorton, John Heseltine, Andrew Holligan, Richard McConnell, Neil Mersh, Ian O'Leary, Clive Streeter.

Additional Illustrators

Simon Calder, Paul Guest, Aziz Khan, Tristan Spaargaren, Ann Winterbotham, John Woodcock.

Cartographic Research

Jane Hugill, Samantha James, Jennifer Skelley, Martin Smith (Lovell Johns).

Design and Editorial

MANAGING EDITOR Georgina Matthews
DEPUTY EDITORIAL DIRECTOR Douglas Amrine
DEPUTY ART DIRECTOR Gaye Allen
PRODUCTION CONTROLLER Hilary Stephens
PICTURE RESEARCH Susan Mennell
DTP DESIGNER Salim Qurashi
MAP CO-ORDINATORS Simon Farbrother, David Pugh
MAPS Uma Bhattacharya, Kunal Singh, Jennifer Skelley, Samantha James (Lovell Johns Ltd, Oxford)
RESEARCHER Philippa Richmond
Azeem Alam, Vincent Allonier, Rosemary Bailey, Shahnaaz Bakshi, Laetitia Benloulou, Josie Bernard, Hilary Bird, Kevin Brown, Margaret Chang, Cooling Brown Partnership, Guy Dimond, Joy Fitzsimmonds, Vinod Harish, Victoria Heyworth-Dunne, Jackie Grosvenor, Annette Jacobs, Nancy Jones, Erika Lang, Francesca Machiavelli, James Marlow, Helen Partington, Sangita Patel, Katie Peacock, Alice Peebles, Carolyn Pyrah, Philippa Richmond, Kavita Saha, Baishakhee Sengupta, Sailesh Sharma, Bhaswati Singh, Priyanka Thakur, Amanda Tomeh, Daphne Trotter, Janis Utton, Dora Whitaker, Irina Zarb.

Special Assistance

Louise Abbott; Anna Brooke, Manade Gilbert Arnaud; Brigitte Charles, Monaco Tourist Board, London; Sabine Giraud, Terres du Sud, Venasque; Emma Heath; Nathalie Lavarenne, Musée Matisse, Nice; Ella Milroy; Marianne Petrou; Andrew Sanger; David Tse.

Photographic Reference

Bernard Beaujard, Vézénobres.

Photography Permissions

Dorling Kindersley would like to thank the following for their assistance and kind permission to photograph at their establishments: Fondation Marguerite et Aimé Maeght, St-Paul-de-Vence; Hotel Négresco, Nice; Monsieur J-F Campana, Mairie de Nice; Monsieur Froumessol, Mairie de Cagnes-sur-Mer; Musée Ephrussi de Rothschild, St-Jean-Cap-Ferrat; Musée Jean Cocteau, Menton; Musée International de la Parfumerie, Grasse; Musée Matisse, Nice; Musée National Message Biblique Marc Chagall, Nice; Musée Océanographique, Monaco; Musée Picasso/Château Grimaldi, Antibes; Salle des Mariages, Hôtel de Ville, Menton, and all other churches, museums, hotels, restaurants, shops and sights too numerous to thank individually.

Picture Credits

t = top; tl = top left; tc = top centre; tr = top right; cla = centre left above; ca = centre above; cra = centre right above; cl = centre left; c = centre; cr = centre right; clb = centre left below; cb = centre below; crb = centre right below; bl = bottom left; b = bottom; bc = bottom centre; br = bottom right; bla = bottom left above; bca = bottom centre above; bra = bottom right above; blb = bottom left below; bcb = bottom centre below; brb = bottom right below.

Every effort has been made to trace the copyright holders and we apologize in advance for any unintentional omissions. We would be pleased to insert the appropriate acknowledgments in any subsequent edition of this publication.

Works of art have been reproduced with the permission of the following copyright holders:

© ADAGP, Paris and DACS, London 1995: 27b, 54br, 59tl, 76t, ca, cb, 77c and b, 78c, 85b, 106b, 119b, 120ca, 144t; © ADAGP/SPADEM, Paris and DACS, London 1995: 76(b), 120 (b); © DACS, London 1995: 26t and b, 27t, 30tr; 73tl, tr, cl, cr and b, 74t, 77t, 78b, 99t, 120cb; 121t; 121ca; 121cb; © Succession Henri Matisse/DACS 1995: 27c, 82t and b, 83t, c and br.

The publisher would like to thank the following individuals, companies and picture libraries for permission to reproduce their photographs:.

ALAMY IMAGES: Dave Watts 231c; ALVEY & TOWERS: 248b; ANCIENT ART AND ARCHITECTURE COLLECTION: 39t and cb, 40bl, 43t; ARCHIVES DE L'AUTOMOBILE CLUB DE MONACO: 52ca; ARTEPHOT, PARIS: Plassart 27c; ASSOCIATED PRESS LTD: 29cb.

LA BELLE AURORE: 32b, 37t; HOSTELLERIE BERARD: 230cr; BRIDGEMAN ART LIBRARY: Christie's, London 47crb, 50–51; Giraudon 47t, 48bl; Schloss Charlottenburg, Berlin 179t.

CAMPAGNE, CAMPAGNE!, PARIS: Jolyot 92br; JL Julien 31bl; Meissonnier 159b; Meschinet 138c; Moirenc 247; Pambour 171t, 172t; Picard 159t; Pyszel 90t; CARTE MUSEES COTE D'AZUR: 237cl; CEPHAS: Mick Rock 208br, 209ca and br; JEAN-LOUP CHARMET, PARIS: 28cl, 29tl; © Antoine de Saint-Exupéry/Gallimard 29ca; 37b, 42bl, 46ca and cb, 49t and cla, 50tl and tr, 52t, 53t, 132cl, 140t, 153t, 160cl; BRUCE COLEMAN: Adrian Davies 114bl; JLG Grande 136bca; George McCarthy 19tl; Andrew J Purcell 115cb and bl; Hans Reinhard 137t, 171bl, bc and br; Dr Frieder Sauer 114c; Robert Wanscheidt 160bl; K Wothe 160bc; Paul van Gaalen 136bra; CORBIS: Owen Franken 231t; John Hicks 11br; Chris Lisle 11tl; JOE CORNISH: 23tr, 188, 234; JULIAN COTTON PICTURE LIBRARY: Jason Hawkes aerial collection 13, 56–7; CULTURE ESPACES, PARIS: 86t and ca; Véran 87t.

PHOTO DASPET, AVIGNON: Musée du Petit Palais, Avignon 44t, 45bc; Palais des Papes, Avignon 44crb and b; DIAF, PARIS: J-P Garcin 33cb; J-C Gérard 228 t and b, 151b; Camille Moirenc 162c; Bernard Régent 26t; Patrick Somelet 158b; DIRECTION DES AFFAIRES CULTURELLES, MONACO: 91c.

EUROPEAN COMMISSION: 241; MARY EVANS: 9 inset, 28t, bl and br, 29bl, 45br and t, 48b, 57inset, 189inset, 235inset; JANE EWART: 22cb, 23c, 24tl, 25cb, 58tl, 76cb, 127b, 163ca and cb, 203b, 237b, 244br; EXPLORER ARCHIVES, PARIS: L Bertrand 38cb; Jean-Loup Charmet 67t, 124c, 147b; Coll. ES 42t, 46cb and bl; Coll. Sauvel 15t; G Garde 33ca; J P Hervey 64t; J & C Lenars 39c; J-P Lescourret 165c; M C Noailles 65b; Peter Willi 40ca; A Wolf 43clb.

FONDATION AUGUSTE ESCOFFIER, VILLENEUVE-LOUBET: 74c; FONDATION MAEGHT, SAINT-PAUL-DE-VENCE, FRANCE: Claude Germain 77t and c; Coll. M et Mme Adrien Maeght 77b; FRANK LANE PICTURE AGENCY: N Clark 170b; Fritz Polking 18tr; M B Withers 136bla.

GALERIE INTEMPOREL, PARIS: Les Films Ariane, Paris 54–5; EDITIONS GAUD, MOISENAY: 70bl, 86b, 87bl and br, 142t, 181c; GIRAUDON, PARIS: 27t, bl and br, 28cr, 32t, 36, 40br, 48ca and br, 133b, 145b, 172c; Lauros-Giraudon 38ca, 45cb, 46tr (detail), 46–7, 49clb, 51clb, 53clb (all rights reserved), 73tl and tr, 110bl, 125b, 134t, 144t, 146t; Musée de la Vieille Charité, Marseille 38tr; Musée de la Ville de Paris, Musée du Petit Palais/Lauros-Giraudon 26bl; Musée des Beaux-Arts, Marseille 48–9, 49b, 152b; Musée du Louvre, Paris 8–9; Musée du Vieux Marseille, Marseille 48cb, 50ca; GRAND HÔTEL DU CAP FERRAT: 191t; RONALD GRANT ARCHIVE: Warner Brothers 29br; GROTTES DE ST-CÉZAIRE: 65c.

ROBERT HARDING PICTURE LIBRARY: 35b, 246t; HOTEL EDEN ROC, CAP D'ANTIBES: 191b; HULTON-DEUTSCH COLLECTION: 28c, 29clb, 52br; Keystone 94t.

ILLUSTRATED LONDON NEWS PICTURE LIBRARY: 50b.

CATHERINE KARNOW, SAN FRANCISCO: 110c; THE KOBAL COLLECTION: United Artists 71tl.

DANIEL MADELEINE: 183b; MAGNUM PHOTOS: Bruno Barbey 228c; René Burri 55clb; Robert Capa 82c; Elliott Erwitt 91br; Guy le Querrec 225b; MAIRIE DE NÎMES: Jean-Charles Blais 132t (all rights reserved); Francis Bacon 225b (all rights reserved); MANSELL COLLECTION: 39b, 42br, 43b, 51cla, 52bl; EDITIONS MOLIPOR, MONACO: 94b; courtesy of SBM 51crb, 94c; MUSÉE DE L'ANNONCIADE, ST-TROPEZ: E Vila Mateu 119b, 120–21; MUSÉE D'ANTHROPOLOGIE, MONACO: J-F Buissière 38tl; MUSÉE ARCHÉOLOGIQUE DE LA VAISON-LA-ROMAINE: Christine Bézin 41clb; MUSÉE D'ART MODERNE ET

D'ART CONTEMPORAIN, NICE: 54br, 85b; MUSÉE FABRE, MONTPELLIER: Leenhardt 135b; MUSÉE DE LA PHOTOGRAPHIE, MOUGINS: 66b; MUSÉE MATISSE, NICE: © Service photographique, Ville de Nice 82t and b, 83t, c and br.

REPRODUCED BY COURTESY OF THE TRUSTEES, THE NATIONAL GALLERY, LONDON: 26c; NATURE PHOTOGRAPHERS: Carlson 16ca; Michael Gore 16b; NETWORK PHOTOGRAPHERS/RAPHO: Mark Buscail 184t.

L'OEIL ET LA MÉMOIRE/BIBLIOTHÈQUE MUNICIPALE D'AVIGNON: Atlas 24, folio 147 42cb; OXFORD SCIENTIFIC FILMS: Mike Hill 136blb; Tom Leach 160br; Frank Schneidermeyer 136brb.

JOHN PARKER: 21bl, 24b, 58tr, 108t, 157; PICTURES COLOUR LIBRARY: 185b; PHOTO RESOURCES: CM Dixon 41cbr; PLANET EARTH PICTURES: Richard Coomber 136bcb; John Neuschwander 114br; Peter Scoones 19b; POPPERFOTO: 29tc, 72b.

RANGE: Bettmann 28crb, 29tr and crb; RETROGRAPH ARCHIVE, LONDON: © Martin Breese 30tr, 69b; ROGER-VIOLLET, PARIS: 47cla, 51t, 52cb, 163b.

SERVICE DE PRESSE DE LA VILLE DE CAGNES-SUR-MER: 78c and b, 79b; ROGER SMITH, EZE: 86cb, 87c; SNCF/FRENCH RAILWAYS LTD., LONDON: 55b, 249b; FRANK SPOONER PICTURES: Robin 67b; P Siccoli 54cb; Gamma/T Pelisier 38b; Gamma/Christian Vioujard 67cra and clb; SYGMA: 75t; 68b; H Conant 54bl; J Donoso 67crb; Diego Goldberg 55crb; Keystone 52–3; 53cla and b; Leo Mirkine 55cl.

EDITIONS TALLENDIER, PARIS: Bibliothèque Nationale 42–3; TERRES DU SUD, VENASQUE: Philippe Giraud 2, 44clb, 45c and bl, 46tl and br, 64b, 70br, 81ca, 105b, 166t, 167cb, 168b; TONY STONE IMAGES: Joe Cornish 14; TRAVEL LIBRARY: Philip Enticknap 93t and br.

WALLIS PHOTOTHÈQUE, MARSEILLE: Clasen 55t, 67cla; Constant 182b; Di Meglio 115ca; Giani 96t, 225t; Huet 185t; LCI 31br, 176t; Leroux 16b; Poulet 96cl; Royer 96cr and b; Tarta 193b.

ROGER WILLIAMS: 101, 138b, 165t, 170c, 181b, 185ca.

Front endpaper: all commissioned photography.

JACKET
Front - CORBIS: Owen Franken main image; DK IMAGES: bl.
Back - JOHN PARKER: cla; THE TRAVEL LIBRARY: Philip Enticknap bl; WALLIS.FR: © ILICO tl; Leroux clb.
Spine - CORBIS: Owen Franken t; DK IMAGES: Kim Sayer b.

All other images Dorling Kindersley. For more information see www.DKimages.com

SPECIAL EDITIONS OF DK TRAVEL GUIDES

DK Travel Guides can be purchased in bulk quantities at discounted prices for use in promotions or as premiums. We are also able to offer special editions and personalized jackets, corporate imprints, and excerpts from all of our books, tailored specifically to meet your own needs.

To find out more, please contact:
(in the United States) **SpecialSales@dk.com**
(in the UK) **Sarah.Burgess@dk.com**
(in Canada) DK Special Sales at **general@tourmaline.ca**
(in Australia)
business.development@pearson.com.au

Phrase Book

In Emergency

Help!	**Au secours!**	oh se**koor**
Stop!	**Arrêtez!**	aret-**ay**
Call a doctor!	**Appelez un médecin!**	apuh-**lay** uñ medsañ
Call an ambulance!	**Appelez une ambulance!**	apuh-**lay** oon oñboo-**loñs**
Call the police!	**Appelez la police!**	apuh-**lay** lah poh-**lees**
Call the fire brigade!	**Appelez les pompiers!**	apuh-lay leh poñ-**peeyay**
Where is the nearest telephone?	**Où est le téléphone le plus proche?**	oo ay luh tehleh**fon** luh ploo **prosh**
Where is the nearest hospital?	**Où est l'hôpital le plus proche?**	oo ay l'opeetal luh ploo **prosh**

Communication Essentials

Yes	**Oui**	wee
No	**Non**	noñ
Please	**S'il vous plaît**	seel voo **play**
Thank you	**Merci**	mer-**see**
Excuse me	**Excusez-moi**	exkoo-**zay** mwah
Hello	**Bonjour**	boñ**zhoor**
Goodbye	**Au revoir**	oh ruh-**vwar**
Good night	**Bonsoir**	boñ-**swar**
Morning	**Le matin**	matañ
Afternoon	**L'après-midi**	l'apreh-**meedee**
Evening	**Le soir**	swar
Yesterday	**Hier**	eeyehr
Today	**Aujourd'hui**	oh-zhoor-**dwee**
Tomorrow	**Demain**	duh**mañ**
Here	**Ici**	ee-**see**
There	**Là**	lah
What?	**Quel, quelle?**	kel, kel
When?	**Quand?**	koñ
Why?	**Pourquoi?**	poor-**kwah**
Where?	**Où?**	oo

Useful Phrases

How are you?	**Comment allez-vous?**	kom-moñ talay voo
Very well, thank you.	**Très bien, merci.**	treh byañ, mer-**see**
Pleased to meet you.	**Enchanté de faire votre connaissance.**	oñshoñ-**tay** duh fehr votr kon-ay-**sans**
See you soon.	**A bientôt.**	byañ-**toh**
That's fine.	**Voilà qui est parfait.**	vwalah kee ay parfay
Where is/are...?	**Où est/sont...?**	oo ay/soñ
How far is it to...?	**Combien de kilomètres d'ici à...?**	kom-**byañ** duh is keelo-**metr** d'ee-**see** ah
Which way to...?	**Quelle est la direction pour...?**	kel ay lah **deer-ek-syoñ** poor
Do you speak English?	**Parlez-vous anglais?**	par-**lay** voo oñg-**lay**
I don't understand.	**Je ne comprends pas.**	zhuh nuh kom-**proñ** pah

Could you speak slowly, please?	**Pouvez-vous parler moins vite, s'il vous plaît?**	poo-**vay** voo par-**lay** mwañ veet seel voo play
I'm sorry.	**Excusez-moi.**	exkoo-**zay** mwah

Useful Words

big	**grand**	groñ
small	**petit**	puh-**tee**
hot	**chaud**	show
cold	**froid**	frwah
good	**bon**	boñ
bad	**mauvais**	moh-**veh**
enough	**assez**	as**say**
well	**bien**	byañ
open	**ouvert**	oo-**ver**
closed	**fermé**	fer-**meh**
left	**gauche**	gohsh
right	**droit**	drwah
straight on	**tout droit**	too drwah
near	**près**	preh
far	**loin**	lwañ
up	**en haut**	oñ **oh**
down	**en bas**	oñ **bah**
early	**de bonne heure**	duh bon **urr**
late	**en retard**	oñ ruh-**tar**
entrance	**l'entrée**	l'on-**tray**
exit	**la sortie**	sor-**tee**
toilet	**les toilettes, les WC**	twah-let, vay-**see**
unoccupied	**libre**	leebr
no charge	**gratuit**	grah-**twee**

Making a Telephone Call

I'd like to place a long-distance call.	**Je voudrais faire un interurbain.**	zhuh voo-dreh fehr uñ añter-oorbañ
I'd like to make a reverse-charge call.	**Je voudrais faire une communication PCV.**	zhuh voo**dreh** fehr oon kom-oonikah-**syoñ** peh-seh-veh
I'll try again later.	**Je rappelerai plus tard.**	zhuh rapel**eray** ploo tar
Can I leave a message?	**Est-ce que je peux laisser un message?**	es-**keh** zhuh puh leh-**say** uñ mehsazh
Hold on.	**Ne quittez pas, s'il vous plaît.**	nuh kee-**tay** pah seel voo play
Could you speak up a little please?	**Pouvez-vous parler un peu plus fort?**	poo-**vay** voo par-**lay** uñ puh ploo for
local call	**la communication locale**	komoonikah-**syoñ** low-**kal**

Shopping

How much does this cost?	**C'est combien s'il vous plaît?**	say kom-**byañ** seel voo play
Do you take credit cards?	**Est-ce que vous acceptez les cartes de crédit?**	es-**kuh** voo zaksept-**ay** leh kart duh kreh-**dee**

Do you take travellers' cheques?	**Est-ce que vous acceptez les chèques de voyage?**	es-**kuh** voo zaksept-**ay** leh shek duh vwa**yazh**
I would like ...	**Je voudrais...**	zhuh voo-**dray**
Do you have?	**Est-ce que vous avez?**	es-**kuh** voo zav**ay**
I'm just looking.	**Je regarde seulement.**	zhuh ruh**gar** suhl**moñ**
What time do you open?	**A quelle heure vous êtes ouvert?**	ah kel urr voo zet oo-**ver**
What time do you close?	**A quelle heure vous êtes fermé?**	ah kel urr voo zet fer-**may**
This one	**Celui-ci**	suhl-wee-**see**
That one	**Celui-là**	suhl-wee-**lah**
expensive	**cher**	shehr
cheap	**pas cher, bon marché**	pah shehr, boñ mar-**shay**
size, clothes	**la taille**	tye
size, shoes	**la pointure**	pwañ-**tur**
white	**blanc**	bloñ
black	**noir**	nwahr
red	**rouge**	roozh
yellow	**jaune**	zhohwn
green	**vert**	vehr
blue	**bleu**	bluh

Types of Shop

antique shop	**le magasin d'antiquités**	maga-**zañ** d'oñteekee-**tay**
bakery	**la boulangerie**	booloñ-**zhuree**
bank	**la banque**	boñk
book shop	**la librairie**	lee-**brehree**
butcher	**la boucherie**	boo-**shehree**
cake shop	**la pâtisserie**	patee-**sree**
cheese shop	**la fromagerie**	fromazh-**ree**
chemist	**la pharmacie**	farmah-**see**
dairy	**la crémerie**	krem-**ree**
department store	**le grand magasin**	groñ maga-**zañ**
delicatessen	**la charcuterie**	sharkoot-**ree**
fishmonger	**la poissonnerie**	pwasson-**ree**
gift shop	**le magasin de cadeaux**	maga-**zañ** duh ka**doh**
greengrocer	**le marchand de légumes**	mar-**shoñ** duh lay-**goom**
grocery	**l'alimentation**	alee-moñta-**syoñ**
hairdresser	**le coiffeur**	kwa**fuhr**
market	**le marché**	marsh-**ay**
newsagent	**le magasin de journaux**	maga-**zañ** duh zhoor-**no**
post office	**la poste, le bureau de poste, les PTT**	pohst, boo**roh** duh pohst, peh-teh-teh
shoe shop	**le magasin de chaussures**	maga-**zañ** duh show-**soor**
supermarket	**le super-marché**	soo pehr-**marshay**
tobacconist	**le tabac**	tabah
travel agent	**l'agence de voyages**	l'azhoñs duh vwayazh

Menu Decoder

l'agneau	l'an**yoh**	lamb
l'ail	l'eye	garlic
la banane	ba**nan**	banana
le beurre	burr	butter
la bière	bee-**yehr**	beer
le bifteck, le steack	beef-**tek**, stek	steak
le boeuf	buhf	beef
bouilli	boo-**yee**	boiled
le café	kah-**fay**	coffee
le canard	kan**ar**	duck
le citron pressé	see-**troñ** press-**eh**	fresh lemon juice
les crevettes	kruh-**vet**	prawns
les crustacés	**kroos**-ta-say	shellfish
cuit au four	kweet oh foor	baked
le dessert	deh-**ser**	dessert
l'eau minérale	l'oh **meeney**-ral	mineral water
les escargots	leh zes-kar-**goh**	snails
les frites	freet	chips
le fromage	from-**azh**	cheese
les fruits frais	frwee freh	fresh fruit
les fruits de mer	frwee duh mer	seafood
le gâteau	gah-**toh**	cake
la glace	glas	ice, ice cream
grillé	gree-**yay**	grilled
le homard	om**ahr**	lobster
l'huile	l'weel	oil
le jambon	zhoñ-**boñ**	ham
le lait	leh	milk
les légumes	lay-**goom**	vegetables
la moutarde	moo-**tard**	mustard
l'oeuf	l'uf	egg
les oignons	leh zon**yoñ**	onions
les olives	leh zo**leev**	olives
l'orange pressée	l'oroñzh press-**eh**	fresh orange juice
le pain	pan	bread
le petit pain	puh-**tee** pañ	roll
poché	posh-**ay**	poached
le poisson	pwah-**ssoñ**	fish
le poivre	pwavr	pepper
la pomme	pom	apple
les pommes de terre	pom-duh tehr	potatoes
le porc	por	pork
le potage	poh-**tazh**	soup
le poulet	poo-**lay**	chicken
le riz	ree	rice
rôti	row-**tee**	roast
la sauce	sohs	sauce
la saucisse	sohsees	sausage, fresh
sec	sek	dry
le sel	sel	salt
le sucre	sookr	sugar
le thé	tay	tea
le toast	toast	toast
la viande	vee-**yand**	meat
le vin blanc	vañ **bloñ**	white wine
le vin rouge	vañ **roozh**	red wine
le vinaigre	vee**naygr**	vinegar

Eating Out

Have you got a table?	**Avez-vous une table libre?**	avay-**voo** oon tahbl leebr
I want to reserve a table.	**Je voudrais réserver une table.**	zhuh voo-**dray** rayzehr-**vay** oon tahbl
The bill, please.	**L'addition, s'il vous plaît.**	l'adee-**syoñ** seel voo **play**
I am a vegetarian.	**Je suis végétarien.**	zhuh swee vezhay-**tehryañ**
Waitress/ waiter	**Madame, Mademoiselle/ Monsieur**	mah-**dam**, mah-dem wah **zel**/muh-**syuh**
menu	**le menu, la carte**	men-**oo**, kart
fixed-price menu	**le menu à prix fixe**	men-**oo** ah pree feeks
cover charge	**le couvert**	koo-**vehr**
wine list	**la carte des vins**	**kart**-deh vañ
glass	**le verre**	vehr
bottle	**la bouteille**	boo-**tay**
knife	**le couteau**	koo-**toh**
fork	**la fourchette**	for-**shet**
spoon	**la cuillère**	kwee-**yehr**
breakfast	**le petit déjeuner**	puh-**tee** deh-**zhuh-nay**
lunch	**le déjeuner**	deh-**zhuh-nay**
dinner	**le dîner**	dee-**nay**
main course	**le plat principal**	plah prañsee-**pal**
starter, first course	**l'entrée, le hors d'oeuvre**	l'oñ-**tray**, or-**duhvr**
dish of the day	**le plat du jour**	plah doo zhoor
wine bar	**le bar à vin**	bar ah vañ
café	**le café**	ka-**fay**
rare	**saignant**	**say**-noñ
medium	**à point**	ah **pwañ**
well done	**bien cuit**	byañ **kwee**

Staying in a Hotel

Do you have a vacant room?	**Est-ce que vous avez une chambre?**	es-kuh voo-**zavay** oon shambr
double room	**la chambre pour deux personnes, avec un grand lit**	shambr ah duh pehr-**son** avek un groñ lee
twin room	**la chambre à deux lits**	shambr ah duh lee
single room	**la chambre pour une personne**	shambr ah oon pehr-**son**
room with a bath, shower	**la chambre avec salle de bains, une douche**	shambr avek sal duh bañ, oon doosh
porter	**le garçon**	gar-**soñ**
key	**la clef**	klay
I have a reservation.	**J'ai fait une réservation.**	zhay fay oon rayzehrva-**syoñ**

Sightseeing

abbey	**l'abbaye**	l'abay-**ee**
art gallery	**la galerie d'art**	galer-**ree** dart
cathedral	**la cathédrale**	katay-**dral**
church	**l'église**	l'ayg**leez**
garden	**le jardin**	zhar-**dañ**
library	**la bibliothèque**	beeb**leeo**-tek
museum	**le musée**	moo-**zay**
railway station	**la gare (SNCF)**	gahr (es-en-say-ef)
bus station	**la gare routière**	gahr roo-tee-**yehr**
tourist information office	**les renseigne-- ments touristiques, le syndicat d'initiative**	roñsayn-**moñ** too-rees-**teek**, sandee-ka d'eenee-sya**teev**
town hall	**l'hôtel de ville**	l'ohtel duh veel
private mansion	**l'hôtel particulier**	l'ohtel partikoo-**lyay**
closed for public holiday	**fermeture jour férié**	fehrmeh-**tur** zhoor fehree-**ay**

Numbers

0	**zéro**	zeh-**roh**
1	**un, une**	uñ, oon
2	**deux**	duh
3	**trois**	trwah
4	**quatre**	katr
5	**cinq**	sañk
6	**six**	sees
7	**sept**	set
8	**huit**	weet
9	**neuf**	nerf
10	**dix**	dees
11	**onze**	oñz
12	**douze**	dooz
13	**treize**	trehz
14	**quatorze**	ka**torz**
15	**quinze**	kañz
16	**seize**	sehz
17	**dix-sept**	dees-**set**
18	**dix-huit**	dees-**weet**
19	**dix-neuf**	dees-**nerf**
20	**vingt**	vañ
30	**trente**	tront
40	**quarante**	karo**ñt**
50	**cinquante**	sañko**ñt**
60	**soixante**	swaso**ñt**
70	**soixante-dix**	swasoñt-**dees**
80	**quatre-vingts**	katr-**vañ**
90	**quatre-vingts- dix**	katr-vañ-**dees**
100	**cent**	soñ
1,000	**mille**	meel

Time

one minute	**une minute**	oon mee-**noot**
one hour	**une heure**	oon urr
half an hour	**une demi-heure**	oon duh-mee urr
Monday	**lundi**	luñ-**dee**
Tuesday	**mardi**	mar-**dee**
Wednesday	**mercredi**	mehrkruh-**dee**
Thursday	**jeudi**	zhuh-**dee**
Friday	**vendredi**	voñdruh-**dee**
Saturday	**samedi**	sam-**dee**
Sunday	**dimanche**	dee-**moñsh**